OTHER BOOKS BY JOSEPH D. PATTON, Jr.

Service Management: Principles and Practices
    (With W. H. Bleuel)

Preventive Maintenance

Product Service Management

Maintainability and Maintenance Management

Service Parts Management

LOGISTICS
Technology and Management

THE NEW APPROACH

A COMPREHENSIVE HANDBOOK FOR
COMMERCE
INDUSTRY
GOVERNMENT

By Joseph D. Patton, Jr.

Foreword by JOHN GOODRUM
        Col. (Ret.) U.S. Air Force
        Former Executive Director of the
        Society of Logistics Engineers

The Solomon Press, New York

*To Family and Friends
Who Have Supported
My Efforts*

Copyright © 1986 by Publishers Creative Services Inc.

All Right Reserved.

No part of this book may be reproduced in any form by any method, either in existence or yet to be devised, without the written permission of the copyright owner. Inquiries should be addressed to:

The Solomon Press
Publishers Creative Services Inc.
89-31 161 Street; Suite 611
Jamaica, New York 11432
United States of America

The author and publisher wish to thank the copyright owners who have given their permission to use copyrighted material. Any ommissions or errors in giving proper credit are unintentional and will be corrected at the first opportunity after the error or omission has been brought to the attention of the author or publisher.

Library of Congress Cataloging-in-Publication Data

Patton, Joseph D.
   Logistics technology and management.

  Bibliography: p.
  Includes index.
  1. Business logistics. I. Title.
                         HD38.5.P38 1986   658.7   86-15624
ISBN 0-934623-02-3

Contents

List of Figures	*xii*
List of Tables	*xv*
Acknowledgment	*xvii*
Foreword by John Goodrum	*xix*
Chapter 1 **Logistics Terms and Definitions**	**1**
Glossary	*1*
Chapter 2 **Systems for Logistics**	**19**
Systems Engineering	*19*
Support Elements	*20*
Complexity and Optimization	*21*
Risk Reduction	*22*
Methods of Planning, Scheduling, and Control	*24*
Techniques	*24*
Chapter 3 **Life-Cycle Costs and Profits**	**29**
History of LCC	*30*
LCC System Program Definition	*32*
Financial Analysis Process	*35*
Life-Cycle Profits	*40*
Factors To Be Considered	*41*
Quantification	*42*
Financial Analysis	*43*
Establishing an Analysis Procedure	*43*

Chapter 4 Information Systems — 45
- Problems in the Information Process — 46
- Information Users — 47
- Field Information — 48
- Data Processing — 49
- Management Needs — 49
- DP Advances — 50

Chapter 5 Program/Project Planning and Management — 52
- Organization — 52
- Activities — 54
- Guidelines — 54
- Key Measurements — 54
- Problem Identification and Correction — 55
- Phased Programs — 55

Chapter 6 Specifications — 57
- Coverage — 59
- Failures — 59
- Maintainability/Maintenance/Serviceability — 59
- Administration — 59
- Special Events — 61
- Costs — 61

Chapter 7 System Design and Development Process — 63
- The Structural Process — 64
- The Design Morphology — 65
- Production-Consumption Cycle — 69

Chapter 8 Reliability, Availability, and Maintainability — 76
- Availability — 76
- Customer Perceptions — 77
- Reliability — 79
- Costs — 88
- Essentiality — 88
- Maintainability and Maintenance — 90
- Achieving Maintainability — 93
- Allocation — 98

Contents   vii

    Maintainability Demonstration   *100*

Chapter 9 Design Reviews   **102**
    Purpose of Final Reviews   *103*
    Planning   *106*
    Conduct of the Review   *106*
    Purchasing Reviews   *107*

Chapter 10 Configuration Management   **108**
    What is CM   *108*
    Verification   *109*
    Documentation   *110*
    Hardware and Software   *112*
    Change Control   *116*

Chapter 11 Acquisition and Production/Construction Support   **118**
    Production Concepts   *119*
    Procurement   *120*
    Procurement Logistics   *121*
    Proposals and Quotations   *122*
    Make or Buy   *123*
    Special Purchasing Programs   *124*
    Industrial Engineering   *125*
    Progress/Learning Curve   *128*

Chapter 12 Forecasting   **133**
    Time Horizons   *133*
    Forecasting Methods   *134*
    Techniques of Technological Forecasting   *141*
    Statistical Techniques   *144*

Chapter 13 Quality   **151**
    What Is "Quality"?   *151*
    Cost, Quality, and Schedule   *152*
    Improvement Through Emphasis   *152*
    Quality Costs   *153*
    QC Elements   *154*
    Determining the Quality Standards   *155*

Variability	*156*
Control Charts	*164*
Design of Experiments	*165*
Audits	*165*
Chapter 14 Modern Maintenance Methods	**167**
Advances	*168*
Production-Line Approach to Service	*172*
Throwaway Maintenance	*172*
Electronic Repairs	*173*
Do It Yourself	*174*
Use to Failure	*175*
Chapter 15 Inventory Management	**176**
Management Objectives and Goals	*176*
Demand	*177*
Location	*180*
Turnover	*180*
Essentiality	*181*
Stocks	*182*
Inventory Management Under Certainty	*184*
Reorder Point Determination	*185*
Operating Days	*186*
Finite Replenishment Rate	*189*
Inventory Management Under Uncertainty	*189*
Monte Carlo Analysis	*192*
Value of Information	*194*
Contingency Procedures	*195*
Safety Stocks	*195*
Allocation of Needed Supplies	*196*
P and Q Models	*196*
Inventory Audits and Records	*197*
Stock Records	*197*
Parts for Supporting New Products	*201*
Money Constraints	*201*
Establishing Initial Demand	*202*

Contents

Chapter 16 Physical Distribution	**205**
Marketing Concept	205
Marketing Mix	206
Channels of Distribution	206
Order and Information Systems	208
Chapter 17 Packaging, Handling, and Warehousing	**212**
Packaging	212
Protection	213
Material Handling	215
Automation	216
Pallets and Containers	216
Warehouse Functions	218
Types of Warehouses	218
Planning a Warehouse	220
Warehouse Operations	223
Chapter 18 Facility Planning and Site Selection	**225**
Acquiring a Building	225
Management Functions	227
Production Location	227
Inventory Locations	229
Simulations	234
Chapter 19 Traffic and Transportation	**237**
Modes	237
Legal Forms	239
Modal Combinations	240
Rates	241
Documentation	242
Traffic Management	243
Chapter 20 Personnel and Organizations	**245**
What Motivates People	245
Personnel Requirements	246
How Many People	247
Hiring	249

Counseling	*250*
Skills Inventory	*251*
Labor Relations	*251*
Training	*251*
Organizations	*255*

Chapter 21 **Customer Interfaces** — **274**
Product Needs	*275*
Life-Cycle Profits	*279*

Chapter 22 **Product Introductions** — **281**
Introduction Support Planning	*284*
Installation Emphasis	*285*
Test Marketing	*286*
Support Impact on Introduction	*288*
Security	*290*
Conclusions	*290*

Chapter 23 **Repair, Rejuvenation, and Disposal** — **292**
Equipment Replacement Decisions	*292*
Repair/Discard Analysis	*296*
Repair/Discard Models	*298*
Graphic Screening Techniques	*299*
Impact on Maintainability	*300*
Rejuvenation	*301*
Disposition	*307*

Chapter 24 **Logistics Models** — **309**
Definition of a Model	*309*
Basic Advantages of Using Models	*310*
Checking for Model Limitations	*311*
Applying Models Throughout the Product Life Cycle	*311*
Using Models for Determining Sensitivities	*313*

Appendix **Classes of Models** — **318**
System Operational Analysis and Logistic Support Models	*318*
Level-of-Repair Analysis Models	*319*

Life-Cycle-Cost Models for Procurement and Program	*319*
Spares and Inventory Policy Models	*320*

References   **321**

Bibliography   **322**

Index   *333*

List of Figures

2.2	Typical System Development Cycle	23
2.3	Bar Schedule, A Form of Gantt Chart	25
2.4	Project Network Structure	27
3.1	Life-Cycle Costs for Home Appliances	31
3.2	System Life Cycle	33
3.3	Pareto Analysis	34
3.4	Evaluation Priorities	36
3.5	Life-Cycle Cost Analysis	38
5.1	Project Management Structure	53
6.1	Elements of a Corrective Maintenance Cycle	60
7.1	Design-Planning Phases	65
7.2	Phases of the Designer-Planner Project Life	66
7.3	Process Planning System	71
8.1	Electromechanical Reliability Curve	81
8.2	Reliability Nomograph	82
8.3	Life-Cycle Cost	89
8.4	Primary Subsets of Maintenance Activities	91
8.5	System Development Cycle	92
8.6	Reliability-Maintainability-Availability Trade-Off Curves	94
8.7	Reliability-Maintainability-Availability RMA Trade-Off Curves	95
8.8	Reliability-Maintainability Trade-Off	96
8.9	Maintainability Hierarchy	99
8.10	Maintainability Demonstration Variation	101
9.1	Design Review Relationship for Program Phases	105

List of Figures

10.1	Documentation of a Typical Commercial Product	111
10.2	Standard Model/Program Phase/Documentation Relationships	113
10.3	The Product Design Documentation Hierarchy	114
11.1	Flow Sequencing by Branch and Bound	126
11.2	One Form of Linear Programming for Assignment	127
11.3	Eighty Percent Learning Curve	130
11.4	Eighty Percent Learning Curve on Log-Log Paper	131
12.1	A Systems View of Forecasting	135
12.1	Cost of Forecasting Versus Cost of Inaccuracy	136
12.3	Moving Average	144
12.4	Input/Output Analysis Modeling	148
12.5	Least-Squares Regression Line	150
13.1	Desirable Trends in Quality Costs	154
13.2	Continuous Probability Distributions	157
13.3	Area Under the Normal Curve	159
13.4	Ideal Sampling Plan Performance	161
13.5	Actual Sampling Plan Performance	161
13.6	Sampling Plan Indices	163
14.1	Condition Monitoring to Predict Optimal Maintenance Performance	169
14.2	Service as a Complete System	170
15.1	Relative Costs of Carrying and Ordering Inventory	185
15.2	Reorder Point Determination	187
15.3	Demand Histogram	188
15.4	Resupply Histogram	190
15.5	Cumlative Distributions of Demand and Lead Time	193
15.6	Part Availability	198
15.7	Stock Performance Report	200
16.1	Marketing Mix	207
16.2	Channels of Distribution for Consumer Goods	209
16.3	Channels of Distribution for Industrial Goods	209
16.4	Elements of an Order-Processing System	210
17.1	Compatible Cartons	214
17.2	In-Transit Mixing	220
17.3	Pallet Placement	221
17.4	Typical Warehouse Layout	222
18.1	Relationship of Inventory Locations and Delivery Time	231
18.2	Optimal Coverage from a Distribution Center: A-B-C-D	234
18.3	Flow Diagram of a Warehouse Location Heuristic Program	236

20.1	Development of Labor Needs	248
20.2	Developing Products Training Programs	253
20.3	Training	254
20.4	Functional Assistance in Organizations	262
20.5	Typical Aerospace Product Support Organizations	272
20.6	A Typical Program/Project/Task Organization	273
22.1	Distribution of Units and Sales During a Product's Life Cycle	282
22.2	Alternative Decisions Following Results of Market Tests	287
22.3	Classes of New Products Adopters	288
23.1	Decision Points for Repair/Discard Analysis	297
23.2	Graphic Screening for Repair/Discard	300

List of Tables

2.1	Support System for Launch of a New Commercial Product	21
2.2	Product Introduction Activity Printout	28
3.1	Life-Cycle Costs	30
3.2	Product-Life Controlling Factors	35
3.3	Service LCC Model Factors	39
3.4	Undiscounted Cost ($) Per Year of Ownership	40
3.5	LCC Problem Answer	41
6.1	Sample of Specifications, Forecasts and Impacts	58
7.1	Comparison of Physical Distribution Elements with Those of Integrated Logistics Support	74
8.1	Component Reliability	84
8.2	Failure Rate	87
8.3	Untitled	100
11.1	Modification Labor Hours for 80 Percent Progress, Function	129
15.1	Parts Resupply Times	180
15.2	Untitled	181
15.3	Down Time Opportunity Costs	182
15.4	Cumulative Costs of Down Time	183
15.5	Demand Data	186
15.6	Resupply Data	191
15.7	Stock Supply Versus Demand Simulation	194
19.1	Relative Operating Characteristics	239

20.1	Five Basic Types of Meetings	270
23.1	Average Annual Cost	295
23.2	Average Annual Costs Less Revenue Advantage	295
23.3	Quantitative Factors in Repair/Ciscard Models	302
23.4	Effect of Repair/Discard Considerations on Maintainability Design Factors	304

Acknowledgments

This book is the culmination of a ten year effort. It had its beginning during the summer of 1976. Those were the startup days of Patton Consultants, Inc. At that time we realized that a unique educational program and set of course materials would help establish our credibility as consultants and educators; and provide a product and service that could be marketed as a ongoing venture. As a supporter of the Society of Logistics Engineers (SOLE), I saw the great need for training logisticians, and specifically for an overview of the knowledge necessary to pass the Certified Professional Logisticians (CPL) examination. That strategy has been proven correct. Our best estimate is that about 16,000 people have used the materials; through both individual purchases and organization licenses.

Special thanks go to Ed Slebodnick and his associates at Boeing Aerospace Company who purchased the first corporate license based on seeing the first few chapters. I dictated and wrote while Susan O. Patton typed furiously (in every sense of the word) and our two young children Jennifer and Joseph III tried to help. Too many lessons left Rochester, New York by courier on a Monday to be taught in Seattle, Washington on Thursday. Looking back from the technological vantage point of word processors equipped with spelling checkers and precise justification, I recall the malfunctions of several used electric typewriters, and how much easier the document preparation was when we finally got a new IBM Correcting Selectric typewriter. Our clients also perceived improvements in quality.

D. Jane Biggs took over the secretarial responsibility for revisions and much of the art for the second edition, and then the third edition that was licensed to the Society of Logistics Engineers for use by their entire membership. Control Data, General Dynamics, Honeywell, Hughes, IBM, Lockheed-Georgia, Martin-Marietta Aerospace, McDonnell Douglas, Sanders Associates, Taylor Instruments, Rockwell, Vought, Westinghouse, Xerox, every branch of the Armed Forces, several other government agencies, and even the Japanese Management Association were licensed to use the material for internal training. Several hundred people took the course individually, under the supervision of Lawrence S. Beale and myself. The material ws further refined through a fourth and fifth edition, with most of the word processing and production activities done by Beverly C. Phillips with the assistance of Herbert C. Feldmann, CPL to assure accurate and complete information.

Appreciation is also due to many other people who allowed their ideas to be used and who supported our efforts with constructive criticism. They are listed in alphabetical order, and without an organization affiliation since there have been many changes over the years.

Steve Barndt	Ben Ostrofsky
Ron Baudendistel	Henry Parlett
Ben Blanchard	Lou Rosenstein
Douglas Brown	John Stanhagen
Bob Cannady	Bob Stein
Dix Cloward	Bob Street
Ed Curll	Paul Tulley
John Goodrum	Dick Webster
Bob Hilton	Lee Webster
Ed Lowery	

Sidney Solomon and Raymond Solomon of Publishers Creative Services and The Solomon Press deserve credit for persevering through this fifth book with the author. Just as logistics and the life-cycle process should begin with the very first conception of an idea and extend through the end of its life, so this knowledge of logistics stimulated my first and (for now, at least) my last effort to develop a logistics book from our courses and materials. I hope *Logistics Technology and Management* contributes to the development of logistics technology and management.

JOSEPH D. PATTON, JR.
JUNE, 1986

Foreword

A nursery rhyme begins, "For the want of a nail the shoe was lost, for the want of a shoe the horse was lost, for the want of a horse the rider was lost . . ." History is replete with examples of both good and bad logistics: the magnificent supply divisions that supported the Roman legions, Hannibal's recognition that food for his elephants would be vital to sustain those animals so necessary for crossing the Alps, massacre of soilders when they forgot the screwdrivers to unband their ammunition.

Logistics is just as critical for peace as it is for war. If we could do a better job of getting available food and clothing to persons in need, many conflicts could be avoided. A recent attempt at marching across the United States to demonstrate a concern for peace bankrupted the organizers and stalled after only a few weeks because preparations for water, showers, and even the route of travel, were inadequate. Modern wide-bodied aircraft can be unloaded and reloaded in much shorter time than could previous flying machines, but have only limited means to unload passengers or baggage if they do not have access to the special docks. Millions are starving to death in East Africa while food is rotting on the docks.

We are becoming more concerned with the life cycle costs and benefits of durable goods. As one well-known ad says, "You can pay me now, or you can pay me later." In many cases the amount paid later far exceeds what would have been a prudent investment at the initial design and production phase. The ideas behind this "womb to tomb" concept are not new. In the Bible, Luke is quoted as saying, "For which of you, intending to build a tower, sitteth not down first and counteth the cost, whether we have sufficient to finish it" (Luke 14:28). Looking to the future, the geography for our sources of materials and goods, and our marketplaces, are expanding from local communities to around the world. Vertical integration, where, for example, an automobile company owns the mines that produce the steel to make the assemblies that produce the cars, is declining;

with the more prominent form becoming corporations composed of only product business management, marketing and service. A product may be conceived in the United States, designed in Italy, manufactured in Japan, and marketed around the world. The intricacies of such widely disbursed transactions obviously require superior logistics.

This book *Logistics Technology and Management: The New Approach* is the fifth generation of logistics material by Joseph D. Patton, Jr. The first edition of *Logistics Technology and Management* was written in 1975 to meet the training needs of logisticians who were interested in the broad coverage of topics viewed by the Society of Logistics Engineers (SOLE) as necessary for qualification as a Certified Professional Logistician (CPL). The material was originally provided as individual correspondence courses supported by Patton Consultants, Inc. and as licensed, reproducible materials that were used by many major corporations, every branch of the United States military, and the Society of Logistics Engineers for their membership. As the logistics profession evolved and new theories and practices were developed, the materials were refined through five editions and then extensively revised to this new hardcover book format.

Every person engaged in planning, developing, implementing, and supporting products and operations, whether civilian or military; commercial, governmental, or industrial, is encouraged to read this book and use the ideas for improvement of all mankind.

John Goodrum
Colonel (ret) United States Air Force
Former Executive Director, Society of Logistics Engineers

CHAPTER

1

Logistics Terms and Definitions

*L*ogistics as defined by the Society of Logistics Engineers (SOLE) is "the art and science of management, engineering, and technical activities concerned with requirements, design, and supplying and maintaining resources to support objectives, plans, and operations." The author participated in the many hours of effort that resulted in that conceptual definition and yet still finds it necessary to amplify the definition with familiar examples.

Much credit must be given to Fred Gluck who, in 1970, developed a 530-page "Compendium of Authenticated Logistic Terms and Definitions" from government and military documents. Louis C. Rosenstein abridged that compendium and modified many of the definitions to nonmilitary usage. We have added terms and definitions used in product support and customer service and in financial, economic, and statistical analyses. While not unique to logistics, they are vital to the profession. Logistics terms and definitions are rapidly changing in answer to the needs of communicating about this emerging profession.

GLOSSARY

A

Access Gaining entry in order to contact part of the system.

Acquisition A very broad term generally including quantity determination, procurement, and distribution to satisfy logistic needs. It can also include contract definition, development, design and test, evaluation, production, installation, purchasing, and contract administration.

Administration Conduct, direction, or internal management of any organization.

Alignment Placing of a variable setting to a condition within tolerance.

Availability Probability that a system or equipment will, under specified conditions, operate satisfactorily. Also, the percentage of time or occurrences a product will operate properly. Inherent availability (A_i) is "pure as designed." It considers only corrective maintenance time. Achieved availability (A_a) includes preventive maintenance time but an ideal support environment. Operational availability (A_o) is total downtime, which includes administrative and supply times.

B

Block stowage loading Method of loading whereby all cargo for a specific destination is stowed together. The purpose is to facilitate rapid off-loading at the destination, with the least possible disturbance of cargo intended for other points.

Business logistics Term generally applied to the logistics of a strictly commercial (i.e., buying and selling) organization. It omits the factors of concern to the manufacturer or producer, and to some extent those of concern to the user or customer. It has been defined by Heskett, Ivie, and Glaskowsky as "the management of all activities that facilitate movement and the coordination of supply and demand in the creation of time and space utility."

C

Calibrate To verify the accuracy of test equipment and assure performance within tolerance, usually compared with a reference standard that can be traced to a primary standard.

Capital Durable items with life or value that allows them to be used a long time.

Carrier Transport organization including railroad, sleeping car, and express companies; private car lines, freight forwarders, motor carriers; barge and steamship companies; air carriers; and pipeline companies.

Cataloging Functions, processes, and operations involved in item identification, classification, stock numbering, and documentation in accordance with a uniform system. Also known as codification. It establishes item identity and interchageability and is the basis for inventory control.

Change impact analysis Logic and reasoning processes that permit quantification of the results of a change in order to predict the outcome before the change is attempted.

Checkout Determination of the working condition of a system.

Concept Basic idea or generalization.

Configuration Physical and functional characteristics of systems, equipments, and related items of hardware or software, and the relative arrangement and contours of these—the shape of a thing at a given time. The specific parts used to construct a machine.

Consumables Those materials that are used up during a product's operation.

Consumer/user logistics Basic elements of logistics of concern to the user, operator, or consumer.

Contract administration Performance of contracting personnel in accordance with applicable law and regulations. May include legal, fiscal, quality, production and cost control, pricing, and other assigned functions.

Contract definition Phase of a system's life cycle during which preliminary design and engineering are verified or accomplished, and firm contract and management planning performed, in connection with major industrial or government–industry projects.

Contractor Any individual, partnership, company, corporation, or association having a formal agreement to furnish things or services, at a specified price or rate.

Corrective maintenance (also see *Unscheduled maintenance and repair*) Unscheduled maintenance or repair actions performed as a result of failures or deficiencies.

Cost effectiveness Relative value of a system—the costs of acquisition and utilization versus system effectiveness.

Critical Category of items that are essential to performance. (The "significant few.")

D

Deadweight tonnage (also see *Register tonnage*) Actual carrying capacity of a ship, including stores, fuel, water, and cargo. A deadweight ton (DWT) equals 2240 pounds, or a "long ton." Displacement loaded ship (i.e., weight of ship, fuel, stores, and cargo in long tons) minus displacement light (i.e., weight of ship, fuel, and stores) equals cargo capacity in long tons.

Definition or analysis phase of development Step preceding full-scale development during which the preliminary engineering and contract management planning is done.

Development Working out and extending the theoretical, practical, and useful applications of a basic design, idea, or scientific discovery. The design, building, modification, or improvement of the prototype or original model of a vehicle, engine, instrument, or the like.

Direct costs Expenses that can be associated with specific products, operations, or services.

Disposal Getting rid of excess or surplus property under proper authorization. It may be accomplished by, but is not limited to, transfer, donation, sale, abandonment, destruction, or recycling.

Distribution Functional phase of logistics that includes the dispensing of materials, supplies, equipment, products, or services.

Downtime Portion of calendar time during which specific equipment is not in condition to function.

E

Economic order quantity (EOQ) Amount of an item that should be ordered at one time to get the lowest combination of inventory carrying and order/production costs.

Economic repair Capability of being restored to sound condition at a cost less than the value of the estimated remaining useful life of the item concerned, based on life expectancy, acquisition, replacement cost, and other relevant factors.

End article or end item Hardware not intended to be installed in, or as part of, another piece of equipment that is capable of performing an operational function.

End user Individual or organization that employs an article or system to accomplish the purpose for which it was designed and intended. This is normally the terminal point of the logistics system intended to accomplish a task, except for the disposal phase.

Engineering Profession and process in which a knowledge of the mathematical and natural sciences gained by study, experience, and practice is applied with judgment to develop ways to utilize, economically, the materials and forces of nature for the benefit of mankind. (Also see logistics engineering, reliability engineering, maintainability engineering, maintenance engineering, systems engineering, value engineering, and management engineering; human, industrial, manufacturing, plant, and methods engineering.)

Engineering change Design change that requires revision to the contract specifications or engineering drawings, or documents referenced therein.

Engineering data Design-related drawings, supporting indexes, specifications, referenced standards, and related technical documents and software used in the design, manufacture, fabrication, or erection of an item, or prepared by a design activity relating to design, performance, manufacture, test, or inspection.

Environment Aggregate of all conditions and influences, including physical location and operating characteristics of surrounding or nearby equipment, actions of people, conditions of temperature, humidity, salt spray, acceleration, shock, vibration, radiation, and contaminants in the surrounding air.

Equipment All items of a durable nature that are capable of continuing or repetitive utilitarian use by an individual or organization.

Expense Items that are directly charged as a cost of doing business since they are used over a short period of time.

Exponential Statistical distribution of logarithmic form that often describes the pattern of events over time.

F

Facilities Physical plants such as real estate and the improvements thereto, including buildings and associated equipment.

Failure Inability to perform the basic function; inability to perform within previously specified limits; malfunction.

Failure analysis Logical, systematic examination of an item, or its design, to identify and analyze the probability, causes, and consequences of real or potential malfunction.

Failure modes and effects analysis (FMEA) Reliability analysis of what items are expected to fail and the consequences of failure. FMECA adds evaluation of the failure criticality.

Failure rate Number of failures per unit measure of life (cycles, time, miles, events, etc.) as applicable for the item.

Feedback Utilization of all or part of the output of one phase of an activity as input to another phase, to influence the final or eventual output. Often the output is in the form of information relative to performance, reliability, maintainability, or understanding.

First in/first out (FIFO) Use of the oldest item in inventory next. Contrasts with LIFO. FIFO accounting values each item used at cost of the oldest item in inventory.

Fixed costs Expenses such as office facilities and training that do not vary directly with activity rates.

Forecast Prediction of future conditions.

Fractionation of inventory Supply management process whereby stocked items are classified as to relative rate of issue, cost, or other significant factors, to achieve best results in connection with requirements review, distribution, and procurement.

Function Separate and distinct action required to achieve a given objective, to be accomplished by use of hardware, computer programs, personnel, facilities, procedural data, or a combination thereof—or an operation a system must perform to fulfill its mission.

Functional level Breakdown of the physical hierarchy of a product. Typical levels of significance from smallest to largest are part, subassembly, assembly, subsystem, and system.

G

General and administrative (G&A) Category of expenses, usually added as a percentage of direct labor and material costs, to cover support and management costs.

General cargo Goods acceptable for loading (normally in ships) in general, nonspecialized areas, such as goods in boxes, barrels, bales, crates, packages, bundles, or on pallets.

General support equipment That which has maintenance application to more than a single model or type of system, subsystem, device, article, or equipment.

Gross weight Combined weight of a container and total contents, or of a vehicle including fuel, lubricant, coolant, on-vehicle material, payload, and operating personnel.

H

Hardware Physical object or objects, as distinguished from capability or function. Generic term dealing with physical items of equipment, tools, implements, instruments, devices, sets, fittings, assemblies, components, parts, raw materials, etc., as opposed to funds, personnel, services, programs, plans, etc., termed "software." (See *Software*.)

Heavy lift ship Cargo vessel specially designed to be capable of loading and unloading heavy and bulky items

Highway capability Number of vehicles (i.e., highway vehicle capacity) or number of short tons payload (i.e., highway tonnage capacity) that can be moved over a highway with proper consideration for type of roadway, maintenance, hills, curves, weather, other traffic, and type of vehicle employed.

Highway capacity Maximum traffic flow on a given roadway using all available lanes.

Human engineering Consideration of human capabilities and limitations for the planning, design, development, and testing of systems, equipment, and facilities to obtain the best mix of safety, comfort, and effectiveness compatible with established requirements.

Human factors All scientific biomedical and psychosocial facts and considerations that constitute characteristics pertaining to the nature of human beings.

I

Identification Means by which items can be recognized as having a given set of characteristics, and named or numbered accordingly.

Indirect costs Expenses not directly associated with specific products, operations, or services: usually considered overhead.

Industry Term generally applied to production, modification, and test facilities in the private sector, or companies, partnerships, corporations, and so forth, including such facilities (as contrasted with those exclusively concerned with exchange, buying, and selling) that are usually considered as "commerce" or "business."

Industrial engineering Composite of activities responsible for the design and development of a production capability.

Installation Fixed or relatively fixed facility location together with its real estate, buildings, structures, utilities, equipment, etc. Also, that period of initial setup and adjustment and performance of a product in the customer's environment.

Insurance items Stocked articles or material that may be needed occasionally or intermittently, but not subject to periodic replacement or wearout, for which prudence requires that there be some stock on hand at certain central points.

Integrated logistic support (ILS) Composite of elements necessary to assure the effective and economical sustaining of a system or equipment, at all levels of maintenance, throughout its programmed life cycle. It is characterized by the harmony and coherence obtained between each of its elements and levels of maintenance.

Integrated logistic support planning Management of selected activities during acquisition: (1) reliability and maintainability, (2) maintenance planning, (3) support and test equipment, (4) supply support, (5) transportation and handling, (6) technical data, (7) facilities, (8) personnel and training, (9) funding, (10) management data.

Interface Common boundary between two or more items, characteristics, systems, functions, activities, departments, objectives, etc. That portion of anything that impinges upon or directly affects something else.

Isolation Separation of the "good" from the "bad" in order to repair the bad.

Inventory Physical count of all items on hand by weight, number, or other measurement. Also, any items held in anticipation of future use.

Inventory control Phase or function of logistics that includes management, cataloging, requirements determination, procurement, distribution, overhaul, and disposal of material.

Inventory management Phase or function of logistics that controls the input, availability, and disposal of items owned by any organization.

Item Generic term used to identify a specific entity under consideration or similar entities. Items may be parts, components, assemblies, subassemblies, accessories, groups, equipments, attachments, etc.

Item characteristic data Details of what an item of supply is, or how it performs, that differentiate it from other items of supply.

Item of supply Article or material that is recurrently purchased, stocked, distributed, and used, and is identified by one distinctive set of numbers or letters, or combination of both, throughout the organization concerned. It consists of any number of pieces or objects that, within the limits dictated by the logistics responsibilities of the organization, can be treated as if identical.

Item management data Collection of significant representations of information with regard to how, when, where, why, and by whom specific items of supply are, or can be, utilized and managed.

L

Labor Work done by humans.

Labor costs Expenses for labor, including wages, taxes, benefits, and overhead.

Last in/first out (LIFO) Use of newest inventory next. Contrasts with FIFO. LIFO accounting values each item used at the cost of the last item added to inventory.

Lead time Allowance for an amount of time required to accomplish a specific task, or to reach a specific objective.

LTL (and LCL) Less than truckload. (LCL—less than carload.) The absolute weight or volume varies by commodity. Transportation rates are higher for LTL than for full truckload (TL).

Level of supply Quantity of an item authorized to be kept on hand at a storage or distribution point, to meet anticipated demands.

Life cycle Series of phases, from concept planning to disposal, that constitute the total existence of a product.

Life-cycle cost All costs associated with the system life cycle including research and development, production, operation and maintenance, and termination.

Logistics Art and science of management, engineering, and technical activities concerned with requirements, design, and supplying and maintaining resources to support objectives, plans, and operations. (Society of Logistics Engineers)

Logistics engineering Professional art of applying science to the optimum planning, handling, and implementation of personnel, materiel, and facilities, including life-cycle design, procurement, production, maintenance, and supply." (John J. Kostura, *Log. Spec.*, vol. 1, no. 1, Sept. 1969)

Logistics management Process by which human efforts are systematically coordinated to create economic and effective support throughout the planned life cycle of equipment, systems, projects, and operations.

Logistics support That which is necessary to assure the availability of *all* resources required to sustain and maintain the full effectiveness of individuals, organizations, operations, projects, equipments, or systems. In the broad sense, it may involve acquisition, maintenance, disposal, and any or all of the many included functions. Achievement of logistics support is therefore the objective of most modern logistics action or endeavor. At times the term "logistics support" or "logistic support" is used to cover all logistic action, collectively.

Long-range planning The "continuous process of making present entrepreneurial (risk taking) decisions systematically, and with the best possible knowledge of their futurity, organizing systematically the efforts needed to carry out these decisions, and measuring the results of these decisions against the expectations through organized systematic feedback." (Peter F. Drucker p. 132, *Technology Management, and Society*, Harper & Row, 1970.)

Lower of cost or market Conservative accounting valuation that uses the lower of what was paid for an item or what it could be sold for now.

M

Maintainability (M) The inherent characteristic of a design or installation that determines the ease, economy, safety, and accuracy with which maintenance actions can be performed. Also, the ability to restore a product to service or to perform preventive maintenance within required limits.

Maintainability engineering Application of applied scientific knowledge and methods, and management skills, to the development of equipment, systems, projects, or operations with the inherent ability to be effectively and efficiently maintained.

Maintenance Function of keeping items or equipment in, or restoring them to, serviceable condition.

Maintenance concept Statements and illustrations that define the theoretical means of maintaining equipment.

Maintenance engineering Developing concepts, criteria, and technical requirements for maintenance during the conceptual and acquisition phases of a project; providing policy guidance for maintenance activities and exercising technical and management direction and review of maintenance programs.

Management The efficient, effective, economical leadership of people and use of money, materials, time, and space to achieve predetermined objectives.

Management engineering Term that covers the development, operation, and improvement of industrial activities. It is usually applied to a blend of professional, engineering, and management activities.

Manufacturing engineering Defines the production process through specification of: (1) assessment of system and assistance in make or buy decisions; (2) selection of materials; (3) selection of basic processes; (4) specifying, with methods engineers, the sequence of operations; (5) identifying man–machine operations and making human factor decisions; (6) selecting tools, machines, test and handling equipment; and (7) designing special tools, jigs, fixtures, etc.

Material All items or things used or needed in any business, industry, undertaking, or operation as distinguished from personnel.

Mean, arithmetic An average of a series of quantities or values;

specifically, the quotient of their sum divided by the number of items in the series.

Measurement ton or ship ton   A measurement ton (MT) or ship ton equals 40 cubic feet. (Also see *Register tonnage*.)

Median   An average of a series of quantities of values; specifically, the quantity or value of that item that is so positioned in the series when arranged in order of numerical quantity or value that there are an equal number of greater magnitude and lesser magnitude.

Methods engineering   Aspect of analyzing production operations in terms of effectiveness and cost.

MDT (mean downtime)   Average time a system cannot perform its mission, including response time, active maintenance time, supply time, and administrative time.

MTBF (mean time between failure)   Average time/distance/events a product delivers between breakdowns.

MTBM (mean time between maintenance)   MTBF plus the interval between preventive maintenance.

MTTR (mean time to repair)   Average time to fix a failed item.

Model   Simulation of the real thing physically, mathematically, or verbally.

Modification   Change in configuration.

Modularization   Separation of components of a product or equipment into physically and functionally distinct entities, to facilitate identification, removal, and replacement (unitization).

Moving average   Mathematical method of considering recent events.

N

Normal   Statistical distribution commonly described as a "bell curve." Mean, mode, and median are the same.

O

Operations research (or operational research)   Approach of modern science to complex problems arising in the direction and management of large systems of people, machines, materials, and money in industry, business, government, and defense. Its distinctive technique is to develop a scientific model of the system involved, incorporating measurement factors such as chance and risk with which to predict and compare the outcomes of alternative decisions, strategies, or controls to help management determine its policy and actions scientifically. (Stafford Beer, p. 44 *Log. Spec.*, vol. 6, no. 2, Summer 1972)

Operation research techniques   Include but are not limited to mathematical programming, inventory models, simulation, queuing models, and critical path (CPM or PERT) analysis.

Operating costs   Expenses of using an item. Not incurred when the item is acquired but not used.

Overhead Costs that are not directly traced to products, operations, or services.

P

Packaging Use of protective wrappings, cushioning, inside containers, and complete identification marking, up to but *not* including the exterior shipping container. (MIL-STD-129)

Pallets Low, portable platforms of wood, metal, or other material used to facilitate handling, storage, and transportation of individual items or groups of items, as units, by means of forklift trucks or similar material-handling equipment.

Payload Quantity (in tons of cargo or equipment, gallons of liquid, or number of passengers) that a vehicle is designed to transport under specific conditions of operations, in addition to its unladen weight.

PERT An acronym for "program evaluation and review technique," which is based on a product-oriented work breakdown structure and time-dependency network. It is a network-type approach to the evaluation of progress versus plan in terms of time, related to the critical path method (CPM) for analyzing complex projects with respect to best timing or cost.

Physical distribution Movement, inventory control, protection, and storage of raw materials and processed or finished goods.

Pipeline Channel of support, or a specific portion thereof, by means of which material or personnel flow from sources of procurement to their point of use.

Preventive maintenance Inspections, lubrication, modifications, and maintenance activities done on a predictive, on-condition or scheduled basis to preclude failures during operation.

Prime contractor Individual, company, firm, or corporation that has entered into a written formal contract to furnish another individual or organization with products, equipment, or services.

Procurement Process of obtaining personnel, services, supplies, materials, and equipment or facilities.

Producer logistics Basic elements of logistics involving procurement and/or production of assets.

Project/program management Concept for the business and technical management of specified projects or programs based on a designated, centralized management authority, or project/program manager, who is responsible for planning, directing, and controlling the definition, research, development, acquisition (in the broad sense), and initial logistics support of the user to the extent necessary to provide a balanced project or program that will accomplish the objectives effectively.

Provisioning Process of determining and selecting the varieties and quantities of repair parts, spares, special tools, test and support equipment that should be procured and stocked to sustain and maintain equipments and systems for specified periods of time.

Plant engineering Design, development, construction, operation, maintenance and modification of production facilities.

Q

Queuing/queueing Pattern of demand placed on an activity.

R

Random failure Any chance nonperformance whose occurrence is not predictable with respect to time or events.

Reaction time/response time Time required between the receipt of directing order, or an impulse triggering some action, and the initiation of the action.

Rebuild/recondition Total teardown and reassembly of a product to the latest configuration.

Redundancy Two or more parts, components, or systems joined functionally so that if one fails, any or all of the remaining components are capable of continuing with the function accomplishment.

Refurbish To clean and/or replace badly worn parts on a selective basis, and make them usable to a customer.

Register tonnage (also see *Deadweight tonnage*) A ship's gross register tonnage is the measure of its interior or enclosed space in register tons (i.e., units of 100 cubic feet of volume). The net register tonnage is the space available for passengers and cargo. Gross register tonnage equals the net register tonnage plus space for crew, power plant, fuel, and operation of the vessel, measured in 100-cubic-foot units.

Reliability Probability that a system, equipment, device, machine, part, or any other item will perform its intended function adequately, without failure, for a specified time period under specified conditions.

Reliability engineering Application of scientific and management knowledge, methods, and skills to the development of things with the inherent or built-in ability to perform intended functions adequately, without failure, for a specified period of time (or equivalent measure of operation), under specified conditions; and the coordination of such quality with all other systems engineering elements.

Repair Restoration or replacement of parts or components of facilities or equipment as necessary to return the facility or equipment to efficient operating condition.

Repair parts Individual parts or assemblies required for the repair of equipment.

Repairable (or repairable item) Item of durable nature that has been determined, by application of engineering, economic, and other factors, to be feasible for restoration to serviceable condition.

Replacement (or replacement item) Item that is functionally interchangeable with another item, but which differs physically from the original part to the extent that installation of the replacement requires such operations as drilling, reaming, cutting, filing, or shimming.

Resources Personnel, funds, materials, equipment, tools, space, and time available for or required to accomplish specific tasks or to realize specific objectives.

Retrofits Modifications that are performed to a machine to correct a deficiency or modernize it.

Rhochrematics Science of material and information flow including the flow of material from the raw material stage through the production stage, to the consumer.

S

Safety Elimination of hazardous conditions that could injure people.

Safety stock Quantity of an item, in addition to the normal level of supply, required to be on hand to permit continuing operation with a specific level of confidence if resupply is interrupted or demand varies in an unpredictable manner.

Salvage Saving or reuse of condemned, discarded, or abandoned property, and of materials contained therein. As a noun, it applies to property that has some value in excess of its basic material content but which is in such condition that it has no reasonable prospect of original use, and its repair or rehabilitation for such use is clearly impracticable.

Scheduled maintenance Preplanned preventive maintenance actions, according to an established time or use table, performed in an attempt to keep an item in a specified operating condition.

Scrap Property or items, discarded in so far as original use is concerned, that have no reasonable prospect of value except for the recovery value of basic material content.

Service contract Contract calling directly for a contractor's time and materials rather than for a specific end product.

Serviceability Characteristic of an item, equipment, system, etc., that makes it easy and cost effective to perform operating checks, fueling, lubrication, and maintenance, after it is put into operation.

Service parts All parts necessary to install and support equipment after production or acquisition.

Shelf life Period of time during which an item can remain unused in proper storage without significant deterioration.

Shipment Item or group of items from one place, released to a carrier for transportation to a single destination.

Shipping activity Organization that plans for, physically assembles, consolidates, documents, and arranges for movement of items from one place to another.

Software Efforts, plans, or paperwork to support projects, operations, equipment, assemblies, items, etc., including technical data, plans, schedules, manuals, and computer programs. (Contrasts to *Hardware*.)

Spares (or spare parts) Components, assemblies, and equipments that are interchangeable with like items, in equipment, that can be used to replace items removed during maintenance.

Specifications Documents that clearly and accurately describe the essential technical requirements for materials, items, equipments, systems, or services.

Standards Established or accepted rules, models, or criteria by which the degree of user satisfaction with a product or an act is determined, or against which comparisons are made.

Standard deviation Measure of average dispersion (departure from the mean) of numbers, computed as the square root of the average of the squares of the difference between numbers and their arithmetic mean.

Standard item Part, component, material, subassembly, assembly, or equipment that is identified or described accurately by a company, industry, federal, or military standard document or drawing.

Standardization Process of establishing, by common agreement, the engineering criteria, terms, principles, practices, materials, items, processes, parts, and equipment to achieve the greatest practicable uniformity of items recurrently used, bought, stocked, or distributed, and of engineering practices, to ensure the minimum feasible variety of such items and practices, and to effect optimum interchangeability of equipment, parts, and components.

Statistics Collecting, classifying, summarizing, and interpreting of numerical facts by other than accounting methods.

Stock Supply of physical items kept on hand at storage points in a supply system to meet anticipated demands.

Stock control Process of maintaining inventory data on the quantity, location, and condition of items due in, on hand, and due out, to determine quantities available, required, or both, and to facilitate distribution and management of stock.

Stock due in Quantity of items or materials expected to be received under outstanding procuring and requisitioning documents, and the quantity expected from other sources such as transfer, reclamation, and recovery.

Stock due out Quantity of items or materials requisitioned by ordering or using activities that is not immediately available for issue, but that is recorded as a commitment for future issue.

Stock number Consumer or user number assigned by the stocking organization or its parent organization to each group of articles or materials treated as if identical within the using supply system (see *Item of supply*), and repetitively procured, stocked, and distributed.

Subcontractor Any supplier, distributor, vendor, or firm that enters into a formal contract to furnish items, services, parts, or supplies to a prime contractor.

Sunk costs Costs that are already incurred and are therefore irrelevant in the consideration of alternate courses of action.

Supervision Guidance, leadership, and control of the efforts of a group of individuals toward common goal.

Supply Procurement, distribution, maintenance in storage, and salvage of items that are consumed in use or become part of other items, thus losing their identity; and of items, assemblies, equipment, systems, and machinery (excludes procurement of land).

Supply control Direction and restraint for requisitioning, receipt, storage, stock control, shipment, disposition, identification, and accounting, related to items of supply.

Supply management Continuing actions of planning, organizing, directing, controlling, and reporting the use of personnel, money, materials, and facilities to provide supplies and equipment to users or consumers.

Supply support Service parts, consumables, and related materials and documents necessary for scheduled and unscheduled maintenance; taking into consideration location, transportation, time, and overall availability to ensure maximum continuity and effectiveness of operations.

Supply system Organizations, offices, facilities, methods, techniques, and trained personnel utilized to provide supplies and equipment to users or consumers; and to take care of requirements computation, planning, procurement, inventory control, distribution, maintenance in storage, issue, and salvage or disposal of items and materials.

Support Action to sustain or complement any effort, item of equipment, system, project or program, operation, person, or organization, etc.

Support equipment Items required to maintain equipments and systems in effective operating condition under various environments. Support equipment includes general and special-purpose vehicles, power units, stands, test equipment, tools, and test benches needed to facilitate or sustain maintenance actions, detect or diagnose malfunctions, or monitor the operational status of equipment and systems.

System Correlated hardware, software, information, principles, doctrines, ideas, methods, procedures, and people arranged or ordered toward a common objective.

System effectiveness Probability that a system can successfully meet an operational demand within a given time, when operated under specified conditions—or a measure of the ability of a system to achieve objectives.

Systems engineering Application of scientific and engineering methods to the study, planning, design, construction, direction, and evaluation of person–machine systems whereby the relationships and utilization of the various parts of the systems are fully planned before releasing the design of the hardware, in order to achieve the best balance among operational, economic, and logistic support factors.

Systems management Directing, evaluating, planning, organizing, coordinating, and controlling of efforts of the developers and producers of a system, from the decision to develop, through the procurement and production phase, to final distribution, including "feedback" from users concerning operational effectiveness.

T

Technical data and information Engineering and production data, prints, and drawings; documents such as standards, specifications, technical manuals; changes and modifications; inspection and testing procedures; performance and failure data; or other forms of detailed knowledge.

Test and support equipment Special tools and checkout equipment, metrology and calibration equipment, maintenance stands and handling equipment required for maintenance. Includes external and built-in test (BIT) equipment considered part of the supported system or equipment.

Trade-off Action or decision generally concerned with the evaluation of alternatives and with compromises to obtain the best mix of support characteristics, system performance, and total or effective cost.

Training Pragmatic approach to supplementing education with particular knowledge and assistance in developing special skills. Helping people to learn to practice an art, science, trade, profession, or related activities. Basically more specialized than education.

Troubleshooting Locating or isolating and identifying discrepancies or malfunctions of equipment and determining the corrective action required.

Turnaround time Interval between the time a repairable item is removed from use and the time it is again available in full serviceable condition.

Transportation and handling support Special provisions, planning, reusable containers, and training necessary to help ensure adequate packaging, preservation, storage, handling, and transportation of materials, parts, equipment, personnel, data, and facilities.

U

Unscheduled maintenance (UM) or emergency maintenance (EM), or remedial maintenance (RM) or corrective maintenance (CM). Restoration of a failed item to usable condition.

V

Value engineering Organized, applied scientific effort for analyzing the design, manufacture, or construction, procurement, inspection, installation, operation, and maintenance of an item, to achieve the necessary performance, reliability, and maintainability at the lowest overall cost.

Variable costs Costs that change as a function of units or time or resources.

Vendor items Items or parts that are acquired by the equipment manufacturer or prime contractor without the acquisition of the design rights—where the prime contractor's source, or the manufacturer of the item for that source, has and retains proprietary rights with respect to design and processes.

W

Warehousing Operations and storage activities concerned with the receipt, storage, care, preservation, packaging, packing, marking, issue of items, and documentation and record keeping incidental to such operations.

Warranty Guarantee that an item will perform as specified for at least the given time.

CHAPTER 2

Systems for Logistics

"System" is defined as a combination or assemblage of correlated things—facts, principles, doctrines, ideas, methods, procedures, people, etc.—arranged and ordered toward a common objective.

A logical approach to logistics engineering and management requires study of the individual elements that form the functional building blocks, the methods, tools, and techniques used to combine them, and the master overview. Just as a house is constructed by carpenters, electricians, and plumbers using lumber, wire, and pipes: a logistics system is constructed by planners, engineers, and managers using people, material, and disciplines such as design, reliability, inventory control, and phased program planning.

Insufficient attention to logistics needs often results in the elements of the system breaking down, and the consequences can be costly.

Logistics systems have been with us since the beginning of humankind. In his book *Origin of the Races*, Carlton Coon states that "it takes five times as many calories per day to raise a male homo sapien as it does to raise a male mountain gorilla. Clearly, then, one of the most important problems to be solved by early man was the logistics system required for food transportation, inventory, and preparation."

SYSTEMS ENGINEERING

Systems engineering is the process of translating mission, test, production, deployment, support, and operational needs into the most cost-effective mix (i.e., balance). More specifically, mission needs are translated into engineering functional requirements and then expanded into detailed design requirements. Logistics support is a significant consideration in this process.

The systems engineering process is iterative, and encompasses functional analysis, synthesis, and optimization with the goal of achieving the proper balance among economic, operational, and logistics factors. The methods of attaining this goal depend upon the various elements involved, including the type of system or equipment, the extent to which tried and proved hardware and software are used versus new items, the degree of risk, and time pressures. The process is visualized as consisting of (1) formulating a tentative design for a new system, (2) studying it using analytical methods, (3) incorporating the results to create a new and better design, and (4) repeating the process until a completely feasible solution is produced. Systems engineering provides the tools to be applied to logistics support design. The design of system hardware and system support must be concurrent and interactive.

SUPPORT ELEMENTS

The elements of a logistics system are the inputs, process, and outputs. The first step in determining the requirements for a logistics system is to define the output objectives of that system. The single greatest failing in business, government, and industry is not establishing clear objectives and goals before attempting to solve problems. The following steps are easily grouped in what is known as the scientific method of problem solving and decision making.

1. Set objectives.
2. Identify problems.
3. Gather information.
4. Identify alternatives.
5. Analyze and evaluate.
6. Select the "best."

Table 2.1 lists the system steps actually used for the launching of a business machine.

After all possible elements are listed, the interactions (requirements and results) should be detailed. This can be done most effectively by constructing flowcharts and diagrams. There may be several levels of charts, ranging from the most important items delineated for top management to the most detailed assembly and checkout information provided for the installing service engineer. The functional approach assures that all facets of system development and operation are recognized and defined. It should be noted that forecasting may be necessary to determine future requirements.

COMPLEXITY AND OPTIMIZATION

The design of any system can be said to consist of two general activities: design selection and resource allocation. Design selection is concerned with generating an adequate definition of the function to be performed, identifying feasible alternatives for performing the function, and choosing the best or "optimum" alternatives. This is implicit in the systems engineering approach. The corresponding management function is the optimum allocation of resources.

As system complexity increases, the attainment of an optimum design requires close coordination of the two activities. One must guard against suboptimization, or violation of what may be termed the first law of

**Table 2.1
Support Systems for Launch
of a New Commercial Product**

Site specifications—space, electricity, etc.
Tech Rep selection and hire/transfer
Service training
Tools
Service Documentation
User Training
User Documentation
Parts
Repair plans and resources
Consumable supplies
Shipping materials
Rigger instructions
Equipment for hands-on trials
Information systems
Detailed support plan
Specifications, goals and measurements

systems engineering: "The composite result of a number of steps or actions, each optimized with respect to its own criteria, is not necessarily optimium and is sometimes unworkable." Figure 2.1 stresses this point.

Suboptimization can also exist in the design or operation of the support subsystem: the minimization of logistics delays to a level below that which is really needed (which costs money that could be better used elsewhere); the reduction of scrap costs, through repair rather than discarding subassemblies (necessitating excessive investments in documentation, test equipment, spares, facilities, and training); and the tremendous expenditures in personnel and facilities solely to minimize unscheduled maintenance downtime.

Increasing complexity also creates the need for more precise hardware designs and support system management since overdesign and inefficiencies rapidly become unsupportable at the total system level. Further, more accurate systems engineering and management interpretation and evaluation of design and operating data are integral at all levels of system design. The very factors that increase these needs make them difficult to satisfy. Thus it is frequently necessary to resort to empirical refinement of hardware designs through the evaluation of prototypes, field tests, and so forth.

Figure 2-2 shows an overview of a typical system development cycle.

RISK REDUCTION

Every logistician has horror stories about products that were designed and could not be supported. The systems approach greatly reduces this risk. Catastrophic failures are relatively rare and are usually not the worst penalties paid for poor logistics support planning. These failures cause one-time economic losses. The failure of marginal products or support systems creates a far greater drain on resources. The user experiences poor performance, low utilization rates, and abnormally high support costs. The hardware producer encounters difficulty in maintaining delivery schedules, excessive rework expenses, and costly redesign and modification efforts. It is more difficult to prevent marginal performance than catastrophe because of the subtleties involved in the decisions to be made, the difficulty in defining and measuring *a priori* the meaning of "marginal" and "optimum" in quantitative terms, and the many pressures exerted on the engineer, planner, and manager by cost and schedule.

To define and measure what is marginal and what is optimum before the system is in actual use also is difficult, since little data are available in the early stages of product development. Sometimes it is next to impossible even to identify all the factors affecting system use because

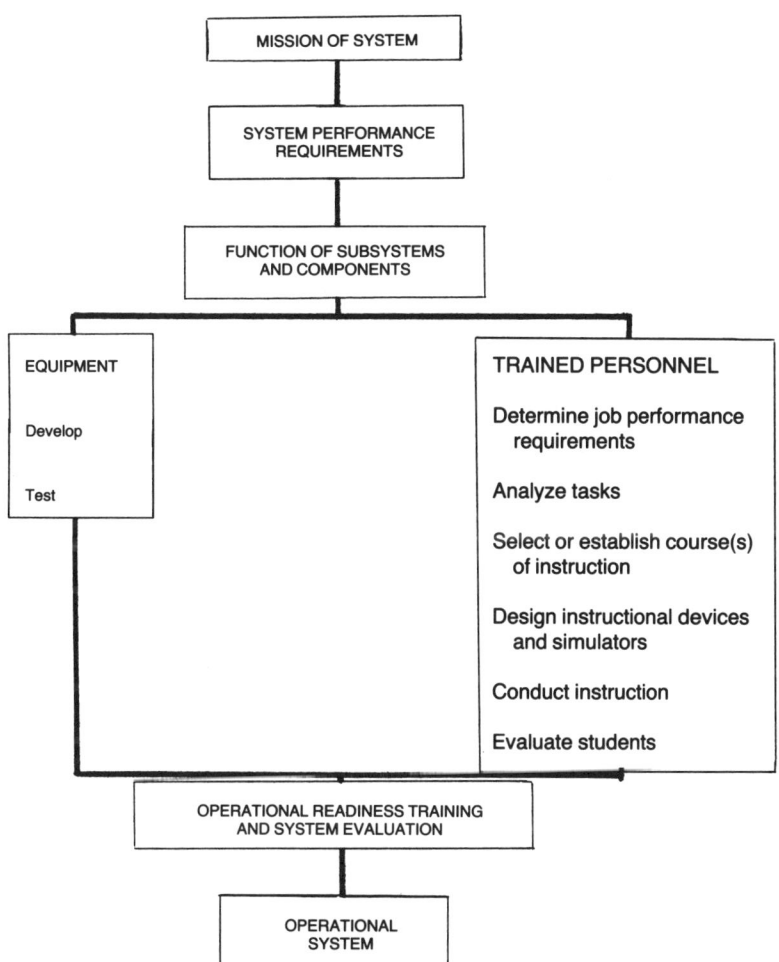

**Figure 2.2
Typical system development cycle**

the use environment can be changed radically once the system is put into service. Therefore it is important to have a change mechanism available to attend to any problems rapidly. There must be contingency planning and structured flexibility.

The systems approach is necessary to identify and evaluate items, considering future consequences. It allows risk to be recognized and at least considered, if not quantified, so that intelligent decisions can be made.

METHODS OF PLANNING, SCHEDULING, AND CONTROL

Plans are generally classified according to chronological time or purpose. Most organizations have operating plans covering a single year—often divided into quarters, months, weeks, or even days—which are termed short range. Long-range plans generally cover three- to five-year periods.

Plans may also be prepared for repetitive, nonrepetitive, and special events. Standing plans may be prepared for use any time an expected situation occurs. The aim of this section is to outline the major methods used in logistics planning, scheduling, and control.

Logistics performance can be measured and evaluated against many factors including:

Time
Cost
Frequency/rate/occurrences

All other factors are grouped under one or more of these categories to evaluate items of availability, reliability, turnover, and so forth. Projects differ from production processes in that they are normally nonrepetitive. They usually confront the decision maker with a unique situation in which prior experience and information for control do not exist. The major planning and control methods not covered in other specific sections are Gantt charts, critical path method (CPM), and program evaluation and review technique (PERT).

These methods require identification of every necessary element in the system, how long it takes to accomplish each task, and what input/output interactions are needed.

TECHNIQUES

Gantt Charts

Gantt charts are the simplest scheduling technique. They do not show interactions, but merely indicate start and stop times for each task.

This technique is most successfully applied to, highly repetitive operations. Gantt charts are used for both long-range production/construction planning and for short-range scheduling on a day-to-day basis. The short-range uses include job progress control charts. The familiar bar schedule is a form of Gnatt chart (Figure 2.3).

Line of Balance (LOB)

Though complementary to Gantt charts, line of balance (LOB) is more product oriented. It is useful in determining percentage of task completion, rather than amount of resources expended. LOB emphasizes major bottlenecks in the production process.

Work Breakdown Structure (WBS)

Events and activities can be organized into work packages, which permits analysis for cost, time, resources, complexity, and schedule. Individual work packages are combined and integrated into the project work breakdown structure, (WBS). The WBS provides an excellent management tool for planning, budgeting, and control.

Critical Path

Critical path analysis is a more powerful and versatile tool. CPM and PERT are variants of critical path analysis. CPM is a deterministic procedure. PERT is a probabilistic procedure. Both CPM and PERT are similar in their logical structure. PERT was developed in 1958 by representatives of the Navy Special Projects Office, Lockheed Aircraft,

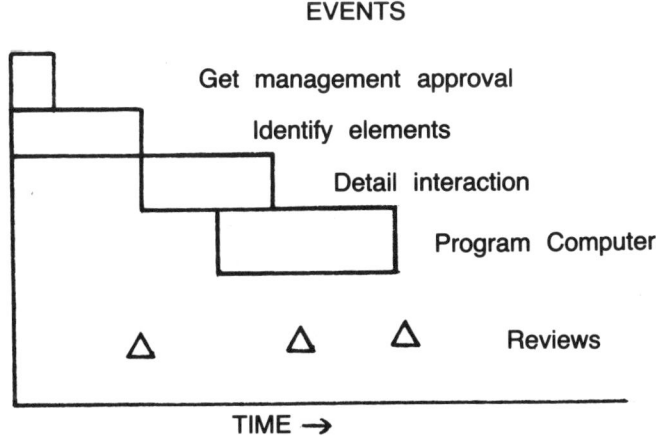

Figure 2.3
Bar schedule: A form of Gantt chart

and Booz, Allen, & Hamilton, Inc., to expedite the Polaris Ballistic Missile Program. It is credited with shortening the original estimated completion time by two years. Since that successful demonstration, the use of critical path analysis has spread rapidly. DoD requires critical path schedules on most major bids. Major applications are in research and development and construction, but uses are increasing for new product introduction, advertising campaigns, and even new store openings.

There are PERT techniques for both time and cost, called PERT/TIME and PERT/COST. In the words of Willard Fagan in *The Origin of PERT*, PERT is a dynamic planning approach "for diagnosing and anticipating the integrated influence of time, resources, and technical performance on the outlook for achieving end objectives."

Projects selected for scheduling and control with PERT or CPM will generally have:

1. A wide range of activities to be coordinated.
2. Completion time pressure, which is in turn dependent on several critical events.
3. A potential need for revisions due to unanticipated events.

Also, the time necessary for completion can be affected by the amount of money or effort available.

Structure

The first step is to develop a project network structure. An action involving *resources* and taking *time* is called an *activity*. Each activity has a beginning and an end, which are signified by *events*. An activity begins with the completion of some prior event and ends with its own completion. The challenge is to list all activities in a project and combine them into an efficient network structure showing in what order the activities are to be performed. A distinction is made between *sequential* (series) relationships and those that are *concurrent* (parallel). See Figure 2.4, where 1, 2, 6, 7 are sequential, but 1, 3, 5, 6 are concurrent with 1, 2, 6.

Time

Accurate times are necessary. CPM uses only one "most probable" time estimate. PERT time probabilities may be handled by several methods, of which the most popular is to get three estimates for each activity time, *optimistic, pessimistic,* and *most probable.* Times used are often $\Sigma[(0.5 \times \text{most probable}) + (0.25 \times \text{optimistic}) + (0.25 \times \text{pessimistic})]$. Any systematic bias should be refined by project coordinators using past experience and any analytical tools at their disposal.

Example

On the basis of most likely times, this shows

$$\text{Path } (1, 2, 5, 6) = 5 + 5 + 2 = 12 \text{ weeks}$$
$$(1, 3, 4, 6) = 7 + 4 + 4 = 15 \text{ weeks}$$
$$(1, 2, 4, 6) = 5 + 2 + 4 = 11 \text{ weeks}$$

The 15-week path is *critical* since it paces the program. Additional effort and cost might be desirable to spend its completion. Events along the noncritical paths have *slack* that can be used to perform the activities more efficiently, if necessary.

The control of PERT and CPM depends on reducing the critical path to the minimum possible time and then tracking all elements. A computer is essential for tracking. A typical section of printout is shown in Table 2.2.

The computer also makes quick work of replans. Probabilities may be used if they will make a schedule more realistic.

PERT/CPM provides powerful methods for planning, scheduling, and control of logistics systems.

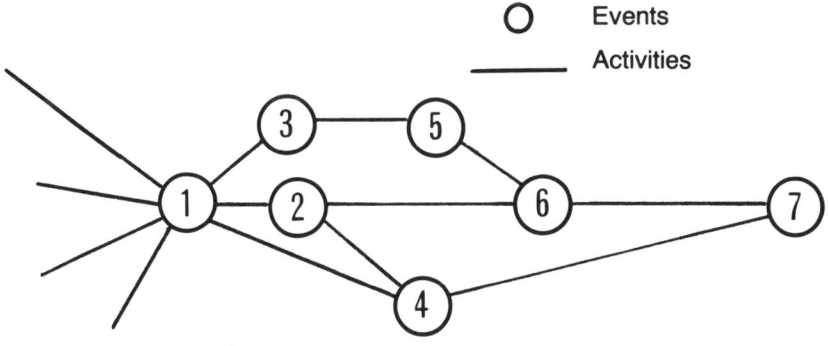

Figure 2.4
Project network structure

Table 2.2
Product Introduction Activity Printout

Plan Date		Actual Date	Activity	Responsible	Event No. 1
Jan. 5	C	1/12	IMO/CIT operator manual	NS/D PATTON	144
Jan. 8	C	1/8	Rigger training	NS/D PATTON	148
	C	1/8	Start Balt cust rep training	NS/D PATTON	149
Jan. 10	C	1/10	Start installation Baltimore demo machines	NS/D PATTON	150
	C	1/10	Rig Balt demo machines regional distribution center to branch	NS/D PATTON	151
	C	1/12	Recondition parts initial list for credit	NS/D PATTON	303
	C	1/10	16 B2 custmr units shipped	NS/D PATTON	347
Jan. 12	C	1/12	Care pkg spares @ Balt	NS/D PATTON	154

CHAPTER

3

Life-Cycle Costs and Profits

*L*ife-cycle costing is a fundamental concept in logistics planning and management. The basic premise is that every product, from idea to termination, can be analyzed and planned in terms of cost. Life-cycle costing considers all resources expended from an item's earliest inception; it is the *total* cost of ownership. Table 3.1 lists items that make up typical life-cycle costs (LCC).

The increasingly popular LCC approach is useful to the individual or organization as a decision-making technique, a trade-off tool, and a philosophy. It has at its center the flexibility to allow the user to evaluate costs in the face of constantly changing factors and uncertain future events. Consider the LCC components for typical household appliances illustrated in Figure 3.1.

The value of this technique can be clearly understood in light of the necessity to reduce risk and recognize changing influences so that effective planning can be executed.

1. The historical emphasis on production or acquisition cost alone is no longer valid. Analogous to an iceberg with the visible portion production costs, "hidden" support costs can often be seven times or more the original build cost.

2. Inflationary trends relate to the cost of money, energy, labor, and materials. Cost constraints, necessitated by decreasing real budget ex-

penditures, can be more efficiently realized by minimizing LCC.

3. The fast pace of technology may reduce present product life and obsolete product value long before startup costs are recovered.

4. Increasing liability costs require safer product planning and support.

5. Consumers are increasingly conscious of operation and maintenance costs over the duration of product life.

6. The U.S. government is requiring life-cycle costing for new military product contracts so support costs can be realistically planned.

7. Control of life-cycle costs can ensure greater life-cycle profits.

8. Analytical techniques with the aid of computers can result in better estimates of the future, and quantify, if not reduce, risk.

HISTORY OF LCC

Practical implementation of the LCC concept began in the early 1960s when the U.S. Department of Defense sponsored studies by the

Table 3.1
Life-Cycle Costs

Research and Development
  Basic research
  Program management
Advanced Development
  Equipment development and test engineering data
Production/construction investment
  Manufacturing—Nonrecurring and Recurring Facilities
  Initial logistics support
Operations and maintenance
  Operations
    Personnel
    Training
  Maintenace
    Personnel
    Scheduled preventive maintenance
    Unscheduled corrective repairs
  Support equipment
    Transportation
    Tools
    Modifications
  Facilities
  Support
    Repair parts and spares
    Facilities
    Tech data
Termination

Logistics Management Institute. As a result, trial procurements were made and DoD guidelines that focused on support LCC were issued. System programs began to include requirements for estimation and analysis of LCC.

There is an increasing awareness of the potential of life-cycle costing for industrial applications and impact on "bottom line" profit. As more consumers demand to know the true total cost of products, LCC will play a more significant role in every stage of a producer's planning.

LCC includes all research and development, investment and capital items, acquisition, production, operation, maintenance, and termination expenses. Many programs and projects have specific phases through which a proposed product moves, with particular check points to ensure performance. Life-cycle costs may be categorized in different ways depending on the elements of the system.

Commercial organizations often add the concept of life-cycle profits. Since revenue − expenses = profit, improving revenues is a significant factor in increasing profits. Life-cycle costs and profit optimization has as its goal increased revenues and reduced expenses. One must realize that if increasing expenses contributes to customer satisfaction and revenues, then the profit "bottom line" will increase.

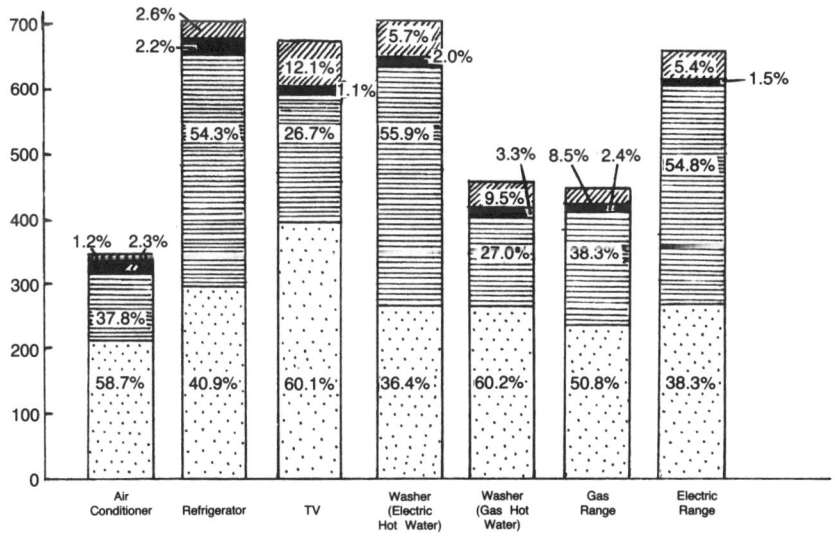

Figure 3.1
Life-cycle costs for home appliances

Timeliness

Timeliness of decisions with respect to alternative actions is crucial. A typical product cycle will have 90-95 percent of total LCC committed by the end of development. If costs are "sunk," then little can be done to alter them without further increasing total expenditures.

Reliability and maintainability are but two of the many factors that pivot on early LCC decision and action. With careful evaluation of all pertinent information, it may be seen in some cases that although front-end cost is higher, total LCC savings will result from reduced failure and maintenance.

LCC SYSTEM PROGRAM DEFINITION

The first step is to delineate the major elements in the item's life cycle. Most products will follow a system life cycle as shown in Figure 3.2.

Once the life cycle is described, a system program can be defined. Purposes and elements include:

1. Scenario of how product will be used and supported (use and support concept).
2. Essential assumptions underlying cost estimates.
3. Historical data on evolution of product design and cost estimates.
4. The establishment of a basis for critical review of product requiements and proposed design and support of those requirements.
5. The highlighting of those design areas with high technical risks and uncertainties.
6. System effectiveness as it relates to life-cycle costs.

The needs, resources, and constraints involved with even a moderately complex product will result in the consideration of thousands of factors. Pareto's principle of "the critical few" (Figure 3.3) provides a good initial emphasis. By concentrating on those swing factors that cost the most or are subject to the most change, LCC planning efforts can be efficiently invested for the greatest potential reward.

The best way to determine all factors is to have several brainstorming sessions with able representatives of all functional areas, and presided over by an experienced logistician. The importance of early involvement of all necessary managerial personnel for LCC to be successful cannot be overemphasized.

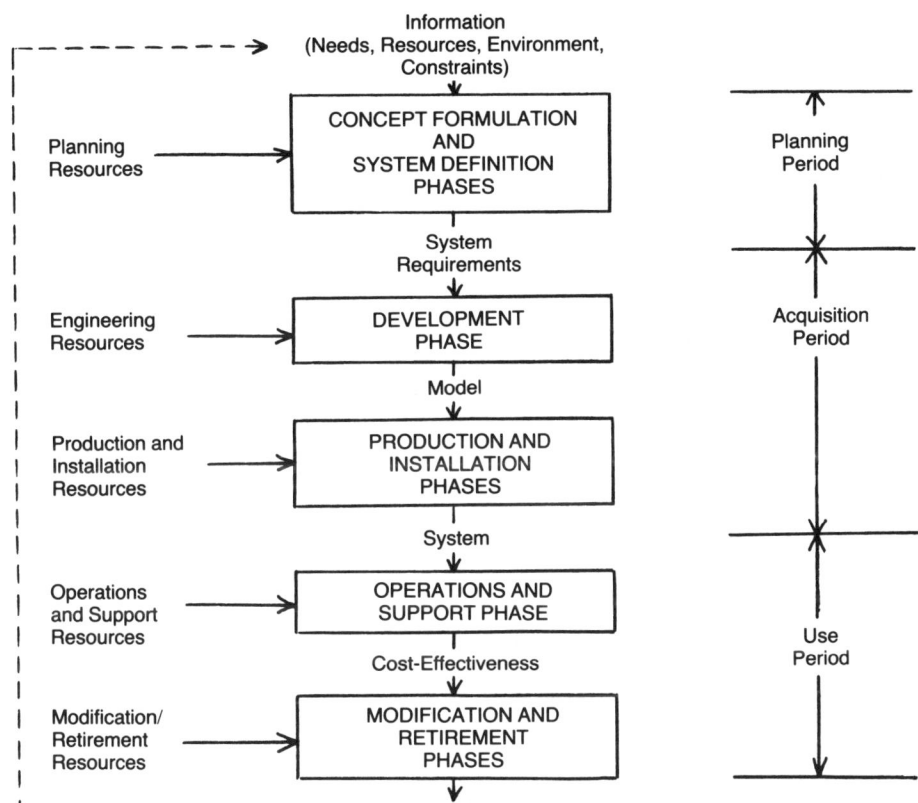

**Figure 3.2
System life cycle**

Product Life

One major time element in the LCC process is determination of product life. Termination time will vary, depending on factors of intended product environment and operational use scenario, in conjunction with considerations from marketing and finance. Table 3.2 shows the basic controlling factors.

A military weapons system or a commercial computer may have a finite life, after which it is technologically obsolete and must be scrapped. Many other durable products leased item may be improved during their life, so that a product such as a telephone set can continue to be very profitable years after its initial introduction. The life of a product sets an important starting point for financial LCC analysis of alternatives and trade-offs. Breakdown of costs for production against operation and service support can then be detailed. A product is normally built once, and serviced many times.

While a discussion of why it is not feasible to maximize product life may seem inconsistent, a quick review is offered:

1. There may be no need. Users may be satisfied with the status quo.

2. The required effort may be excessive in terms of labor or precious materials needed.

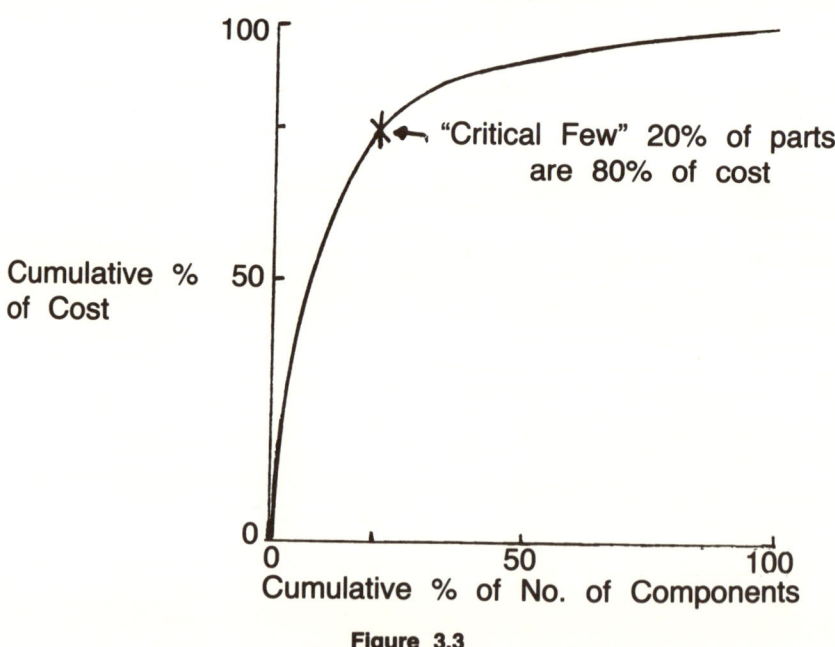

Figure 3.3
Pareto Analysis

3. Cost effectiveness may decrease from a standpoint of both loss of future sales revenue and increased service costs to support the product longer.
4. Present state-of-the-art technology may not be sufficient.
5. The ability to introduce ongoing improvements with production-line modifications may be reduced.
6. The resultant jobs shift and economic dislocation may cause production economies to suffer.

DTC, DTUC, DTLCC

In recent years there has been confusion as to the use of terminology of the concepts design-to-cost (DTC), design-to-unit-cost (DTUC), and design-to-life-cycle-cost (DTLCC). Often one term is used when another is meant.

DTC dates from the historical emphasis strictly on design and production costs for a product. This was due to the uncertainty and/or neglect of future cost considerations for support elements. The newer DTLCC concept is a primary design goal setting a unit cost that both meets given performance requirements and includes all other cost factors for the life cycle. Under DTLCC, once the producer–user relationship is established, the "affordable" costs for each segment of the life cycle are determined and alternatives explored. A target for DTUC can be set. DTUC can be a relatively small part of total life-cycle costs. This is not to diminish the importance of the DTUC concept; while production may only control a small part of the life-cycle cost, it can create many opportunities for future operation and support and life-cycle cost savings. As part of overall life-cycle cost management, both DTLCC and DTUC are techniques that can result in greater life-cycle profits.

FINANCIAL ANALYSIS PROCESS

Once the sequence of a product's life cycle has been determined, a methodology must be developed for a common basis of comparison

Table 3.2
Product-Life Controlling Factors

Product Life	Producer	User
Short-term	Support	Usage
Long-term	Replacement products	Purchase motivators

among possible alternative actions. This process for financial LCC analysis should consist of the following steps.

1. Set desired goals.
2. Define factor constraints in terms of available resources and system effectiveness. These include limitations and efficiencies of finance, personnel, and materials for the situation. For example, there is no sense in attempting to produce a product that will be too costly to maintain over its life, or setting a production schedule that is inefficient. Figure 3.4 details a listing of different evaluation levels of system effectiveness and the equivalent life-cycle cost components.
3. Explore evaluation solution alternatives and tradeoffs. This can include exploration of differing production, operation, and maintenance schedules and times for one product or a comparison of two similar products. Since LCC is a tool, and a sometimes complex and unwieldy one, several short-cuts are used to give quicker answers to specific questions. Trade-off analysis and change impact analysis (CIA) are useful for making decisions on single items or small segments, as compared with the whole life cycle.
4. Develop a financial model. This should consist of the various predicted costs for the development, production, and operation and support as they will occur over time. It will include the various interactions over the product life and allow for feedback.
5. Conduct data analysis. Sources for the data may be actual infor-

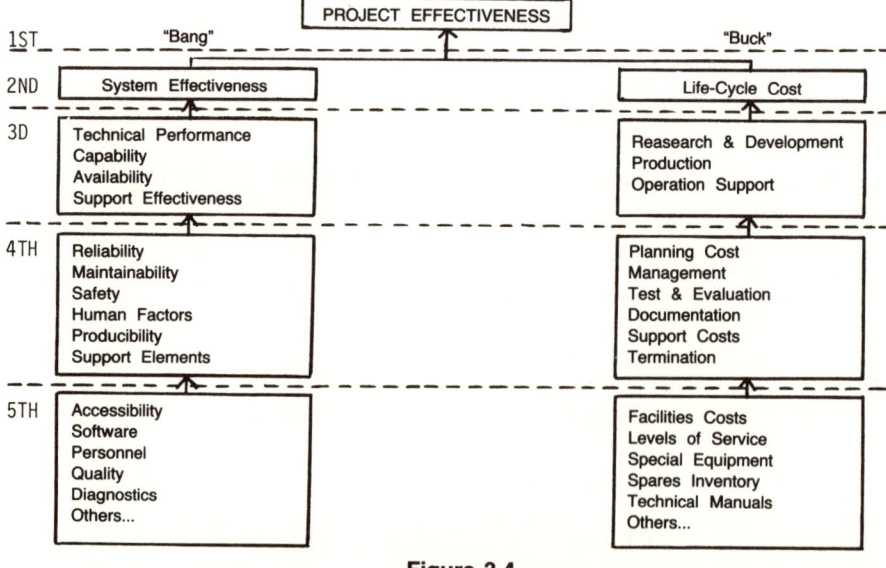

Figure 3.4
Evaluation priorities

mation on previous similar products, best estimates by knowledgeable personnel, or, most likely, a combination of the two. Once cost relationships have been formulated, an actual analysis of the life-cycle costs should be conducted. Present value, profit, and return on investment are common financial measures for achieving this. A detailed example using the present value technique will be discussed at the end of this chapter.

6. Interpret and validate cost analysis results. This is the most important and often least used step of the analysis process. This step allows the opportunity to make certain that cost factors, relationships, and available data or estimates are valid and have been interpreted in a manner on which all involved personnel can agree. Validation can include the use of sensitivity and indifference analysis for variations and uncertainties. Figure 3.5 shows a general cost analysis process.

Models

Many organizations have life-cycle cost models of varying complexity. A listing of the different product phases and costs of one such typical LCC model developed for service evaluations is shown in Table 3.3.

The basic intent of the models is to simulate the numerous product cost relationships during various parts of its life into individual segmented formulas. The segmentation results in an LCC program management tool for practical planning. Variations of inputs to the model, as done in trade-off analysis, can be useful for calculating the costing consequences for different actions.

LCC Problem Using Present-Value Technique

One common example of life-cycle costing is the process of evaluating a new car purchase. The following example details the life-cycle cost streams of three new automobiles. The desired car is expected to last for a period of four years and the average usage will be 15,000 miles per year. You have narrowed your choice to:

Type	Characteristics	Acquisition Cost
A	Medium size and performance, U.S., four-door, 15 miles/gallon	$9,900
B	Small size, high performance, import, two-door, 30 miles/gallon	14,900
C	Medium size, high performance, U.S., four-door, 25 miles/gallon	11,900

38 Life-Cycle Costs and Profits

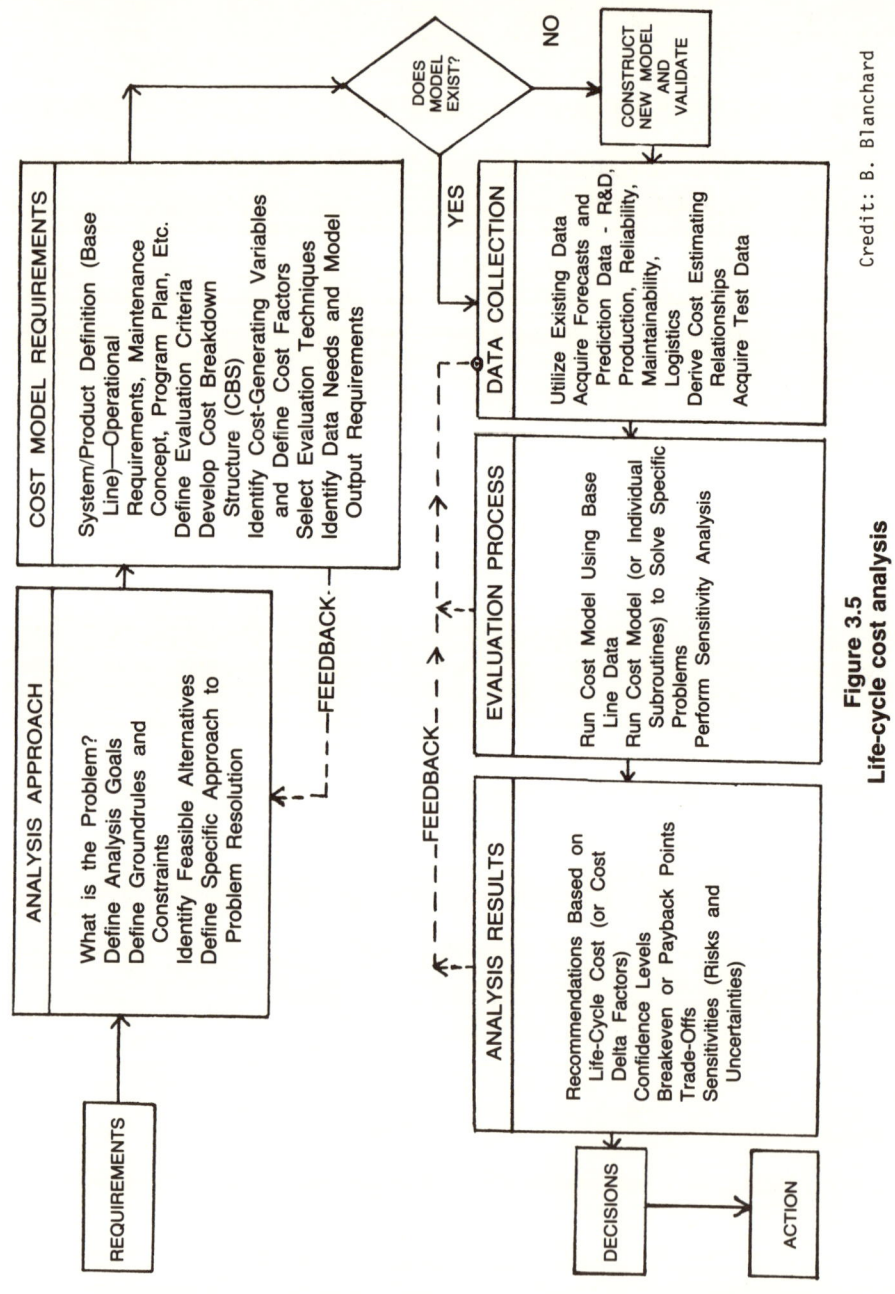

**Figure 3.5
Life-cycle cost analysis**

Credit: B. Blanchard

The following assumptions were made:

1. Salvage value at the end of the four-year life is zero.
2. Discount rate is 10 percent.
3. Depreciation and insurance are not included.
4. In doing analysis, dollars are rounded to nearest whole dollar (i.e., $1.47 = $1.00, $1.52 = $2.00).

Realistic estimates of operation and maintenance costs over the four-year life must be made for each year and car. Then the present-value technique is applied. In this case, the present-value discount factor for 10 percent, one, two, three, and four years in the future is multiplied by that year's actual dollar cost to give a common basis for comparison between the three car alternatives. The sum of the discounted four-year cost for operation and maintenance is added to the purchase price (not discounted since the car is bought at time = 0 years) to result in total life-cycle costs.

A summary of estimated operation and support costs for each car is illustrated in Tables 3.4 and 3.5.

Table 3.3
Service LCC Model Factors

R&D	Design	Production	Operation & Support	Termination
$Fixed	$Fixed	Variable costs	Operating	Remove
•Concept	•Drawings	•Materials	•Energy and materials	•Refurbish
•Feasibility	•Models	•Labor	•Operator training	•Rebuild/ Recondition
•Definition	•Tech data	•Packing	•operator info.	•Scrap
		•Preparation for shipment	•Operator labor	
		•quality control	Support	
		Fixed costs	•Personnel	
		•Facilities	•Installation	
		•Tools/ machines	•Calibration	
		•Overhead	•Repair	
		•Utilities	•Prevention	
		•G&A	•Spare parts	
		•Contingency	•Tools	
		•Profit	•Training	
			Downtime expense echelons:	
			•Operator	
			•Local	
			•Intermediate	
			•Depot/factory	

LIFE-CYCLE PROFITS

While the intent of LCC philosophy is to minimize total cost over product life, a related approach is to maximize life-cycle profits (LCP). Since profits are what is left once expenses have been subtracted from revenues, they will be affected by changes in revenues and expenses. For fixed revenue, as costs rise profits fall, and vice versa. We often concentrate on cutting costs while neglecting revenues. The key to maximizing LCP is a systems approach that attains the greatest balance of revenues against cost.

CHANGE IMPACT ANALYSIS

Change impact analysis, a variation of trade-off analysis, was developed to ensure that any design changes in hardware consider the total life-cycle costs related to that change. This is especially necessary where continuing service is important, as in leasing. Analysis of change goes beyond trade-off since a good decision can probably improve all parameters, whereas "trade-off" indicates that something must be given up in order to obtain improvement in something else. The example used throughout this discussion will focus on the analysis of change to a more costly component in a print copier to obtain lower service costs and increased customer satisfaction through improved reliability. Service cost

Table 3.4

Undiscounted Cost ($) Per Year of Ownership

Criteria	Auto	Yr. 1	Yr. 2	Yr. 3	Yr. 4	Description
1. Operation						Gas costs
	A	1110	1200	1300	1400	$1.10/gal in year 1
	B	555	600	650	700	$1.20/gal in year 2
	C	660	720	780	840	$1.30/gal in year 3
						$1.40/gal in year 4
						(15,000 mi. = mpg $1 gal = cost)
2. Unscheduled maintenance (labor and material)	A	220	370	420	400	Repairs
	B	185	295	250	500	
	C	100	250	300	400	
3. Scheduled maintenance (labor and material)	A	130	150	170	210	Oil changes, lubrication, periodic checks
	B	200	180	180	200	
	C	110	120	180	160	
10% discount rate factor		0.909	0.826	0.751	0.683	Year 0 = 1.000

projections evaluated with unit manufacturing costs are emphasized. The dollar is used as the common unit of measure.

Why should we evaluate changes? Ensuring the selection of the most profitable alternatives has to be dominant in the minds of those seeking maximum value for our resources. This includes government, private foundations, industry, and commercial business. Getting the most for our money should be everybody's objective.

FACTORS TO BE CONSIDERED

The first step is to clarify the change to be made in terms of what, why, how, when, and where. This can be done by looking at sketches, describing the idea verbally, or looking at actual hardware.

The life cycle of each item should be thought through from cradle to grave—definition, feasibility, design, production, operational phases, and so forth.

After the life cycle has been determined, the list of factors should be reevaluated to check for necessary additions or deletions. A list of common factors should be developed and directed to anyone involved. Those who are evaluating trade-offs should employ the agreed-upon figures so that there are fewer opportunities for misunderstanding or selective manipulation.

Typical common factors include:

Supported machine population.
Average machine life.
Base mean use time between maintenance (MTBM).
Base mean time to repair (MTTR).
Labor cost per hour.

Table 3.5
LCC Problem Answer

Automobile	Purchase Price	Consumer Operation and Support Cost				Total Life-Cycle Cost
		Yr. 1	Yr. 2	Yr. 3	Yr. 4	Present Value $
A						
Actual	9900	1460	1720	1890	2010	
Discounted	9900	1327	1593	1419	1373	15,612
B						
Actual	14900	940	1075	1080	1400	
Discounted	14900	854	888	811	956	18,409
C						
Actual	11900	870	1090	1260	1400	
Discounted	11900	791	900	946	956	15,493
Year	0					
10%						
Discount rate factor	1.000	.909	.826	.751	.683	C is lowest LCC

QUANTIFICATION

Dollars should be used as the common denominator because they are the only common item of measure into which all items we use can be converted. For example:

$20 = 100 miles of automobile transportation
       4 main drive motors
       30 minutes of an engineer's labor
       2 special service tools
       or the profit expected after tax on $200 revenue

Ordering factors according to priority is a major step in converting to dollar value. (Items that cannot be expressed in dollars will be covered later in this book.) First noted are items that are necessary because the specification, contract, or management requires them. It is important to make sure that these are genuine needs. Change impact analysis is very helpful in this area.

Other items are ordered in terms of their impact on schedule, performance, and risk.

Performance features can be arrayed according to joint determination by Marketing, Service, Manufacturing, and Engineering. Risk is an important consideration because in many situations a high probability of obtaining only a moderate profit is preferable to a low probability of a high profit. The impact on end profit may also be considered in setting priorities.

A person familiar with a particular area can usually rank factors without study. For many trade-off analyses this is an advantage because it is not a complicated process. The straightforward factors can be separated from the esoteric ones, and at this point all factors can be addressed in order of priority.

Quantifying those subjective factors that were not easily given dollar values—aggravation, availability, feasibility, risk, to name a few—can be achieved by grouping the items together and ranking them relative to one another. At minimum, the influences can be determined to be positive or negative.

If the dollar-valued factors are close on each side of the decision, then the subjective factors may tip the balance. There is no substitute for sound management judgment, however. In the end, it is the manager with experience, who has looked at the facts, who will step in with a recommendation.

FINANCIAL ANALYSIS

Once the majority of items are dollar-valued, the difference in time and payback relationship must be computed to a common base. Present value (PV), profit, and return on investment (ROI) are common financial measures for achieving this. It is desirable to keep decision making at the lowest possible level. For this reason, development of the common factors and use of simple sensitivity and indifference relationships is a great help. A simple ratio such as $100 unit cost equals $1 servicing cost per 1000 copies is good because this simple figure can be thought of and used quickly without referring to complex, sometimes questionable, graphs.

If all costs are incurred at the time of manufacture, and payback is either at that time or spread out uniformly, then the simple sensitivity ratio or graph can be used by the field engineer or advanced manufacturing engineer. If costs of payback follow any other pattern, the assistance of a financial expert is needed.

With appropriate modification, this procedure can be used for almost every decision to be made. One must use judgment to determine whether to take the time to make such an analysis or to employ the facts at hand and use personal experience to make a rapid decision. Bayesian analysis is a very useful technique for quickly determining the consequences of a right versus wrong decision.

The most common decisions involve a change that costs more to build, but that should improve reliability or mean time to repair. Special forms can be developed, if there are many trade-offs to be made following a particular pattern. They are useful when there are many people involved in making trade-offs to ensure that all considerations are covered and that common logic is used. If an item is not applicable, it is omitted.

ESTABLISHING AN ANALYSIS PROCEDURE

A decision should be made at the lowest possible level consistent with unbiased information, so the first step is to identify the point of need. The design engineer is probably the choice. But the design engineer is already under a great deal of pressure and does not need to cope with further complication. What the design engineer does need is to recognize when a decision has to be made and an easy way to contact those in charge of recommendations. A contact in field engineering and one is advanced manufacturing engineering solves this problem. A cooperative atmosphere and two-way communication are necessary to ensure that the design engineer and all functional groups can be made aware when something may pose a potential problem to the other.

One person should be responsible for providing the indifference and sensitivity graphs, constant factors, check list, and other aids to all participating parties.

A formal training session is necessary in the beginning to explain the system, run through several examples of the logic, and have the financial people explain the derivation of the graphs and factors. Follow-up and on-the-job experience is of the greatest significance. Continual communication and honest quantitative decision making can build mutual respect among functional groups. Given a positive environment with managers who believe that quantitative decision making is a must, change impact analysis can be developed to provide an effective method for an organization to determine the dollar value of change.

In conclusion, the techniques of life-cycle cost and profits are valuable analytical tools. Dollars get management attention and are the best way of qualifying decisions.

CHAPTER 4

Information Systems

The wealth of human knowledge doubled between the years 1 A.D. and 1750. By 1900 it had redoubled, and by 1950 it had doubled again. Between 1950 and 1960 knowledge doubled yet another time. According to Ralph Davidson, publisher of *Time*, it continues to increase at an exponential rate. By definition this means that our store of information has increased at an extraordinary pace since, as William Simon points out in his book *Administrative Behavior*, "Whatever the nature of the 'real world' outside man's minds, we know nothing about the world (i.e., there is nothing in our minds about it) until we receive information about it." In effect, any characteristic of a situation that can be observed and recorded represents potential information for decision making. What ultimately determines whether the data are of value to decision makers is the data's perceived contribution toward goal attainment. Even if information were considered irrelevant with respect to present goals, it still might be useful to future decisions. Therefore, management faces the continuous problem of obtaining information and then of converting it into goal-oriented action. One of the most promising tools being developed to aid in decision making is called information theory.

The starting point in information theory is the source, or set of sources. Faced with numerous items of information, the decision maker is free to select those deemed most useful in the particular situation. Transmission of information is facilitated by the use of signs, symbols, and other forms of expressing conditions such as $, ILS, and ?. Their propriety is determined in a specific instance by the degree to which the message serves its purpose and supplements the receiver's previous knowledge. In other words, the quality of the information must meet the expectations of the decision maker.

The capacity of an information channel is measured in bits. A bit is the amount of information that can be conveyed by choosing between two alternatives: for example, between left and right, debit and credit, yes and no, heads or tails, on or off. Bits of information are crucial components of decision making because, by sequentially selecting between the two alternatives available, a decision can be reached by the process of elimination. Through the manipulation of codes, messages can be transmitted within the channel capacity. Present computers can use only coded information, although future models may be able to recognize handwritten and verbal input.

PROBLEMS IN THE INFORMATION PROCESS

The following problems arise in the information process.

1. Reliability
2. Validity
3. Redundancy
4. Quality
5. Relevancy
6. Insufficiency
7. Excess
8. Timeliness
9. Cost

The consideration of each problem can provide a better understanding of the characteristics that should be included in logistic information systems. Reliability reflects degree of consistency; thus the reliability of information can be measured. On the other hand, validity, the degree to which information contributes to the goals of the individual or organization, is not so easily measured. Information becomes distorted as it is transmitted because of filters between the transmitter and receiver. Redundancy is that part of the message that is unnecessary. It increases the volume that has to be handled, which can result in the distortion of the information's significance. Russell Ackoff noted, in his article entitled "Management Misinformation Systems," that most managers, rather than suffering from a *lack* of relevant information, suffer more from an *overabundance of irrelevant information.*

Optimal decision making requires up-to-date relevant information, but such information in sufficient and verified quantities is seldomly readily available. And the search for useful data is time consuming and expensive. Time is most problematic when what is required involves conditions outside of the company, such as technological development, government policies, and competitive practices. Computerized data processing is valuable when large amounts of data must be processed in a short period of time; however, a long time is required to provide program changes, and there are problems in dealing with anything that is not standard.

Finally, the cost of information is a fundamental problem. Gathering information is an expensive undertaking, even when it can be done by personnel within the organization. Many companies cannot justify the costs of consulting firms to assist in providing additional information and different interpretations of what already exists. Moreover, from the perspective of many managers, information gathering does not rate a high priority in the firm or in the employee's job description. Fortunately, most logistics organizations are willing to determine and meet the costs necessary to get good information.

INFORMATION USERS

From the viewpoint of the logistics system, information needs are concentrated in design, manufacturing, and the field sales and service organizations. One of the major jobs of Industrial Sales is to provide information on a continuing basis so that their goods and services will be chosen over others who do not offer the same information.

Control of the production environment has been the subject of many scientists and writers. Frederick Taylor, Henry Gantt, Henri Fayol, Ralph Davis, and Frank and Lillian Galbreth are among the many who have devoted a great deal of attention to scientific analysis and quantitative management. Their findings indicate some of the functions in which information plays a critical role:

Control
Communication
Problem detection and analysis
Correction
Forecasting
Planning
Scheduling

The measurement of output against the standard is what most would recognize as quality control. The American Production and Inventory Control Society (APICS) is a large professional organization dedicated entirely to the use of information within production. The production control system—including control over factory parts and raw materials, materials requirements planning (MRP), just-in-time (JIT) resources, dispatching, and expediting—is an integral subsystem of the total logistics system of the firm.

FIELD INFORMATION

The service organization operates in both the internal and external environments. It must receive accurate information from Design and Production so that the proper support equipment and software are made available, and so that the customers' needs can be accommodated. Every service organization will have a field reporting system with a network of information systems, including routine, exceptions, and specials. Feedback from those systems is vital to assist the service organization in assuring customer satisfaction, to efficient and economical operation, and to the promotion of design and quality improvement. The amount of interest in field information is dependent upon a continuing business and service relationship with the products. A consumer product that will be discarded if it fails receives little long-term attention unless sales falter. Durable goods are of more interest, particularly if they are leased, since service is then a way of protecting the owner's investment. Interest will depend on whether it will be serviced by the selling organization, a franchiser, or an independent organization. In the case of the military, complete information systems exist that report the maintenance time and parts replaced at higher than field echelons. Survey teams often get field reports, or in the case of aircraft, they are accurately maintained by Flight Maintenance and Operations.

The only information that may be available to the manufacturers of home appliances is the sales of replacement parts. They get warranty charge information, which gives them a perspective on the initial repairs of a product. After that initial period, they hear very little unless there are catastrophic failures. Automotive service departments keep detailed records on each automobile, and these may be easily analyzed by factory representatives.

Contract service organizations maintain accurate records of every service call. These reports are completed by the customer engineer after every action. The reports attempt to show not only the parts used, but also what areas were serviced and how much time was required. Feeding back the results of the customer engineer's reports to Engineering and Quality is also critical.

Exception reports are used for special events such as fires, safety hazards, or defects in an initial group of machines after a change has been made.

Special reporting systems are often necessary for such events as special reviews and beginning field trials, when the detail of information and timeliness of existing systems may not be adequate. These special systems are usually used on a select group of people and machines, with sampling results then transformed to predict the entire population.

DATA PROCESSING

In its simplest perspective, data processing involves (1) collection, (2) conversion, (3) verification, (4) manipulation, and (5) output.

Data collection, as a fundamental activity in the process, obtains the facts when they are necessary. Selectivity is required to overcome the information explosion on one hand, and information scarcity on the other. Data collection sources, methods, and content must be reviewed periodically to determine whether the process is attaining management's intended purpose. Particularly when the system is recording information about human beings, change is inevitable and must be accommodated. There are many ways to mechanize data collection, including time clocks, pipeline gauges, and counters. One of the most obvious changes in data collection is the use of the Uniform Product Codes on grocery items, which can be read by a computer rather than a checkout clerk.

Data conversion is necessary since raw data can rarely be used. Conversion simplifies the data content and puts it in a form for easy analysis. Translating devices such as optical character readers are becoming important for high-speed data conversion. Verification is necessary to ensure the desired accuracy. Every credit card, for example, contains a check digit as the last number. Through a complex series of additions, subtractions, multiplications, and divisions on the preceding numbers, the check digit verifies that the numbers are correct. As computer software becomes more "intelligent," systems are checking themselves and interacting with operators to request verification and correction of possible errors.

Data manipulation is done by separating the classification of procedures or transactions, using each type of transaction to produce several outputs, and rearranging data sequences.

MANAGEMENT NEEDS

The goals of management dictate the rearrangements of data. The separate handling of transactions by classes is shown by the segmenting of expenses into departmental functions such as finance, marketing, personnel, R&D, and production. Each of these classifications can be broken down into more finite expense accounts. Data inputs that are rearranged by using each type of business transaction to produce several outputs are shown by considering expenses in terms of units of actual production, inventory, sales, and profit, or as potential investment in future production, inventory, sales, and profits.

The rationale underlying the third way of manipulating data; by rearranging data sequences, is that there is a logical sequence of events. Accounting students, for example, learn systematic and logical frameworks for arranging data into financial statements. PERT (program evaluation and review technique), PACE (performance and cost evaluation), and CPM (critical path method) have forced management to plan production and distribution activities more accurately. These systems operate to improve performance by a rearrangement of path and data.

Output of a data processing activity is the most important item to a manager. As in the previous functions of data processing, selectivity is important to the effective use of data output. The user/manager must guide the systems analyst in creation of a system that will provide necessary output. If a manager wants specific information that follows a set pattern, the computer can be easily programmed to provide it and thus clearly identify undesirable variances and point out corrective action. The major reason most businesses are "data rich and analysis poor" is reluctance on the part of management to sit down with the data processing people and clearly explain needs and guide the process that will give efficient data processing.

DP ADVANCES

While early computer systems were offline and usually required batch processing, there are now widespread online systems. The first implementers of the online data processing system were airline ticket agents. Other uses of online data processing systems now exist in manufacturing, retailing, inventory control, stock exchanges, and even in maintenance of computers. Computer power, speed, and capability continue to increase dramatically relative to size and cost.

Memory systems ranging from tape to magnetic disks to optical disks and even small magnetic strips on credit cards are improving rapidly in speed, capability, and cost. Acquisition and display systems are automatically reading data through magnetic or optical sensors, allowing keyboard-like data entry directly into magnetic storage, and showing requested information rapidly to the operator via VDT (video display tube) or high-speed printer. Computers may now be linked to many terminals through standard voice-grade telephone lines or other communications links that are adapted to high-speed data transmission at reasonable costs.

Because of improved software programming techniques the level of expertise needed to guide and operate computers is on the decline. The machines themselves are becoming capable of doing internal interactions that previously had to be guided by highly trained programmers.

While the ability to process information rapidly is increasing, the temptation to gather masses of data should be resisted. Managers must be directly involved in the information system to determine what, specifically, she needs to know; and then turn that objective over to the information experts so they can deliver the facts.

CHAPTER

5

Program/Project Planning and Management

There are two basic approaches to product development. The classical approach is to develop a product in response to a market need. The other approach is to define and develop a product and then create a market for it. New technologies such as microprocessors, lasers, and fiberoptics are examples of the latter situation. Short takeoff and landing (STOL) aircraft and energy-efficient automobiles are examples of the classical approach of responding to a market need. Though the role of product planning is different for each case, it is even possible to use the approaches simultaneously within a product line.

Product planning normally takes place in the very earliest phases of program/project development. The two words "program" and "project" will be used synonymously to mean the activities directed toward bringing a new product through the acquisition process into the user environment. The product planning function may continue after products are in users' hands, through modifications that improve and enhance the basic product and with follow-on improved products.

ORGANIZATION

Bureaucratic and functionally structured organizations have major problems with bringing new products through development to production and into the marketplace. Committee, matrix (grid), and overlapping forms of organization are only slightly more successful. The most efficient form to date is the structure called project/task/goal. Participants in the project organization share common intent with common goals and supportive tasks. This structure is shown in Figure 5.1.

The project form of organization is used by many government agencies, most of the aerospace industry, and commercial companies concerned with a high rate of new product development and introduction.

A team approach to product planning is most prevalent since the majority of functions must interact. Typical members of a program team will include a program manager, with assistance for planning and control, and functional representatives from engineering, production, logistics, finance, sales, and other support functions. Normally these representatives operate in a matrix environment with two bosses. One boss is their functional manager and the other boss is the program manager. This organizational structure has a disadvantage with split authority, but it has a major advantage in that concentrating team efforts on development of a specified product is the most effective means of meeting objectives.

The time period from concept to production is often five years or more. Risk and uncertainty are reduced at each successive phase, and decisions are made to increase investment commensurate with the chance of success.

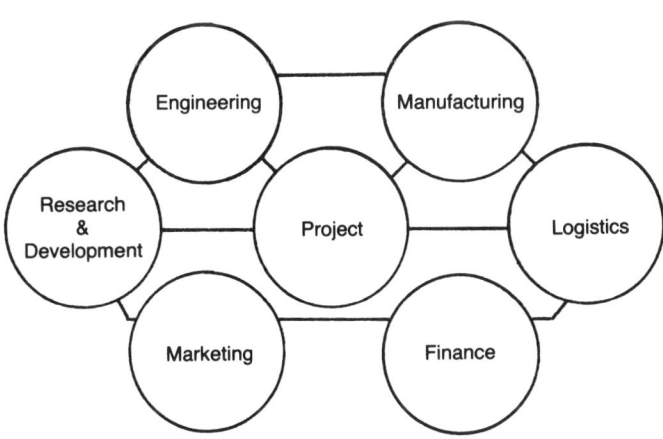

Figure 5.1
Project management structure

ACTIVITIES

The activities required of each organization should be enumerated, following the scenerio of the product's life. Experience with similar products and brainstorming with representatives of involved functions should provide the initial check lists.

To schedule and control activities efficiently, CPM and PERT should be employed. This requires identification of input and output interfaces for each event, and determination of time required for each. Several interactions and negotiations will be necessary to establish a valid network. There may be several levels of events established, with the level of detail greatest at the lowest functional working level and decreasing as it rises in the organization. A four-level structure is good, with only the major summary events shown on the first level for top management. A second level would be used by program management, a third level by functional PMs, and the fourth by the detailed working level organization. As an example, the third level net used by logistics (called national service/distribution) program management for a copier program contains about 300 events. There were over 10,000 events tracked on fourth-level nets.

The level of detail in activities and documents will increase at each phase. For example, a set of performance goals should be prepared in the earliest concept phase. They will be refined and approved at each phase review until they become firm specifications prior to production.

GUIDELINES

There must be corporate or government guidelines to provide a framework for efficient new product development. These should include policies, procedures, handbooks, long-range plans, operating plans, and development manuals.

The involved organizations will have guidelines established by budgets, facilities, growth projections, phase proposals, and reviews.

KEY MEASUREMENTS

Progress versus plans should be evaluated at least monthly. Formal progress reports including task achievement and costs are necessary. Additional reports should be made for phase reviews.

Every phase should have objectives that must be met before the program is advanced. This stairstep progression helps assure achievement before the next payment is made.

Logistics costs should be reforecast at each significant milepost. Major detailed predictions are suggested for each phase review, and only major variances considered each month.

Configuration changes caused by design or manufacturing have major influence on logistics. Engineering requests, specification changes, and engineering changes usually affect R, M, economics, or levels of effort. Therefore, the numbers and scope of engineering documents should be tracked.

Tests, reviews, and demonstrations provide additional information. Maintenance task analysis (MTA) and maintainability demonstrations (MDs), qualification tests, field studies, special audits, and field performance feedback all provide measures of progress against plan.

PROBLEM IDENTIFICATION AND CORRECTION

A deviation from objectives is a problem. Proper identification and detailing are the first step toward solution. After facts are established, the alternatives are enumerated. Then analysis and evaluation should lead to recommendations for corrective action. The reason for program management is to avoid or alleviate problems, so special attention goes to problem solution.

Specific allocation of responsibility is effective. The person who can most quickly advance corrective action should be selected: not necessarily the person who caused, or is causing, the problem. For example, if a frequent part failure is a problem, it could be assigned to the logistics manager as the person who can arrange training and replacement parts to pacify customers while the longer range improvement of the defective parts is accomplished.

PHASED PROGRAMS

Phased program planning and management (PPP&M) is an effective family of techniques and tools that assist new programs to progress rapidly from dreams to realities. PPP&M helps to:

1. Assure all tasks are identified.
2. Establish who is responsible for what.
3. Set schedules and standards.

4. Balance investment against risk and potential payoff.
5. Assure resources at proper time.
6. Promote effective communication.
7. Meet total (system) program objectives efficiently.

CHAPTER 6

Specifications

Specifications form the contract that lists all parameters that must be met in product or system performance. There may be specification packages for the total system, and also for the individual elements of design, manufacturing, marketing, and service support. Service organizations must have a clear definition in writing of what they can expect and what others expect of them. This is similar to the input and output approach taken in functional design specifications.

The first documents created may be called goals, since the parameters should be written, measurable, understandable, challenging and achievable. The goals form a basis for discussion. Goals must be established in the concept and feasibility stages of a product's life cycle, and must be detailed at every successive step, so that when the production phase is started, the specifications are firm and agreed to by all parties. The importance of stringent specifications cannot be overemphasized since the product is going to be designed and built once, but serviced many times. Patton's principle that "the last should be fast and be best of the rest" holds true. Service, being the last, should expect to be faster and better than planned, to make up for deficiencies in quality and schedule. Performance against specifications must be measured often and the deviations identified, along with their profit impact. Table 6.1 illustrates a sample worksheet. Service must be prepared to justify any specifications, and should support demands with facts wherever possible to establish credibility.

Table 6.1
Sample of Specifications Forecasts, and Impacts

	Specifications	Forecast	Deviation	Profit $ Effect of Development	Profit $ Impact of Improvement	Comments
Reliability						
Mean copies between service calls (MCBSC)	1/3400 intro (294 sc/10^6) 1/7000 mature (142/10^6)	1/3000(333)	−400(39)	2.56×10^6 calls = $64 million	$1/10^6 = 64 \times 10^3$ calls = $1.6 million	Priority I
Maintainability						
Mean corrective maintenance time	0.75 hr, 95% ≤ 2.25 hr	x̄ 1.0 same	−0.25 hr	$6.25 × 64 × 10^3 = $400,000.	$6.25/call	Priority II
admin (Mct)	0.25 hr 1.0 hr, 95% ≤ 3.0 hr	1.25	0			
Administrative						
Response time	X̄ 3.3 hr, 95% ≤ 7 hr	x̄ 2.9 hr 95% ≤ 7 hr	+ 0.4 hr	0	0	Can relax and possibly save $
Special events						
Installation	X̄ 0.75 hr, 95% ≤ 1.25 hr	Same	0	0	1 min. = $.42 5 min. × 1 M instals = $2M	
Set up	0.75 hr, 95% ≤ 1.25 hr	Same				
Admin and Trng	1.5 hr, 95% ≤ 1.75 hr					

COVERAGE

Goals and specifications should include typical mission scenarios to bound the performance desired of a product. These terms and conditions of use necessarily limit conditions under which the product is expected to perform. Here, service management must participate because their experience and intuitive judgment will be more realistic and practical than other participants. Service people often see the computer run without air conditioning, the car that has never been lubricated, and the copier that sits on top of the heater on the loading dock. At the same time, we must ensure that efforts are balanced and attention given according to the need and frequency of occurrence and cost.

FAILURES

The most important parameter is failure rate, since a product needs corrective service only if it fails. The main specification for reliability is mean time between failure (MTBF), with time stated in terms most meaningful to the product. That could include:

Time—hours/days/weeks/etc.
Distance—miles/kilometers/knots/etc.
Events—photographs/copies/cycles/etc.

MAINTAINABILITY/MAINTENANCE/SERVICEABILITY

Service management must know what will be required to prevent or alleviate failure, and what to do if corrective action is necessary. Statistically based specifications are necessary for all activities in the scheduled and unscheduled maintenance cycles. The elements may be diagrammed as shown in Figure 6.1.

ADMINISTRATION

Response time, availability of spares, and customer relations time/call may be specified so that all elements of the scenario are covered. These will be the major components of service time and costs.

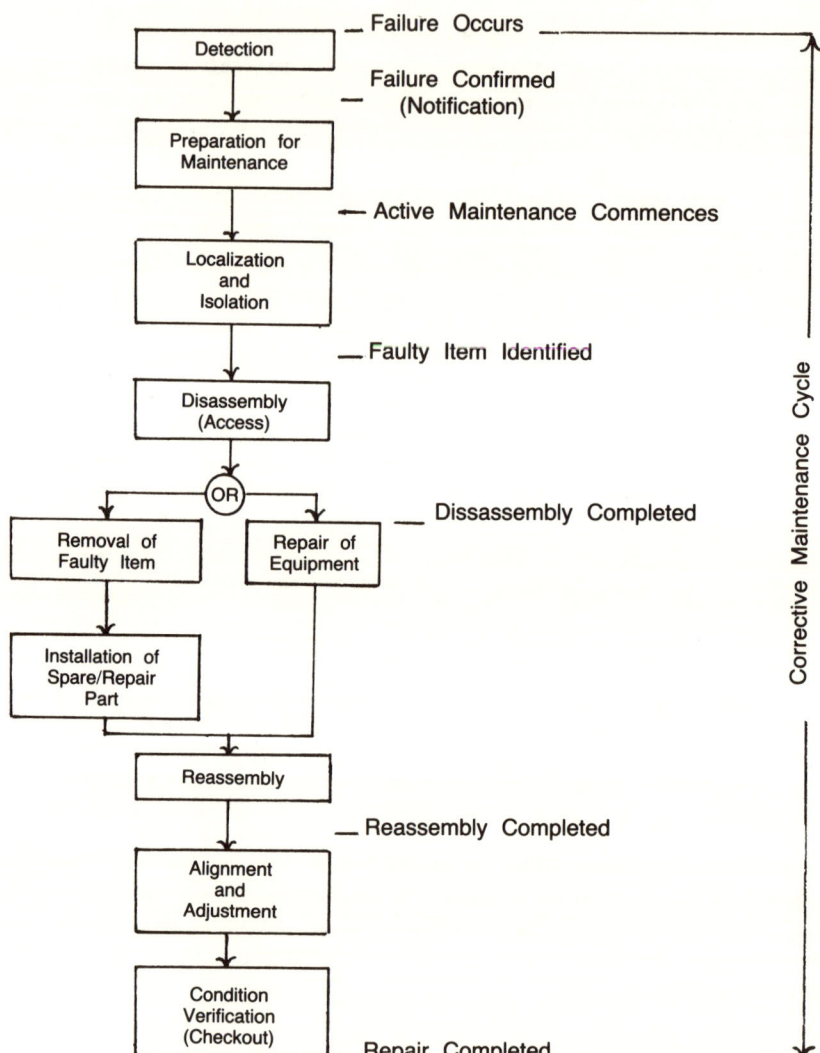

**Figure 6.1
Elements of a corrective maintenance cycle**

SPECIAL EVENTS

Every product has special events that are of significance to the service organization, and therefore require detailed specifications. These may include:

Installations
Removal
Refurbishment
Modifications and retrofits
Service personnel training
Customer training
Tools
Spares availability
Credit for returned items
Required inventory locations

Installations, for example, should include in detail the amount of time needed, any checks and adjustments necessary, special tools or fixtures required, number of personnel, and any essential outside assistance such as riggers.

COSTS

Costs are the bottom-line reason for all the other specifications; however, they are greatly affected by inflation, taxes, and other economic parameters. Ratios tied to use are a good way to specify costs, such as costs per mile or cost per thousand copies. Costs can also be meaningfully expressed as ratios such as expenses: revenues. However, management should ensure that one side of that ratio cannot be unilaterally shifted. Such would be the case if sales prices were suddenly dropped 10 percent, causing a corresponding decrease in revenues. The idea is that the price decrease would cause increased sales and thereby keep the total revenues constant. This is not necessarily so. Return on investment (ROI) is another good specification measure for service, since the amount of resources required can be quite high considering the payback. ROI gives service a good arguing tool for showing marketing and others that many small products and frequent change creates a large burden to service, compared with the potential return. Many organizations are hesitant to specify the cost and financial parameters and instead consider them guidelines. However, if they are not specified, the involved people are not strongly motivated to meet them. At the very least, individual products should have costs specifications so that their sums will add up to the organizational guidelines for costs.

Assuming the service organization is a business center and obtains revenue as well as expenses, it should have its own revenue versus expense ratios specified, since these will influence demand as well as their own supply. There should be a mechanism for transferring costs back and forth between internal organizations so that design, for example, may be stimulated financially to provide changes that will give profits to service. Costs are the major motivating factor that can be attached to all specifications.

CHAPTER

7

System Design and Development Process

The growth of technology in the 20th century has led to complexities in modern planning that greatly affect the efficiency of the resulting activities. Perhaps the most significant recognition occurred during World War II when the design and implementation of new weapons involved large numbers of personnel and very complex equipment for the first time on a recurring basis. Not only did their plans require the solution of technological and scientific problems, but they had to solve the attendant problems of communication among a diverse array of disciplines and people of different training and abilities. It was not to be for approximately 15 years, after many expensive, abortive trials in the development of complex systems, that the armed services delineated an explicit process for the planning, design, and production of new systems. Formal attempts to relate all constituent disciplines included the consumer and operating organizations for the resulting system. At about the same time, the design morphology was set forth by Asimow and a similar set of activities discussed by Hall. The resulting morphology placed, in an orderly fashion, the sequence of decisions that should be adequately resolved in order to emerge with an effective set of plans to meet the identified needs.

When large-scale systems are approached, decisions by the designer-planner almost always are made under the limitations of incomplete data. These limitations usually exist to some extent in each decision step of the process and hence are compounded as many times as there are steps in the process. The decision structure associated with a morphological decision sequence such as that described here cannot guarantee successful results, but can offer a structure that provides for efficient use of the resources available to the designer-planner.

THE STRUCTURED PROCESS

Definitions

Several basic definitions are required to help establish the framework for further activity. First, the word "system" has often been misused and, as a result, has led to difficulties in relating different disciplines to the same problem. Hall defines a system as "a set of objects with relationships between their attributes." Here objects are viewed as the "parts" of the system and "attributes" as the properties of the objects, so that relationships bind the system into the entity being considered. The "parts" of the system do not have to be tangible; for example, a process can be considered a system.

If two systems exist, say X_1 and X_2, and are interrelated to form a third system, say X_3, then X_3 is called the system relative to X_1 and X_2, and these in turn can be considered subsystems of X_3.

Webster defines "plan" as a "method or scheme of action, a way proposed to carry out a design . . . ," and further, "to prearrange the details of doing something." "Design is defined as "purposeful planning as revealed in, or inferred from, the adaptation of means to an end or the relation of parts to a whole. . . ."

In general, planning and designing are synonymous. This being the case, the lack of interchange between planners and designers is anomalous. If planning and designing include the same basic processes, the methods of each should be applicable to the other. We can design a process as well as we can plan a system.

Science and Design—Planning

It is generally accepted that a scientist is a person immersed in a given discipline, knowledgeable in its contents, and interested in enlarging this content by research into the fundamental nature of relationships among characteristics. As such, then, when a scientific theory is formulated, any divergence from the theory can be interpreted as a deficiency or a breakdown of the theory. Thus a scientist must be an absolute perfectionist in all aspects of disciplinary interests.

The designer-planner, however, is a person who must recognize a need and move to meet this need in the most effective manner possible. This implies much the same mastery over disciplinary content as the scientist, but further requires an appreciation for how each discipline fits into overall environmental considerations. The designer-planner must achieve a useful solution to meet the needs within the resources available even though absolute rigor may be (and often is) sacrificed for the good of overall performance. This places the designer-planner in a situation that usually requires much broader awareness of constituent discipline interactions, while the scientist becomes the person knowledgeable in depth in a particular area.

The design-planning phases are illustrated in Figure 7.1.

THE DESIGN MORPHOLOGY

Morphology gets its name from the branch of biology dealing with the form and structure of animals and plants. The design or planning morphology can be considered as the form or structure of the process required to establish and meet defined needs. The definition of such a

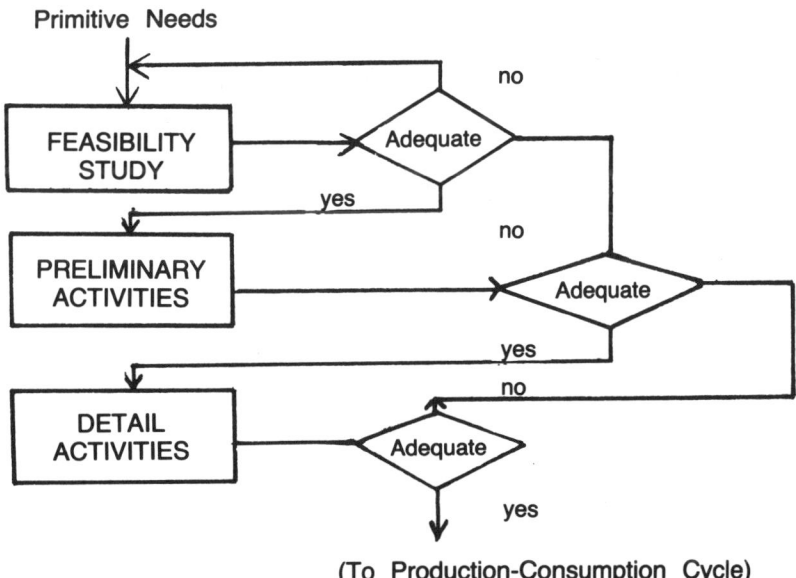

Figure 7.1
Design-planning phases

structure can provide a means for more effective planning, especially when the morphology is identified to a point that "structures" the form and content of the respective decisions at each step in the design process.

The relationship of the design process to the production–consumption cycle is the basis for relating designer-planner activities to user needs. The cycle activities are of particular interest to the system design and also appear to be one of the main patterns in the socioecological system that encompasses the resulting design or plan. Since the elements of the production-consumption cycle relate to user-consumer activities, it becomes necessary for the designer-planner to understand the nature of these activities and then relate existing technology to them so that an effective solution to the problem emerges.

Design-Planning Phases

As illustrated in Figure 7.2, in attempting to plan for the most efficient use of resources, the Asimow phases of design are adapted for the designer-planner. The primary phase must consider the production–consumption cycle and, in fact, the success of the design or plan can often be considered in some manner as a function of the degree to which the requirements of this cycle are included.

A project begins with the feasibility study to establish a solid base upon which to build ideas in depth as one progresses through the

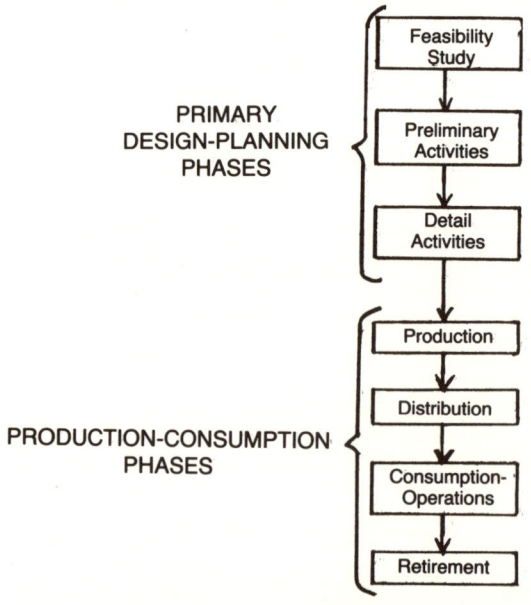

Figure 7.2
Phases of the designer-planner project life

morphology. The feasibility study's purpose is the achievement of a set of useful solutions to the defined problem. A major set of activities in this phase includes the establishment of need and the explicit definition of the problem to be solved by the plan or design. The feasibility study not only serves as the basis for all subsequent steps, but it actually accomplishes several of the initial steps, including the synthesis of solutions, and the screening of these solutions. Hence the set that emerges contains the alternatives to be compared and evaluated. If no useful solutions emerge from the screening, then the solution is "not feasible." Consequently the completed study determines the problem needs, identifies the planning or design problem, and offers a set of useful solutions.

Given a set of useful solutions, choosing the "best" alternatives becomes the purpose of the preliminary activities. "Best" must be defined in terms of explicitly delineated criteria. To accomplish this, criteria must be related to parameters and other attributes of the alternatives, laboratory or field testing may verify relationships of the parameters to the criteria, values must be assigned to the performance of each criterion for the respective alternative approach, and the "best" alternative must then be selected. Analytical aids to the identification of a theoretic optimum alternative are available.

Once identified, the chosen alternative is tested and predictions made concerning its performance in the production–consumption stages of its life. Rate of obsolescence, technical deterioration, and socioeconomic conditions such as competition and state of the art should be evaluated. Any factors affecting the performance in the production–consumption cycle of the chosen alternative should also be considered.

With the alternative chosen, the implementation problems begin. For systems that involve hardware, the detail activities must result in a complete description of a tested and producible design so that the product can be manufactured, distributed, consumed, and retired in the appropriate quantities and in the planned manner. For the implementation of process-oriented problems, the same conceptual approach is in order, but the production–consumption cycle takes on the nature already described.

In general, however, product-oriented systems enable more detailed planning and preparation to be accomplished prior to actual implementation. This means the planning process will be primarily oriented toward product or hardware system implementation, with appropriate descriptive details provided for the interpretation of each activity as part of a meaningful "process" domain.

Preparation for the detail activities requires a thorough review of the available information, as well as study of the organization, facilities, time, and other resources needed to implement the chosen alternative successfully. Elements should be developed to the extent where good communication is enabled with those who will implement the production–consumption cycle. For technological systems this is normally accomplished by means of drawings, audiovisual techniques, or computer-aided devices.

Communication includes instructions for the development or manufacture of the chosen candidate, and information on the assembly of the elements as well. This becomes particularly important when large-scale systems are being considered. As the number of system constituents increases, the possibility for incompatibility of some of the elements increases very rapidly. Therefore, assembly instructions must be provided.

Paramount in the successful implementation of a new system is the anticipation of any major problems, as well as most of the minor ones, to be encountered during the production–consumption cycle. This is normally accomplished by means of specific plans.

The *organization plan* covers all phases of the cycle, and delineates such details as organizational function, number and type of each skill or professional classification, and the responsibilities of each group and individual in the organization. Since the organization plan covers a large number of different activities as well as planning phases, changes to plan elements must be reflected so that one can extract the necessary management information concerning time, personnel, costs, and system status at any phase of the production–consumption cycle.

The *production plan* may be necessary for those systems entering a mass production phase, or for systems requiring transformation of inputs prior to implementation. This plan generally provides facility and equipment requirements, hardware drawings and details, assembly sequence and layout, workforce, inventory and equipment forecasts, quality-control needs, and cost estimates.

The *operations plan* indicates how the system will be deployed or where located; when activities that are necessary to successful operation of the system should occur and how these activities are sequenced; at which points in time the appropriate equipment, facilities, and personnel are involved and the description of their activities; and which logistic elements are necessary for the respective activities. Often logistics becomes such a major consideration that a separate plan is provided to identify adequately the scope and meaning of each logistic element.

In general the plans described do not exhaust the possibilities. A specialized plan may be developed when a certain element becomes of sufficient importance to warrant such consideration. For example, many complex equipment systems require a maintenance plan that combines the elements of logistics, organization, and operations in a manner such that all maintenance operations are clearly and completely delineated.

Having accomplished all the relevant plans necessary for successfully surviving the production–consumption cycle, it may be necessary to continue to analyze the behavior of the system in the predicted environment. This activity almost always occurs with products that are subject to constant modification and revision (automobiles, television sets, and most consumer-oriented products). The results of such analyses can then be used to offer predictions of system performance in the production–consumption cycle and hence predict results. When these predictions are sufficiently different from plan predictions, modifications and revisions are made to the basic system.

Another reason for analysis and prediction results from proposed system changes and innovations. Such proposals are then considered in light of their affect on the total system. Upon proper evaluation the changes are incorporated.

Iterative Nature of Design or Planning

From the recognition of needs in the feasibility study to the last step in retiring the system, a great deal of knowledge is gained concerning the system being developed. Unfortunately, decisions must be made at each step in the process to achieve the necessary conclusions, usually within time constraints. Because of the incompleteness of knowledge at the time decisions are made, they may require reexamination at subsequent points when additional information is gained. This process of reexamination is the iterative nature of design and is recognized as an integral part of the process. Iteration permits many decisions that, when first made, might be inadequate, but with increasing information can be restructured.

The restructuring of a decision then causes a "ripple" effect in the following steps of the process. Each part of the planning or design that is affected must be reexamined to assure the adequacy of subsequent planning.

Principle of Least Commitment

It is because of this "ripple" effect that the designer-planner should pursue a policy of "least commitment." That is, in progressing from step to step or phase to phase in the morphology, no irreversible decision should be made until it must be made. This allows maximum flexibility in each step. More alternatives remain available to the designer-planner so that elimination of "better" alternatives is minimized.

PRODUCTION–CONSUMPTION CYCLE

The production–consumption cycle provides the environment for the application of results of designer-planner activities. The cycle is represented by the chronological sequence of production, distribution, consumption (or operation), and retirement. Each in turn affects the designer-planner, and certain considerations predominate when the designer-planner integrates cycle requirements into methodology. The production–consumption cycle requirements are not only necessary for the designer-planner, but no system can be considered effective without meeting their needs. Therefore, one must be intimately familiar with the cycle for a morphology to be capable of producing acceptable results. The morphology by itself is inert. It exists only as a framework for the decisions necessary to accomplish system development. Knowledge of the involved disciplines remains the basic building block.

In the case of systems containing hardware, the production–consumption activities take on their commonly accepted meanings. Production implies the activities engaged in to make the system elements; distribution suggests the flow of goods into the production facilities and from them to the consumer location. In addition to the product being consumed, consumption may also imply operations for those systems requiring continuing performance that is monitored by humans. Retirement means those activities necessary to remove the system from consumption to a permanently inactive status.

For those systems consisting totally of processes, the production–consumption cycle retains the same basic definitions, but is modified to meet the needs of the particular system. This modification does not change the meaning of the original cycle semantics, but relates them in such a manner as to make possible the use of a structured planning sequence of decision areas.

Production

"At the core of production is the technology of transformations."[5] "Transformation" defines the nature and basis for production, and management of the transformation process is what one means by "production management." While consideration of the industrial or "factory" version of production occupies much of the current literature, if "transformation" is to define production processes as is indicated here, then *all* processes of transformation must also fit the definition of production to some degree. Indeed the concept of production applied to the classical version of the firm, or to the system, indicates the set of activities or products resulting from the transformation process. As the first class of activities in the production–consumption cycle, many of the major needs and constraints for the designer-planner emerge from this phase of the activities. Basically the production problem relates to responding to the questions concerning the organization, facilities and equipment, quality control, and schedules. Areas such as inventory systems, maintenance, and cost control all contribute to needs and constraints for the designer-planner, and provide the framework for the activity in achieving a successful system from the morphology. The designer-planner wants to establish an analytical framework for evaluation of production alternatives in the development of the "best" system, and to relate these alternatives to the set of alternative candidate systems being considered.

Timms and Pohlen identify two main subsystems as comprising process planning: "process design," the macrosystem; and "operation design," the microsystem. Figure 7.3 shows the feedback among the production subsystem elements. Note that iteration among these elements is a necessary ingredient in accomplishing the desired outputs.

Distribution

Distribution accomplishes the "phase-in" of the product or process to the ultimate operators or consumers. It may include various types of distribution facilities, sales organizations, applications, or other activities. The distribution activities should provide flexible and effective methods

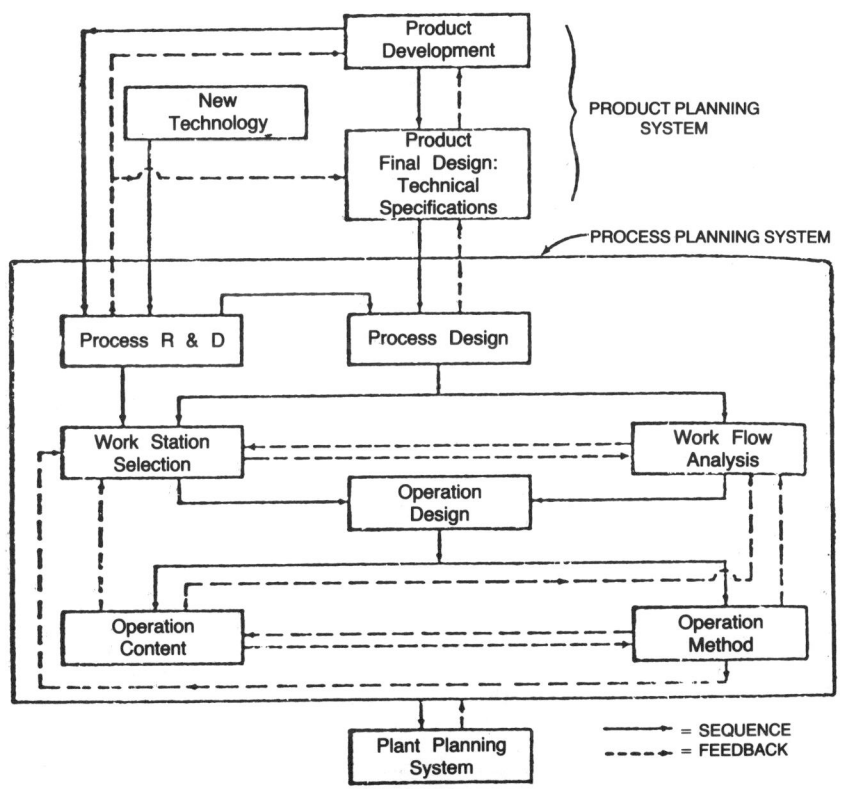

Figure 7.3
Process planning system

for accomplishing the transfer of product or process to the required locations.

When the result of production is a product, the classical areas of packaging, warehousing, promotional activities, shelf-life, among others, pertain. Obviously these factors must be considered during the earlier design stages.

When the result of production is a process (or service), the distribution function takes on a more subtle characteristic. Here phase-in becomes the major consideration and implies the activities necessary for the operators adequately to prepare for the operations that are to follow. "Phase-in" implies the transfer of the process to the environment in which the follow-on activities of operation will occur as well as the adequate accomplishment of the supporting functions necessary to make a smooth transition. These supporting functions can be activities such as communicating all the requirements for process implementation among a widely scattered organization; preparation of sales or other applications data and personnel; warehousing or inventory control of materials or equipment for process implementation at the proper location for efficient operation; and all remaining activities that are needed to implement the process.

A clear illustration of process distribution can be realized by examination of a national franchising organization. One national sandwich chain has planned its activities to the minute, and a reasonably long training program for the independent managers who will be operating the franchise. Quality control is maintained by requiring specified foods, prescribing quality of meats, and, in general, controlling all food products. In addition, sanitation methods are prescribed and activities for cleaning the facility are included in the schedule. A permanent staff inspects every facility at unannounced times during the week. Distribution is accomplished with high effectiveness through adequate planning for transfer of the activities to the many different locations that require it.

Consumption/Operations

Consumption is that portion of the cycle that meets the main objectives of the designer-planner. This is the phase in which the product, having been produced and distributed, is now accomplishing the needs for which the product was produced. In this vein consumption can also be interpreted as operations. That is, many products are not consumed *per se*, but are used in the accomplishment of activities—they are operated. All equipment and most hardware fall into this category. For example, a metal screw is consumed, but a bicycle is operated.

When the system is a process, operation becomes the application of the process. In the case of the franchise, the activities necessary to maintain the predetermined schedule define the operation of the system.

While production and distribution considerations result in constraints upon the designer-planner, these two phases of the cycle are basically well defined. That is, with adequate study most problem areas can be resolved, and those not resolved can be identified and risks evaluated in a relatively straightforward manner. This is generally not the case in consumption or operation. Here, with the consumer taking on the vast indeterminate characteristics of people, the risks assumed by the designer-planner generally are greater, or at least the performance required to plan adequately is more varied. For this reason more study of the consumption requirement is usually necessary. Paradoxically this phase generally determines the major criteria for system acceptance. Herein lies the designer-planner dilemma: how reasonably to limit the expenditure of resources in determining consumption requirements while simultaneously obtaining the best overall performance from the entire morphology. This type of problem is not completely answered by any morphology, but a great deal of headway is made by structuring the nature of the decisions so that a proper perspective is maintained during the decision processes.

Retirement

Retirement is that part of the production–consumption cycle that includes those considerations necessary to facilitate the withdrawal of the system from its intended functions. Withdrawal may imply replacement or only major change, but whatever the reason, this phase has implications for the designer-planner that often lead to major considerations for the design of the system.

Factors such as rate of obsolescence and service life are often the main causes leading to retirement. These factors can be included in the designer-planner activity to plan for the timing of retirement, but the activity itself leads to consideration of many problems, which, although eased by timely evaluation, involve the technologies of the respective areas being thought about.

Consider the environmental pollution problem. What might have been the effect if the industrial designer-planner had adequately considered retirement of the system? Certainly a good part of the current problem would be eased, if not completely eliminated. Hence it can be observed that retirement becomes a vital part of the cycle, and that acceptance of the resulting system can actually be effected by adequacy of retirement planning for the system.

Logistics Implications

Perhaps the main advantage of the design-planning morphology is the attempt to consider the integrated-whole requirement and its necessary activities. Inherent in defining these activities is the adequate consideration of logistics functions that provide reinforcement in accomplishing primary system functions. Logistics activities have grown in importance during the past few decades because of the recognition of this need. However, the diversity of activity in the logistics domain has caused difficulty in identifying its bounds. Those involved in management functions oriented during operations have regarded logistics primarily from the time and place utility aspect. Emphasis is placed on requirements for adequate management of an existing organization relating to problems of physical distribution and its integration into system management. In terms of the production–consumption cycle, this relates to the activities during consumption (or operations) and retirement.

With the advent of large-scale, complex technological systems, severe deficiencies were noted when logistics functions were related exclusively to operations and retirement, and attempts were made, mostly in government agency planning, to integrate these logistic activities into the design-planning stages prior to the production stage. The attempt to integrate logistics activities reinforced the completeness of the morphology, and logistics planning took on the more complete supporting role for all four stages in the production–consumption cycle. Table 7.1 lists the areas generally looked at by the business community for the study of physical distribution (sometimes referred to as "business logistics") as they compare with the areas identified as "integrated logistics support" by government agencies.

For the designer-planner, the more adequate approach depends primarily on the system. For systems involving hardware research, design, and development, the integrated logistics support context may be more appropriate, while for problems involving only management of existing operations, physical distribution activities might be considered. In general, however, designer-planners do better by identifying more areas and

Table 7.1
Comparison of Physical Distribution Elements with Those of Integrated Logistics Support

Physical Distribution	Integrated Logistics Support
	Maintainability and reliability
Transportation	Maintenance plan
Storage of product	Support and test equipment
Manufacturing and converting capability	Supply support
Communications and control	Transportation and handling
	Technical data
	Facilities
	Personnel and training
	Support resource funds
	Support management information

then responding to the demands of such areas. Hence adequate resolution of problems is more likely to be derived through the use of the integrated logistics support premises.

It should be noted that the terms applied to specific phases of a product or system life cycle may differ from those used in this section. Those terms are covered in the sections on design and reviews and life-cycle costs.

CHAPTER

8

Reliability, Availability, and Maintainability

*T*his chapter covers fundamentals of availability, maintainability, and reliability that should be understood by everyone involved with product design, production, and support. By necessity this is a broad overview.

AVAILABILITY

Reliability (R) and maintainability (M) interact to form availability (A), which may be defined as the probability that equipment will be in operating condition at any point in time. The three main types of availability are called achieved, inherent, and operational.

Inherent availability (A_i) is the probability that a system or equipment, when used under stated conditions in an ideal support environment, will operate satisfactorily at any point in time, excluding scheduled maintenance actions and logistics supply and administration downtime. It is expressed as:

$$A_i = \frac{MTBF}{MTBF + Mct}$$

where MTBF = mean time between failures, and Mct = mean corrective maintenance time. Note that Mct is synomous with mean time to repair (MTTR).

Achieved availability (A_a) is the probability that a system or equipment, when used under stated conditions in an ideal support environment (i.e., everything is available), will operate satisfactorily at any point in time. The definition excludes administration and logistics supply time. Achieved availability is more applicable to the early design process where interest is greatest in measuring hardware, reliability, and maintainability characteristics. It is expressed as:

$$A_a = \frac{MTBM}{MTBM + \overline{M}}$$

where $\overline{M}$ = mean active maintenance time. This includes unscheduled corrective maintenance and scheduled preventive maintenance time.

Operational availability (A_o) is the probability that a system or equipment, when used under stated conditions in actual operational environment, will operate satisfactorily when called upon. It is expressed as:

$$A_o = \frac{MTBM}{MTBM + MDT}$$

where $MTBM$ = mean time between maintenance and MDT = maintenance downtime. MDT includes time for active maintenance, logistics supply, and administration.

CUSTOMER PERCEPTIONS

The designer and the laboratory technician may have very different understandings of the impact of availability, maintainability, and reliability than do the customers or sales and service personnel. The reason for placing the early emphasis on customer perceptions is that satisfaction of the customer/user must be a logistician's goal if the profit objective is to be reached. Satisfied customers use products well and buy more. Dissatisfied customers complain, cause excessive support costs, cancel orders, and do not produce revenue. Customer-perceived availability is a very complex interaction of failures, of which hardware failure rate is only a part. Detailed examination of several commercial products shows that, in fact, the design is responsible for only about 20–40 percent of the problems in field reliability and maintainability. Manufacturing has an influence of 10–30 percent due to poor quality and deficient configuration management. The field sales and service force has the remaining impact.

A product can never be more reliable than the inherent design. The design establishes the hereditary capacity for the product, which may be met by excellent production and support activities. However, there is a high probability that the design will only be degraded by the following functions. This degradation is usually established in the form of "K factors." These are relative ratings of how performance will vary between laboratory and factory and field. In tightly controlled programs such as the NASA Space Shuttle missions, the K factors are very close to 1.00. (The catastrophic Challenger explosion, though tragic, was not unexpected.) However, for many commercial product programs where large numbers of diverse customers may be involved, the K factors can be as low as 0.5. Every significant element of a product system should be evaluated to determine its K factor, and improve the correlation in the future.

Expectation establishes the framework in which a customer accepts or rejects a product. They are based on advertising, talks with sales and service personnel, and experience with related equipment. This is why a product or system must be just as reliable in failure terms at introduction as the equipment it will replace. Competition has set standards against which products will be compared. A customer who is given the correct information and made aware of product advantages and shortcomings will accept failures much more readily than the customer who has been led to believe that everything will be perfect.

Smooth, rapid installation of hardware, including availability of all supplies, software, and training of customer personnel, is vital to creating a good initial impression. This is equally true of delivery and adjustment of a new television set or thorough dealer preparation of a new automobile.

There is definite evidence that time between service is a factor that registers in the minds of most customers. Unscheduled breakdowns requiring corrective action are undoubtedly most aggravating. However, a user is very sensitive to any need for maintenance. Operational availability (A_o) is what the customer really cares about. As an automobile driver, you are certainly interested in having an ignition system that allows your car to run well for 20,000+ miles, and in having it go at least 6000 miles between oil changes and lube jobs. The number of miles, copies, or hours between failures is generally unknown and is not of interest to the customer at the time work has to be done. Usage patterns make this very complex. For example, a CPA's office copier makes many copies during the tax season, but very few during the remainder of the year. Doctors' offices make most use of their machines during the end-of-the-month billing period. These customers want just as much time or even more between any failures during their busy periods as during the slack times. Intervening periods such as weekends or holidays apparently have an effect, so that time-perception thresholds exist according to calendar time. Unfortunately engineering designers cannot operate against the calendar time specification and must have it related in terms of hours, or miles, or copies in order to do their work. A relationship between time and design factors must be established so that specifications are related to the time or event base.

Preventive maintenance that takes a machine out of action temporarily is often regarded by a customer as just as aggravating as any unscheduled maintenance call. Service is always better off if service personnel never have to see the customer. However, every object will break down some time and maintenance will be required. And customers on service contracts do want to see some activity for the money they pay.

Equipment may be defective for some time before it is noticed by the customer and a call for service is made. Downtime is important; however, its impact depends on the customer's need at that time. The feeling seems to exist that time to restore a product to good service is secondary to response time. In other words, the customer is somewhat satisfied as soon as action is taken to restore the system, even though it may be some longer time before the system is actually back in operation. Response time by a computer customer engineer or an office machine repairperson is important in the customer's eyes. Whether it takes 15 minutes or four hours to get the machine back into operation has additional effect on the customer. It does, of course, affect service cost! The frequency of downtime appears to be much more important than the total amount of time a machine is down. That means reliability is of paramount importance and must be weighed more heavily than maintainability. The interaction of factors is complex and there has been very little published market research on the subject. To determine what levels should be specified for availability, maintainability, and reliability, without placing excessive demands that are inefficient use of resources, every organization should determine the relevant factors and sensitivity of their customers. The factors must be identified and quantified so that sensitivities can be established along with the related costs and profits to provide the best possible combination of alternatives for the business.

RELIABILITY

Reliability is usually defined as the probability that a system or product will give satisfactory performance for a specified period of time when used under stated conditions. It is usually expressed in terms of mean time between failures (MTBF) or mean life. The "time" may be expressed in actual clock time, information bits, financial transactions, liters, grams, or any other parameter particularly applicable for your business. If reliability is high, it may be expressed as failures per million

(10^6) hours. That is the reciprocal of the number of hours between failures, which may be a more practical term for your business. Many people can better comprehend that an automobile runs 6000 miles between maintenance actions, than the inverted term, 166.67 maintenance actions per 10^6 miles. Complete reliability is rarely achieved since humans and hardware are rarely perfect. Anything less than 100 percent reliability means that a failure will occur and the deficiency must be corrected.

Failure rate (λ) will be relatively constant throughout the middle period of a product's operational life. When a product is first produced, there are usually fewer failures as the hardware and support systems are "debugged." The reverse happens when the equipment begins to "wear out," and failures increase. This produces the bathtub curve shown in Figure 8.1.

The failures that occur during early operation have been countered by burn-in of components through special processes or in actual operation at a functional level. The semiconductor industry, for example, realizes that baking components for several hours at high temperatures and subjecting them to thermal shock will help eliminate early failures before they become part of a more expensive assembly. If replacement parts are subject to significant early failure, or if the service engineer may damage something during replacement, there is cause to consider hands-off-until-failure, rather than scheduled preventive maintenance.

The reliability exponential distribution is $R = e^{-\lambda t}$, where e = natural log base 2.7184, λ (lambda) = failure rate per hour ($\lambda = MTBF$), and t = total hours of operating time. In the exponential distribution, time to failure is the random, continuous variable. This differs from the Poisson distribution where the random variable is the number of failures in a given time period, and the variable is discrete. Most electronic and mechanical component failure rates follow the exponential distribution. The relationship between MTBF in hours, λ, reliability, and operating time is shown in Figure 8.2.

Building in Reliability

Inherent reliability must be designed into the hardware and software as part of the system engineering process. This process begins with establishing goals and specifications, allocating the reliability among functional areas, predicting the results of their efforts, reviewing, testing, and feeding back change information. If, for example, the goal of an entire system is 200 failures per million hours of operation, those 200 failures should be allocated to all involved activities that may influence reliability in any way. This includes design, manufacturing, and the field; and within those areas failures should be broken down to functional design subsystems, and even to individual design activities. The allo-

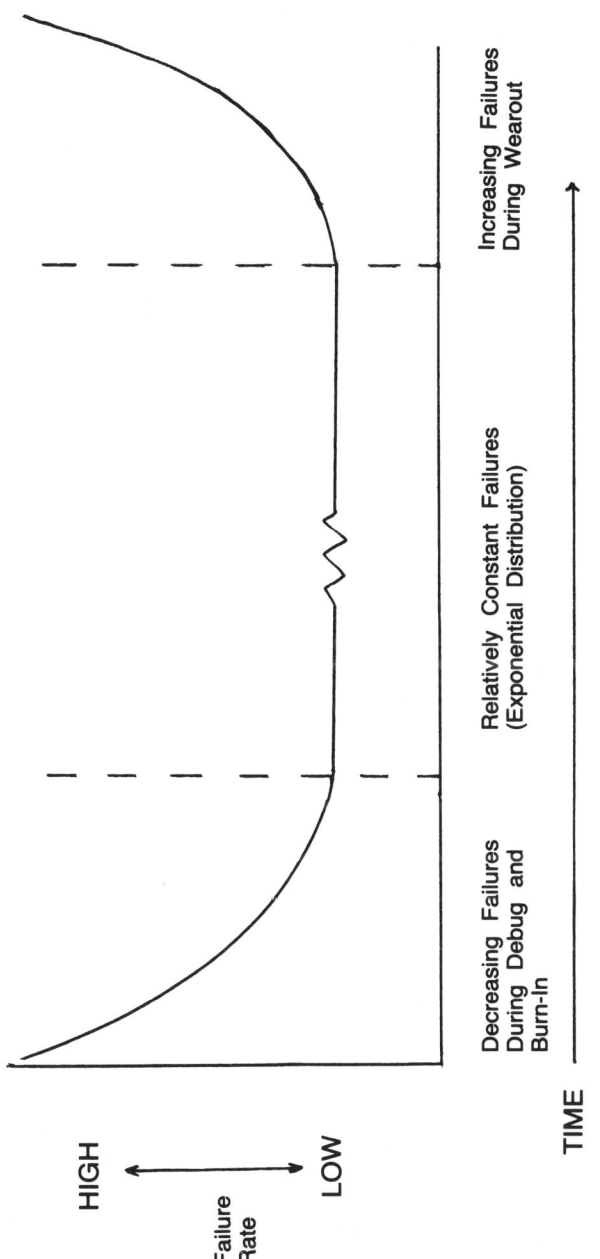

**Figure 8.1
Electromechanical reliability curve**

cation will be done according to their contribution to the final results. Areas where design is familiar, and failure-rate information is available or can be readily accessible, may be more precisely allocated than can areas where design is new and reliability is complex.

Mathematical models are available to assist in the complex calculations that accompany many system allocations and predictions. There are four relationships that should be understood:

1. *Series*: If any item in the system fails, the entire system will fail.

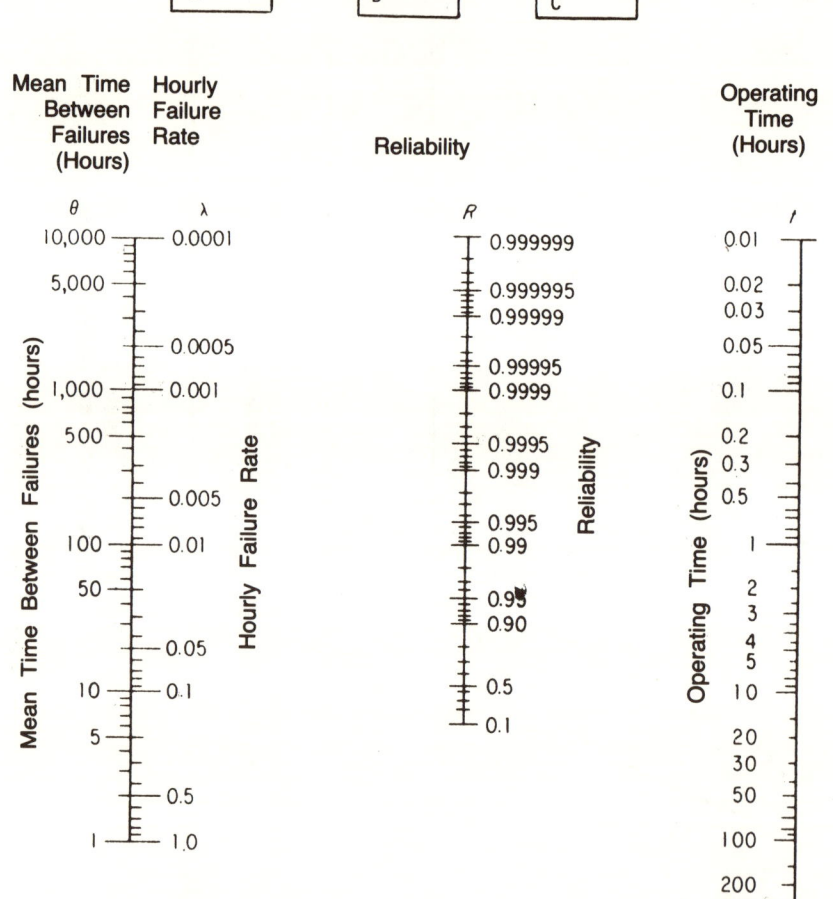

To solve equation $R = e^{-t/\theta}$, connect t and θ with straight line and read value of R.

**Figure 8.2
Reliability nomograph**

$$R_T = (R_A)(R_B)(R_C)$$
$$= .90 \times .90 \times .80$$
$$= .648$$

2. *Parallel combination:* The system will continue to operate if one block fails and will go down only if both fail.

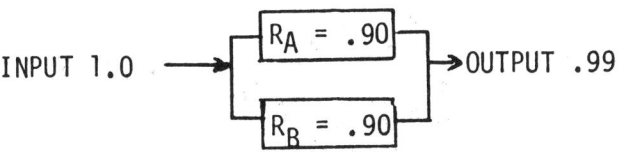

$$R_T = R_A + R_B - (R_A)(R_B)$$
$$= .90 + .90 - (.90)(.90)$$
$$= 1.8 - .81$$
$$= .99$$

3. *Dual-parallel:* Either A and B or block C must operate.

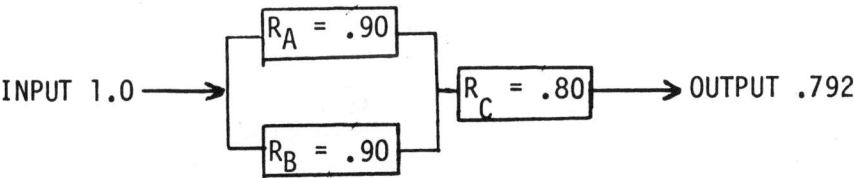

$$R_T = R_A R_B R_C + R_A R_B (1 - R_C) + R_A R_C (1 - R_B) + R_B R_C (1 - R_A)$$
$$+ R_C (1 - R_A)(1 - R_B)$$
$$= (.90 \times .80 \times .85) + (.90)(.80)(1 - .85) + (.90)(.85)(1 - .80)$$
$$+ (.80)(.85)(1 - .90) + .85(1 - .90)(1 - .80)$$
$$= .612 + .108 + .153 + .068 + .017$$
$$= .958$$

Note that this may be more simply solved by treating R_A and R_B first as a series and then R_{AB} with R_C as parallel.

4. *Series-parallel:* Either block A or B must operate along with block C.

$$R_T = R_A R_C + R_B R_C - R_A R_B R_C$$
$$= .72 + .72 - .648$$
$$= .792$$

It can also be solved as parallel then series, with the same results.

The technique of allowing parallel relationships is known as redundancy and is one method of achieving a fault-tolerant design.

Example

The following example is constructed such that it employs the various circuit combinations and techniques that were delineated in the previous paragraphs. The example is presented as an aid to basic reliability familiarization. See Table 8.1.

For any type of system, a reliability block diagram may be constructed so that the effect of failure of any component on the system may be analyzed. Such a diagram is shown below.

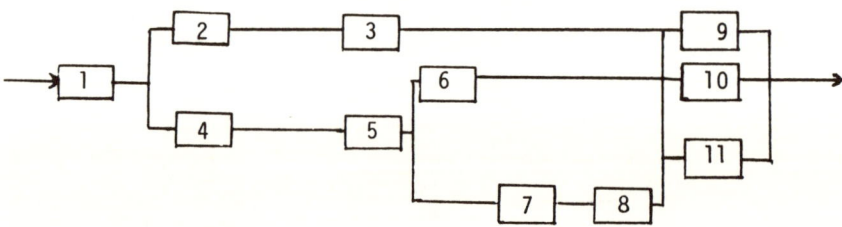

The first step in calculating the reliability of the system is to obtain the failure rate per hour of the individual items, and hence their reliability. These values are presented in the table. Once this is accomplished,

Table 8.1
Component Reliability

Component	MTBF (in Hours)	Failure Rate per Hour (λ)	Reliability per Hour $(R(t))(1 - \lambda)$
1	500	.0020	.9980
2	200	.0050	.9950
3	300	.0033	.9967
4	400	.0025	.9975
5	800	.0013	.9987
6	500	.0020	.9980
7	500	.0020	.9980
8	900	.0011	.9989
9	600	.0017	.9983
10	500	.0020	.9980
11	300	.0033	.9967

the parallel circuits are combined. The resulting series circuit is then simplified and the system reliability obtained.

Step 1: Reduce the parallel combination of items 9, 10, and 11 to single item A, in series with the remaining circuit.

$$R_A(t) = 1 - (1 - R_9(t))(1 - R_{10}(t))(1 - R_{11}(t))$$
$$= 1 - (1 - .9983)(1 - .9980)(1 - .9967)$$
$$= .9999+$$

The block diagram is now:

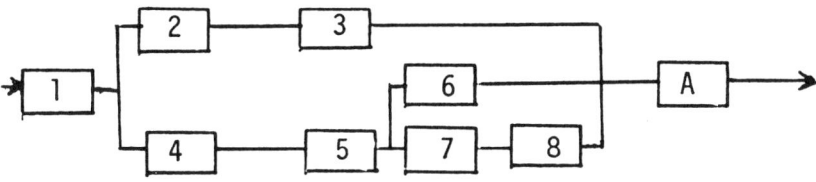

Step 2: Reduce the series parallel combination of items 6, 7, and 8 to a single item k.

$$R_k(t) = 1 - (1 - R_6(t))[1 - R_7(t) R_8(t)]$$
$$= 1 - (1 - .9980)[1 - (.9980)(.9989)]$$
$$= .9999+$$

The resulting block diagram is:

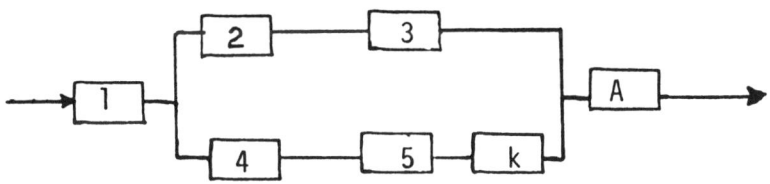

Step 3: Reduce the series combination of items 2 and 3 to a single item L.

$$R_L(t) = R_2(t) \times R_3(t)$$
$$= .9950 \times .9967$$
$$= .9917$$

The resulting block diagram is:

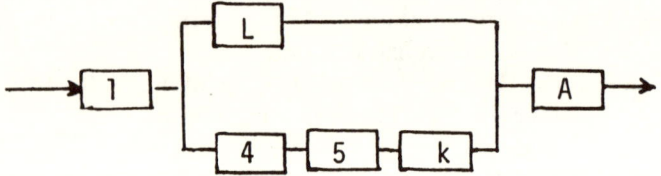

Step 4: Reduce the series combination of items 4, 5, and k to a single item S.

$$R_S(t) = R_4(t) \times R_5(t) \times R_k(t)$$
$$= .9975 \times .9987 \times .9999+$$
$$= .9961+$$

The resulting block diagram is:

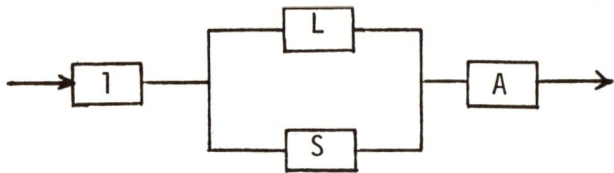

Step 5: Reduce the parallel combination of items L and S to a single item B.

$$R_B(t) = 1 - (1 - R_L(t))(1 - R_S(t))$$
$$= 1 - (1 - .9917)(1 - .9961)$$
$$= .9999+$$

The resulting block diagram is:

INPUT → [1] — [B] — [A] → OUTPUT

$$R(t)_{total} = R_1(t)\, R_B(t)\, R_A(t)$$
$$= .9980 \times .9999+ \times .9999+$$
$$= .9978+$$

INPUT ────→ $R(t)_{total} = .9978$ ────→ OUTPUT

The reliability allocation provides the criteria for the designer and establishes the initial frame of reference for logistics support in terms of anticipated maintenance rates on the subsystems and system.

Once the reliability goals have been allocated, the design process involves selecting the component parts, considering their stresses, tolerances, and known performance. Reliability emphasis in design would include

1. Simplification. Every component has a failure rate, so the fewer components used the better.
2. Use of standard components and material. The standard component has a known reliability that is often better than that of nonstandard items and allows better prediction of failure rates and support requirements. It also assures fewer unique components with related lower provisioning and maintenance costs.
3. Evaluation of all components and materials prior to design acceptance. This includes studying the effects, stresses, tolerances, and other characteristics of the component in its intended application.
4. Reliability. Utilize only those component parts capable of meeting reliability objectives.
5. Human factors. Consider the impact of people on the equipment.

Reliability prediction can be accomplished as soon as a design is posed, by piece-part analysis. Mil-Hdbk 217 provides failure rates for generic classes of components that allow the piece parts to be counted and simply multiplied by the failure rate, with the sum giving an estimate of the system failure rate. For example, a simple system made up of the following components would be calculated as in Table 8.2.

The predicted values for MTBF or failure rate (λ) must be frequently compared against the requirements, and areas of incompatibility evaluated for possible design improvements. Predictions must be a major part of design reviews.

Failure modes and effects analysis (FMEA) is performed during early design to determine how a module is likely to fail and what will happen if it does fail. This is a systematic approach that permits evaluation of failures and points out critical failure areas so that the designer can be guided and will allow special emphasis for modification. The FMEA can be used to generate logic troubleshooting diagrams for maintainability.

Table 8.2
Failure Rate

Part	Quantity	Failure Rate Per 10^6 HR	Total
Resistor	5	.035	.175
Capacitor	1	.011	.011
Transistors	10	.25	2.5
Diode	3	.2	.6
Integrated circuits	12	.5	6.0
		Total failure rate	

Once the design has been completed, reliability becomes the charge of manufacturing. Materials management, quality control, fabrication and assembly techniques, handling procedures, and final packaging are all areas where manufacturing can degrade product reliability. Then, when a product gets to the field, the operator and support personnel can cause further degradation through ineptness, lack of training, use of wrong components, and mishandling of tools. It is a valuable activity to compare the reliability and failure modes and effects of similar products presently in the field with those undergoing design, so that major deficiencies can be avoided and shortcomings accommodated.

COSTS

Reliability is an expensive discipline. The number of tasks, resources applied, and amount of management attention required are very costly. However, lack of reliability is even more expensive. Costs are available for any business to determine past effects of failures. Figure 8.3 shows the life-cycle cost for a typical military program versus item reliability. Equipment that breaks down frequently causes high service involvement, is not utilized, and is not reordered.

There may be many types of degradation considered as part of reliability. For example, in a recent survey of office typewriters, 46 percent of the respondents equated copy quality with reliability. There are levels of criticality. A machine totally out of action is without question the highest level. However, a typewriter producing copies of quality enough to be used internally but not good enough for sending to clients may be equated as a different subgroup.

ESSENTIALITY

Essentiality was first developed by a combined study group from George Washington University, the U.S. Navy, and Lockheed Aircraft while developing the Polaris Submarine Missile Program. The concept was evolved so that the submarines that would be under sea for long periods of time would recognize the failure of items that could cause major impact on mission performance and should have redundant components or carry necessary replacements, whereas items of little consequence could be disregarded. For example, the inertial guidance system was critical and had to have adequate backup, but a radio for listening

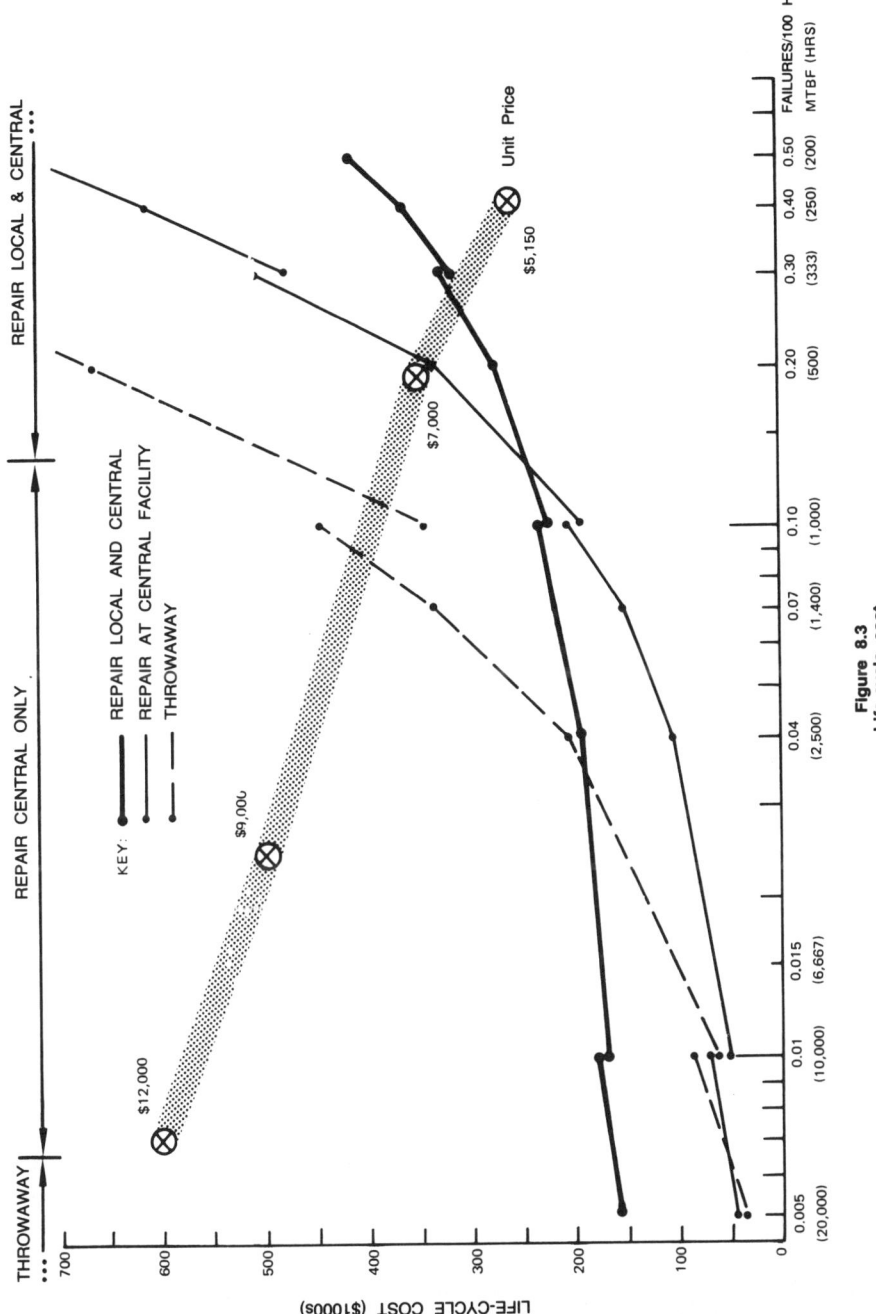

**Figure 8.3
Life-cycle cost**

to commercial stations was not so critical. This concept has been transferred to commercial businesses with a typical four-point rating being:

1. Safety and legal failures that could cause great damage.
2. Equipment not operable and not producing revenue.
3. Equipment operating at substandard level.
4. Minor cosmetic problem.

Obviously essentiality levels 1 and 2 require rapid corrective action, whereas level 3 might be fixed when a customer engineer is next at the account and level 4 might not be corrected until the machine is returned to the repair center.

The result of any failure, or the requirement for some action to prevent or alleviate failures, leads us to maintainability and maintenance.

MAINTAINABILITY AND MAINTENANCE

Maintainability usually refers to those features of a product or system that contribute to its ease of repair. Often called "serviceability," it is primarily a function of equipment design and is implemented most effectively prior to or during manufacture. Maintenance, on the other hand, refers to those activities actually performed upon a product to prevent failure, or in the event of failure, to restore it to a satisfactory level of operation. Maintenance, therefore, relates primarily to support of a product after it is in the hands of the user. The major maintenance activities are shown in Figure 8.4. Maintainability, (M) is also statistically expressed as the probability that a machine will be repaired within a specified time in a specified maintenance environment, using specified tools, procedures, and technical skill levels."

Maintainability engineering is defined by the three military services. NAVORD-OR-39223 defines maintainability engineering as: "The engineering discipline which formulates an acceptable combination of design features, repair policies, and maintenance resources, to achieve a specified level of maintainability, as an operational requirement, at minimum life-cycle cost." AFSCR-80-9 says it is: "A management discipline which requires research, education, and information exchange emphasis in all phases of system life, starting with the conceptual phase." AR-705-50 defines it as: "The application of scientific knowledge and engineering skills to the development of items of equipment so as to provide an inherent capability to be maintained (i.e., the possession of favorable maintenance characteristics). Maintainability engineering must be integrated with the other elements of 'system engineering' so as to provide the necessary effectiveness considering all costs over the entire life-cycle of the item."

Maintainability is now considered one of the essential ingredients of the logistics system and a factor in both systems effectiveness and cost effectiveness. The role of maintainability in the systems development cycle is shown in Figure 8.5.

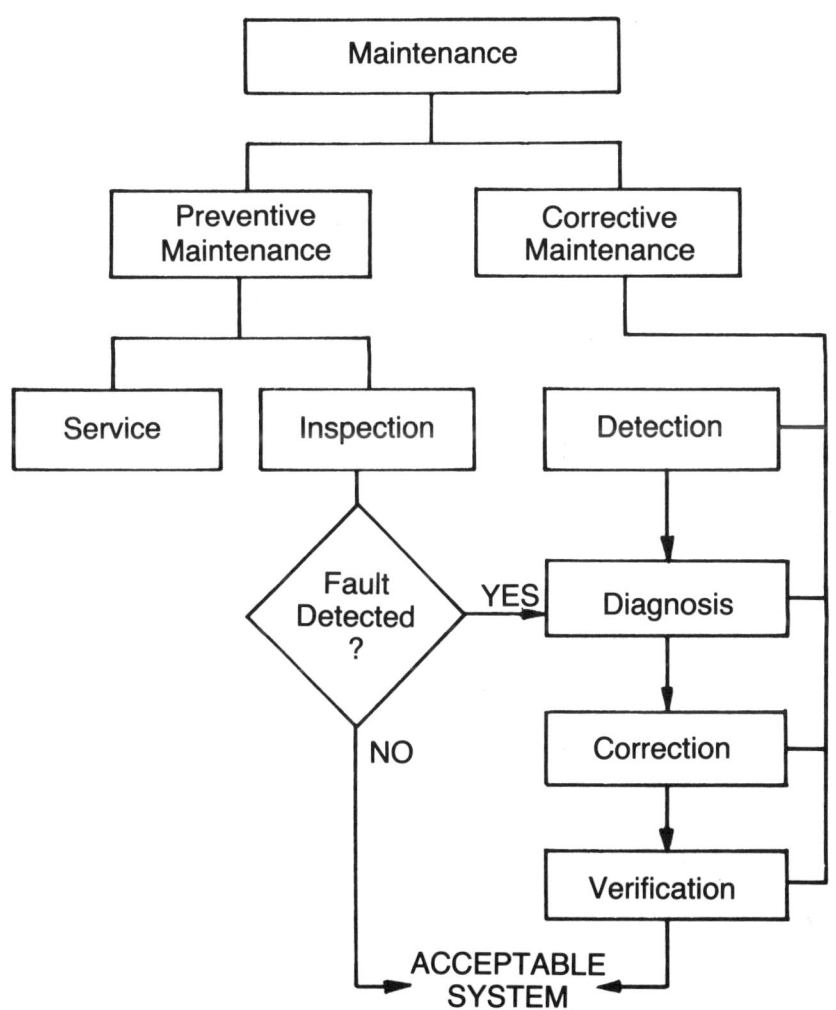

Figure 8.4
Primary subsets of maintenance activities

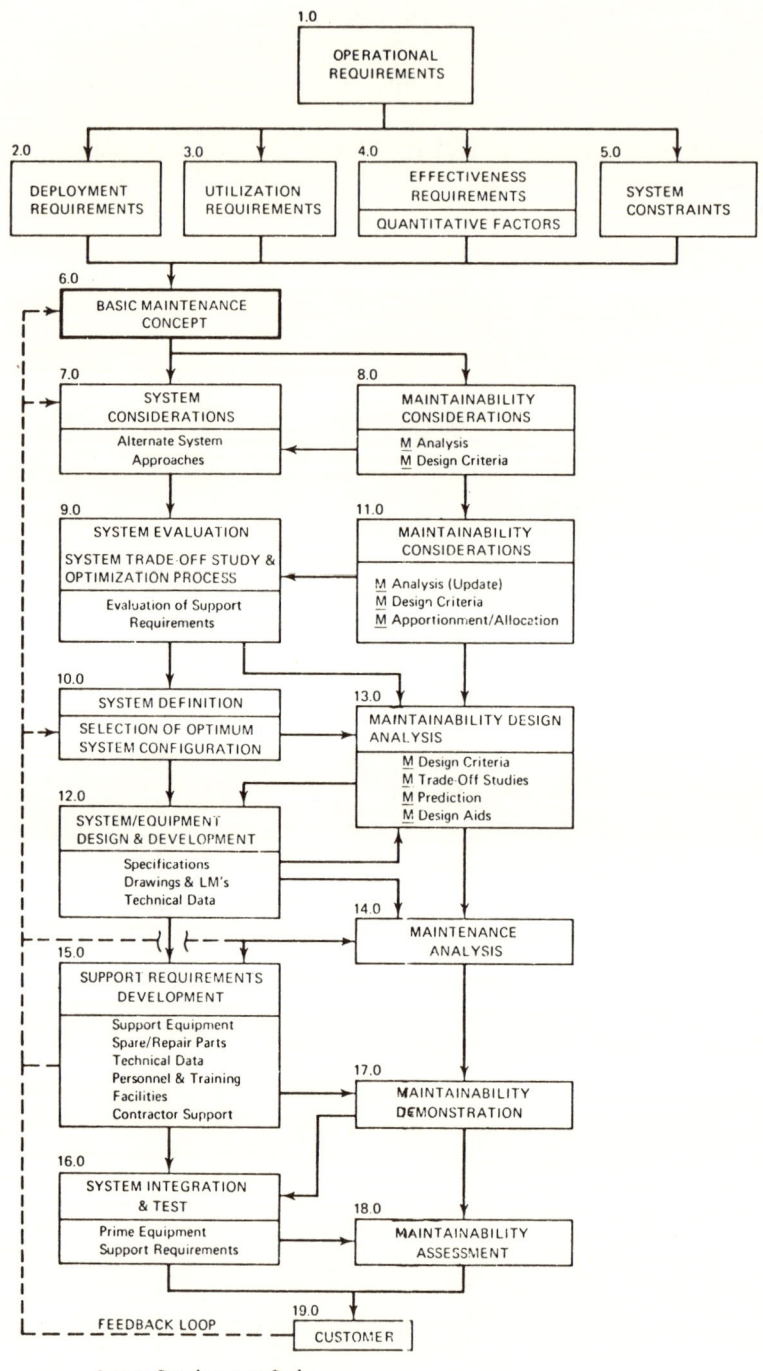

**Figure 8.5
System development cycle**
(Reproduced by permission of authors: B.S. Blanchard, Jr., and E. Edward Lowery.)

TERMS

The measures of maintainability most commonly employed are:

MTBM—mean time between maintenance, including both scheduled preventive maintenance and unscheduled corrective maintenance. MTBM is also considered a reliability parameter since it includes consideration for reliability MTBF as well as MTBR.

$$MTBM_c = MTBF \quad MTBM = \frac{1}{1/MTBM_c + 1/MTBM_p}$$

MTBR—mean time between replacement of an item due to corrective or preventive maintenance, and usually requires a spare part.

$\overline{M}$—mean active maintenance time, including unscheduled and scheduled maintenance (Mct, Mpt), but excluding logistics supply and administrative wait times.

$\overline{M}ct$—mean corrective maintenance time = MTTR, = $\overline{M}_u$, where u is unscheduled.

$\overline{M}pt$—mean preventive maintenance time = $\overline{M}s$, where s is scheduled. During $\overline{M}pt$ the system may be in full operating condition or it may be down.

MTTR—mean time to repair = $\overline{M}ct$ = $_\Sigma Mct$.

Mmax—maximum active corrective maintenance time, usually specified at the 95 percent confidence level.

MDT—maintenance downtime, which is the total time during which equipment is not in condition to perform its intended mission, MDT includes active maintenance time (M), logistics supply time, and administration time.

ACHIEVING MAINTAINABILITY

Like reliability, maintainability must be inherent in the design during early stages. Maintainability engineers must interact with design engineers and maintenance personnel, with continual feedback among all parties. Product or systems specifications will call out the parameters to be met. In some cases availability may be specified, leaving the decision of balancing reliability and maintainability and maintenance up to the system engineering team. Figures 8.6, 8.7, and 8.8 show general trade-off curves. There will always be additional guidelines and contraints, which should be detailed in the maintenance concept.

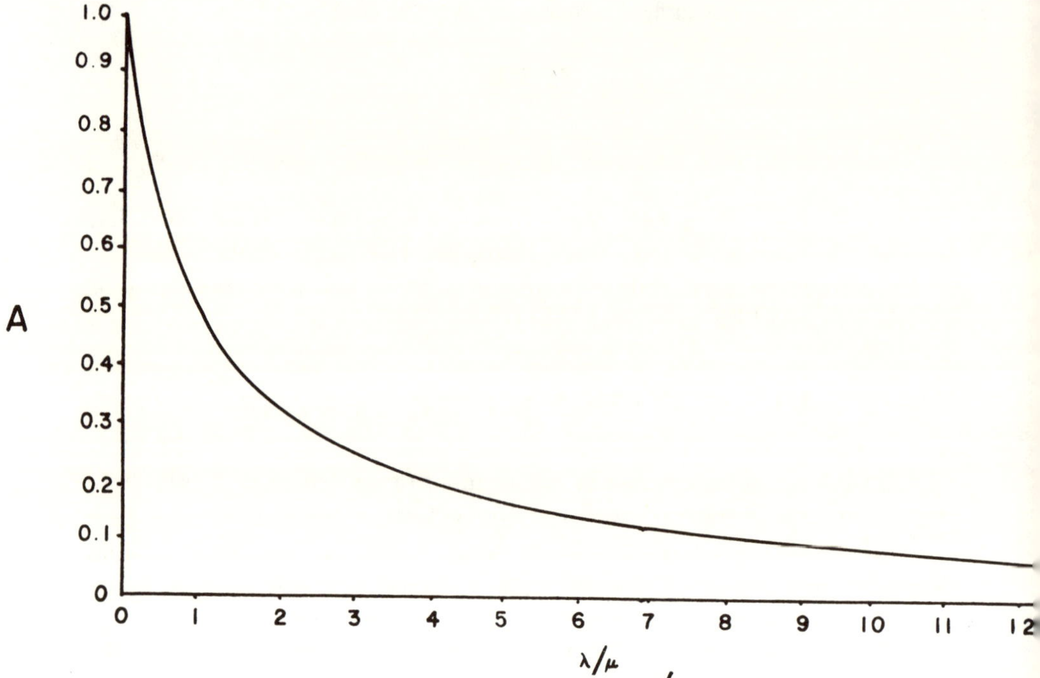

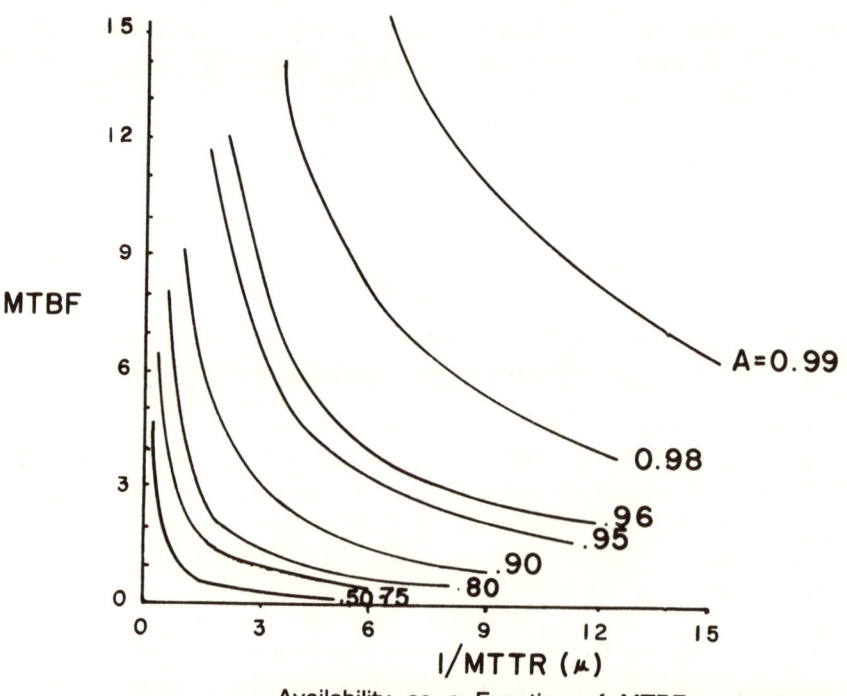

Availability as a Function of λ/μ

Availability as a Function of MTBF and 1/MTTR

Figure 8.6
Reliability-maintainability-availability trade-off curves

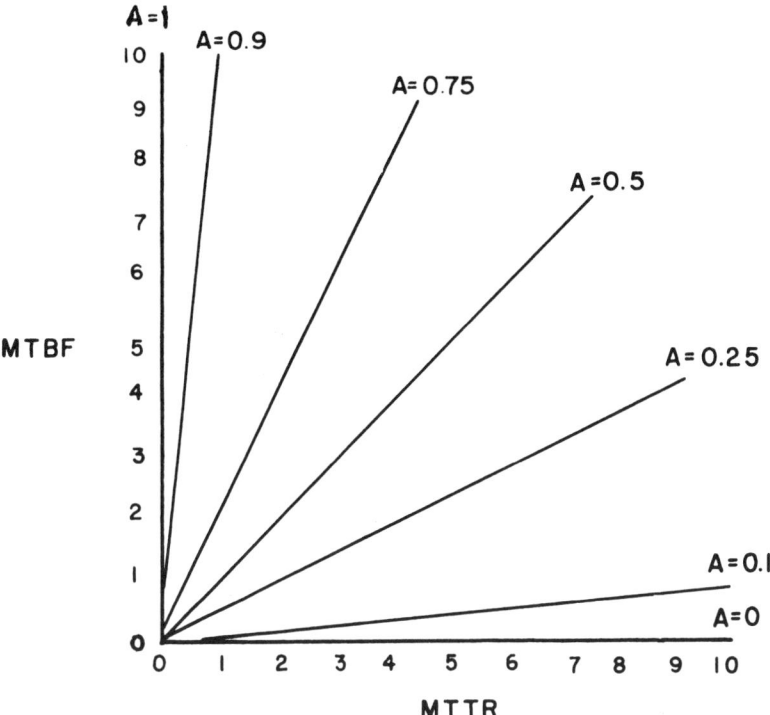

(A) Availability as a Function of MTBF and MTTR

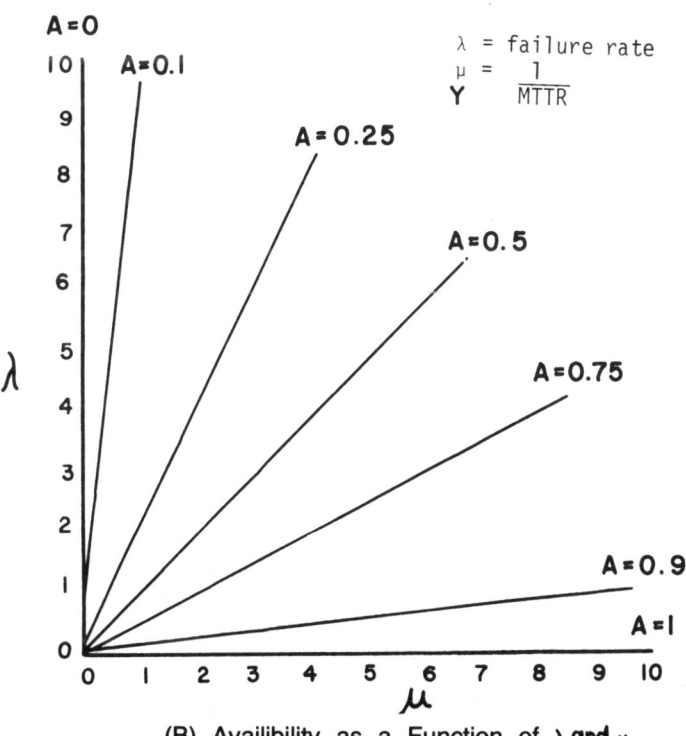

(B) Availibility as a Function of λ and μ

Figure 8.7
Reliability-maintainability-availability RMA trade-off curves

Reliability, Availability, and Maintainability

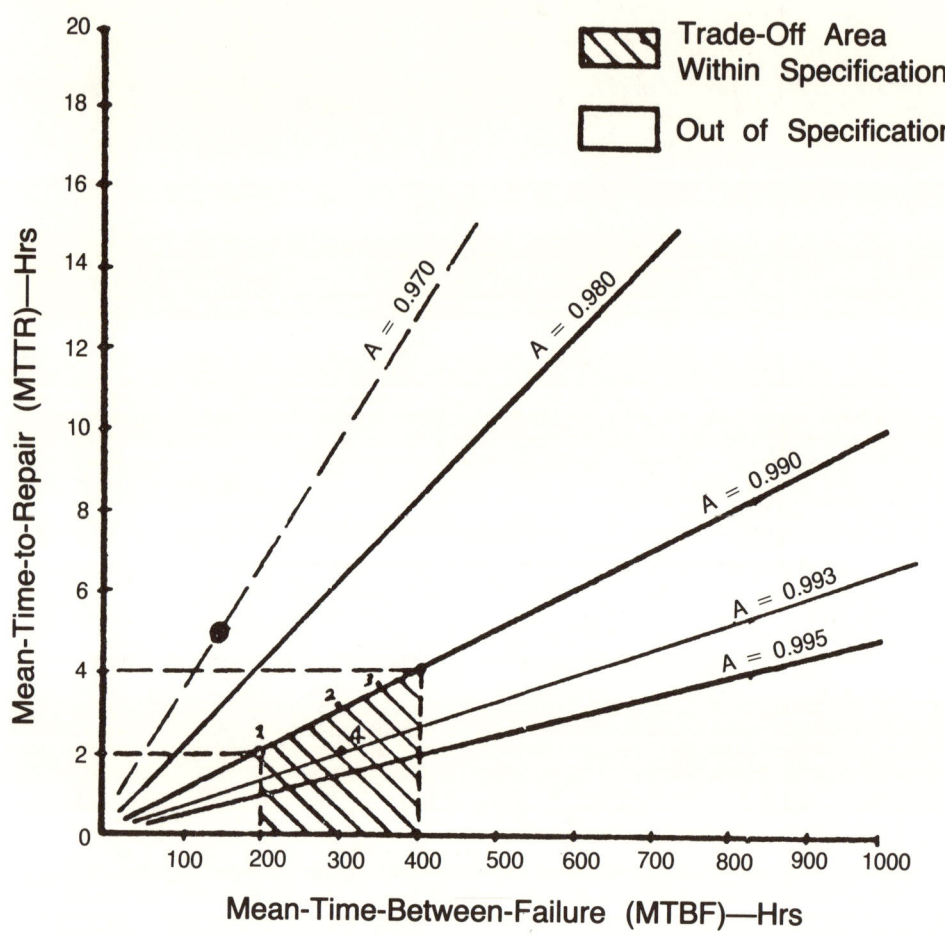

Requirement

A = 99%

MTBF = 200 Hrs Min.

MTTR = 4 Hrs Max.

**Figure 8.8
Reliability-maintainability trade-off**

Consideration, decisions, and probably trade-offs will be necessary for many items, including:

1. *Reliability versus maintainability.* This considers the question: What is the most cost-effective and customer-satisfying balance between failure rate and speed of restoration?
2. *Repair level.* Involves allocating maintenance tasks and resources to the various maintenance levels such as organizational, intermediate, and depot.
3. *System level.* The question is: At what level, piece part, module, assembly, or complete system should maintenance be performed?
4. *Repair/replace-discard.* This trade-off is concerned with determining and applying economic decision criteria to decisions on whether a failed item should be repaired or thrown away. It is also concerned with whether an item should be repaired, should be fixed on site, or possibly a new component should be installed and the defective one repaired at another location and then returned to stock.
5. *Scheduled versus unscheduled maintenance.* As was discussed earlier, items with predictable wear-out characteristics may be cleaned, adjusted, lubricated, or replaced at predictable times in order to prevent catastrophic failure. Thus your automobile requires oil changes, greasing, and new filters, spark plugs, and points to keep it running well. It should be noted that scheduled maintenance intervals are determined based on probability and statistics that have deviations around the mean. The replacement interval should be placed not at the mean or median, but at an earlier point depending on the trade-off between customer satisfaction and cost. In many situations it is the better choice, because of the variability in failures, to allow an item to fail and then perform unscheduled corrective maintenance.
6. *Automation.* Built-in or automatic test checkout and diagnostic equipment may be incorporated depending on its value to the system. Many computer systems, for example, are connected to central checkout systems so that they may be checked periodically from remote locations to ensure proper functioning. Early-warning devices such as error-frequency detectors and dirt-measuring devices may assist in identifying the need for preventive maintenance. Early warning devices are especially effective where conditions of use and customer operation vary a great deal.
7. *Standardization.* This is concerned with whether uniform components should be used on all systems in order to reduce spares inventory, training, tools, and documentation.
8. *Modularization.* Components may be repaired and replaced at a piece-part or a higher level. The decision depends on failure rate, cost, field engineering ability, space, need to minimize time to restoration, critical adjustments, and so forth.

9. *Costs.* Every trade-off is based to some extent on economic criteria in addition to performance and effectiveness. Life-cycle costing assists in determining the trade-off between acquisition and operation and support costs.

10. *Allocations of times and responsibility.* The various elements of maintainability must be divided among responsible organizations that can assure their achievement.

ALLOCATION

Responsibility for achieving the specified conditions is allocated, as mentioned, to responsible functions. Sifting through the scenario of a typical unscheduled maintenance call will assist in determining proper allocation. When the machine has failed, the user determines whether the deficiency can be corrected unaided, and if not, calls the service representative. The user then waits impatiently until the repairperson arrives. There is an initial customer relations period during which the user relates the symptoms and discusses what the problem might be. The problem then is diagnosed and corrected. Other problems may be observed in the machine, or it may be more efficient to perform preventive maintenance while the equipment is down. In either case the actions are additional to the corrective maintenance ($\bar{M}ct$). After the equipment is thoroughly checked and operating properly, the user and management should be informed. If any operator training is necessary, that should be done and the users should realize that supplies or consumables must be ordered. Finally, there are records to be kept of the reason for the service call, action taken, how much time was consumed, and any replaced parts. The administrative aspects of a call—notifying repair personnel, traveling to user locations, discussions with machine operators and customer management, record keeping—are significant time consumers. Depending on the product involved, actual on-machine repair time ($\bar{M}$) may be only 50 percent of the on-site time and less than 25 percent of the total time (MDT), including travel. It thus can be seen that service operations (maintenance management) are a major part of the action.

The hardware components must have maintainability allocated according to a logical hierarchy. Within the total system, maintainability will be distributed by subsystems, assemblies, subassemblies, and so forth. A typical allocation could be as in Figure 8.9.

An allocation table is helpful, such as Table 8.3.

$\bar{M}ct$ for equipment $POR = \dfrac{1.486}{3.466} = .429$

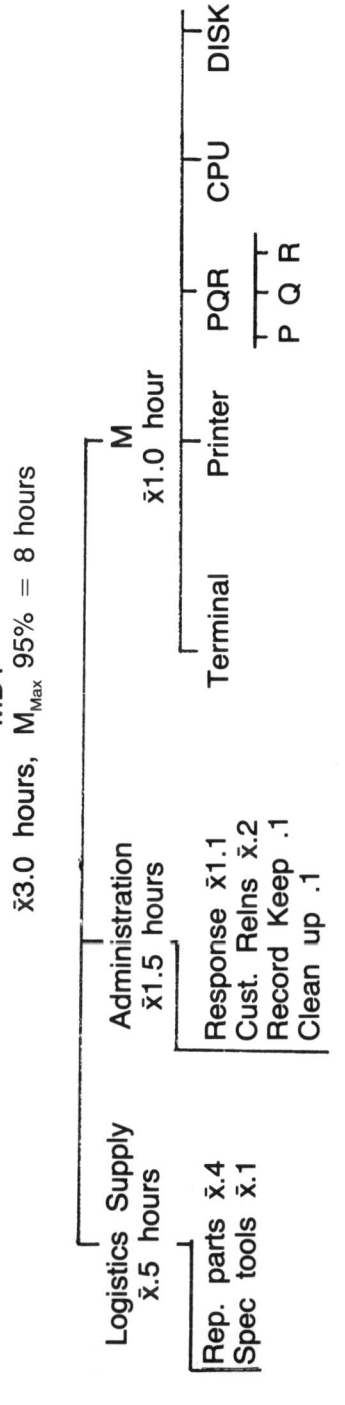

Figure 8.9
Maintainability hierarchy

Table 8.3

Item		Quantity (Q) per System	Fail. (λ) per 10³ Hr.	Cont. of Tot. Fail. λQ = C_f	% Contrib.	M̄ct (hr)	Cont. of Total M̄ct
Widgit	P	1	0.246	0.246	7	0.50	0.123
	O	2	1.124	2.248	65	0.25	0.562
	R	1	0.972	0.972	28	0.83	0.801
Total				3.466	100		1.486

Chances are that allocation is over target, so a cooperative effort is needed with reliability engineering to reduce the failure rate of widget O and a maintainability effort to reduce M̄ct for R and O. Predictions may be made once design is initially established. The techniques of industrial engineering allow time and motion to be built up from individual steps. Historical information on experience with the company's own products is most valuable for making accurate estimates.

MAINTAINABILITY DEMONSTRATION

The maintainability of a design may be demonstrated first on paper through the predictive process and must be later proven through hands-on trials. As soon as hardware can be shown to function properly, demonstrations should be conducted using experienced technical personnel. The second level of demonstration involves field service people who are given special training on the early hardware. As the design develops, additional demonstrations should be conducted to prove that the equipment can be maintained in a customer environment. Representative sample tasks are selected for demonstration based on expected contribution to the total maintenance requirement. Failures may be induced to ensure adequate coverage. At every stage corrective action is initiated to alleviate problems. There will be major initial changes as gross oversights are corrected. As the design becomes refined, the changes will become more subtle, but may be just as value effective.

Alternatives for conducting demonstrations include at least four variations of environment, personnel, and resources as shown in Figure 8.10. Initial demonstration (block 1) will usually be conducted by the producer at the producer's facility using facility people and support equipment. The trials then usually move to customer environment as shown in block 2, but are often still under control of contractor personnel. Demonstration may be conducted by the user's own personnel in the producer's environment, if necessary, due to schedule or cost or technology. Finally, operational demonstration will be conducted for acceptance by the user in the user's own environment as shown in block 4.

Validation checks should be made on field results through information systems, so that the organization can be continually assured that maintainability and maintenance are within specifications and are cost effective.

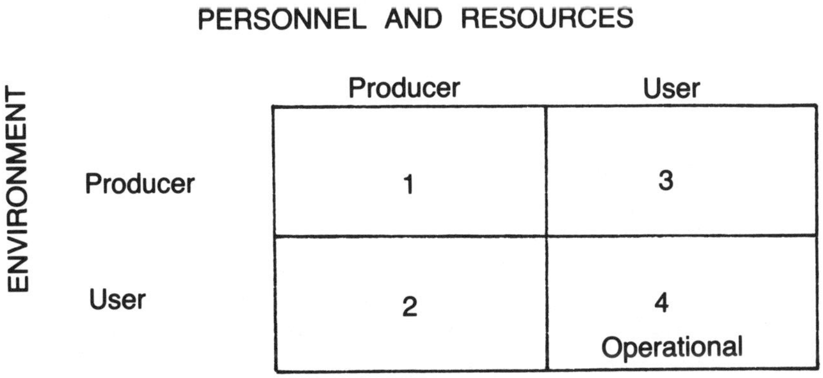

PERSONNEL AND RESOURCES

	Producer	User
ENVIRONMENT — Producer	1	3
ENVIRONMENT — User	2	4 Operational

Figure 8.10
Maintainability demonstration variations

CHAPTER 9

Design Reviews

Design reviews are the evaluations of drawings, sketches, mock-ups, assemblies, models, and other elements of an equipment or system. The evaluations are performed to assess potential and existing problems, or the lack thereof, related to:

1. Functional capability.
2. Manufacture of the equipment.
3. Logistics support.
4. Specific attributes, including reliability, maintainability, human engineering, systems engineering, and safety.

An official design review is usually a formal meeting attended by representatives from the various areas of interest. As the result of this joint meeting, major trade-off decisions are made and directions decided upon to effect improvements. The formal design review serves as a check point on the day-to-day design operation to ensure that all facets of design and supporting interests are being adequately considered.

Rather than holding separate reviews for each of the technical discipline support areas such as reliability and maintainability, the most effective way is to consolidate all the needs into a total system review effort. Separate design reviews result in confusion, schedule delays, wasted effort, and cost, and do not usually incorporate all the factors necessary to make trade-offs.

PURPOSE OF FORMAL REVIEWS

Many purposes, all related to communications, are served by formal design reviews.

1. Program baseline. Formal reviews provide the opportunity for all functions and organizations to communicate with each other and agree on the status of the project at that time.
2. Audit. The proposed hardware and software design is reviewed to ensure it is meeting goals and specifications.
3. Interface compatibility. Potential problems with the interfaces between engineering and manufacturing and the field may not be detected until everyone sits down for a formal review.
4. Latest developments. It is easy for one organization to change direction slightly due to new technology, organizations, and so forth, and assume that everyone else knows this is being done. A design review provides an opportunity for this information flow.
5. Formal records. Detailed minutes that record the status of development, major issues, problems, considerations, trade-off possibilities, and decisions should be widely distributed.
6. Synergism through common direction. Any organization is much more efficient if all components are pulling in the same direction and understand what others are doing.
7. Risk reduction. Formal reviews allow information to be evaluated and decisions to be made before large investments in personnel and parts are initiated.
8. Anticipation. Questions and criticisms from customers are considered, so that integrated solutions can be developed.
9. Standardize. Maximum utilization of standards should be assured wherever applicable or feasible.

When

Formal design reviews should be scheduled to coincide with phases of the design process. Normally a design review will be conducted prior to a total program review for phase transfer so that the design function can adequately state progress and problems. The frequency and type of design reviews will vary from program to program. The common formal design reviews are:

1. Conceptual.
2. System.
3. Preliminary.
4. Critical.

or

1. Conceptual
2. Intermediate.
3. Final.

Figure 9.1 shows the relationship of design reviews to program phases.

The conceptual design review should be held very shortly after a contract is awarded, or at the transfer from concept to feasibility phase. This information session is important to logisticians since most life-cycle costs are already determined by the completion of the concept phase. The purpose of the conceptual design review is to examine the management and technical approaches relative to the system development to ensure that they can meet customer requirements and can be supported. The maintenance concept and data on availability, maintainability, and reliability will be included.

System design reviews are generally held during the last part of the definition phase just before the formal drawing release. The complexity of the system under review may dictate several formal reviews in order adequately to cover all items. The system design review shows, in addition to the potential for meeting customer's requirements, whether the documentation is using the best overall design approach.

A preliminary design review should be held in the design phase when all layouts, drawings, diagrams, and hardware prototypes are available for demonstration and examination. It should take place prior to finalizing the detailed design. Trade-offs, constraints, and problem areas should be identified and reviewed in order to make decisions and seek solutions prior to freezing the design.

Several industrial/government contractors have combined the systems design review and the preliminary design review into a comprehensive intermediate design review. The intermediate design review is a "working" session that requires data including dimensional sketches, layouts, schematics, wiring diagrams, and details of high-risk designs.

The critical/final design review is held to evaluate the final detailed drawings prior to issue for production. It will verify the functionality, produceability, and supportability of the basic design and attempt to catch any oversights before the start of actual manufacturing. The critical/final design review should be coordinated with reliability and maintainability demonstrations, which are considered qualification tests and normally occur at the end of the design or preproduction phase. Since heavy investment is under way at this point, design must be "frozen" and all items given a final reevaluation in order to minimize risk. The critical/final design review and should specifically cover any changes that have resulted from corrective action initiated in the preliminary/intermediate design review.

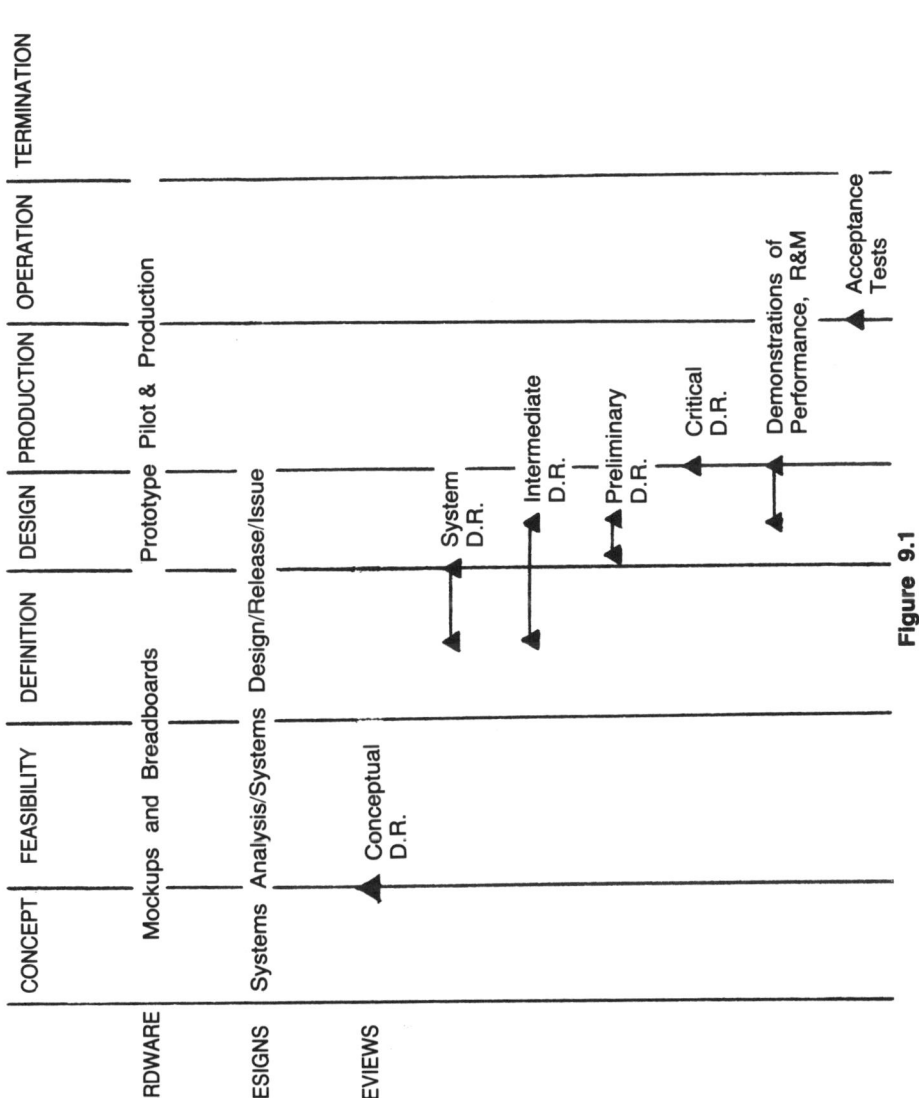

Figure 9.1
Design review relationship for program phases

Additional design reviews may be held as necessary to assure that all specifications and customer requirements can be efficiently met. If any major item is not satisfactory, follow-on reviews could be held to address that specific item.

PLANNING

The success of a formal design review depends on the preparation accomplished prior to the review itself. Coordination should include establishing:

1. Specific date and place for review.
2. Agenda, including the objectives and specific topics to be discussed.
3. Supporting information and data, which participating organizations will want to review prior to formal sit-down.
4. Attendance, which should be as small as possible and still represent those persons who have a direct contribution to make. Since it is a decision-making review, all participants must be authorized to make decisions for the organizations they represent and accept responsibility for follow-on action. A chairperson, normally the design engineering manager, must be designated. The customer may be invited to participate or, in fact, may specify the time and place of the review.
5. Opportunity for physical evaluation of hardware, because it is usually advantageous for the sponsoring organization to have a hands-on demonstration prior to the formal review.
6. Requirements designating who will take minutes and prepare follow-on reports.
7. Funding to assure that financial responsibility is identified and costs are properly planned.

To ensure the success of the design review, a management check list of all necessary items should be compiled. All contributing functions will want to conduct their own internal reviews just before the formal design reviews. This helps assure that anyone who deserves to input has a chance to participate in the process.

CONDUCT OF THE REVIEW

A formal design review is a critical milestone in product acquisition. It is essential that it be conducted in a manner that assures maximum effectiveness. With adequate planning the actual review can follow the agenda and flow smoothly even though the hardware and software under review may not have performed as well as expected. The chairperson of the design review board is in charge and with this will come the responsibility for establishing and maintaining firm control and keeping the meeting focused on the agenda topics. Where design problems are identified, the review team may point out possible approaches to solutions; however, detailed engineering designs should not be attempted at design reviews. The chairperson should assign responsibility for follow-up action and ensure that the responsibility is agreed to by appropriate organizations, and schedules and controls are established to assure their completion.

PURCHASING REVIEWS

An extension of design reviews is prompted by the problem of equipment being purchased for factory use with little consideration given to its support requirements. Similar situations occur when companies acquire new product lines to be supported. A check list of maintenance considerations should be evaluated as part of the purchasing decision before new equipment is acquired. Special considerations should be added for specific environments and unique requirements.

Advance attention to support considerations through design and purchasing reviews can help assure that total life-cycle costs of ownership are minimized.

CHAPTER

10

Configuration Management

From the invention of the wheel, with its attendant problems of trying to get two wheels the same size on one axle, to the advent of mass production, the need for configuration control and management has increased accordingly. The epitomy of standardization was Henry Ford and his Model T, which was "available in any color you wanted, so long as you wanted black." Even today, parts are available for the car built 60 years ago because the demand was supportable through good specifications, drawings, and component identification. Unfortunately, the reverse is often true with consumer products, even with durable goods built today.

WHAT IS CM?

Generically, configuration management (CM) systems establish a means to ensure the identification, control, accounting, and verification status of all aspects of a product. We tend to think of CM as referring to hardware only. However, it does include all related software and support items. A typical CM plan will be composed of at least:

1. Specifications.
2. Verification and confirmation.

3. Product documentation.
4. Hardware and software configuration.
5. Change control.

Specifications have been considered as a separate topic. The remaining items will be addressed in the following section.

VERIFICATION

Verification, sometimes called confirmation or baseline, ties together all the elements of configuration management and provides a powerful tool to program management for the precise and timely control of product configuration. Verifications are designed to relate directly to transfers between phases of phased program planning. For example, a production verification would be established at the end of the definition phase and be based mainly on prototype acceptance testing. The significance of that verification step is the demonstration of the ability of prototype units to comply with the system performance specifications before the typically rapid escalation of program expenditures and risk for tooling, gauging, and parts procurement. The verification criteria must be established at the beginning of that phase as the objectives to be met before the program advances to the next phase.

Questions should be asked and answered satisfactorily, including:

1. Is the ultimate market established?
2. Will the product goals and technology as presently planned satisfy market needs, cost objectives, and performance advantages set for the product?
3. Are process and product meeting established guidelines?
4. Has the hardware configuration and design verification testing been completed commensurate with these requirements?
5. Has product documentation been completed and does it reflect available hardware?
6. Has integrated logistics support planning been completed commensurate with phase and program requirements?

By taking snapshots at the designated times, these verifications allow management to evaluate product achievements against preestablished targets, assess risks, and anticipate downstream impact so that decisions and plans for the future can be made. It is rare that all targets are fully met. If they are not, the deviation should be clearly identified together with plans for the necessary corrective action, and the associated risk should be clearly defined. It is often possible to effect the phase transition and begin work in many areas on the new phase while deficient areas run parallel high-risk paths to catch up with the moving program.

The transfer qualification criteria must be prepared with the joint participation of all organizations and functions involved with the product/program development. There should be formal reviews conducted at those times so that all questions and answers (or lack thereof) are out in the open. This is particularly true when service organizations may be about to receive products from engineering and manufacturing. If the product is being done on contract, both vendor and buyer personnel must be in agreement before advancing to the next phase or signing the contract.

DOCUMENTATION

Product documentation is typically defined as all the information necessary to enable design, manufacture, test, and support of a product during its useful life. As such, documentation covers a number of areas, aspects, and disciplines, including:

1. Specifications.
2. Design disclosure.
3. Action documents and systems.
4. Program administration.
5. Product support.
6. Reference policies, procedures, and standards.

These are detailed in Figure 10.1.

The objectives of a product documentation system are to define the hardware and software, and communicate its functional, operational, and physical characteristics. These objectives support the manufacturability and serviceability of a product and assure that relevant design information is recorded and maintained.

Documentation control varies with the scope, nature, and detail of the particular document. Generally the documents required relate to the functional inputs needed by organizations and functions to do their jobs and are often presented as part of the output of their efforts; for example, the design engineering function will prepare engineering orders and drawings that follow rigid guidelines available in most companies to assure uniformity between individuals and departments. All drawings and applicable changes must be circulated to involved functions.

Since manufacturing may not be able to deliver the product exactly as drawn, there should be concessions and deviations documents that describe potential differences. It is important that all responsible orga-

Configuration Management

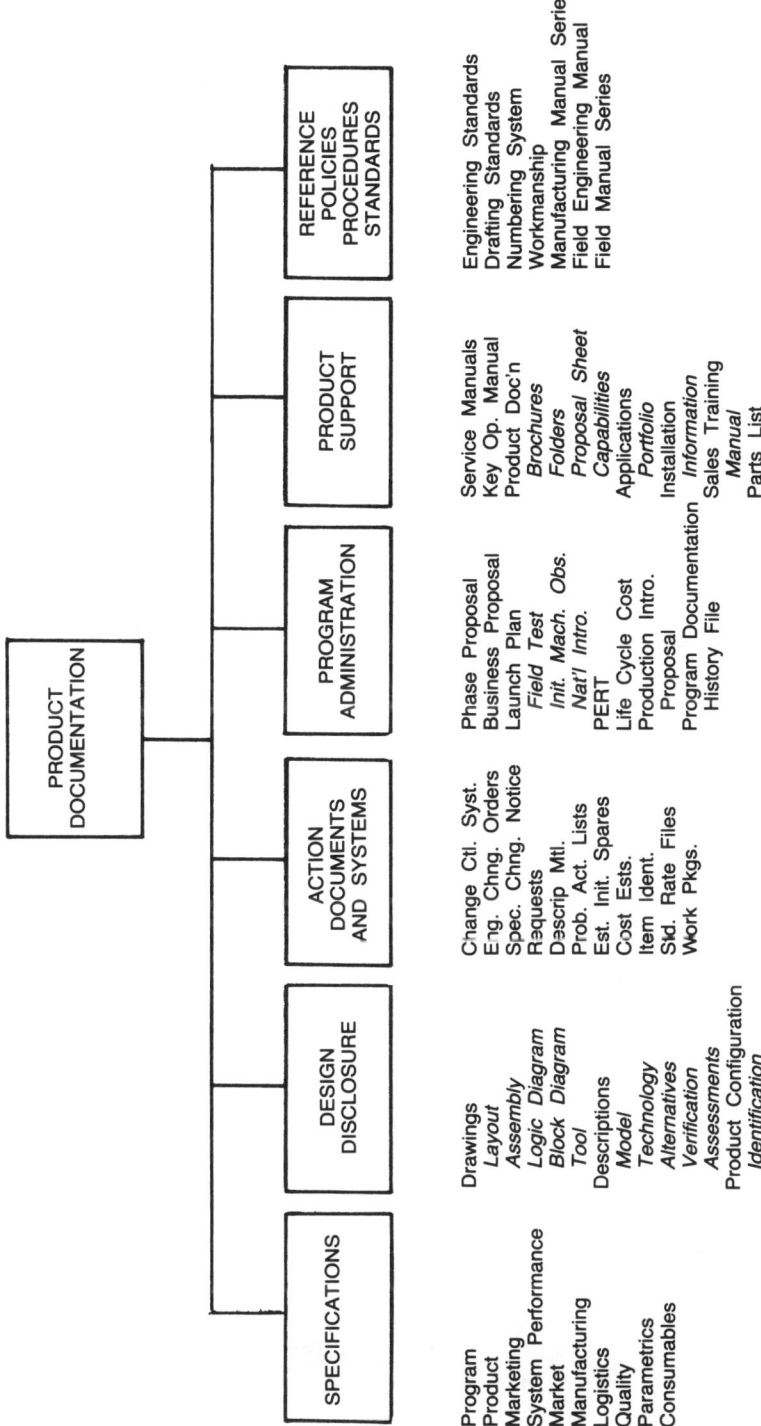

Figure 10.1
Documentation of a typical commercial product

nizations have review and sign-off rights to any change! While a designer may feel that a particular revision does not change form, fit, or function, it may well have a significant affect as viewed by the service engineer.

As shown in Figure 10.2, the detail and involvement of documentation will increase significantly with each phase in the product's development cycle, reaching its fullest intent at the production phase. The hierarchy of documentation for product design is shown in the final assembly layout, Figure 10.3.

HARDWARE AND SOFTWARE

Hardware and software configuration management attempts to establish criteria for the identification and classification of equipment, networks, systems, units, modules, and accessories. It sets up mechanisms to control the configurations of these items and track subsequent changes to their structure. End-item identification and the storage and retrieval of inventory configuration information are a vital part of the system.

It is probable that there are three significant differences in the product configuration, defined typically as "as-designed," "as-built," and "as-maintained." The as-designed form is the drawings, which are prepared by engineering and communicated to manufacturing and field support activities. When the machine leaves manufacturing, it may be slightly different from the as-designed configuration, due to discrepant parts or human error, and therefore is described as as-built. After a product has been in the field, operated by customers, serviced, and possibly modified, it may pass to a as-maintained configuration.

The basic element of control is the part number. This unique code should be assigned according to a companywide system that is compatible with that of suppliers, customers, and other related organizations. Contractors to the government, for example, follow the federally dictated parts number sequence. Any organization just establishing part numbers must be cautious since part numbers, once established, are very difficult to alter. If a company should later become involved with others through purchase, acquisition, or sale, the change to the surviving system could be very traumatic. Wherever possible, every part should be clearly marked with its specific number. Part numbers should be all numeric, as short as possible, and not be structured with intelligent components.

Since most products are made up of many parts, subassemblies, assemblies, modules, and so forth, a number of small changes on individual pieces result in many combinations and permutations. If these are of form, fit, or function that is not significant, then the problem is merely one of identification. If, however, there are significant differences, then further control is necessary. Block control is one method. Block is

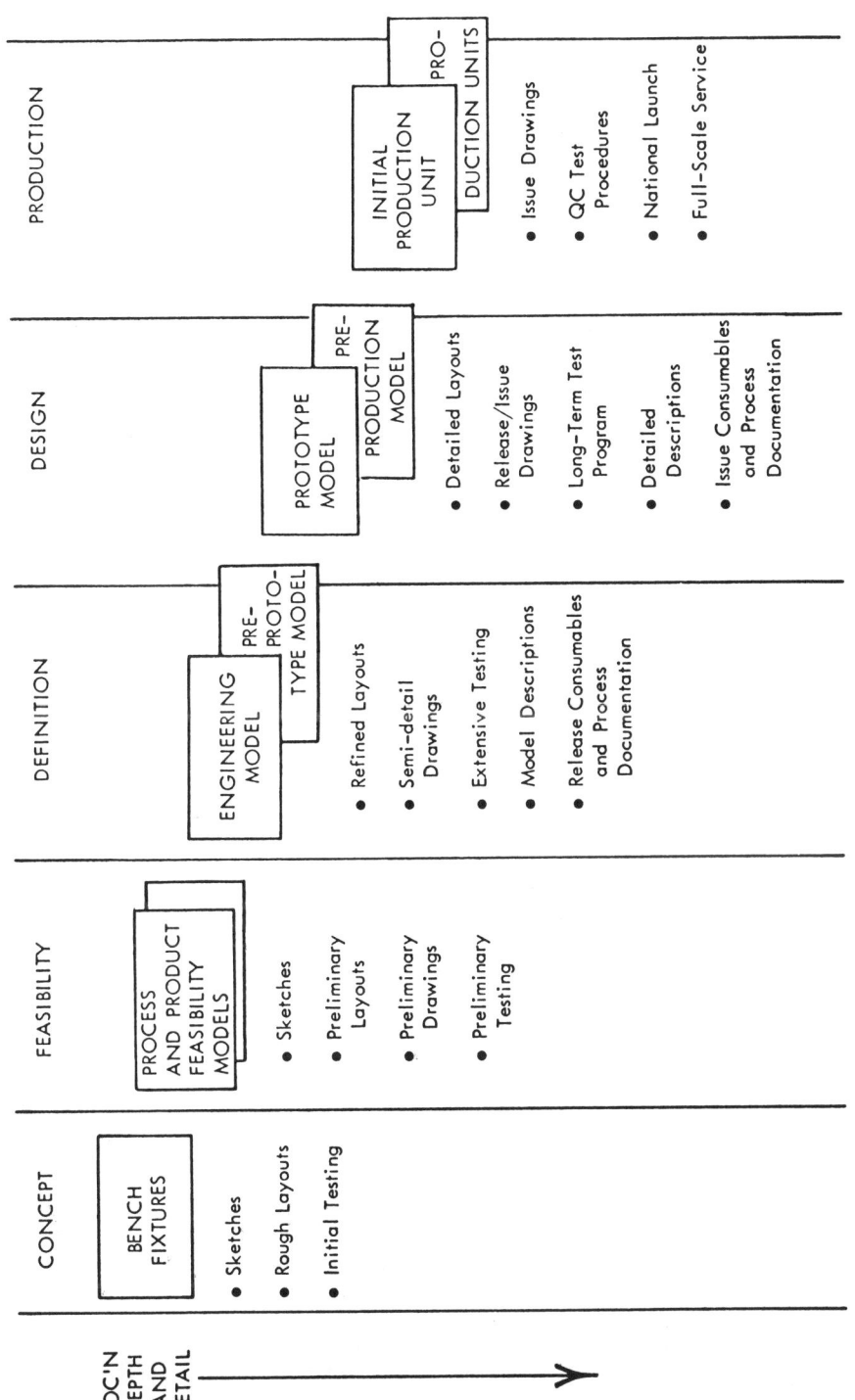

Figure 10.2 Standard model program phase documentation relationships

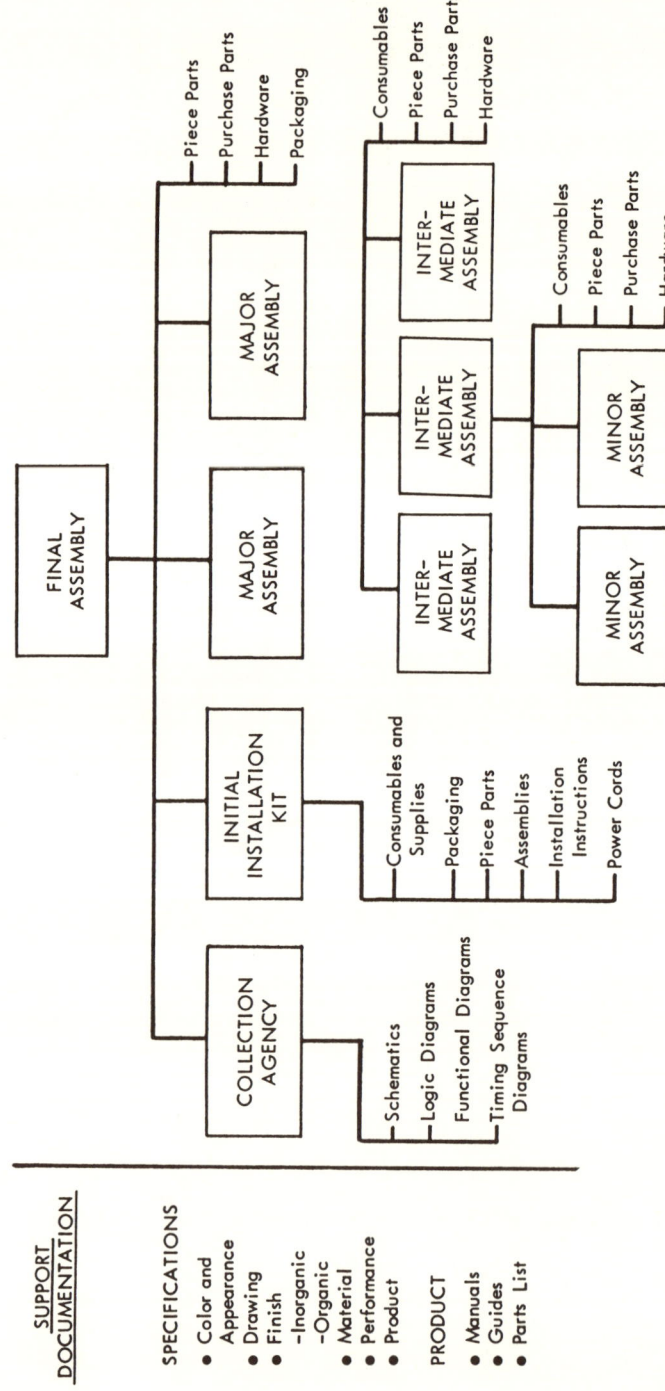

Figure 10.3 The product design documentation hierarchy

a term that describes a specific configuration level of a machine being manufactured and shipped to the field for installation, or a group of machines that possess similar performance characteristics and configuration. Manufacturing is significantly constrained when block production is ordered since all parts in production must conform to that configuration level before a product can be shipped. This presents severe scheduling problems and probable scrappage. Manufacturing normally prefers to roll in changes; that is, let them occur as they run out of one part configuration and the successor configuration becomes available. It may be necessary to control all units or modules that make up a system to assure compatibility when they are connected and expected to work well with each other.

The previously mentioned documentation of engineering orders and change orders is a vital link in assuring control of hardware and software configuration. There must be a single system with single-point responsibility for making changes, and all other functions must funnel their changes into this single area. Any deviation or concession for a documented waiver temporarily to manufacture or use certain parts should be discontinued at a specific point in time or quantity, or else be changed to an engineering order. Making end runs around the formal system by many temporary measures defeats the control.

The hardware and software documentation and configuration are critical to the service organization in preparing manuals. The service organization is interested in documentation that will aid in maintaining and repairing equipment. The process of transforming the information on engineering drawings into service documentation and training programs is accomplished by technical writers, illustrators, and educators. The best person for the writing and educating job is one who has carried a tool bag and fixed products. This person can make intuitive judgments about the level of detail necessary, and can explain the practical significance of checks and adjustments that may differ from the theoretical or pure engineering approach.

Documentation provided to a service engineer must be accessible without being patronizing. There are many ways to disseminate information, including ladder charts, flow diagrams, and schematics. Recent trends are toward functional documentation as pioneered by the McDonnell Douglas Aircraft Company. Designers think in a functional logic format, taking inputs into their subsystems, manipulating them to perform certain functions, and then providing outputs to other elements of the system. They think in terms of both a physical entity and what it is achieving. Functional documentation can take this information directly from the engineer and make it usable for servicing with relatively little translation. This helps communication between the field and internal design functions, since they can all use the same terms and numbers for components and functions. Service documentation and hardware configuration are covered further in the section on personnel and training.

CHANGE CONTROL

To document properly the dynamic growth of a program through the life cycle, a drawing may average five to ten changes. Of course, a few of the components and drawings account for most of the changes, and the majority of changes are for correction of relatively insignificant items such as thread sizes and incorrect addition. That could typically be 60 percent of all changes, with another 25 percent for well-thought-out logical minor changes that can be easily discussed and approved. The remaining 10–15 percent cause most of the trouble, and require most of the design and analysis time. All of these changes must be controlled.

Change documents are necessary as a formal mechanism to alter any drawing. These are called by names such as engineering change order (ECO), EO, or CO. There may be an engineering request (ER) document used by other organizations for requesting changes to be made by engineering. Changes to be made on installed equipment are documented on a field change order (FCO). Whatever the name, the intent is to document any changes formally. The function that approved the original drawing should approve any change to it, and before doing so, should perform change impact analysis. This guarantees screening of all proposed changes to ensure that they are, in fact, improvements and can be positively accommodated by all functions.

Often during the production process, changes are initiated to correct a deficiency, improve a product, or accommodate a discrepant component. In most cases a change in one element of the system will directly affect other elements. For example, a change in the design configuration of prime equipment will, in all probability, affect the design of test and support equipment, the type and quantity of spares, and replacement parts, technical data, facilities, and so forth. A change in the production process may impact reliability of the product, which, in turn, affects test and support equipment, spare parts requirements, labor rates, maintenance allocations, and many other elements of logistics support.

There are many reasons for configuration to change: (1) the equipment may be produced without a fixed design configuration having been formally reviewed, demonstrated, verified, and fixed; (2) the original mission may have been amended, requiring an alteration in the equipment; (3) technical developments may allow improvement; (4) suppliers may discontinue their supply or send discrepant components at the last minute. In most cases the need for changes can be avoided by proper planning. However, there will often be discrepant materials, and after report and review, some form of concession or deviation notice provides authorization for their limited use.

Major changes in equipment (discussed earlier under block change control) should be permanently identified by an assigned modification or retrofit code number and affixed to a tag located on a permanent part of the system. Any time an alteration is made to an installed product, this change in the as-maintained configuration should be marked on the retrofit label and the information reported to central record control.

Finally, all elements of configuration for a particular piece of equipment must be retrievable in connection with that product's serial number. This can be important for maintenance, so that the proper documentation, tools, and repair parts are available; for sales, so that the customer can depend on receiving a piece of equipment that has the capability desired; and for legal liabilities, so that a product recall or warning can be accurately made on short-time turnaround. Configuration management is a very complex, but necessary, part of product design, manufacturing, and field support.

CHAPTER

11

Acquisition and Production/Construction Support

A segment of logistics called *Industrial logistics* deals with the logistics support required in the production of an item. The elements for production and construction are very similar to those already studied—with significant additions, notably in the areas of procurement and production control. If we define production as the transformation of goods or services into a more usable form, this producing function includes manufacturing an automobile, writing an insurance policy, and cooking a meal.

Production normally connotes many elements that must be arranged in a particular sequence to produce the desired end product. Those elements and their most efficient arrangement are the major challenge to a designer-planner. The preparation of a meal allows a relatively high degree of flexibility. For example, in making pancakes it differs little in what order flour, eggs, milk, and butter are added so long as the required amounts are used and blended together. In producing an automobile, however, the assembly must start from the basic center component and work outward. In technology-driven processes such as an oil refinery, the process may be dictated by the physical chemistry. The designer-planner is much more constrained in the latter processes and will have fewer candidate systems, but will nevertheless study the process requirement and develop an assembly sequence that is efficiently tailored to match inputs and outputs with resources, facilities, equipment, and people.

PRODUCTION CONCEPTS

Production can usually be classified as either a continuous process or an intermittent batch concept. A continuous production process flows material in a fairly consistent stream. Mining, pharmaceuticals manufacture, and oil refining are examples of continuous-flow processes.

Most production lines that appear to be a continuous mass production system are, in fact, intermittent processes made up of many smaller steps. These steps have been balanced together to form an efficient sequence.

The three main concepts of intermittent manufacturing are known as:

1. Job shop.
2. Intermediate "flow-through."
3. Assembly line.

Under a job shop system, equipment is organized by types and allows a production order, at least in principle, to follow any sequence of departments through the plant. Job shop organization is characterized by extreme flexibility, a lot of paperwork to control and dispatch orders, and large in-process inventories to act as buffers against workload variations in individual departments. On the other hand, an assembly-line system has a tight schedule, rapid flow, and difficulty in making changes to the product going through the line. The assembly-line system depends on very tight control over available parts stock in relation to scheduled flow, and on-site supervision. In fact most businesses have neither the extreme variability nor the unpredictability of demand that requires the job shop operation, nor can they properly engineer products to match the assembly-line needs.

An intermediate system known as the flow-through concept is gaining recognition by many manufacturers, although they may have been using it without having defined it as such. The flow-through concept depends on elements of the following:

1. Products are grouped into patterns.
2. The time a product spends on a particular machine will vary from product to product and requires machine utilization factors to estimate machine hours required and capacity.

3. Machines and process centers are then arranged by product group to provide an estimated capacity within the same physical location.

4. A central organization processes all production orders.

5. Occasional special transfers of orders are possible to accommodate medium-term imbalance.

Automated data processing greatly assists the computation necessary for efficient flow-through scheduling. The automobile assembly line, which can produce cars in different body styles, colors, engines, and accessories to match a customer's specific order, is a good illustration.

Inventories, as previously discussed, are vital to:

1. Smooth the production flow.
2. Allow separation of sequential operations.
3. Minimize material handling.
4. Permit high utilization of equipment.
5. Keep fresh material flowing to the production process.

Accurate material requirements planning (MRP) greatly reduces inventory held consistent with just-in-time (JIT) delivery of needed parts and materials.

PROCUREMENT

One of the most important functions in industrial production is the organization called Purchasing, Buying, or Procurement. Whatever its name, it carries more dollar responsibility per person than any other industrial, commercial, or governmental function.

George Algain, editor of the *Purchasing Handbook*, defines Procurement as corporate management's group of professional and expert specialists for the procurement of materials, supplies, tools, and services required by all other groups in the enterprise in the overall process of adding value.

Purchasing must consider quality as well as price since it must strive for the best possible "value." In fact in evaluating most bids and proposals, the qualification of the bidder and the quality or "fitness for use" of the goods or services to be purchased must be acceptable before the price can even be considered.

A procurement organization has many functions, including:

—Providing purchasing services.
—Obtaining effective value.
—Financial commitment control.
—Negotiations.
—Information.

Procurement interacts with many other functions, including Engineering, Production, Receiving, Accounting, Legal, Marketing, Service, and Program Management.

Purchased materials represent a major portion of costs in most manufacturing firms. As a percentage of sales, materials costs can range from a low of 35 percent for electronic components to a high of 66 percent for metal containers. The purchasing department is the function that conducts contract negotiations between the firm and its suppliers. They are the focal point through which all vendor negotiations must flow in order to assure consistent statements and information in accordance with company strategies and policies. For example, communication with vendors on quality problems should be initiated by the vendee's purchasing department and the vendor rather than by quality control, engineering, or other functions. Procurement will chair any meetings and be responsible for the decisions.

PROCUREMENT LOGISTICS

The first step toward any procurement action is to detail what must be procured. The design specifications and drawings define the material or product to be purchased. Quality assurance will assist Design, Manufacturing, and Purchasing in determining the optimal level of quality assurance and conformance. Purchasing will prefer design documentation that allows flexibility and competition through standard items and nomenclature. Specifications requiring single-point purchase constrain procurement and present a risk to the company since alternate courses of supply would permit price competition, security, disaster protection, and competitive motivation. Purchasing will often provide a list of qualified suppliers and their products so that design and production can be somewhat predicated on the best available items. How much to order is a function of Production and Inventory Control as discussed earlier, but the procurement department should consider transportation logistics in deciding from what locations the items should be purchased and what effect transportation costs will have on the end product.

When to procure is a primary function of Production and Inventory Control but there will be information feedback regarding price discounts, rebates, and other pricing decisions that should influence the quantity purchased, as well as contractual agreements that may give an economic advantage for various patterns of order, delivery, and payment. Negotiations are expensive, so negotiating once to cover many orders might prove expedient. Even processing purchase orders for known price items can cost from $15 to $75. "Blanket buying" is a concept in which a commitment is made to purchase a large volume of material over a long period of time in order to get the best volume price, but delivery is made in smaller units, which reduces inventory on hand and spreads the purchasing cost over the entire period. Such large once-a-year contracts are normally put out to invite bidding on a fixed-price basis. The request for bids would include specifications as to when, where, and in what quantities the materials are to be delivered so that they can be efficiently handled by the using organizations.

PROPOSALS AND QUOTATIONS

When a purchasing department is directed to acquire an item or service, its actions depend on whether it is a normally stocked item, a new item, or a routine reorder procedure. The sequence for purchasing a normally stocked item is as follows.

1. Purchase order (PO) prepared by user.
2. Request for quote (RFQ) sent to vender.
3. Vender returns the quote.
4. Purchase order issued by user to producer vender.
5. Vender returns acknowledgement copy of PO.
6. Vender ships the ordered item and invoice.
7. Receipt reported.
8. Recipient pays billing invoice.

The procedure for reordering standard items is as follows:

1. Purchase requisition prepared by function needing the item.
2. Purchase order (PO) prepared by procurement and sent to vender.
3. Vender ships item and invoice.
4. Receipt of item recorded.
5. Invoice paid.

New items present a more complex ordering sequence, particularly if there are degrees of quality or service available. A simple process is shown in the following list.

1. User originates purchase requisition.
2. Request for quotation (RFQ) or request for proposal (RFP) sent to interested venders.
3. Vender returns quote.
4. Purchase order (PO) sent to selected vender.
5. Vender acknowledges PO.
6. Vender ships item and invoice.

7. Receipt reported.
8. Invoice is paid.

Extensive supply of goods or services normally requires a request for proposal (RFP). These documents may cover many pages and considerable detail on what is to be delivered. This form would be typical for such things as providing a new data processing system for a governmental agency or contracting to provide a new weapons system. A proposal normally has two separate sections; the first outlines how the job will be fulfilled and the second details cost. The format of a typical proposal includes:

• *Cover letter*, which should be one page, covers the organization bidding, proposal highlights, and who is authorized to represent the bidder.
• *Short introduction* and summary includes an outline of the general approach to the statement of work. It should contain a brief statement of the salient features of the proposal response.
• *Understanding of the problem* discusses the understanding of the requirements, implementation, and the methodology that would be employed.
• *Task plan, time table, and person-hours* includes the estimates of the period of performance and task delineation with a technical discussion of each phase. This section will generally include a detailed statement of the work to be performed under each contract requirement, any specific statements of compliance or exception to requirements, and the degree of major difficulties anticipated.
• *Background and experience* shows where the bidders describe their experience in meeting similar jobs and their cost, schedule, and technical performance records.
• *Resumés of individuals* include the experience, educational background, demonstrated capabilities, and availability of the personnel that would be assigned to the program.
• *Cost* enumerates the detailed costs and schedules. The cost structure could be cost plus fixed fee (CPFF), fixed price, standard labor rate, not-to-exceed price, or incentive.

MAKE OR BUY

A "make or buy" decision is made by an organization to determine whether materials should be manufactured or purchased. The comparative cost to make or buy an item is the primary evaluation criterion, so that the total cost is minimized per the equation

$$C_iD + \sqrt{2C_bC_hD\left(1 - \frac{D}{R}\right)}$$

where

C_i = item cost
C_b = buying cost or line set up expenses
C_h = holding cost
D = demand
R = Replenish rate

Consider a gizmo laid out for comparison as follows:

	Make	Buy
Item cost—$	6.00	6.10
Lead time—days	12	16
Order 1 setup cost—$	50.00	8.00
Replenish rate/day	18	∞ (unlimited)
Holding cost per period—$	0.004	0.004
Demand per period	3	3

$$TC_{min} = C_iD + \sqrt{2C_bC_hD\left(1 - \frac{D}{R}\right)}$$

Make = $6.00(3) + \sqrt{2(50)(\$.004)(3)(1 - 3/18)}$ = $19.00

Buy = $6.10(3) + \sqrt{2(8)(0.004)(3)}$ = $18.74   Minimum cost

The cost considerations are, of course, only one criterion necessary for the decision. Manufacturing also requires investment in machines, people, abilities, raw materials, and so forth, with related overhead and nondirect expenses. There may be considerations for additional control since a company making its own material has better control over schedule, quality, and utilization. On the other hand, buying an item means the company does not have to invest in those resources and allows the funds to be diverted to more profitable investments.

SPECIAL PURCHASING PROGRAMS

Reciprocal agreements are often entered into so that the company purchases items from customers who buy its products. It is a necessary marketing tool to maintain trade relations, but from a logistics point of view it increases the number of suppliers and the supply points to be served and decreases the average shipment size. These reciprocal agreements trade off increased logistics costs for increased sales. Every company has its critical few items that must be carefully controlled, but the majority of these are relatively low in cost. Most procurement departments have a rule of thumb that allows them to buy large quantities of low-cost, high-volume items such as common hardware in order to reduce total involvement. Another system, called systems contracting or blanket purchasing is often used for maintenance, repair, and operating supply (MRO) items that may be needed from company storerooms several times a day. Stationary supplies, such as paper clips, pencils, and typewriter ribbons, are examples of items that can best be handled under a systems contract. An organization awards a contract to a supplier for a complete family of related items and gives all internal customers an in-company catalog that describes the items that may be requested. The individual needing an item submits a simple requisition, which is passed through purchasing direct to the vender. The vender then fills the requisition from the inventory directly to the user.

Another system is the purchase order draft (POD). Kaiser Aluminum Corporation found that 75 percent of the 18000 checks written each month to venders were under $200 and accounted for only 4.5 percent of the total disbursements. With the POD system, the user prepares a purchase order and sends it with a blank check to the vender. When the order is shipped, the vender makes out the check for the proper amount and cashes it. The customer audits the receiving reports and bank statements. Loss rate using the POD system has been very low. A similar method, called cash-in-fist (CIF), is being used to pay freight carriers. Under CIF a blank check is part of the bill of lading and the carrier simply computes shipping charges, makes out the check for the proper amount, and cashes it.

Other systems utilize venders' sales/stock personnel to check the user's inventory and replenish it as necessary through requisitions they prepare and send simultaneously to the user's purchasing department for approval and their own producing company for shipment. Under yet another arrangement, a vender may stock and staff the inventory storeroom and fill all orders from stock, with bills submitted periodically on the basis of issued requisitions. Computers naturally speed the entire procurement process, particularly where interaction is necessary between orders, bills of materials, inventories, the order levels, purchase order preparation, and tracking of receipts, receiving inspection, and accounts payable to assure that the procurement process operates as an integrated system.

INDUSTRIAL ENGINEERING

The composite of activities necessary for the design, development, and operation of the production capability is termed industrial engineering. These activities normally include:

1. Plant engineering.
2. Manufacturing engineering.
3. Methods engineering.
4. Production planning and control.
5. Quality control.

Plant engineers are normally responsible for determining the capacity and location of the production facilities, their utility requirements, capital needs, internal layouts, and maintenance.

Manufacturing engineering determines the best way to build the engineering design. It defines and specifies the production process, including selection of materials, processes, methods, tools, handling equipment, and test equipment. Manufacturing engineers are very concerned with making sure that human factors are adequately taken into account.

Methods engineering works closely with manufacturing engineers to establish work methods, time, and cost standards. It is responsible for assuring efficiency and cost in the production operation. Methods engineering normally includes the estimating function, which provides cost data for life-cycle cost analysis. Industrial engineers working in methods engineering utilize the well-known techniques of time study, work factor analysis, and method time and motion (MTM) studies. These standards are used to set productivity, requirements, incentives, and bonus structures. Methods engineering uses techniques of flow sequencing by branch and bound as shown in Figure 11.1 below, and linear programming as shown in Figure 11.2. Obtaining the best possible sequence of operation flow sequencing by branch and bound can be done either manually or by computer to establish the minimum cost/effort of producing N jobs through M machines. Note that the number of possible choices is reduced by one at each step.

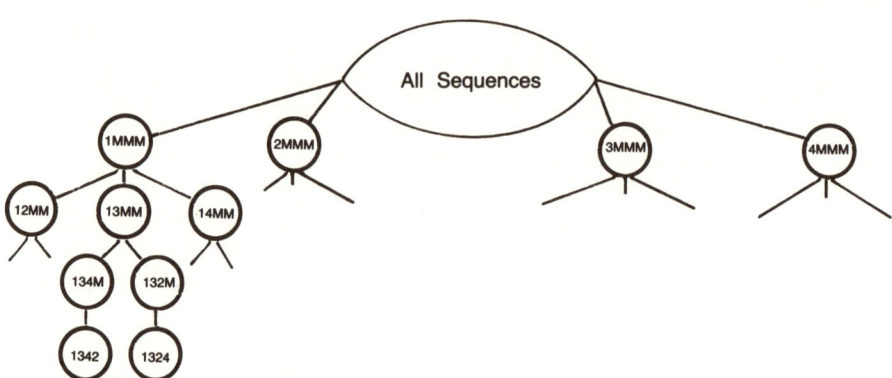

Figure 11.1
Flow sequencing by branch and bound

1.

	Job (Columns)			
Equipment	A	B	C	D
(Rows) 1	16	14	15	18
2	12	13	16	14
3	14	13	11	12
4	16	18	15	17

2. Reduce Rows

	Job			
	A	B	C	D
1	2	0	1	4
2	0	1	4	2
3	3	2	0	1
4	1	3	0	2

3. Reduce Columns

	Job			
	A	B	C	D
1	2	0	1	3
2	0	1	4	1
3	3	2	0	0
4	1	3	0	1

4.

	Job			
	A	B	C	D
1	0	+	0	0
2	+	0	0	0
3	0	0	0	+
4	0	0	+	0

5. Least Cost

```
  12
 +14
 +15
 +12
  ──
  53
```

Figure 11.2
One form of linear programming for assignment

Linear programming is very useful for assigning specific operations to machines so that the least-cost total system is obtained. As illustrated in Figure 11.2, the matrix must be established with equal numbers of rows and columns, each showing the cost, time, or other uniform parameter per each way of achieving it. The second step is to reduce every row so that at least one item is 0. This is done by subtracting the smallest number in each row from every number in that row. Then every column is reduced by the same method of subtracting the smallest integer. With the fourth step the 0 item is selected for each job and will provide the lowest cost or time combination for the total solution. If more than one selection is possible, as in column C where either row 3 or row 4 could have been selected, we will notice that row 4 is not available from any other column, but row 3 is. Therefore, row 4 should be selected as the choice for column C and row 3 goes with column D. The least-cost selections are then merely added to give the total. There will be no other solution giving less cost.

Matrices that are not square, that is, the rows do not equal the columns, can be solved through the construction of dummy rows or columns as necessary, and reduction through the use of minimum zero lines with the smallest number subtracted from the open rows or columns and added at the intersections. The dummy variables are not a possible selection, so any selection which refers to a dummy variable is not valid and some tool or location will not have its requirement fulfilled. You see this in the solution block 8a or 8b in which row 6 is invalid solutions.

Production planning and control determine the production lot quantities, batch sizes, economic inventory levels, and a work order processing system that is necessary to assure proper material flow to all operations.

PROGRESS/LEARNING CURVE

The manufacturing progress curve is often referred to as a learning curve. Actually improvements usually come from tool design, methods, materials, and procedures, as well as from employee learning. The concept of quantifying progress is also useful in training, maintenance, and many other logistics concerns.

Learning curves are based on the fact that the average cost to produce a unit drops by a fixed percentage as the total number of units produced doubles. All progress functions will have the same shape, even though they may differ in the percentage improvements between doubled quantities and the direct labor hours required to produce the first unit. The relationship between direct labor hours and units produced can be shown as a curve with only a few plotted points. The curve will directly illustrate the information needed for a specific number of units. Two variations of learning curve techniques are useful for support logistics. One allows the determination of the time required to do any task of the series. The other computes the average cost of each of a following group of units. An example will help explain. A field modification must be done on 500 computer installations. Past experience with similar modifications showed an 80 percent progress function. As a trial eight installations were done under simulated field conditions, with labor time required of 40, 32, 27, 24, 23.5, 22.3, 21.7, and 20 hours, showing very close to an 80 percent learning curve. Those results were extended past the planned 500 installation as shown in Table 11.1.

The hours for all units were summed to get the cumulative direct labor hours, and then divided by the number of units produced to give the cumulative average.

The information for the first 64 units is plotted on arithmetic graph paper in Figure 11.3.

Plotting on log-log paper helps because the curve becomes a straight line, as shown in Figure 11.4. This is so because equal ratios are equally spaced on the logarithmic scale. For example, the distance from 2 to 4 will be the same as from 4 to 8 and 8 to 16.

The formula for the progression function is:

$$Y_X = KX^{LS/2}$$

where Y_X = number of direct labor hours to install the Xth unit
K = number of direct labor hours to install the first unit
X = the unit sequence number
$LS/2 = \dfrac{\log \text{ learning curve factor}}{\log 2}$

Table 11.1
Modification Labor Hours for 80 Percent Progress, Function

Unit Number	Unit Direct Labor Hours	Cumulative Direct Labor Hours	Cum Average Direct Labor Hours
1	40	40	40
2	32	72	36
3	27	99	33
4	24	123	30.75
5	23.5	146	29.2
6	22.3	169	28.2
7	21.7	190	27.1
8	20	210	26.2
16	16	352	22
32	12.8	581	18.2
64	10.2	946	14.8
128	8.2	1528	12.0
256	6.6	2463	9.6
512	5.2	3948	7.7

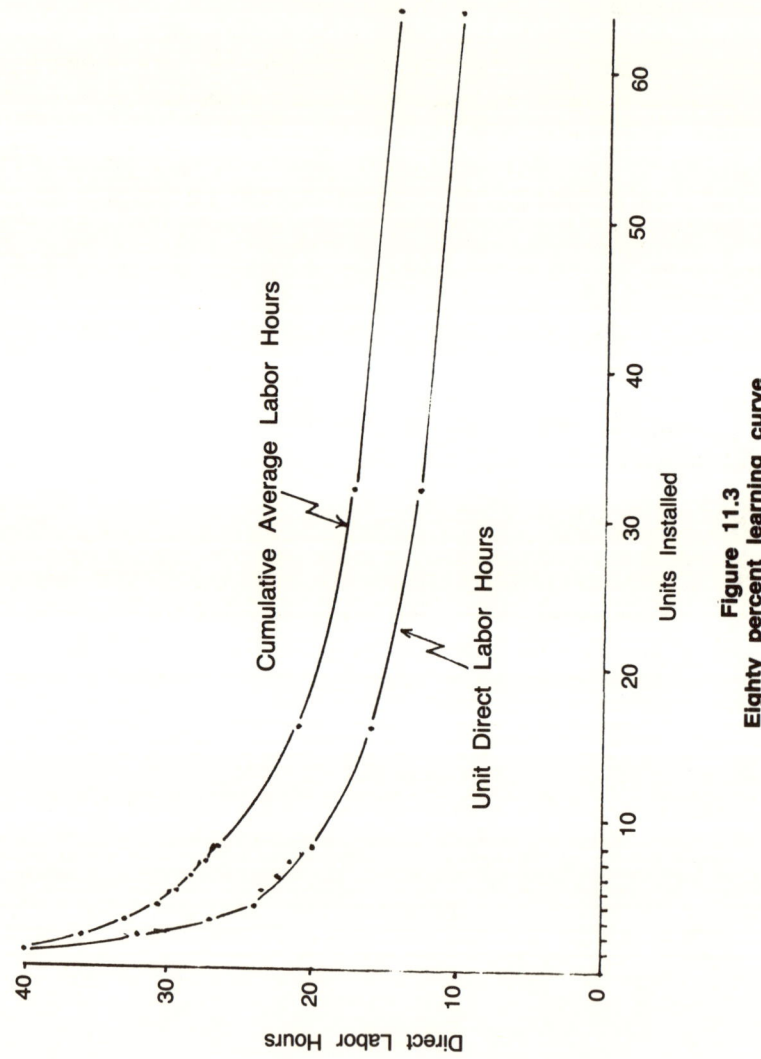

Figure 11.3
Eighty percent learning curve

Acquisition and Production/Construction Support 131

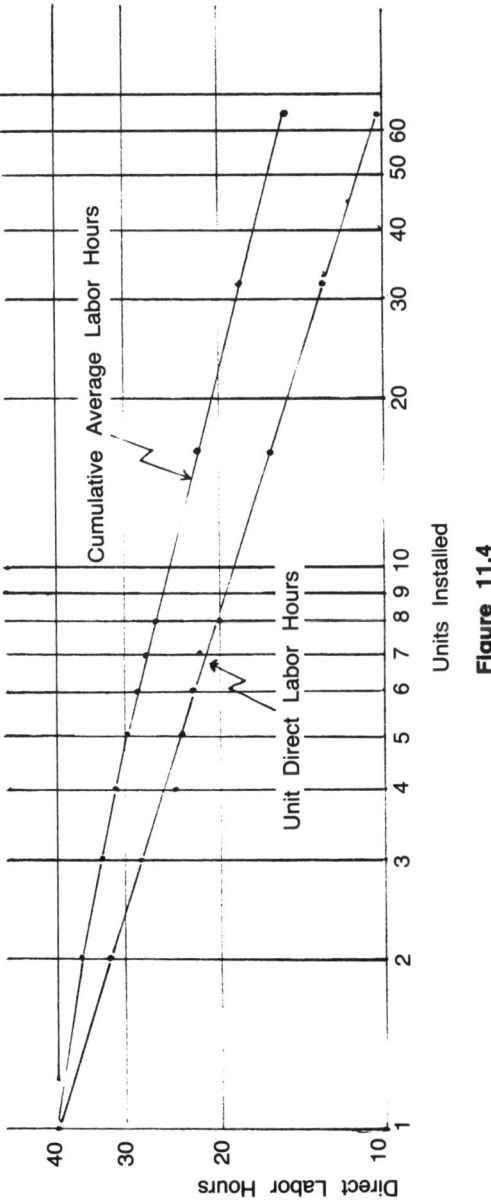

Figure 11.4
Eighty percent learning curve on log-log paper

To calculate the time predicted for the tenth installation in our example:

$$Y_{10} = 40(10)^{\frac{\log 0.80}{\log 2}}$$

$$= 40(10)^{-0.322}$$

$$= \frac{40}{10^{0.322}}$$

$$= \frac{40}{2.099}$$

$$= 19.06$$

Thus the time required to do any task of the series may be either read from the chart or calculated using the formula $Y_X = KX^n$.

The second learning-curve variation is used for determining average times or costs of groups and for evaluating economies of scale. For an 80 percent learning curve, the average per-unit cost of the first 100 units will be 80 percent of the average per-unit cost of the first 50. Similarly, if a production quantity of spare parts again doubles (to 200 units), the average per unit cost of all 200 will equal 80 percent of the value computed for the first 100 units.

The equation used is:

$$\bar{C}_T = C_I \left(\frac{N_B}{N_A}\right)^{LS/2}$$

where

$\bar{C}_T$ = mean total costs
C_I = initial unit cost
N_B = present total number of units
N_A = previous total number of units
$LS/2 = \dfrac{\log \text{learning curve factor}}{\log 2}$

Using our example again, to determine the average time required to install 20 units if the first 10 averaged 25 hours:

$$C_p = 25\,(20)^{\frac{\log 0.8}{\log 2}}$$

$$= 25\,(2)^{-0.322}$$

$$= 20 \text{ hours average for first 20 units}$$

CHAPTER 12

Forecasting

*F*orecasting can be defined in a general way as the estimation, calculation, and prediction of future events. To those concerned with industrial processes, however, the term takes on a more precise definition: Forecasting is the estimation, calculation, and prediction of the values, changes, and even the existence of variables that affect the process.

TIME HORIZONS

Forecasting requirements can be generally classified into three time horizons, each necessitating different assumptions and methodology, and each with different objectives.

2. Long-term forecasts are required for decisions on facility locations, capacities, and changes in the future process. They involve studies of social, economic, and technological trends.

2. Two- to five-year forecasts are required for decisions on capacity adjustments, funding, and changes in user preferences in the economy and in technology, and demanding more precision than longer term forecasts.

3. Forecasts for the immediate future are short-range operating decisions based on forecasts of various factors that affect the current operation process.

a. Demand.
b. Operation costs (based on demand).
c. Workforce requirements.
d. Equipment requirements and the availability of equipment (through models).
e. Probable states of nature.
f. Probability distributions on the states of nature.

The sequential relationship between forecasting and planning is often confusing and should be analyzed in the light of the type of forecast required and the organization's present situation and future alternatives. Figure 12.1 shows a systems view of forecasting.

If forecasting an estimate of national economic activity, for example, the sequence

$$FORECAST \rightarrow PLAN$$

is valid, as the plans of a single organization have a negligible effect on the economy, or if the organization has limited alternatives available. The sequence is not valid, however, if the forecast is of a factor that is influenced by the action of the organization, such as the impact of a marketing program on a company's sales. In this case the correct sequence would be:

$$PLAN \rightarrow FORECAST$$

FORECASTING METHODS

Successful forecasting attempts to reduce the areas of uncertainty that surround management decision making with respect to such items as costs, profits, sales, production, pricing, capital investment, and so forth. The method selected depends on how much accuracy is desired, what variables are to be forecast, the time period involved, what data are available, cost/value of forecast, and what amount of sophistication is available to the decision maker. This is shown in Figure 12.2.

Principles of forecasting include:

1. Forecasts are more accurate for larger groups of items.
2. Forecasts are more accurate for short periods of time.
3. Every forecast should include an estimate of error.
4. A forecasting method should be tested before it is applied to a system.

Forecasting

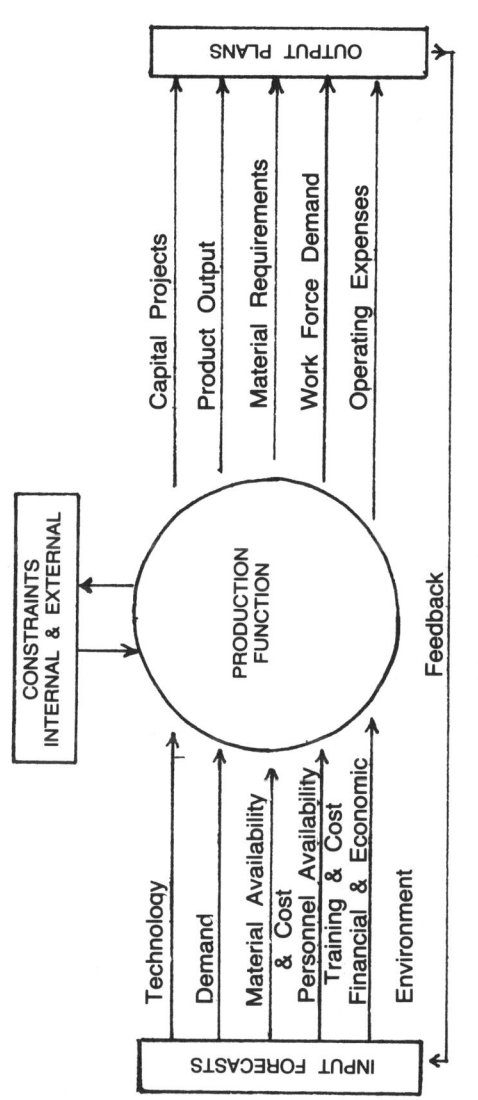

**Figure 12.1
A systems view of forecasting**

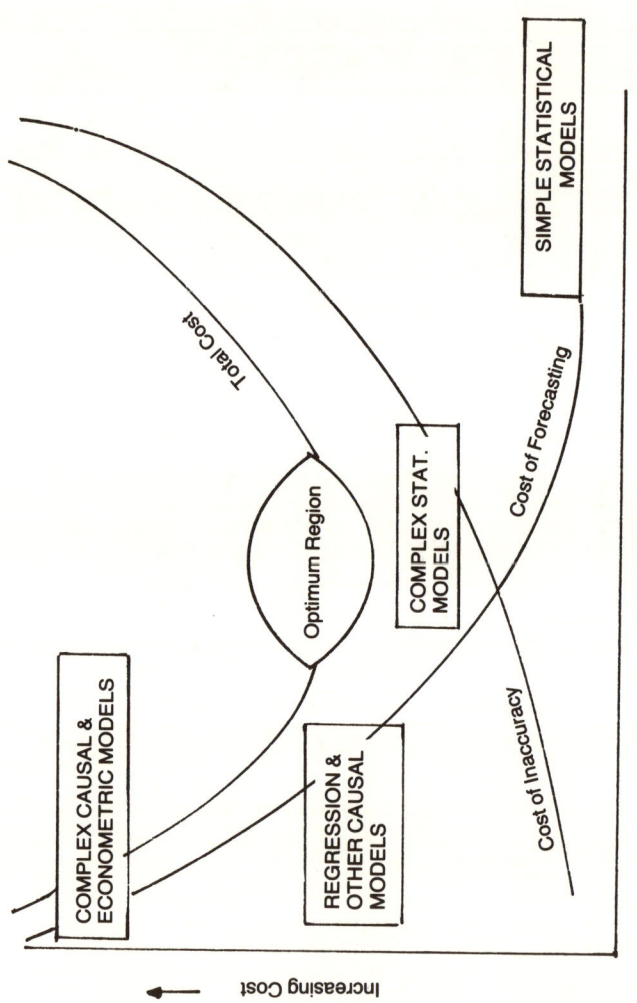

**Figure 12.2
Cost of forecasting versus cost of inaccuracy**

In general the following methods are available to forecasters.

1. Mechanical.
2. Barometric.
3. Survey.
4. Linear regression.
5. Input/output analysis.
6. Econometrics.

Mechanical Methods

Mechanical methods of forecasting may be defined as unsophisticated and unscientific projections based on guesses or mechanical extrapolations of historical data. As a method of prediction, they may include procedures ranging from coin tossing to determine an upward or downward movement to the projection of trends, autocorrelations, and other, more complex mathematical techniques. Typically they are distinguished from other forecasting methods in that they are essentially mechanical and are not closely integrated with relevant economic theory and statistical data. Nevertheless they are widely used by professional forecasters, probably because they lend an air of sophistication and precision for the mathematically naive. Some of the more widely used methods are discussed in the following.

Factor-Listing Method

One of the earliest forms of forecasting common in the 1920s and '30s and still used by many business firms today, this approach presents an interesting point of departure for the discussion of other techniques because it illustrates how naive some methods can be. The factor-listing method is a procedure whereby the analyst simply enumerates the favorable and unfavorable conditions that will affect business activity with no provisions for the quantitative evaluation of each of the factors. It completely ignores the weighting of the true forces that have a bearing on business change.

Time-series analysis

A time series is a sequence of values corresponding to particular points, or periods, or time. Data such as sales, production, and prices, when arranged chronologically, are ordered in time and referred to as time series. The simple line chart is the most common graphic device for depicting a time series, with the dependent variable such as sales, production, or price scaled on the vertical axis, and the independent variable "time" expressed in years or months or any other temporal measure, scaled on the horizontal axis. In analyzing time series, the problem is to discover and measure the forces that have caused a series to exhibit its particular fluctuations, in the hope that the causal factors may be projected into the future and forecast. Time-series procedures have certain specific uses when employed as part of the forecaster's total kit of analytical tools.

Barometric techniques

Whereas mechanical methods of forecasting, particularly time-series analyses, imply that the future is some sort of extension of the past, the use of barometric techniques is based on the idea that the future can be predicted from certain happenings in the present. Specifically barometric methods usually involve the use of statistical indicators—selected time series which, when used in conjunction with one another or combined in certain ways, provide an indication of the direction in which the economy or particular industries are heading. The series chosen thus serve as barometers of economic change. Two particular applications of the barometric approach are commonly employed: leading series and pressure indexes.

Leading indicators

Leading indicators tend to reflect future changes in economic activity with some consistency. The movements of the series indicate that various economic factors exist that tend to move through the course of the business cycle in consistent but different time sequences. A number of leading series are available in different publications, such as *The Business Conditions Digest* published by the U.S. Department of Commerce. Leading series may provide a useful guide for predicting the future course of the economy, but they have some limitations.

1. They are not always consistent in their tendency to lead.
2. It is not always possible to tell whether a series is signaling an actual turning point or merely exhibiting an unimportant variation.
3. They indicate only the direction of future change, while disclosing little or nothing about the magnitude of the change.

Leading indicators are at best a supplement to other forecasting devices.

Pressure Indexes

Pressure indexes represent the various ratio and difference measures that have been developed by economists as guides to forecasting in the belief that amplitude differences play a significant role in the analysis of business cycles.

1. Ratio of raw materials inventories to new orders for finished goods, as a forecaster of raw material prices.
2. The spread between common stock yields and corporate bond yields as a predictor of stock prices.
3. The difference between the rate of family formation and the rate of housing inventory growth as an indicator of the long-term demand for new housing.

Pressure indexes are valuable as warning signals of impending developments, but are not helpful in forecasting the magnitude of the change. When used in conjunction with other forecasting methods, pressure indexes can accomplish much in establishing guideposts for better prediction.

Survey Methods

The survey technique of forecasting is a subjective method of prediction, amounting largely to a weighted or unweighted averaging of attitudes or expectations. The underlying assumption is that certain attitudes affecting economic decisions can be defined and measured well enough in advance so that predictions of changing trends can be made. The results are arrived at by asking people who are directly involved about their expectations as to future events. Some of the best known surveys are discussed here.

Economic Forecasting

1. Surveys of business people's intentions with respect to what to spend on plant and equipment.
2. Surveys of customers' finances and buying plans.
3. Surveys of business people's plans regarding inventory changes.

Sales Forecasting

1. Executive polling, whereby the opinions of top management are combined and averaged.
2. Sales force polling. These surveys are based on the assumption that salespeople are more knowledgeable of the market, and thereby give reliable forecasts.
3. Consumer intentions surveys.

In addition to being a highly subjective technique, surveys are expensive and time consuming.

Linear Regression

Regression analysis determines the equation of past data and assumes a similar relationship for the future.

Input/Output Analysis

Input/output analysis is a technique developed in economics to study the levels of interdependence of the input and output of the various industries in the economy, and to predict the changes that would occur in the output requirements of one industry given a known change in another.

Econometrics

Econometrics explains past economic activity and predicts future economic activity by deriving mathematical equations that express the most probable interrelationship between a set of economic variables. The equations are a simplified abstraction of a real situation, and are employed as a predictive system that yields numerical results. When our theoretical understanding and statistical data are good, econometrics can illuminate the darker areas and enhance our ability to predict. It is more analytical in nature and process oriented in approach than any other method, because its chief concern is to identify and measure changing cause-and-effect relationships over time. It is the only approach that is logically suitable for incorporating or utilizing the best features of the other techniques or variables in the model.

Technological Forecasting

Technological forecasting is taking its place alongside other methods of forecasting that aid modern management. To be useful, forecasts do not necessarily need to predict the precise form technology will take in a given application at some specific future date. Like any other forecasts, their purpose is simply to help evaluate the probability and significance of possible future developments so that managers can make better decisions.

"Technology" is not a piece of hardware or a chemical formula. It is the knowledge of physical relationships systematically applied. This knowledge can range from the initial glimmerings of how a basic phenomenon can be applied to the solution of a practical problem to an end product in a mature operating system. Even in the latter case, the performance characteristics of any operating system are normally improved in small, continuous increments. What may appear to be a "step function" advance in a technology is usually nothing more than an accumulation of small changes not worth individual attention until the total can make a significant contribution.

It is usually futile for a forecaster to try to predict exact technological developments, but ranges of likely characteristics can be predicted, and the factors on which they depend presented. Forecasts made in this manner help to identify potential problems and opportunities so that advance action may be undertaken to improve the organization's position when the projected events occur. Forecasts—no matter how accurate—are useless unless they influence action.

TECHNIQUES OF TECHNOLOGICAL FORECASTING

Demand Assessment

Studies suggest that demand, not excess technological capacity, is the driving force behind technological change. In fact, a technology is only utilized if it responds to a need.

Demographic and sociological analysis outlines future needs such as traffic control, pollution, energy, communications, and food.

Conditional demand analysis predict the conditions under which new technology will be needed and the probability of this event occurring. The conditions surrounding oil recovery from shale illustrate this as a function of foreign crude oil supplies, economic trade-offs versus other forms of energy, exploration and refining costs, and international oil prices.

Opportunity identification techniques look at common situations and investigate ways in which technology and ideas might do the job as well or better. What needs are presently unfilled? What costs/values are out of line?

Theoretical Limits Test

Pushing known apparatus or phenomena to theoretical limits can reveal potential implications. For example, laser transmission of energy from the sun can be envisioned, and the necessary advances determined. One must be cautious about "science fiction" forecasting that has little real value. A good way to check the logic of forecasts is to have a group of experts refine their estimates through successive approximations, both individually and collectively. This is called the Delphi approach.

Parameter Analysis

Technological forecasts should predict whether technical systems can reach or exceed key levels or parameters of performance by some future date. To develop effective parameter forecasts, there are guidelines that should be followed.

1. Select a limited number of significant performance characteristics that can be quantified.
2. Include ranges as well as most likely values.
3. Decide on a consistent point in development such as full-scale demonstration.
4. Document the major assumptions.
5. Include an estimate of the probability of meeting the projection.

Techniques for parameter analysis include the following.

Predicting technological changeover points.

Selection of critical performance factors and limits where change is desirable will identify an area in which advances normally occur. One must be cautious about relying too heavily upon overt characteristics. The initial, most obvious components may be deceptive as in the case of the piston aircraft engine manufacturer who ignored turbojets because their efficiency and fuel economy was low. This was true, but the "cost per ton/mile" and "cost per seat/mile" were very attractive, and jets rapidly replaced piston aircraft.

Analysing unique properties of a product.

This identifies situations where substitution should occur. For example, Kevlar (™ DuPont) synthetic thread is much stronger and lighter than steel and with these unique properties can be used in many useful products, ranging from boat sails to bulletproof vests.

Trends in plotting technical-economic performance.

This technique should indicate to management when a new technology will cross critical thresholds. For example, greater demands for electric energy create needs for more transmission. Ecologists are pushing for buried wires and power companies want to comply where feasible. New tunneling technologies will make buried power lines attractive at some time in the future that can be forecasted.

Analyzing substitution growth curves.

This can show how rapidly one technology will take over from another. The familiar "S" curve is the usual pattern. Substitution occurs slowly at first, then faster as acceptance grows, and then slows down again as saturation is reached. It is interesting to note that major substitutions of one technology for another normally take decades, rather than years, as is generally supposed. Television, jet aircraft, and computers show this long substitution cycle.

Systems Analysis

Weaknesses in present operating systems can be identified and calculations made for other ways to meet the needs better. Impact studies and hypothetical or probable future problems can be defined to see "what if?" and "if we do this, what will result?"

Surveys of Scientific Effort

The National Science Foundation and other information sources provide information on what areas of science are receiving most attention. Published papers and technical symposia provide guidance in state-of-the-art developments and "how we do it."

Competitive Evaluations

The monitoring of patents, advertisements, and press releases is common but the information is rarely coordinated into useful form. Three approaches can be used to improve efforts.

Technological mapping.

All possible means of accomplishing an end are diagrammed and known status determined for each possibility. Colors indicating relative activities and strengths can give visual emphasis to attractive approaches.

Strategic Evaluation of facility and equipment investments, mergers, and acquisitions indicates the direction in which a company is heading. Several major companies have had big failures when investments were made on a purely financial basis without recognizing that the facility would soon be technologically obsolete.

Life-cycle models can show the speed and degree of influence on the marketplace. Thorough analysis of all possible approaches can lead to identification of weakness and sources of strength.

Technological forecasting can improve decision making through better understanding of probable future events, driving forces, and critical parameters. Payback usually exceeds costs many times and the information can be used to make better, more profitable actions.

STATISTICAL TECHNIQUES

Moving Averages

Method

A moving average forecast is obtained by summing the data points over a desired number of periods. As the forecast moves in time, the oldest value is dropped and the most recent added.

Extending the moving average to include more periods increases the smoothing effect but decreases its sensitivity to recent data.

A forecast can be obtained with moving averages by using the last calculated value as the forecast or by projecting a moving average trend line to the current period. See Figure 12.3.

Assumptions

It is assumed that outside forces and trends will continue during the forecast span as they did in the past.

Advantages

1. Data required are minimal.
2. Calculations are readily computerized.
3. Little analytical skill is required.
4. Preparation is inexpensive and rapid.
5. Method is objective.
6. An estimate of probable error in the forecast is possible.

Disadvantages

1. Cannot predict turning points.
2. Assumes a strong continuity of the future with the past.
3. Does not make use of the forecaster's knowledge of outside developments.

Data	3 Period Moving Average	Centered Moving Average
190		
210	214	
242	248	264
291	281	
310		

Figure 12.3
Moving average

4. Does not contribute to managerial efforts to understand causal factors.
5. Decreases sensitivity to newest data.

Weighting may be applied if recent data is considered more valuable than older data. For example 60%, 30%, 10% applied to the above data would be [(242 × .6) + (210 × .3) + (190 × .1) = 227.

Exponential Smoothing

Method

Exponential smoothing uses a constant (α) that puts emphasis on recent demand.

$$F_n = \alpha(Y_{n-1}) + (1 - \alpha)(F_{n-1})$$

Since F_{n-1} was dependent on past data, this can be expanded to:

$$F_n = \alpha y_{n-1} + \alpha(1 - \alpha)Y_{n-2} + \alpha(1 - \alpha)^2 Y_{n-3} + \ldots \alpha(1 - \alpha)^p Y_{n-n}$$

where F_n = forecast for next period
F_{n-1} = forecast for previous period
α = smoothing constant
Y_{n-1} = actual value for previous period

It can be seen that this function is a linear combination of all past data weighted according to the smoothing constant. Values for α must be between 0 and 1. If $\alpha = 0$, there is no change since the previous period's forecast is used. If $\alpha = 1$, the next forecast is the same as the most recent data. A response similar to a moving average of period N is obtained if $\alpha = .5$.

Assumptions

It is assumed that outside forces and trends will continue during the forecast span as they did in the past.

Advantages

1. Data required are minimal.
2. Only current data and the previous forecast are necessary for a forecast for the next period.
3. Little analytical skill is required.
4. Preparation is inexpensive and rapid.

5. Method is objective.
6. Estimate of probable error in the forecast is possible.

Disadvantages

1. Cannot predict turning points.
2. Assumes a strong continuity with the past.
3. Does not make use of the forecasters knowledge of outside development.
4. Does not contribute to managerial efforts to understand causal factors.

Time-Series Decomposition

Method

Time-series decomposition attempts to break down time-series data into trend, cycle, seasonal, and residual components. These, in turn, are multiplied together to obtain a forecast.

The trend is often obtained by using the method of least squares to determine the best curve through all relevant historical data points in the time series. Cyclic and seasonal components are then determined to explain some of the variation from the trend line.

The decomposition of the data into cycles of fixed period and waveshape have not proved successful in forecasting. This is caused partly by the government's discretionary influence in breaking business cycles.

Seasonal influences may be attained by averaging data of the desired period and determining the fraction of the yearly total that is obtained in each period. This can be difficult if such factors as average workdays per month, the dates of holidays, and other significant events are to be taken into account. Trends may also develop in the seasonal component. Tests are available to determine if this is the case.

The variation that remains is the error of the forecast. This can be quantified and a probable range of the forecast determined.

Assumptions

It is assumed that the constants determined in the forecasting equation do not change significantly with time.

Advantages

1. Required data are minimal.
2. Calculations can be computerized.
3. The method is objective.

4. Extrapolations are reasonably accurate if conditions are stable.
5. Identification of a trend and seasonal pattern reduces forecasting errors.
6. The decomposition allows for causal analysis of the various components.
7. Decomposition allows for the prediction of seasonal turning points.

Disadvantages

1. The trend, cycle, and seasonal components must not change over time.
2. Computers are practically a necessity.
3. The analysis gives no information on the effect of external forces on the forecast.

Control of Time-Series Forecasting

Once a method of forecasting has been decided upon, the forecasts must be continually checked against actual data to be certain that conditions have not changed. If it is assured that the forecast is the mean of all observations at a certain point in time, and that the variance does not change in time, it is possible to determine an estimate of that variance.

$$S_y = \sqrt{\frac{\Sigma(Y - Y_F)^2}{r}}$$

where
 Y = historical data points
 Y_F = forecasted points
 r = degrees of freedom

With this information it is possible to set up control charts to check for unexpected variations of the actual data from the forecast.

Leontief Input/Output Analysis

The output of any industry is needed as an input in many other industries, and even for that industry itself. Therefore, there is an interindustry dependence for "correct" output levels. This interdependence may be handled by an input/output analysis. The input coefficient, a_{ij}, indicates how much of the ith commodity is used for the production of each unit of the jth commodity. Input/output analysis modeling as shown in Figure 12.4 can forecast change effects among industries.

Assumptions

1. Each industry produces only one homogeneous commodity unless interpreted as two or more commodities in fixed proportions.
2. Each industry uses a fixed input ratio.
3. Production in every industry is subject to constant returns to scale.
4. Where these assumptions would produce obvious discrepancies for a particular industry, that industry may be conceptually at least broken down into separate industries.

Advantages

1. The model readily provides a solution to the interdependence of industries and consequently can forecast the change (magnitude and direction) of output requirements for one industry given a *known* change in another industry.
2. The table of input coefficients may remain reasonably stable over time, thus minimizing research effort.
3. Computers can handle the inversion of large-scale matrices.

Disadvantages

1. A fundamental point that was ignored in such an analysis is the actual process of adjustments and readjustments of the industries involved (such as bottlenecks or inventory levels).
2. The model's performance in forecasting is limited by the degree to which the assumptions are unrealistic and become a factor.
3. Difficulties in establishing accurate relationships or finding good estimates may exist for many industries.

	\multicolumn{4}{c}{Output}
Input	I	II	III	N
I	a_{11}	a_{12}	a_{13} ...	a_{1n}
II	a_{21}	a_{22}	a_{23} ...	a_{2n}
.	.	.	.	.
N	a_{n1}	a_{n2}	a_{n3}	a_{nn}

**Figure 12.4
Input/output analysis modeling**

Least-Squares Linear Regression (LSLR)

In cases where a linear relationship is known to exist or may be reasonably assumed, LSLR may be used for forecasting. If we specify:

$$Y_i = B_1 + B_2 X_{2i} + \cdots + B_k X_{ki} + u_i \quad \text{for } i = 1, 2, \ldots, n$$

for n observations on the variable $Y = f(X_2, X_3, \ldots, X_k)$. Putting this in matrix notation,

$$Y = \begin{matrix} Y_1 \\ Y_2 \\ \cdot \\ \cdot \\ Y_n \end{matrix}, \quad X = \begin{matrix} 1 & X_{21} \cdots X_{k1} \\ 1 & X_{22} \cdots X_{k2} \\ \cdot & \cdot \\ \cdot & \cdot \\ 1 & X_{2n} \cdots X_{kn} \end{matrix}, \quad B = \begin{matrix} B_1 \\ B_2 \\ \cdot \\ \cdot \\ B_k \end{matrix}, \quad u = \begin{matrix} u_1 \\ u_2 \\ \cdot \\ \cdot \\ u_n \end{matrix}$$

Thus $Y = XB + u = X\hat{B} + e$,

where
$$\hat{B} = \begin{matrix} \hat{B}_1 \\ \hat{B}_2 \\ \cdot \\ \cdot \\ \hat{B}_k \end{matrix}, \quad e = \begin{matrix} e_1 \\ e_2 \\ \cdot \\ \cdot \\ e_n \end{matrix}$$

and an estimate for all of the coefficients, $\hat{B}_i$, is $\hat{B} = (X'X)^{-1}X'Y$. Using these estimates of the coefficients (calculated from past data), we may use forecasts of the independent variables to obtain Y, the dependent variable.

Assumptions

1. A stochastic term is justified by at least one of the following:
    a. That we choose to represent Y as an explicit function of just a small number of what are thought to be the more important X's and let the net effect of the excluded variables be represented by u.
    b. That over and above the total effect of all relevant factors, there is a basic and unpredictable element of randomness.
    c. That a source of error exists in the observation or measurement.
2. For the K coefficients, the $K - 1$ explanatory variables, and a sample size of n: X has rank $K < n$
$$E(u) = 0$$
$$E(uu') = \sigma^2 I_n$$
X is a set of fixed numbers

3. The principle of minimizing the value of the residuals, e, squared is the best criterion for fitting the line. (See Figure 12.5.)

Advantages

1. A nonlinear expression may be linear if the variables are transmuted; that is, take the logs of both side for an equation such as $Y = e^{BX}$.

2. A great deal can be done with the data available. Significance tests and confidence intervals can be constructed and calculations of the coefficient of determination and the partial correlation coefficients may be found.

3. Computer routines are available.

4. Econometric theory provides methods to handle measurement errors and special relationships among the explanatory variables.

Disadvantages

1. This method may well lead to biases or inefficiencies since the values of many of the variables involved may be the simultaneous interaction of relationships and be best handled by systems of equations.

2. It may be as difficult to obtain forecasts of the explanatory variables as it is for the dependent variable.

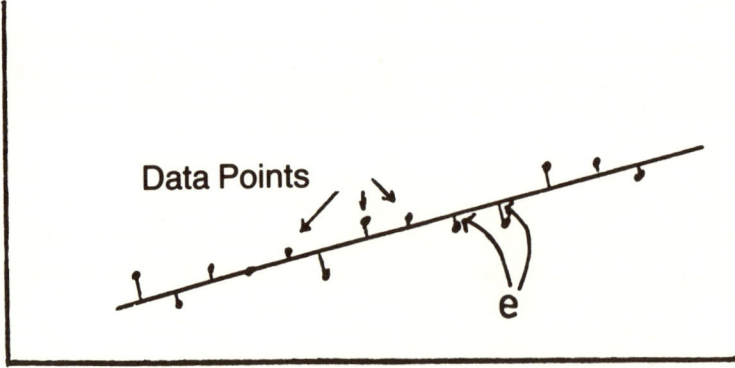

**Figure 12.5
Least-square regression line**

CHAPTER 13

Quality

WHAT IS "QUALITY"?

Quality is herein defined as the entire collection of activities through which we achieve fitness for use. It also has several other meanings, which causes confusion. Among them are that Quality control (QC) and Qaulity assurance (QA) mean the collection of quality activities assigned to the company organization that concerns itself primarily with the quality function. Since organization forms differ, the terms QA and QC have many different meanings. QC can also mean the methods, tools, knowledge, and skills through which quality activities are carried out and the name of the organization that devotes itself to the quality function. While the words differ considerably between military, industrial, and commercial organizations, quality concepts are remarkably alike and universally accepted.

Any dimension, property, physical parameter, or attribute that can be seen, felt, tasted, smelled, heard, or sensed in any other way, and that contributes to fitness for use, is a quality characteristic.

As any hardware or software progresses from concept through development stages toward the marketplace, there are common elements of:

Research
Development

Production
Process control

Design   Vendors
Configuration management   Inspection
Production planning   Test
Acquisition   Sales
Instrumentation   Service
                                 External feedback

COST, QUALITY, AND SCHEDULE

Most management and business decisions involve trade-offs between cost, quality, and schedule. A poor quality program can have adverse effect on both costs and program timing. A good quality program may cost more initially, but will reduce life-cycle cost by controlling quality losses and deliveries that could be adversely affected by poor quality. A good quality program will detect problems early enough to prevent action that will preclude a compromise in cost, quality, or schedule. Therein lies an emphasis on the prevention of quality problems rather than reactive correction.

IMPROVEMENT THROUGH EMPHASIS

Quality, like many other concerns, benefits from attention. And, as with most logistics elements, there are always a "vital few" characteristics that contribute most to success or failure. The principle of the critical few is sometimes called the Pareto principle, although it could more correctly be attributed to Lorenz or Juran.

Several movements in recent years have emphasized some aspects of quality that were not previously stressed. These include:

1. *Statistical quality control.* This movement is generally thought to have started with the creation of the statistical control chart by Dr. W. A. Shewhart in 1924. Statistical sampling plans are a further development of the movement.

2. *Total quality control.* This movement emerged in the early 1950s and recognized that a quality program must be comprehensive in scope and include "new design control, incoming material control, product control, and special process studies."

3. *Reliability.* The product design phase of the quality problem received emphasis through the reliability movement, which began in the mid-1950s. Techniques for quantifying reliability have been emphasized.

Quality

4. *Maintainability.* Maintainability is a rather new discipline with its origins in about 1954 and the first standards issued in the mid-1960s. It is now considered one of the essential ingredients of a logistics system and a factor in both systems effectiveness and cost effectiveness.

5. *Zero defects.* This was a motivational movement directed toward eliminating defects through quality manufacturing.

6. *Product assurance (product effectiveness).* This movement of the early 1960s emphasized the relationship and interactions of complex products and particularly the relationship of reliability, availability, maintainability, and cost.

Each of these movements emphasized some aspect of quality that was not previously stressed, and each has made a contribution to the quality field. The underlying functions and basic principles of these quality movements are very similar to those in logistics.

QUALITY COSTS

The basic concept of quality costs is recognition and organization of certain quality-related costs to gain knowledge of their major contributing segments and the direction of their trends. This is similar to the concept of life-cycle costs. Costs are broken down into four primary areas in order to weigh input and outputs: (1) prevention—costs associated with personnel engaged in designing, implementing, auditing, and maintaining the quality system; (2) appraisal—costs associated with measuring, evaluating, or auditing products, components, and purchased materials to assure conformance with quality standards and performance requirements; (3) internal failures—costs associated with defective products, components, and materials that fail to meet quality requirements and cause manufacturing losses; and (4) external failures—costs generated by defective products being shipped to customers.

The basis of quality cost budgeting is to consider the four cost segments and their general trend, rather than to budget each element. The basic relationship among the four cost segments is that dollar investments in prevention and appraisal can substantially reduce both internal and external failures. Minimizing external failures is most important to a business, since they determine customer acceptance and goodwill. The preferred approach to target setting is to establish a broad target for reducing quality costs that permits some latitude in handling expenditures. This encourages investments in prevention and appraisal that will accomplish an overall reduction. A desirable relationship of quality cost changes is shown in Figure 13.1.

QC ELEMENTS

The framework of quality costs gives a good basis for outlining the major elements involved in Quality Control.

Category A: Prevention
    1. Quality engineering
        a. Quality control engineering
        b. Process control engineering
    2. Design and development of quality measurement and control equipment
    3. Quality planning by function other than quality control
    4. Quality training
    5. Data processing, reporting, and support services

Category B: Appraisal
    1. Receiving or incoming tests and inspection
    2. Laboratory acceptance testing
    3. Inspection and test
    4. Checking labor
    5. Setup for inspection and test
    6. Inspection and test materials
    7. Product quality audits
    8. Outside endorsements or approvals
    9. Maintenance and calibration of test and inspection equipment used in control of quality

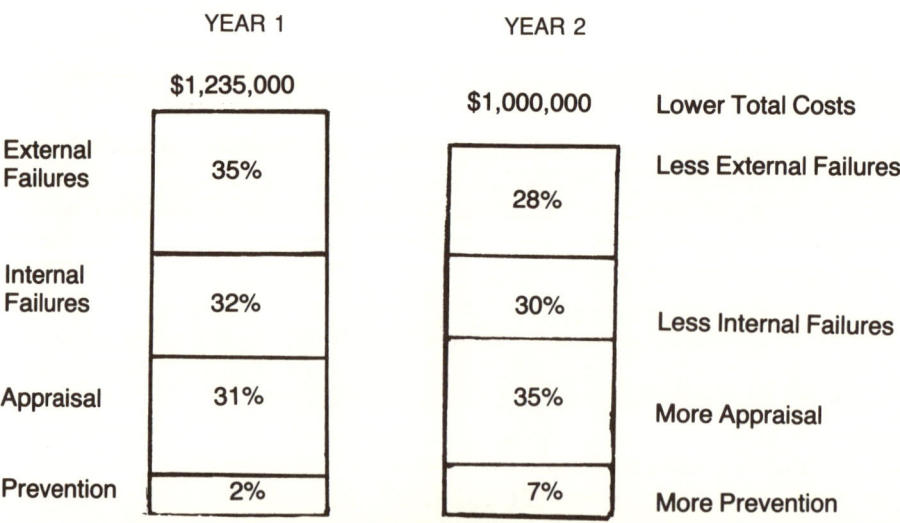

Figure 13.1
Desirable trends in quality costs

10. Review of test and inspection data
11. Field performance testing
12. Internal testing and release
13. Evaluation of field stock and spare parts
14. Calibration and maintenance of production equipment used to evaluate quality
15. Data processing inspection and test reports
16. Special product evaluation
17. Test and inspection materials

Category C: Internal failure
1. Scrap
2. Rework and repair
3. Troubleshootimg or failure analysis
4. Reinspect and retest
5. Scrap and rework due to fault of vendor
6. Discrepant material activity
7. Downgrading

Category D: External failure
1. Complaints
2. Product or customer service
3. Products rejected and returned
4. Returned material repair
5. Warranty replacement
6. Marketing error
7. Engineering Error
8. Factory or installation error

DETERMINING THE QUALITY STANDARDS

When an engineering drawing specifies a tolerance, it defines the desired precision for a product, and all related machining and labor will be greatly influenced. Standards for precision are often specified by competitive practice of the customer. The problem of economics in tolerancing is then one of finding the best way to attain the specified precision. If there is no quantified standard, then market requirements should be established and the lowest cost practical standard should be used for materials, such as chemical purity and electrical component grades. If there are no standards established, the lowest cost option should be used if it can meet market requirements. The tolerance will often determine the manufacturing process. For example, a hole can be punched and give tolerances of $+0.004$ and -0.002; but if a tolerance of $+0.0002$ and -0.000 is required, additional steps using a punch and bore with honing or lapping will be required and increase costs about ninefold. The tolerance is the deviation allowed on either side of the midpoint value.

Tolerances and precision greatly affect interchangeability. Interchangeability increases costs because of added engineering design effort, manufacturing engineering greater precision requirements, and more extensive fabrication controls. It has trade-off benefits of reducing the human skills necessary to fit components, the time required to fit during assembly, and the cost of field maintenance when replacing parts. The economics of interchangeability in a production facility differ from those in the field. In a production plant, the facilities are readily available for taking care of components that do not fit. They may be thrown away or easily adjusted. If a production facility desires to use greater tolerances in order to reduce costs, it may do so, but a special effort must then be made to prepare special parts with reduced tolerances for shipment as field spares. The level of quality required should be based on costs and practicality.

VARIABILITY

Variation is inherent in every known process. Some items, such as atomic clocks and primary standards, have little variation, but most of the economically practical world must accept a varying lack of precision. It is rarely possible to measure all elements of a universe or population. Usually a group of units or portion of material from the population serves to provide information that can be used as a basis for making a decision concerning larger quantities. It is usually assumed that the sample is a random one, with each possible sample of n measurements having an equal chance of being selected. Each item will be evaluated on either attributes or variable data. Attributes is a term used to designate a method of measurements whereby units are examined by noting the presence (or absence) of some characteristic in each of the units in the sample under consideration, and by counting how many units do (or do not) possess it. Inspection by attributes may take one of two forms: the unit of product is classified simply as defective or nondefective, or the number of defects in the unit of product is counted with respect to a given requirement or set of requirements. "Variables" is a term used to designate a method whereby each unit is measured to determine the numerical magnitude of the characteristic being looked at. This involves reading a scale of some kind; for example, grams, centimeters, or degrees. Countinuous probability distributions are employed to make predictions using variable data.

A probability distribution function is a mathematical formula that relates the value of a characteristic to its probability of occurring within the population. Most continuous characteristics follow one of four common probability distributions illustrated in Figure 13.2: normal, exponential, Poisson, or Weibull. There are other continuous distributions, such as F, t, and chi-square, which are also used to analyze data but are not really helpful in predicting the probability of occurrence of the *actual values* of the characteristic.

When the sample data are laid out in ascending or descending order, or a histogram plotted, the shape of the sample data will provide some indication of the probability distribution that the population follows. "Goodness-of-fit" tests provide a quantitative means of evaluating any distribution assumption, but a more practical way is simply to plot the information on graph paper.

DISTRIBUTION	FORM	PROBABILITY FUNCTION
a. Normal	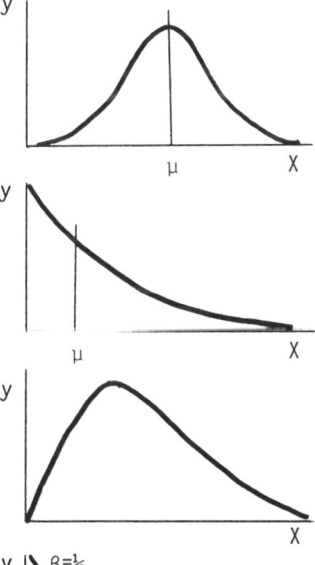	$y = \dfrac{1}{\sigma\sqrt{2\pi}} e^{-\dfrac{(x-\mu)^2}{2\sigma^2}}$ μ = population average σ = population standard deviation e = 2.718 π = 3.141
b. Exponential		$y = \dfrac{1}{\mu} e^{-\dfrac{x}{\mu}}$ μ = population average
c. Poisson		$y = \dfrac{a^x e^{-a}}{x!}$
d. Weibull	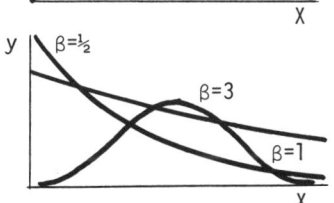	$y = \alpha\beta(x-\gamma)^{\beta-1} e^{-\alpha(x-\gamma)^\beta}$ α = scale parameter β = shape parameter γ = location parameter

**Figure 13.2
Continuous probability distributions**

To make predictions about a normally distributed population, estimates of the average (mean) and the standard deviation of the population are used together with a tabularized probability function. The estimate of the mean of the normal population is simply the mean of the sample ($\bar{X}$) taken from that population.

Therefore, mean $\bar{X} = \dfrac{\Sigma X}{n}$ where

$\bar{X}$ = sample mean
X = individual observations
n = number of observations
Σ = sum of

Normally Greek symbols are used to denote population values and roman symbols denote sample values. The standard deviation of a population is obtained by incorporating a correction factor $n/(n - 1)$. This gives the standard deviation formula

$$s = \sqrt{\dfrac{\Sigma(X - \bar{X})^2}{n - 1}}$$

In general the standard deviation (s) is the most useful measure of variation. The standard deviation is best viewed at this time as an arbitrary index that shows the amount of variation in a set of data.

For quality control and logistics prediction purposes, we are usually interested in the amount of area under the normal curve, given that we know the mean and standard deviation. Areas under the normal curve based on standard deviations from the mean are shown in Figure 13.3.

Statistical tables are available that show the fractional area under the normal curve for various numbers of standard deviations (σ) from the mean. The common term "outside the $\pm 3\ \sigma$ limit" means the item is in the last 0.27 percent of the population. The number of standard deviations selected as a criterion is purely a matter of judgment. The United States uses $\pm 3\ \sigma$ as standard while some countries use $\pm 2\ \sigma$ and others use $\pm 4\ \sigma$. Remember that these predictions refer to the population and not to the sample. The percentage of a *sample* within a set of limits can be quite different from the percentage within the same limits in the population. This is an underlying principle of testing hypothesis.

The shape of the exponential distribution curve differs greatly from that of the normal (bell) curve. In an exponentially distributed population, 63.2 percent will be below the average and 36.8 percent above. The average is not always at the 50 percent point! The characteristic of a higher percentage below the average indicates applications for the exponential distribution. For example, the exponential describes failure

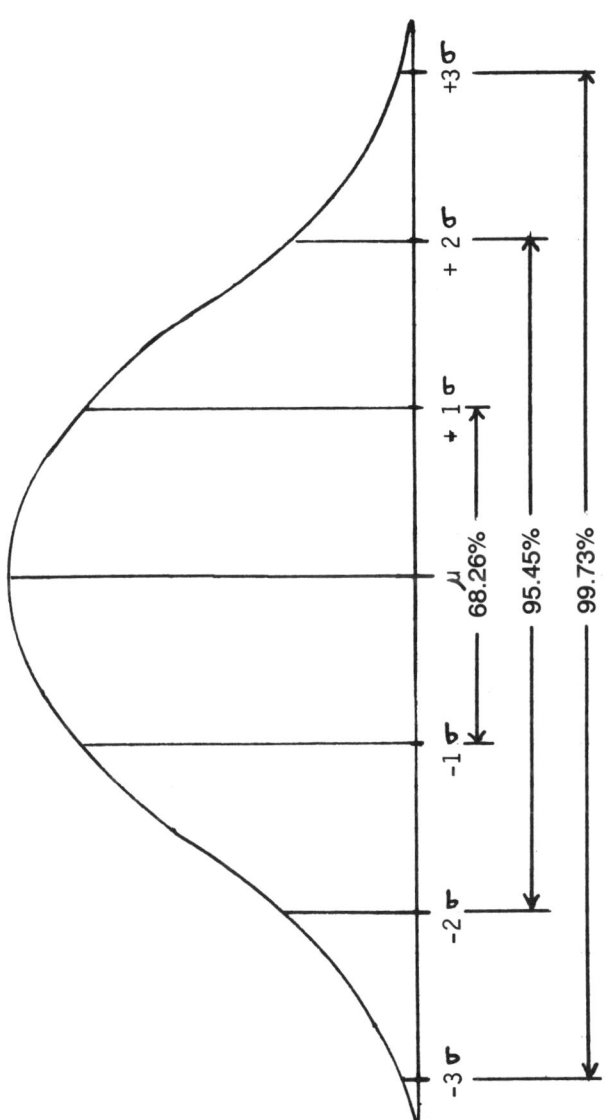

Figure 13.3
Area under the normal curve

rates of electronic components where short-time failures are more numerous than long-time ones. Statistical tables exist for determining the exponential distribution values under the curve based on individual observation, X.

The Weibull family of distributions varies greatly depending on the value of X. This is often assumed to be 0 to simplify the equation. The shape parameter (β) reflects the pattern of the curve. Note that when it is 1.0, the Weibull function reduces to the exponential. Also note that when β, the shape of the parameter, is about 3.5 (and $\alpha = 1$ and $\gamma = 0$), the Weibull closely approximates the normal distribution. The Weibull is very popular because its ability to cover several important distributions reduces the problem of examining a set of data and deciding which of the several choices would be most appropriate.

Weibull distribution predictions are usually made by using special Weibull probability paper. The solution n is to plot the data on Weibull paper, and if all the points fall approximately in a straight line, draw the line, and read the probability predictions directly from the graph. Weibull paper is a plot of a log function of the usage characteristic X versus the cumulative percent frequency of S. For small samples of 20 or less, the data point is plotted against the "median rank" found in a statistical table.

The Weibull technique is helpful for predicting results. When statistical theory is balanced with engineering experience and judgment, Weibull may be employed to extrapolate beyond the actual test data and make life predictions without accumulating a large amount of test time. This is good for predicting which components will be most troublesome early in a warranty period and provides a technique for predicting the critical few components early enough to allow corrective action.

Although making predictions about the population on the basis of samples from that population has definite economic advantages, it also has risks. There can be two errors in decision making: (1) A good lot may be rejected. This is called a producer's risk, or type 1, or alpha error. (2) A bad lot may be accepted. This is called a consumer's risk, or type 2, or beta error. There is no practical way to be sure that the material accepted is entirely free of defects. Sampling involves the risk that the sample will not reflect conditions in the lot. The operating characteristic (OC) curve for a sampling plan quantifies these risks. The OC curve for an attribute plan plots the fraction defective in a lot versus the probability that the sampling plan will accept a lot with the specified fraction defective. An ideal OC curve is illustrated in Figure 13.4, but a more common curve is shown in Figure 13.5. Both curves are based on rejecting a lot with more than 4 percent defective and accepting one with fewer than 4 percent.

An OC curve can be constructed by determining the probability of acceptance for several values of incoming quality p. Probability of ac-

Quality 161

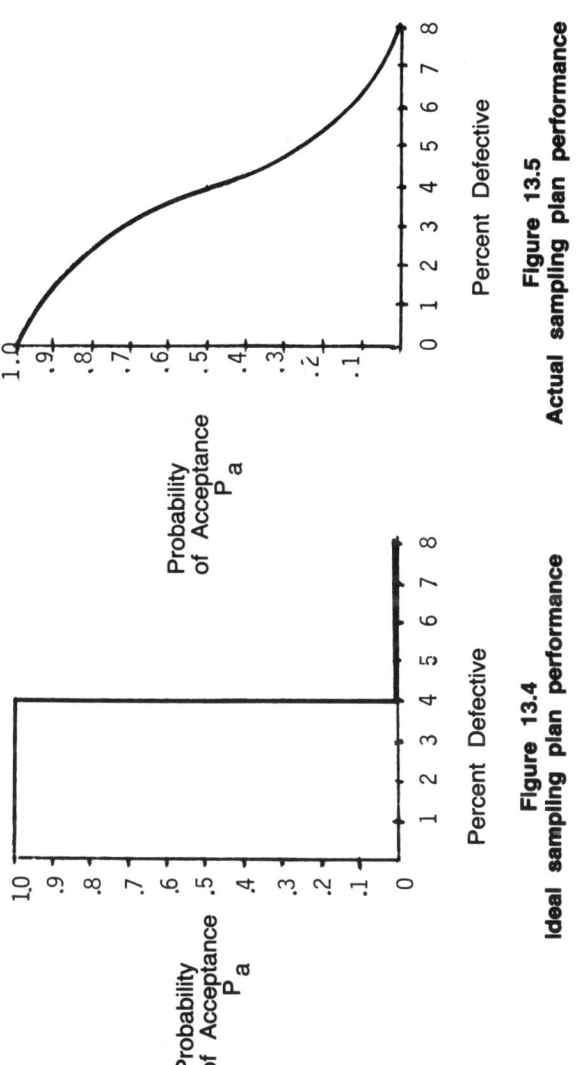

Figure 13.4
Ideal sampling plan performance

Figure 13.5
Actual sampling plan performance

ceptance is the probability that the number of defectives in the sample is equal to or less than the acceptance number for the sampling plan. Three distributions can be used to find the probability of acceptance: hypergeometric, bionomial, or Poisson. The Poisson distribution is preferable because of the ease of calculation. It requires a large sample size (at least 20) and small probability of occurrence ($p = 0.1$). The Poisson distribution used for acceptance sampling is:

$$P_a \begin{matrix} \text{Exactly} \\ r \text{ defectives} \\ \text{in sample size } n \end{matrix} = \frac{e^{-np}(n_p)^r}{r!}$$

If, for example, 20 items are selected from a lot of 400 and the lot is truly 5 percent defective, probabilities are:

$$np = (20)(0.05) = 1.0$$

$$P_a(0, 20) = \frac{2.718^{-1}(1)^0}{0!} = 0.368$$

$$P_a(1, 20) = \frac{2.718^{-1}(1)^1}{1!} = 0.368$$

$$P_a(2, 20) = \frac{2.718^{-1}(1)^2}{2!} = 0.184$$

$$P_a(2 \text{ or fewer in } 20) = \phantom{\frac{2.718^{-1}(1)^2}{2!}} = 0.920$$

A sampling plan should never be adopted without first reviewing its OC curve. "Rule of thumb" sampling plans are frequently found inadequate when evaluated by the OC curve. Standard OC curves for sampling plans are contained in MIL-STD-105 and other publications for ease of reference.

Published plans can be categorized using one of four indexes.

1. Acceptable quality level (AQL). This usually means the lowest quality level that is still considered satisfactory. Since an AQL is an acceptable level, the probability of acceptance for an AQL lot should be high. This is illustrated in Figure 13.6. A demerit system may be useful if a product can have a number of different defects of varying seriousness. A weighted demerit rating can be attached to each type of defect and product quality measured in terms of demerits.

2. Rejectable quality level (RQL). This is unsatisfactory quality and is synonymous with the term, "lot tolerance percent defective" (LTPD) as used in Dodge-Romig plans. Since the RQL is an unacceptable risk, the probability of acceptance should be very low. This probability is known as the consumer's risk and is generally standardized at 0.1. The consumer's risk is *not* the probability that the consumer will actually receive product at the RQL. The consumer will, in fact, not receive one

lot in 10 defective at 0.1 RQL. What the consumer actually gets depends on the actual quality in the lot before inspection and on the probability of acceptance.

3. Indifference quality level (IQL). This is a quality level somewhere between the AQL and RQL at which the probability of acceptance is 0.5.

4. Average outgoing quality limit (AOQL). At the extreme of either very good or very bad, the outgoing quality will tend to be very good because it will either be all right to begin with or the sampling plan will cause all lots to be rejected and detail inspected. Between these extremes is the point at which the percent of defectives in the outgoing material will reach its maximum. This point is known as the AOQL.

Sampling forms include (1) single (2) double, and (3) multiple. In a single-sampling plan, the decision to accept or reject is based on inspection of a single sample drawn from the lot. In double-sampling plans, a smaller initial sample is taken. A decision to accept or reject can be reached if the number of defectives is either very small or very large. If it is either, a second sample would be taken. Since the second sample is required only in marginal cases, the average number of inspections per lot is generally lower than with single sampling. In multiple-sampling plans, one or two or several still smaller samples are inspected as required to reach and accept or reject decision. Double- and multiple-sampling plans usually mean less inspection but are more difficult to administer.

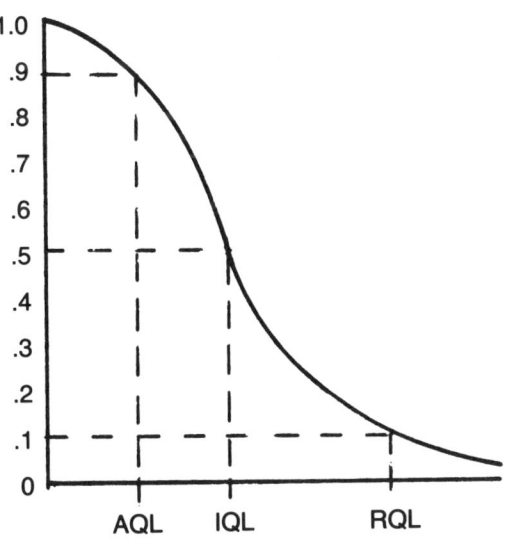

Figure 13.6
Sampling plan indices

What level should be established for the AQL, AOQL, or LTPD? The decision is based on balancing the cost of finding and correcting a defective against the loss incurred if a defective slips through an inspection procedure. The break-even point for inspection is recommended for the AQL. It is calculated as follows:

$$\frac{\text{Cost to inspect one piece}}{\text{Damage done by one defective}}$$

It may be helpful to classify defects as critical, major, or minor, as is done in MIL-STD-105, and assign different AQLs to different groups of defects.

CONTROL CHARTS

Control charts are very useful as a graphic technique that shows rapidly whether the hypothesis of "no significant difference" is accepted or rejected. Control charts may be classified by the characteristic being examined as:

1. Average measurements ($\bar{X}$ chart)—Averages are more sensitive to change than are individual values.
2. Range (R chart)—This measures the distance between the highest and the lowest values.
3. Percent defective (p chart).
4. Number of defects in the sample (c chart).

Control charts can be constructed for any statistical measure, so there are many variations of these four basic charts. Initial control limits are usually set 3σ above and below the expected average value. Statistical tables for control chart trial limit factors facilitate the initial setup. If all points fall within control limits, then it is concluded that only chance variation is present. If any points fall outside the control limits, then there must be an assignable cause for the variation in the process.

The question is often asked, "Can data outside the limits be eliminated from computation?" There is no justification for eliminating data unless corrective action has been taken and confirmed so that the cause is eliminated. A paper study may be made to determine whether the process could be capable of meeting tolerances if all the assignable causes were somehow eliminated. This will indicate when the effort is worthwhile or when a complete breakthrough is necessary to change the entire process to within limits.

DESIGN OF EXPERIMENTS

"Design of experiments" denotes the plan of an experiment that recognizes statistical aspects. Classical methods of experimentation vary only one factor at a time while everything else is held constant. Modern procedures are designed to allow several factors to be varied simultaneously. Experimental conditions are analyzed rather than precisely controlled, experimental error is stated in quantitative terms, bias is reduced by randomization, and fewer measurements are needed for valid practical information.

The analysis of results is performed by a technique called analysis of variance (ANOVA). The total variation in the experiment is divided into three groups:

1. Factors under investigation.
2. Interactions between factors.
3. Experimental error.

Variation of the factor under investigation is compared with the experimental error and a conclusion reached as to whether it is acceptable using the F test from statistical tables. If the calculated test value falls within the acceptance region, the hypothesis of "no interaction" is accepted. If the calculated F value falls outside the acceptance region, the hypothesis is rejected, normally showing that the differences are significant. Regression analysis, which is the study of relationships among variables, is another important analytical tool for testing experimental hypothesis.

AUDITS

An audit to appraise the quality system of an activity, a product, or an entire plant may be undertaken when a problem is known to exist. It may be routine or a surprise to "keep people on their toes" and assure that problems are not occurring unnoticed. A quality audit is similar to an accounting audit in that it must be undertaken by people independent from the activity being audited. Audits are expensive, but are an effective form of prevention. They can also be very useful to focus attention on a particular activity. An audit is not undertaken to criticize, but rather to accomplish necessary corrective action. The human relations problems are especially important. A good technique is to assure that everyone understands the objectives of the audit before it is undertaken and that audit results are shown to the involved people before the report is issued. Corrective action will often take place even before the debriefing session.

"Results orientation" is important in the entire profession of quality control. Number gathering and fine-tuned analysis using advanced statistical techniques is meaningless unless they result in practical improvement.

Persons interested in further study of quality control are advised to contact local colleges for undergraduate and graduate courses, which are often included in applied statistics departments. The American Society for Quality Control (ASQC) sponsors many education and training courses and conducts programs leading to certification as a quality engineer (CQE). The state of California has opened registration as a professional engineer (PE) to quality engineers.

CHAPTER

14

Modern Maintenance Methods

The maintenance concept is one of the first policies that should be planned and published for the guidance of designers, logisticians, and everyone else involved in design and development of new products and support systems. In the real world, the maintenance concept usually evolves after the fact and reacts to, rather than leads, design. Too often we must service the design since we failed to design the service.

Significant recent advances have taken place concerning technology, quantitative information, and ideas regarding service.

Technological developments such as thermoplastics and high-tensile metals that afford longer life under stress conditions, minature electronic components with great capability at low cost, and development of computers, jets, lasers, and other new devices mean that new ways are available for accomplishing objectives. Quantitative information is increasing at a rapid rate, with the major problems being to understand it and communicate it meaningfully to those who have use for it. In the early 1950s, several American companies joined resources and investigated the nature of reliability. A number of concepts evolved from this effort, including the reliability bathtub curve as shown in Figure 14.1.

Early failures, which are often the result of poor-quality manufacturing or defects introduced during service, are minimized by burn-in. Some equipment, such as piston aircraft engines, was broken in for several hours by doing "slow time" to set the piston rings properly. This run in was usually performed near an airport so the plan could glide to a landing if the engine failed during the critical first hours.

The middle part of the bathtub curve is commonly called "random failure" or "constant failure rate failures." It is generalized as being due to many possible causes of failure with the probability of any one being quite small. Then if wear-out occurs and contributes to failures, the failure rate will increase as shown in the last part of the curve. This is caused by metal fatigue, corrosion, decreased elasticity, decreased resistance, decreased dielectric constants, weakening cathode electron emissions, and other physical characteristics that diminish with time or cycles or operation. As more and more experience is gained on equipment and data gathered for analysis, qualitative intuition gives way to quantitative facts.

New ideas are continually being developed concerning new ways for servicing equipment. As service becomes a larger and more expensive component of our economy, interest in reducing service costs is increased. The systems approach to service gives consideration to its many facets and influences, which must be integrated into a whole package. Figure 14.2 shows the architecture for service segments of a large commercial communications organization. The matrix is divided three ways; by environments, by business types, and by service systems. The business environments are the geographic density in which the products will be serviced. Different procedures are obviously necessary for servicing the many systems that might exist in a skyscraper in New York City versus servicing one product on a remote western ranch. The business areas are divided according to the purpose of the specific product: size, technology, capability, and customer need. Service systems are divided into management, hardware, technical, and logistic to assure that all necessary items are covered.

ADVANCES

Technology, information, and ideas have been developed into the following guidelines for maintainability and maintenance.

1. Safety is paramount.
2. Only design changes can improve inherent reliability and safety.
3. Beyond cleaning tasks necessary for customer comfort and product appearance, do only the maintenance tasks necessary to preserve safety or reliability. (If it works, don't fix it.)

The increasing failures shown in the bathtub curve of Figure 14.1 are really a very minor problem. Since operating conditions, materials, lubricants, usage, intervals, and other affecting parameters vary considerably, wear-out can only be accurately detected by sensors or by using

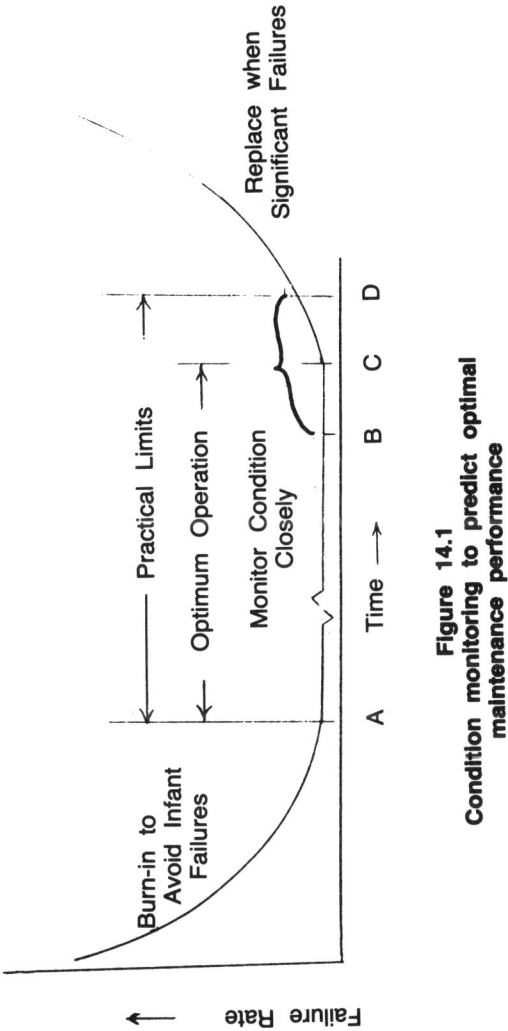

Figure 14.1 Condition monitoring to predict optimal maintenance performance

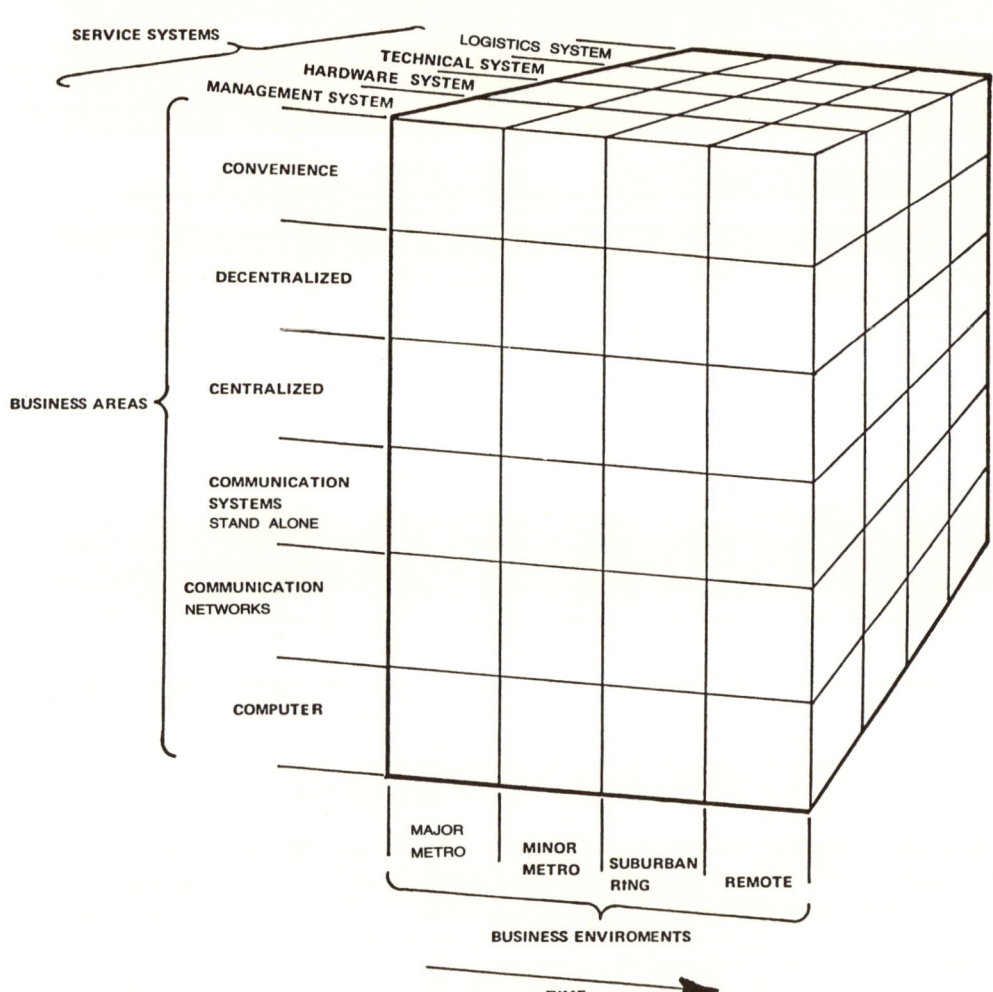

**Figure 14.2
Service as a complete system**

until failure. Those are two modern service concepts. The idea of indiscriminate replacement based on projected possible failures is being succeeded by "on-condition" or "condition monitoring" techniques. Inspection detects when a particular equipment is approaching wear-out and, therefore, when preventive maintenance is needed. Instead of lumping a family of components together, on-condition inspection determines the wear-out point of each component. Incipient failures are detected by determining whether some threshold value of an observable characteristic has been exceeded. Since wear-out usually occurs gradually, the on-condition inspection interval is shorter than the interval between the occurrence of the threshold value and failure.

Sensor technology and analytical evaluation of lubricants and exhausts are becoming useful means of evaluating wear-out of hidden components. Naturally, when any of these devices detects that the safe threshold has been exceeded, a positive indication must be given to the person in charge, or the equipment should go into a fail-safe mode. Referring again to Figure 14.1, the optimum operation will be during the random failure center portion of the bathtub curve. In reality the point denoted A can be accurately determined because of the large amount of data available. Point C is much more difficult to determine because the failure rate of single components may be masked, and less information is available both because of the reduced number of components and problems in getting accurate field information. It is also difficult to determine when an increasing failure rate is in fact statistically significant. Service managers will generally resist replacing expensive parts unless they know that replacement will reduce total service costs. The tendency, therefore, is to leave the components in operation until the point approximated by D. If it is practical to check the wearing component during other service, the conditions should be monitored closely beginning with time B, which will be about two standard deviations in time before the mean point at which failures are projected to increase. The difference between optimum and optimal is that optimum is theoretical and optimal is practical and satisfactory while probably not theoretically perfect.

A predictive maintenance inspection is performed to discover a pending failure. To be effective, it requires (1) a threshold value of some parameter beyond which a failure is probable, and (2) an appreciable operating time between the occurrence of the threshold value and the failure.

Inspections are generally ineffective to detect constant failure rate failures since the interval between the threshold value of the parameter and occurrence of failure is small. Therefore, constant failure rate failures can rarely be anticipated by scheduled inspections or avoided by scheduled maintenance. Scheduled maintenance does not improve inherent reliability. For example, inspecting your automobile tires will determine whether alignment is good and they are wearing evenly, and will allow you to have a defect corrected if appearance indicates a problem. However, the inspection will not prevent your tire from going flat if it is punctured by a nail.

PRODUCTION-LINE APPROACH TO SERVICE

Theodore Levitt, in his *Harvard Business Review* article that won the McKinsey award in 1972, points out that most people think about service in humanistic terms, but about manufacturing in technocratic terms. This, he feels, is why manufacturing industries are forward looking and efficient while service industries and customer service are, by comparison, primitive and inefficient. Service is presumed to be performed by individuals for other individuals, generally on a one-to-one basis. Manufacturing is presumed to be performed by machines, generally tended by large clusters of individuals whose sizes and configurations are themselves dictated by the machine's requirements. Service is performed in the field by distant and loosely supervised people working under highly variable and often volatile conditions. Manufacturing occurs in the factory under highly centralized, carefully organized, tightly controlled, and elaborately engineered conditions.

People assume, and rightly so, that these differences largely explain why products produced in the factory are generally more uniform in appearance and quality than the services produced or delivered in the field. One cannot as easily control agents or their performance in the field, and different customers want different things. Yet, once conditions in the field get the same kind of attention that conditions inside the factory generally get, many new opportunities become possible. First, however, management must revise its thinking about what service is and what it implies. Discretion is the enemy of order, standards, and quality. Many variations and frequent change can reap havoc with service in the field just as with any manufacturing operation. Customer service is rarely discretionary. If it is consciously treated as "manufacturing in the field," it will get the same kind of detailed attention that manufacturing does. It will be carefully planned, controlled, automated, audited for quality, and reviewed for performance improvement and customer reaction. Moreover, the same kinds of technological labor-saving and systems approaches that now thrive in manufacturing operations will get a chance to help improve service.

THROWAWAY MAINTENANCE

Many products, ranging from television sets to military weapons, are designed with replaceable modules that are to be thrown away rather than repaired when failed. Many considerations go into this decision, including:

Cost of spares
Usage
R&M
Personnel and training
Technical publications
Sport equipment
Physical distribution
Pipeline quantities
Facilities
Material availability
Capacity for repair

Unfortunately the typical customer engineer avoids throwing anything away, especially if costs are under scrutiny and will appear less if a part is fixed instead of a new part ordered or there is an immediate need and a replacement cannot be obtained right away. In either case the part will be repaired and all the detailed analysis in favor of throwaway disregarded.

If the supply system does not provide adequate replacements as needed, then repairs become practically mandatory. Although not very successful to date, a 100 percent throwaway maintenance program is possible. Realistic analysis, backed up with adequate spare parts, documentation, and training, is vital, and management must assure that the concept of throwaway maintenance is followed. New electronic technologies for microcircuits and large-scale integrations will relieve the problem. They are, fortunately, very reliable and lower in cost, since they are virtually impossible to repair. It will become increasingly more important to do realistic analysis during the concept and design stages to assure that throwaway maintenance is advantageous, but success will mean logistics savings and more useful products that are easier to service.

ELECTRONIC REPAIRS

Printed circuit boards (PCBs) are used in many products and often must be repaired. They are treated here as a special case, since 20–60 percent of boards returned from the field are misdiagnosed. Testing of misdiagnosed boards that are actually good costs more than does testing and repair of bad boards where the fault can be quickly found. The question is: Why was the board returned? Did it actually not work in a specific equipment, or was it replaced through faulty troubleshooting or to placate a customer? Several companies have the policy of repairing bad boards that are returned but scrapping boards that test good. This is excessively expensive.

A preferable method is to diagnose all returned boards, and if a faulty component is identified, engrave it and carefully mark the position. The component is removed and tested separately. If it is defective, it is replaced with another component. If it is not defective, it is put back in the board and the PCB retested for design defects. All repaired boards and those on which a defect could not be found should be subjected to thermal shock. This means rapidly taking a board from ambient temperature down to $-20°C$ and holding it there for about 20 minutes—then heating it rapidly to $65°C$ and holding it there for 20 minutes before returning it to ambient for test. This procedure will weed out an additional 15 percent of defectives normally due to mechanical failures from inadequate strain relief and poor production quality. Component selection is a minor part of unreliability. Production quality causes most problems, with design deficiencies next. Information to date indicates that the failure rate of the first year is three times higher than in following years. Indications are that the failure rate then remains steady for about 14 years before wear-out sets in. Even then the wear-out is due mostly to problems caused by initially poor production design or technique. Complex components and boards generally cause fewer problems because more attention is given to them.

Repaired boards should be serialized so they can be identified if they are ever returned. It is difficult to get people to serialize new boards because of the effort demanded, but it must be done to track field returns. If a serially numbered board is returned a second time for repair and a defect cannot be found, the board should be scrapped. If a defect is found and corrected, the repaired board will probably be more reliable than a newly produced one since early failures have been weeded out. A good rule of thumb for pricing PCB repairs is 25 percent of the parts' cost. This means that if you add up the cost of all components on the board and multiply by 0.25, you will at least break even on testing, parts, labor, and facilities. Note that it costs at least $100 to return any defective part for repair, so parts worth less than that should be discarded at the place of failure, unless needed for technical evaluation or valuable materials.

DO IT YOURSELF

Many customers are interested in doing as much as possible themselves before they succumb to an expensive service call. This should be encouraged, so long as it does not present a safety hazard or potential equipment damage, since it gets the product back into service quickly and satisfies the customer. A small product can easily be transported by the customer or a pick-up and delivery service to a central service center. Expensive customer engineers do not need to waste their time traveling, and repairs are done where test equipment and spare parts are readily available. Automatic diagnostic equipment, which is too expensive to provide to each individual customer engineer, can be used at such a repair center.

The ideal situation is that in which no customer service needs any tool other than a thin coin, and all customer education is through self-guiding features of the equipment. Built-in warning and test equipment is possible if it can be economically justified. If the equipment is portable and shipped ready-to-use, the customer can install it and remove prior equipment. Consideration should also be given to like-for-like exchange of equipment if it becomes necessary for the customer to bring it to the repair center. "Loaner" equipment should be available if the customer's machine will be in repair for a long time.

There should be toll-free telephone lines with qualified customer service personnel to answer queries, guide customers in performing minor maintenance, and order any parts or information the customer may require. For the do-it-yourself strategy to succeed, the operation must be simple. While the technology may be very complex in concept and design, the customer's responsibilities and available opportunities must be uncomplicated.

USE TO FAILURE

Modern in-service reliability analysis shows that the real incidence of an adverse age/reliability relationship is much lower than intuition implies. Far more problems have been encountered by using low-reliability people to service high-reliability products. A good rule to follow is, "Fix anything that is defective; check the condition of critical items; and if it is working right, don't touch it!"

CHAPTER

15

Inventory Management

An effective inventory management program depends on:

1. Determination of management objectives and goals.
2. Assessment of basic business needs.
3. Understanding and use of methods, techniques, and models.
4. Forecasting.
5. Gathering, analyzing, and reporting information.
6. Establishing contingency procedures.
7. Design of follow-on and peripheral elements.
8. Internal and external testing.
9. Cost and service level controls.

MANAGEMENT OBJECTIVES AND GOALS

The objectives of logistics activities usually concern customer service and cost. To the manager of a grocery stroe, newsstand, or lunch counter, customer service means having the items the customer wants to buy. To a product support manager, it may mean having enough spare parts available to fix down machines.

Operational availability (A_0) is a popular topic mainly because it may be too low—often because the mean logistics delay time (MLDT) is too high. MLDT is often the downtime while a field customer engineer is waiting for necessary replacement parts. Customer-oriented measures of product availability focus on service as perceived by the customer. They include percent of orders completely filled, back ordered, shipped on time, and shipped within specified time periods.

The first management objective to be determined is what percent of all line item orders should be filled within what time. The only way to satisfy all demands is to stock an infinite supply of spare parts. But since an infinite supply of spare parts would cost an infinite amount of money, this solution is obviously unacceptable. On the other hand, zero spares will produce a low assurance against stock-outs, but never 0 percent, because even though we have no spares there exists the possibility that no spares will be demanded. Thus we cannot have 0 percent assurance or 100 percent assurance, but we can obtain many different assurances between 0 and 100 percent by varying the number of spares stocked. Increasing the number of spares increases the assurance against stock-outs; decreasing them decreases the assurance. Then we can set our goal at meeting demands 95 percent of the time from immediate stock with the remaining 5 percent met within 24 hours. The time can usually be reduced by expeditious ordering, production, transportation, and special handling, all of which cost money. Since we realize that a high probability of parts support is expensive, we must continually determine sensitivity, optimum levels, and cost constraints to get the most for our money. Management will usually have an objective of performing within budget, which translates into a specific goal of providing the spares inventory for, say, $1 million per year.

When you need one widget from inventory, you are really interested only in whether there is one or zero widgets in the stockroom. If there is one item, you are satisfied. If there are no items you are dissatisfied. However, additional items in the stockroom incur carrying costs, which will amount to over 25 percent of an item's value per year. It covers the cost of handling, information, storage space, and insurance, and the cost of capital (alternate uses of funds). If your demand is fulfilled, you are happy. If you are on the supply end of the supply–demand function, you have other concerns: Can I fill the next order promptly? What is my safety stock? Have I reached my reorder point? What is the economic order quantity? Is demand changing?

It is up to the inventory manager to advise management of sensitivities to cost, time, and support so that management can decide what balance is desired.

DEMAND

Demand is not synonymous with usage. For a new item, it is probably the sum of sales to customers plus defective or damaged items that cannot be sold. For spares support, usage will be the failure rate plus replacement due to incorrect diagnosis or damage by faulty repair efforts, parts received defective, and quantities necessary to fill the "pipeline." The usage is above and beyond the technical failure rate and requires the prediction assistance of experienced personnel.

Parts for New Products

Initial sparing of parts for new products is always a challenge because of the dynamic changes caused by introductions to the market place, uncertainties of customer demand and usage, a high rate of revision, retrofit and modification, inadequate documentation, manufacturing start-up problems, and general lack of experience.

The key elements in establishing demand are the usage rate (natural failures + induced failures + misdiagnosis + received defectives), system usage, and quantity per system to determine total usage quantities. During the early stages of a program, additional adjustment factors may be used, including reliability growth, usage profile, secondary failures, user-responsible failures, learning curves, and wearout. If items are to be replaced during scheduled maintenance, those needs must be added to the unscheduled usage.

Development of these factors will require extensive cooperative efforts among the spares specialist, field engineer, design engineer, product planner, manufacturing engineer, and marketer. The maintenance concept provides the initial base for planning. The scenario of operation may, however, not specifically coincide with the base for determining the provision of allowances. For example, with airborne equipment the base most commonly used is flight hours per week or month. However, some equipment on board the aircraft is used only during a small portion of the flight and conversion factors must be developed to predict the failure rate on the basis of equipment operating hours. The factor will vary from system to system, and even by organization, depending on the mission profile and equipment utilization.

The ground operating time for test diagnosis may also be a significant factor that can be three to four times greater than the actual mission time. Remember that supplies and spares are necessary for failures occurring during tests and training, as well as during missions. Heavy reliance should be placed on field data from similar systems since such data will include many of the human factors and other "real-life" considerations that influence usage rates.

This diagnosis factor takes into account the fact that units are often removed from a system when they are thought to be defective but are in fact good. This is known in quality control as a type 1, alpha, or producer error. This factor is influenced by the capabilities of built-in test (BIT) equipment, system complexity, operating environment, documentation, training, and tools. Again, experience with comparable field systems and thorough maintainability analysis will guide usage determination.

Reliability growth will usually follow a predictable pattern. In many cases early production units do not have the high reliability that is expected with later units. Problems include poor manufacturing quality, unstable processes, and customer engineer ineptness during the learning period. Prescreening, burn-in, preinstallation, and other techniques may be used to improve reliability as actually seen by the first customers, but replacement parts are necessary for failures during these early operating periods.

Secondary failures due to feedback loops may be established by a failure modes and effects analysis (FMEA). Experience shows that secondary failures are so few that they do not justify much analytical effort based on "what if?" but could cause significant problems as a result of, for example, electrical spikes or heat from failure damaging adjacent components.

User-responsible failures are an important factor with many products. Equipment must be "idiot-proofed" because people try it first and read instructions only in case of failure. The consumer protection responsibility of product design necessitates extreme care in design and testing of products to assure that the user will not be hurt. A producer can be sure that if anything can go wrong, it will.

Wear-out, if it is predictable, can be used to establish a scheduled replacement interval for parts so that they can be replaced when convenient before they have induced a catastrophic failure. Preventive maintenance expenses are more than compensated for through improved customer satisfaction, reduced labor, and better planning.

How Many Items to Order?

The usage rate based on failures plus modification factors must be further expanded to consider the replacement level, other suitable parts, repair or scrap, level of repair, location, and essentiality.

The use of other substitutable parts is enhanced through standardized design and support. The more common parts there are in a system or product family, the better the chance will be of fulfilling a part need from any of several sources.

Whether a part is to be scrapped or repaired has a major influence on the number of spares required. If a part is scrapped, then a spare is necessary to replace every one to be used. If a replaced part is returned for repair, then the repair and recycle time determines the quantity. Low-volume, low-cost parts should be designed for throwaway maintenance.

Spares location also interacts with organization, structure, facility planning, item selection, and operations, which have an influence because the more places there are to stock parts, the more parts that are required.

It does not make sense to stock all parts at every level. An important consideration is the ability to have accurate information on where a part is available within a short period of time, so that needs may be satisfied from several possible locations within the system. For example, every generator may have its own spare fuses and fan belt. The customer engineer who services many generators may not need to carry those items because when more are needed than are available at one generator, they can be borrowed from another generator for later replacement. The engineer may then be able to go to a team stockroom and replace the supply. That stockroom may be directly supported by a central distribution center.

LOCATION

As illustrated in Table 15.1, time to resupply is a function of the source location, with expected time based on actual field data for existing products.

Table 15.1
Parts Resupply Times

Stock Location	Typical Time to Supply to Machine Work-Hours
Machine	0
Customer engineer	3
Team	4
Branch	8
Distribution center	24
Factory	72

TURNOVER

Inventory turnover is an important function since no item should lie dormant at any location. High-volume retailers such as supermarkets should turn over their inventory at least once a month. The spares supply of a television repairperson, aircraft mechanic, or computer customer engineer should turn over at least 3.5 times per year. If the parts are not being used at that high a rate, they should be considered for dropping from the spares list, and should certainly be moved to the next higher stocking point for consolidation. The evaluation of what parts should be held where and in what quantities should undergo continual revision since much time can be lost (but not reported in typical reporting systems) getting necessary replacement parts.

ESSENTIALITY

Essentiality is a factor adopted from the George Washington University Logistics Research Project on the Polaris Missile System, where it was first used to evaluate the effect of various components upon fulfillment of the defense mission. It is a very useful concept. Many organizations now utilize four essentiality levels as shown in Table 15.2. The additional cost of service or the opportunity lost depends on essentiality. If, for example, a level 1 or 2 part is required, additional expenses for special service calls and expediting as necessary will be encouraged to get the equipment back in operation, since it is not fulfilling a mission or producing revenue, or may be exposing the owner to potential lawsuit in case of an accident. In the case of a computer necessary to run a payroll, there may be little problem for the first hour, but then the potential cost is $100 for the next hour, with $75 each additional hour since replacement equipment must be found and used, goodwill is lost, and income is forgone. Determining that pattern is necessary for making the management decisions discussed earlier. Where a very high machine base rent is charged for equipment, the customer is going to want a rebate if the equipment is down very long. In many cases, if the machine is down for one hour, at least 75 percent of the work will be saved and run when the machine is repaired and only 25 percent of the contribution margin actually lost. As the machine is down for longer periods, proportionally more potential work will be turned over to other equipment. In the case of military defense systems, a NORS (not operationally ready supplies) level of 30 to 40 percent is reported as all too common! For essentiality level 3, the effect will probably be negligible for a few days, during which time the part could be easily supplied and replaced

Table 15.2

Level	Meaning
1	Safety hazard or legal liability.
2	Equipment out of action.
3	Degraded operation; still functioning but at a reduced rate.
4	Failure not an immediate problem, however, the part should be replaced before it contributes to major degradation, or is cosmetically undesirable.

at the next opportunity. Level 3 would include a machine that will operate only at 1000 iph instead of the normal 1500 or at degraded quality. Essentiality level 4 may not be replaced until the equipment is returned for major overhaul or may be fixed at the next scheduled visit. The impact of this downtime effect can be shown for an industrial product that rents for an average of $35 per hour and has an estimated goodwill of $25 per hour. Fee formulas used are shown in Table 15.3. This assumes losing the potential $35 contribution income for essentialities 1 and 2 at a rate of 25 percent the first hour, increasing 5 percent each additional hour t in the form of loss = goodwill $25t$ + forgone income $35\{.25t + \Sigma 0.05(t - 1)\}$.

Table 15.4 shows cumulative down time losses.

It can be easily seen that costs can increase rapidly when expensive equipment is down for lack of parts. The cost of a one-hour delay of a jet airliner is over $1000 plus the effect on delayed passengers. A steam turbine shutdown costs an electric company over $20,000 per day and a nuclear power generator down costs over $1 million per day.

STOCKS

When is a car not a car? In terms of logistics, when it is in Pittsburgh at the time it is needed in New York. When it is yellow instead of the desired red. When it is in a back lot and it should be in the showroom. In short, utilities are created in goods when they are at the right place at the right time and in the quality and quantity desired, at a reasonable cost.

Stock-keeping units (SKUs) are handy references since each differs in shape, size, color, fragrance, strength, reliability, or other characteristics (e.g., fanbelt-12 inch, heat resistant, grooved). An SKU inventory refers to the stock of an individually described SKU, which may contain any number of units. A stock-keeping unit location (SKUL) is the number of units inventoried at one facility. One or more SKUs make up a product line and the sum of all SKUs at all SKULs is the total inventory for a company.

Table 15.3
Down Time Opportunity Costs

Essentiality Level	Opportunity Lost, Dollars per Hour
1 and 2	$25t + 35 \{0.25t + \Sigma .05 (t - 1)\}$
3	$25t + 35 \{ 35 \{0.25t + \Sigma .05 (t - 1)\}$
4	Negligible up to 14 days, during which time the part should be easily supplied.

Inventories may be classed as basic demand, in-transit, safety, speculative, or dead, depending on the reason for which they are held. Basic demand stocks are those required for filling orders under conditions of certainty where demand and replenishment time can be predicted accurately.

In-transit stocks are en route from one inventory location to another. They may be considered as a part of basic stocks even though they are not available for sale until they arrive at a given destination. Many modern transportation functions include in-transit as a means of warehousing the supplies where arrival time may be accurately predicted.

Safety stocks are held in excess of the basic inventory because of uncertainties in either demand for the SKU or the replenishment time, or for disaster or security reasons.

Speculative stocks are created to balance cyclical production, such as foods produced during a short harvest season, or for acquiring commodities, such as raw materials, which may change significantly in price or availability. An inventory of steel accumulated in expectation of a strike could be considered both a speculative stock and a safety stock.

Dead stocks are those for which no demand has occurred over a specified period. If no further demand is anticipated, they should be scrapped and their value written off.

FIFO (first in/first out) and LIFO (last in/first out) are common to inventory. Normally FIFO is used to assure regular use of items in inventory and avoid obsolescence, excessive shelf life, and deterioration. However, accounting policies can impel a change to LIFO for improved financial reporting during periods of rapid inflation. The monetary LIFO valuation may be different from the physical movement (LIFO or FIFO) unless there is identification of specific inventoried items such as serial-numbered equipment, in which case both must be LIFO or both FIFO. A "pool concept" may also be used in which no control is exerted. Be alert to avoid FISH (first in, still here)!

The term "ABC inventory policy" refers to a collection of prioritizing practices to give varied levels of attention to different types of inventories.

Table 15.4
Cumulative Costs of Down Time

Time-Work Hours	Essentiality Levels 1 and 2	Essentiality Level 3	Essentiality Level 4
1	$ 33.75	$16.88	0
2	69.25	34.63	0
3	106.50	53.25	0
4	145.50	72.75	0
8	319.00	159.50	0
24	1293.00	646.50	0

The priorities may depend on sales dollar or unit volume, essentiality, unit cost of inventory items, usage rate, strategic value, customers served, control shoft life and ease of storage.

INVENTORY MANAGEMENT UNDER CERTAINTY

Inventory policy decisions would be relatively simple if customers organized their requirements for an equal number of all items every day of the week, and further, if the time required to schedule produce, and transport replenishment stock were known and constant. While these conditions are rare, the model should be understood so that real-world variations can be applied. The two major influences regarding quantity of a product to order are the cost of placing an order and the cost of carrying inventory. The cost of placing an order or setting up a manufacturing run is assumed to be constant regardless of the size of the order or run, so the cost per unit will decrease as order size increases. However, as order size increases, it will take longer to deplete the quantity ordered and the average inventory level will be higher; therefore, it will cost more in carrying charges.

With fixed known demand, the average level of inventory fluctuates half as much as the change in reorder quantities. We can see that the more we order each time, the higher the average amount will be on hand and the higher our carrying charges will be for interest, warehousing, insurance, storage space, taxes, obsolescence, and damage. However, the relative costs of carrying and ordering inventory vary inversely as shown in Figure 15.1.

The problem can be represented mathematically by stating total costs as

$$C = \frac{QUR}{2} + \frac{AD}{Q}$$

where

C = total inventory cost
Q = quantity ordered
U = average cost per unit
R = annual inventory carrying rate as a percent of product cost
A = the setup or ordering cost
D = period demand (quantity per period)

This simply says that $QUR \div 2$ is annual carrying costs of one-half the quantity ordered, (Q) times the unit cost (U) times the annual inventory carrying charges (R). It also says that AD is the annual ordering or set up cost in terms of the number of orders per year D times the cost per setup or order (A).

The optimum value for Q is found by setting C equal to the minimum value Q and taking the first derivative of a cost equation that solves for $Q\sqrt{2AD}$. The formula for optimum quantity is often called the Wilson lot size formula, or Camp's formula, but most commonly is known as the economic order quantity (EOQ) formula.

Try an example: if the setup cost for a small production line is $500 and annual unit demand is 2,250 units which cost $4 each and have carrying charges of 25% per year, how many should be ordered at one time?

$$EOQ = \sqrt{\frac{2AD}{RU}} = \sqrt{\frac{2 \times 500 \times 2250}{0.25 \times 4}} = 1500$$

Thus the line would be set up and 1500 units produced each time, which would occur about every nine months.

REORDER POINT DETERMINATION

Ideally we would like to have the first of the new units available just as the next order is received following stock-out of the earlier supply. If our sample demand was a normal 2000 over 365 days per year, that

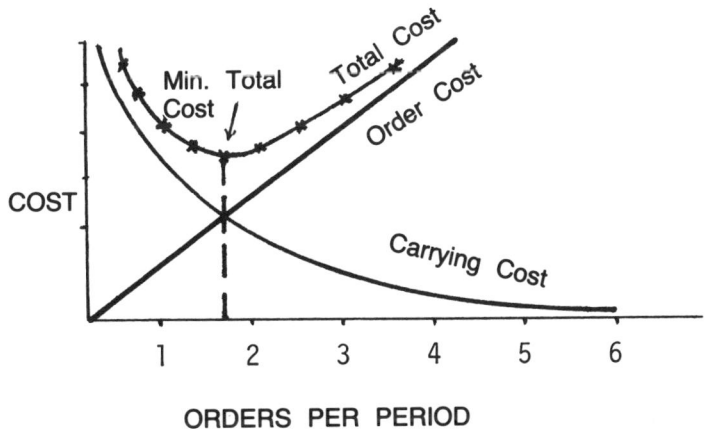

Figure 15.1
Relative costs of carrying and ordering inventory

would be 5.5 units per day. Working backward, if we had a perfect transportation time of seven days, a production time of three days, and an order processing time of four days, we would place the order on the 59th day, knowing that we would receive it 14 days later the 73rd day. This is shown in Figure 15.2.

Just by formatting the data in Table 15.5, the president can see that he can fill 81.6 percent of the orders immediately by having three OLBITS in stock during any day. Having four OLBITS gives 10 percent more for 91.6 percent. Doubling that quantity to eight OLBITS gains 7 percent better service, and having five times that many gains the remaining 8.4 percent necessary to give 100 percent immediate delivery. Figure 15.3 is a histogram of the same data.

The replenishment cycle also varies in length, due mainly to sporadic delivery schedules. The actual delivery data are shown in Table 15.4.

OPERATING DAYS

Even though there are 365 days in a normal calendar year and some activities take place on all but major holidays, production and handling normally do not include weekends or holidays, leaving about 250 effective operating days per year, abbreviated "0" Days.

365 days per year
− 104 Saturdays and Sundays
− 11 holidays
 250 operating days

Table 15.5
Demand Data

Demand	Number of Days	Total Units	Frequency %	Cumulative Frequency %
0	50	0	20.0	20.0
1	57	57	22.8	42.8
2	65	130	26.0	68.8
3	32	96	12.8	81.6
4	25	100	10.0	91.6
5	4	20	1.6	93.2
8	13	104	5.2	98.4
16	1	16	.4	98.8
20	3	60	1.2	100.0
	250	583		

Inventory Management

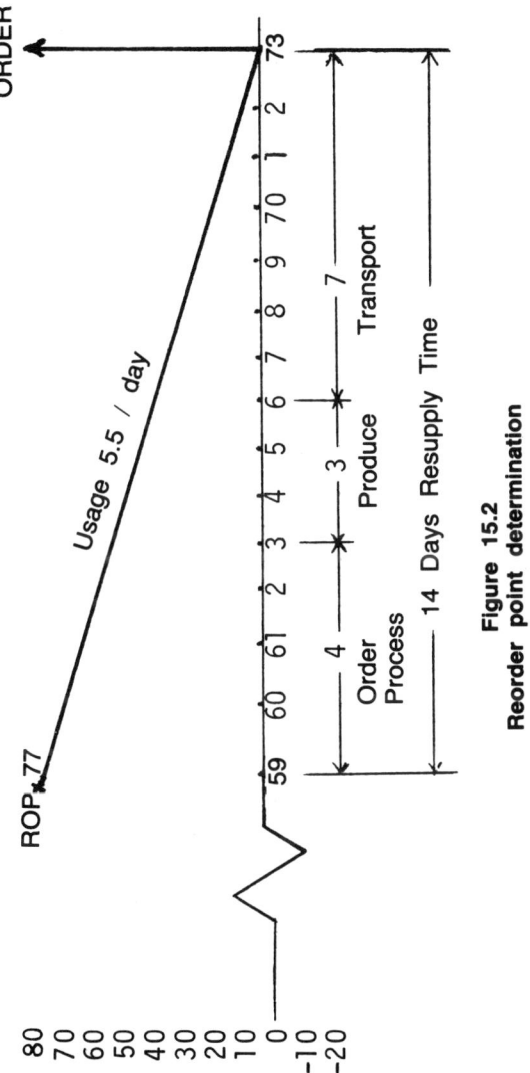

**Figure 15.2
Reorder point determination**

188 Inventory Management

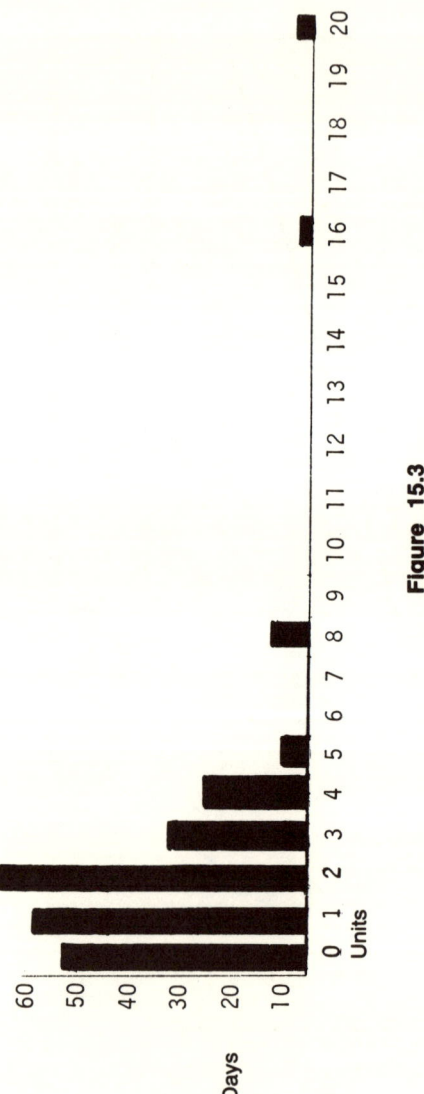

**Figure 15.3
Demand histogram**

FINITE REPLENISHMENT RATE

Where a production process requires long periods of time to build the desired number of parts, there will be an accumulation of inventory during production cycles that exceed the outgo. Maximum inventory will occur after Q/P if P equals production rate per day and Q/P equals number of days to complete an order of size Q. During this period inventory is amassing at the rate of $P-D$. Daily usage equals D (which is units per year) with the D over 250 days per year. Maximum inventory will occur after Q/P days and will equal $\{(P - D)/250$ units per day gain $\times$ Q/P days$\}$. Average inventory again equals inventory divided by 2.

For example, if the delivery rate (P) is 3000 per day and demand (D) is 416,000 per year with holding costs (R) of 22 percent, set up cost (A) of \$80 each, and unit value (U) \$0.05,

$$EOQ = \sqrt{\frac{2 \times 80 \times 416{,}000}{.22 \times 0.05 \left(1 - \frac{416{,}000}{250 \times 3000}\right)}} = 116{,}565$$

INVENTORY MANAGEMENT UNDER UNCERTAINTY

Theory is fine, but reality does not always follow its guidelines. We do not usually know what the demands will be for our parts, how long reorder time will be, what breakdowns and delays will occur in transportation, and whether the handling will be affected by the fact the order comes through late on a Friday afternoon. There may be great variability in all these factors. We can adjust two parameters: order quantity and when the order is placed. Since the initial impact comes from the demand, the order timing is more important. Order quantity determines the frequency with which we expose ourselves to potential stock-out conditions as well as the average items in inventory, but it is the point (in terms of units left on hand) at which we place our order that will determine our ability to fulfill demands. Herein lies the need for understanding distributions, means, and variance.

The Geneseo Electro-Optical Company (GEO) sells inspection, test, and control devices. One of the most popular items is the OptoLecBIT for inspection of jet and turbine engines. To determine demand the president tabulates orders for OptoLecBITs (OLBITS) over the past year. He notices a seasonal trend reaches a peak in February just after the new year's budgets are approved. He also notices minor patterns based on days of the week and end of the month but decides to disregard these in figuring demand for the last year, consisting of 250 operating days.

Mean $\overline{X} = \dfrac{\Sigma c}{N} = \dfrac{144}{20} = 7.2$ days

Standard deviation $\sigma = \sqrt{\dfrac{\Sigma(\bar{x} - x)^2}{N}} = \sqrt{\dfrac{\Sigma D^2 N}{N}}$

$= \sqrt{\dfrac{99.20}{20}} = \sqrt{4.96} = 2.23$

Note that Σc = sum of delivery days required. N = number of deliveries. We can now see that the range of deliveries is between five and 15 days with a mean of 7.2 days and standard deviation of 2.23 days.

For simple management information, the arrival times of deliveries are plotted in Figure 15.4. Each time a delivery is received, it can be added to the chart so the information is continually updated. It could help also to have the charts prepared for each supplier, factory, distribution center, or other useful control group. Any information in this graphical form makes it easy for management to recognize trends and potential problems, motivates the organizations involved to do better since they are on display, and assures the continual attention necessary to assure adequate arrival times.

It may be desirable to differentiate current from past information so that more attention is given to the most recent. Mathematical techniques such as exponential smoothing and moving averages may be used to weight new data more heavily; however, it should be understood that

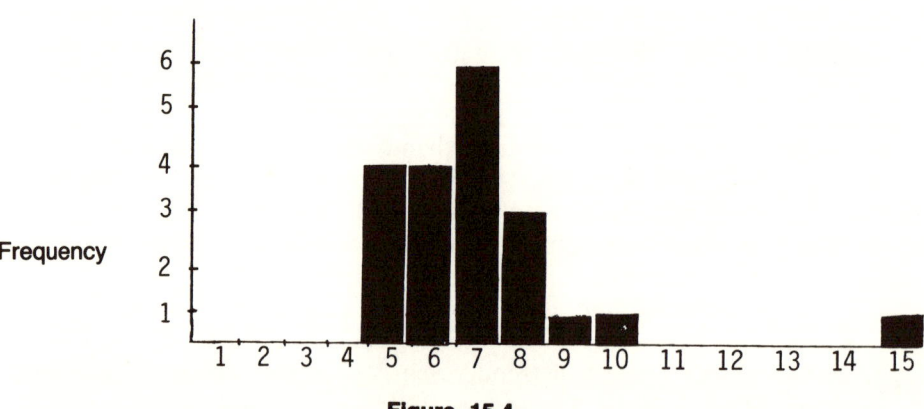

**Figure 15.4
Resupply histogram**

management may desire both averaging, which shows long-term trends with less emphasis on current data; and a system that shows significant changes in the information, such as would be shown by a geometric moving average (exponential smoothing).

Since reorder quantity is set at 30 units due to the capacity of delivery trucks, the question is how often (in terms of the remaining SKUs) we should place a reorder.

The probability of demands can be read off the frequency chart in Table 15.6. GEO management has established a goal to fill 90 percent of the orders from stock on hand. Looking at the demand table, we see that this requires four available OLBITS at any time, which would give a cumulative frequency of 91.6 percent. What are the chances of encountering various levels of usage during the order cycle? The rules of probability give us a basis for computing the chance. For example, what is the chance of having a demand for four units every day during the seven-day average order cycle? The extremely small probability of about five per 100 million is only part of the situation, since we are interested in the cumulative probability of more demand than supply.

From our earlier work, we can see that the average demand was 2.33 units per day over the last year (583). Each delivery gives enough glass for 30 units. But a 3.0 percent breakage rate brings that 30 down to 29.1 finished units. That means we should reorder every 12.5 days (29.1). If our average delivery time, which is also the median or typical delivery time, is seven days, the first order should be placed five days after the arrival of the last order, which is seven days before we expect to need the units.

The question we must now ask is, "What is the probability of stocking-out before the new units arrive?" If demand should suddenly increase during the time prior to placing the order, the order could be placed immediately. However, once that time has elapsed, it could be made up only at the cost of very high expediting expenses. If demand

Table 15.6
Resupply Data

Days (a)	Number of Deliveries (N) (b)	Cumulative Delivery Days (c)	Deviation per Delivery (D) ($\Sigma c/\Sigma b$) − (a)	D^2	D^2N
5	4	20	2.2	4.84	19.36
6	4	24	1.2	1.44	5.76
7	6	42	0.2	0.04	0.24
8	3	24	0.8	0.64	1.92
9	1	9	1.8	3.24	3.24
10	1	10	2.8	7.84	7.84
15	1	15	7.8	60.84	60.84
	20	144			99.20

is known to be certainly predictable, then we can see from Table 15.6 that ten days' delivery time will account for about 95 percent of the situations (19 of 20). Therefore, if we want a 95 percent service level, we must order ten days in advance of expected need, which is at a reorder point of 23 units (demand of 2.3 per day times 10 days). It can thus be seen that an additional stock of seven units (23 minus 16) is necessary to provide the difference between a 50 percent and a 90 percent service level if demand is constant.

Let us assume the worst possible happens. We place our order at the conservative point of 23 units and have a ten-day delivery time, but we want to know the probability of hitting the high point in our demand cycle that would exceed the available 23 units and result in customer dissatisfaction. This can be visualized by looking at the cumulative distributions of demand and lead time taken from Tables 15.5 and 15.6 and plotted in Figure 15.5.

We can simply take the probabilities for demand and lead time, multiply them by each other, and get the probability of that combination and sum all worse cases. Another approach is to look at tables of cumulative Poisson probabilities using the mean (μ) of 2.3 and we can see that the 1.00 probability level is encountered when X is above eight units.

MONTE CARLO ANALYSIS

The inventory flow process may be simulated by a Monte Carlo analysis of inventory flow over time. The simulated flow will probably not exactly parallel the real-world process that it models, but the results are very useful for checking expected values. Let us assume that we have a reorder level of 23 SKUs and that EOQ equals 29. We start the simulation process with a fresh order of 29 OLBITS on hand. To determine the initial demand, we choose a value at random from the demand distribution. This value is subtracted from inventory, resulting in a new stock level for the end of the period. If the new stock level has reached the order point, an order is placed. If not, no action is required. We then proceed to period two with a new random demand and determine its effect on inventory. When the reorder point is reached and a new order placed, a random value is selected from the lead-time distribution. In following calculations, the lead time decreases by one for each period so that it reaches zero and we then assume a new stock of 29 units has arrived and is added to inventory. It is possible for demand during this time to exceed the items on hand, at which time we are in

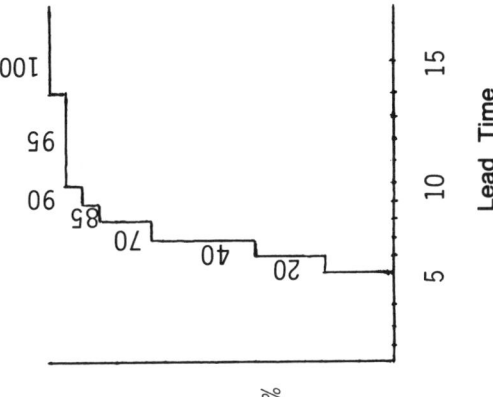
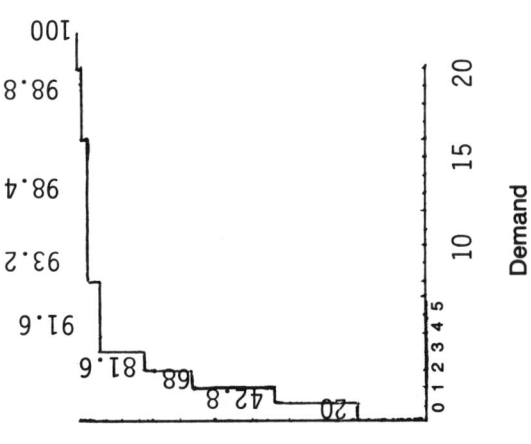

Figure 15.5
Cumulative distributions of demand and lead time

a negative, back-order situation. Table 15.7 shows a basic simulation.

If the information value is worth the time and effort, and a computer is not available, then two containers, one for demand and one for lead time, could contain slips of paper or any numbered items in the same proportion as the distribution. Then, at each period, demand would be determined by drawing a slip of paper from the container at random and using that value for that period's demand. The slip of paper would be returned to the container. The same would occur for lead times when reorder is necessary.

VALUE OF INFORMATION

A question that must be asked at this point is, "What is the expected value of this information?" We spend time and money to do accurate calculations that can be upset by the whims of nature. If we are preparing inventory for a Polaris submarine that is vital to our nation's defense and operates on critical schedules, then the information is worth precise calculations. If we are worried about OLBITS, an approximation is sufficient. If we had not been so lucky in the tenth period (good inventory management!), what would have been the consequence of stocking-out? Management must determine what the costs are of not having the item in stock. If it is an OLBIT, especially when the order is large, chances are that lead time will be sufficient to allow the order to arrive or other arrangements to be made.

Table 15.7
Stock Supply versus Demand Simulation

Period	Initial Stock	Demand*	Inventory End Period	Lead Time
1	29	0	29	—
2	29	5	24	—
3	24	1	23 (reorder)	7*
4	23	2	21	6
5	21	4	17	5
6	17	0	17	4
7	17	1	16	3
8	16	1	15	2
9	15	15	0	1
10	0	1	28 (29 # 1)	0
11	28	2	26	—
12	26	2	24	—
13	24	3	21 (reorder)	9*
etc.				

*Random selection from distribution.

CONTINGENCY PROCEDURES

A possible stock-out condition should be anticipated, and in fact expected, if we are operating an efficient inventory system with relatively high holding costs. The necessary inventory can be replaced through transhipping from other distribution sources, buying from a similar distributor, expediting handling and transportation of an order already on its way, or even rapid start-up of a production line. Every inventory control organization should have plans prepared in advance to answer, "What if?" Problems of location strategy and production/acquisition are additional issues, but the point here is that plans must be in place for determining the source or sources with priorities from which replacement parts should be expedited, the need for expediting (which is normally based on essentiality), and how available stocks are allocated if all locations are in short supply. Remember that time and place utility require that the part be available. It does no good to have an item in Washington, D.C., when you need it in Spokane! But it may make sense to consolidate quantities of parts in a few sources so that all needs may be filled in a short time rather than an erratic practice that fills some needs immediately but takes a long time for others.

SAFETY STOCKS

One answer to the need for spares when the inventory is in back-order status is safety stock, preferably held at a central location where it can be expeditiously handled as necessary. It must be remembered that safety stocks cost as much money as any other inventory since they are not being turned over. There may be reasons, such as disaster backup, that call for safety (insurance) stocks, but there also may be reasons, such as short shelf life or obsolescence, that items should not be held in large quantities. Safety stocks are normally accomplished by setting the reorder point high enough to establish a greater probability of providing the item from inventory. Such was the case in our GEO example where we shifted from the inventory level of 15 to 23. A more acceptable alternative is to project replacement orders more accurately and arrange for alternate means of acquiring back-ordered items. The need for expediting will be influenced by the demand for the item, alternate sources, penalty in lost revenue, or ill will if not supplied, and the cost of providing expedited services as opposed to normal. Any time the cost of an expedited shipment is less than the expected loss, the order should be expedited.

In organizations with multiple inventory locations, it may be possible to obtain required items from another location's "excess stock." Excess is defined in several ways, but usually represents items in excess of what should be required before the next order arrives. A well-controlled inventory program will not have excess items. However, it is possible that demand could turn out to be less than expected, and, therefore, inventory may be available in excess of actual needs. An organization must be careful to do no more transferring of inventory than is absolutely necessary. Juggling inventory causes high handling and transportation costs, money that could be better spent on direct shipment. The alternatives should be compared with the economics of delaying shipment until the product becomes available from the main source.

ALLOCATION OF NEEDED SUPPLIES

When sufficient quantities are not available, operations research techniques show that the available supply should be uniformly spread over requesting locations so all achieve the same level in terms of time demand. This is not always practical however. There are priority customers. Some customers will insist on full orders with no partials allowed, or special influences may affect the demand. It is also necessary to note that some individuals are greedy and others are team players, so that some overseeing authority is usually necessary to set the policy for multilocation inventories.

P AND *Q* MODELS

We have determined that there are 3 basic forms of inventory models, which we will call *Q* for fixed quantity, *P* for fixed order *p*oint, and *T* for fixed *t*ime. Solving the models requires that two of the three elements, order point (*P*), order quantity (*Q*), or order time interval (*T*) must be fixed to solve for the third. The *Q* model uses fixed order point and quantity with variable time interval. The *P* model fixes the order point and varies the time interval or quantity. A form of variable interval model is now being utilized to review stocks frequently but actually order only when a reorder point is encountered. Most popular inventory control models incorporate features of both the *Q* and *P* models, such as the "optional replenishment model," which uses a fixed order point with a fixed order interval system. This min-max model is useful because the fixed order point (minimum value) may be determined by subtracting a quantity from the maximum value that represents an efficient purchasing quantity. This was shown in our GEO company example where a truckload of glass for 30 OLBITS was most efficient.

Inventory Management

This method allows orders to be efficiently placed and reduces procurement cost, but if stock-out costs are significant, the optional replenishment model may have to have the minimum quantity increased to guard against a stock-out. The true test of any inventory model is whether it can provide the needed level of service at an acceptably low cost.

INVENTORY AUDITS AND RECORDS

The information from any inventory management system is only as good as the facts behind it. As the computer people like to say, "Garbage in gives gospel out." The most important criterion for any inventory system is that it provide the necessary information so that it can be easily understood and benefit the organization. The records may be a small black book in the worker's pocket, or a massive computer file.

Most people do not like to keep records. They must be motivated through an understanding of how the record keeping will help them. Particularly in product service, accurate record keeping is vital if parts are to be available when they are needed so that logistics downtime can be avoided. Someone must be placed in position of responsibility with authority over inventory.

Quantities and locations should be rapidly available. Computer systems make this knowledge immediately accessible (Figure 15.6).

This form of perpetual record will identify at a glance whether an item is available, when new ones were ordered, and where items are going. The same form serves for adding items to inventory, since orders received or excess parts returned can be added to the running record. This system should be audited by management frequently and at surprise intervals to ensure that records are being accurately maintained and to stimulate correction action if they are not.

Many companies, whether or not required to by law, conduct an annual inventory to assure record accuracy, count physical items for valuation, and adjust records as necessary. However, regular cycle counting is preferable and avoids ever closing a stock facility. Inventory, like many other items, receives as little attention as necessary and is improved only when special attention is focused on it.

STOCK RECORDS

With the advent of decreasing costs for automated data processing, many firms are using interactive computer systems that tie customer order entry to credit, billing, and inventory control. When a customer calls, the firm can immediately check, usually via a VDT terminal, to

```
PART ID: 770001    DESC: BEARING    ,ROLLER 7MM STAINLESS STEEL
SELECT BY: ORGANIZATION(O)/STOREROOM(S)/EMPLOYEE ID(E)/ALL(A): A
CODE/ID: ALL        NAME: ALL

                                   ON    ON     ON      IN    BACK
CODE/ID  NAME                      HAND  ORDER  RESERVE REPAIR ORDER  EXCESS
TOTAL                              26    144    8
B112     MAIN STOREROOM            8     72
FENG     FIELD ENGINEERING         4            4
N448     NORTH STOREROOM           4     36     2
S158     SOUTH STOREROOM           4     36     2
79871    JAMISON                   2
81811    SAMPSON                   2
92785    LEMBO                     2
```

Figure 15.6
Part availability Display

assure that the desired items are in inventory. If the customer desires that item and has good credit, the simple push of a button can prepare all information and papers necessary to debit inventory, reorder if necessary, prepare shipping invoices, and bill the customer. The important function is that every change in inventory status must be recorded and the quantity actually on the shelf must agree with the quantity listed on the stock record. Analysis of activity provides an ongoing evaluation of how well parts needs are being met (Figure 15.7).

It should be noted that there is a definite cost for adding any item to inventory. Surveys find different organizations using costs ranging from $250 to $5000. The majority are $2500 ± $500. Any organization should establish the cost accurately to guide the level of spares, modularity, and other inventory decisions.

The cost of a single purchase order is placed at a minimum of $30; Ford Motor Company found its average was $575!

Organizations providing product support usually have inventories carried by their technical representatives. The normal report completed after every service call indicates by number what parts were used and whether the tech rep wants them replaced. If so, the orders for parts used are usually consolidated weekly and automatically shipped to a convenient location. The level of spares kept by any individual is greatly affected by the confidence one has in getting simple, rapid resupply. Other factors, such as the amount of space available to store spares, influence the quantity held. When technical representatives were shifted from large cars to compacts as an economy move, economies also resulted in inventory because there was less room for spare parts.

Each supply or spare part must have a configuration identification so that it can be accurately and easily noted on inventory records. This could be a part number, which is easily copied, or a pick tag which can be pulled off and tabulated separately. Such systems are encountered in retail stores. In many places the receipt is tabulated for reorder purposes. In others a tag is pulled off every item purchased and is deposited for later record keeping. The latest development is the Universal Product Code, which is being used to automate checkout systems in supermarkets. You have probably seen the rectangular array of bars and numbers on food packages. At the check-out counter, a laser beam scans the symbol and sends information to a computer, which looks up the price, produces a receipt, and updates inventory. Point-of-sale equipment is not cheap. A system with a computer and eight checkout stands costs about $100,000 and stores estimate it will take two to four years to get back the investment. Only a store that takes in at least $2 million a year can justify the expense of even a smaller system, but 18,000 food stores in the United States do that much business. Savings are estimated at 1 to 1.5 percent of sales for a total of about $200 million to $300 million a year. A point-of-sale system for a department store with 80 terminals

```
STOREROOM OR ALL: ALL          NAME: ALL
DATE FROM: 3/01/86    TO:  3/31/86

          DEMAND ACCOMMODATION %      :              84

          DEMAND SATISFACTION %       :              93

          TOTAL TRANSACTIONS          :            1300

          TOTAL PART VOLUME           :            2600

CURRENT DATA AS OF  3/31/86
          TOTAL STOCK LIST LINES      :            4000
          % STOCK LIST ZERO BALANCE:                 10
          TOTAL NON-STOCK LIST LINE:               1000
          AVERAGE STOCK PER LINE      :              17
          EXTENDED VALUE ON HAND      :$      3,500,000
          % OF EXCESS LINES           :              15
          EXCESS VALUE                :$        750,000
```

**Figure 15.7
Stock performance report**

and an in-store computer will cost about $400,000. When the cash register rings up a sale of four pairs of size 9 men's socks, the computer immediately adjusts inventory records. For the first time retail store managers have the information to accurately manage the business.

PARTS FOR SUPPORTING NEW PRODUCTS

Unique situations are encountered when products are being developed, tested, and initially tried in the field. There are three basic problems to be solved: (1) quantity of spare parts, (2) location of spare parts, and (3) cost of spare parts. These three problems are interrelated. The approach is to solve the location and quantity simultaneously and then determine total costs. Getting accurate values is one of the most difficult parts of the process. Through work with product design and development engineers, the logistician should be able to obtain information for each necessary spare part.

MONEY CONSTRAINTS

Money is always a constraint. The probability always exists that not enough money will be available for everything we want. Cash flow may dictate that fewer dollars should be spent early even though it is expected to cost more later. To be prepared for operating budget analysis, the print-out of parts can be arranged for ease of evaluation. After computations are performed for location and quantity of parts, the total cost of those initial parts should be computed, then the total expected usage and cost for the service period set down. Parts should then be grouped by essentiality levels and arranged by increasing part cost within each level. This gives a display of parts in order of descending relative value. It is then a simple matter to go down the list, starting with most essential parts, and cut off where the budget dictates.

It should be noted that budgets are often arbitrary; the logistician should then compute the effectiveness with the limited funds and present the cases to management for approval or possibly additional funding for additional spares. Another approach is marginal analysis, sometimes called incremental analysis, which is a tool commonly employed by economists to measure the value of additional units of goods or services in economic terms. It will tell us whether the extra cost gives us extra benefit. Assuming we have good information on the demand for spares, we can compute the additional assurance against stock-out provided by increasing each additional part. For example, if zero spares gives a 50 percent assurance against stock-out, adding one spare increases the assurance by 30 percent, the second spare by 16 percent, and so forth. We divide the increase in probability gained by stocking a spare by the cost of that spare; the resulting number gives us a relative value measure. The largest relative value number gives the greatest increase in probability per dollar cost and is the best choice. Relative value provides a quantitative measure for helping decide where money should be invested.

ESTABLISHING INITIAL DEMAND

Forecasting parts requirements is difficult, and it is important to understand the cooperation that must take place between the spares specialist and the maintainability and maintenance designers, manufacturing engineers, and equipment designers. Many products will have initial parts usage determined by field engineering or a field spares organization and then turn the responsibility over to a continuing distribution function after six months or so.

The determination of spare parts normally involves the following steps:

1. Equipment review.
2. Preprovisioning analysis.
3. Provisioning conference.
4. Postprovisioning analysis.
5. Follow-up and feedback.

Equipment review is vital so that logisticians understand the system that must be supported. Study of a system specification, review of contractual requirements, facility visits, design evaluation, reliability analysis, and review of maintenance data from early testing are all important. As the most sensitive factor is the usage rate, the provisioning specialist must carefully evaluate all information dealing with reliability and usage of proposed systems, as well as comparable ones already in the field. Confidence must be established between the engineers providing reliability information and the provisioning specialists who are going to use it.

During preprovisioning analysis, initial ideas are screened to define the problem. The first screening, based on unit cost and failure rate compared with the break-even curve, should decide whether an item should be thrown away or repaired. The Navy Economic Level of Repair Screening Model considers 11 factors.

1. Spares inventory.
2. Packaging and transportation.
3. Item cost and retention.
4. Support equipment.
5. Support equipment space requirements.
6. Repair workspace.
7. Inventory storage space.
8. Repair material.
9. Labor.
10. Training.
11. Documentation.

If a part should be repaired, then level-of-repair analysis should be performed to determine whether it should be by a technical representative or by higher authority. Computer programs are available to determine the minimum life-cycle cost repair policy for a hardware system, considering repair action in the user site, at regional bases, or at a central depot.

After the analysis is prepared, the provisioning specialist should present recommendations to the provisioning team for review. The analysis will have determined sensitivities and probably identified alternatives, such as deratings or possible standardizations, and items for special improvement attention. Initial information will be prepared on logistics downtime, not operationally ready-supplies (NORS), service level, and cost of sparing.

When the provisioning conference is concluded and agreement reached on provisioning parts breakdown, maintenance coding, removal rates, and so forth, additional optimization should be attempted through the use of computerized models. Total system evaluation should be performed for level of repair, evaluation of optimum spares, evaluation of the inventory list, support simulation, and total system performance against specifications.

Probably the most important aspect of this procedure is the task of follow-up and feedback. A new product will analyze dynamic change as equipment is refined, modifications incorporated, more information obtained on usage rates, and vendor quality problems identified. All these must be incorporated into analytical revisions. Many sources of information, including test laboratories, field sites, and failure modes and effects analysis (FMEA), will provide information that will effect the spares provisioning. Special attention is necessary during the introductory periods to ensure that adequate spares are available. This is particularly important because of increased customer and market sensitivity during introductory periods.

Allowance should be made for local adjustments to inventory. The headquarters planner certainly cannot expect to be infallible. The people in the field have more direct exposure and are in many ways more qualified to determine what spare parts they should carry. Usually they will try for more, and the headquarters planner will try to cut back. However, with education and understanding, a cooperative effort can be fostered and a balanced inventory achieved.

CHAPTER 16

Physical Distribution

*P*hysical distribution is defined by the AMA as: "The movement and handling of goods from the point of production to the point of consumption or use." Responsibilities found in physical distribution departments include:

Traffic and transportation	Material handling
Warehousing	Purchasing
Shipping and receiving	Exporting
Inventory control	Invoicing
Order processing	Packaging
Production planning and scheduling	Pricing
	Industrial engineering
Customer service	Personnel
Research and analysis	Accounting and financial control
Forecasting and planning	

MARKETING CONCEPT

The marketing concept is simply a planning philosophy that seeks to identify customer needs and direct the firm's resources to serve them at a profit. All systems of a company—engineering, production, marketing, finance, and logistics—must aim at this fundamental goal. Three statements form the foundation for the marketing concept:

1. Customer needs are more basic than products.
2. Products must be viewed in an end-user concept.
3. Volume is secondary to profit.

There is an old adage that "you can't sell what you can't provide, and there is no use providing what you can't sell." The potential market must be studied in depth to determine the customers' true needs and wants, and then products and services can be designed to meet them. The product may be equipment passing through the distribution system, or it may be a service of the system itself. There are four utilities a product must have: form, time, place, and possession. Production and engineering create the form, marketing creates the possession, and physical distribution creates time and place. This means providing the right thing in the right place at the right time. Profits result only if all four utilities are integrated and satisfy the customer.

Keep in mind that the marketing concept is a corporate orientation and not directly related to the performance of the marketing department. Physical distribution may be organized in any reporting fashion and still be guided by the marketing concept. It is, however, by direction that distribution is often organized under marketing, along with sales, service, advertising, and so forth. Physical distribution is also found in organizations all its own, in a logistics department, and in production; depending on its function and importance to the firm.

MARKETING MIX

Marketing mix is the term given to the parts of a firm's marketing plan. The major elements are shown in Figure 16.1.

The name "mix" comes from the fact that all items are blended into an integrated effort. The mix provides the customer with a total package of goods and services.

CHANNELS OF DISTRIBUTION

The distribution part of the marketing mix has two components—the physical movers and the transaction creators. Some large companies, particularly in the industrial durables segment, control all channels from production to end user. Most firms, however, use intermediaries to sell and move their goods or services. They are involved in both movement and legal exchange of title. Merchant middlemen are the wholesalers, retailers, distributors, jobbers, and drop shippers who buy and sell on their own initiative and deal with the risks of ownership.

Physical Distribution

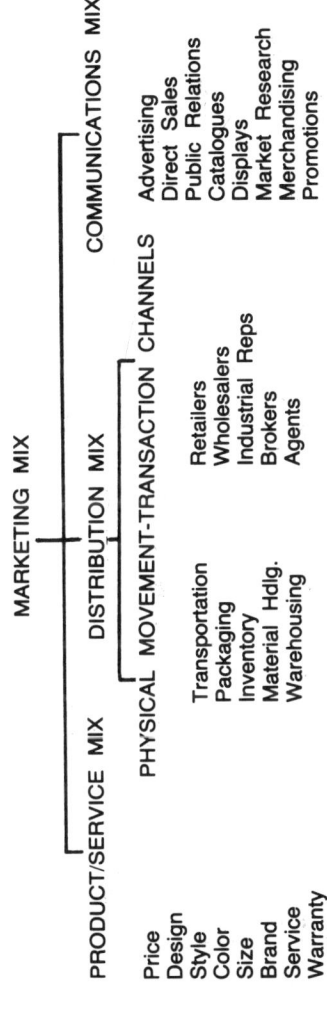

**Figure 16.1
Marketing mix**

The full-function wholesaler is typically an independent businessperson who buys goods in large quantities directly from the producers, and sells them to retailers, who will sell them to end users. Industrial goods differ from consumer goods in that they are typically durable items of strength and long life used in the production of further goods. Industrial distributors deal mostly with manufacturers, utilities, transportation firms, repair shops, and specific industry segments such as restaurants and beauty parlors.

Drop shippers are limited-function wholesalers who operate on speculation that goods they purchase in large quantities may be sold for a higher price in the future. Coal, wheat, soy beans, lumber, and construction materials are typical of materials bought and sold by the drop shipper, who often owns the goods but never actually takes delivery. Instead, the shipment goes directly from the supplier to the customer. A central purchasing function might, for example, order a large quantity of merchandise and have the items drop shipped in smaller amounts directly to the firm's retail stores.

Rack jobbers are important to supermarkets, news stands, and similar stores that sell nonperishable, but perhaps time-related, items. These salespeople drive to their accounts, check the rack contents, replenish sold items from their inventory, and bill the retailer for items sold. The salesperson assures that the racks are properly arranged and all items price-marked. The store owner has the items on consignment, so only space for the rack is provided and in return the store owner gets a commission for each item sold.

The division between wholesale and retail has become blurred, with many stores realizing that cash-and-carry can relieve them of high labor costs and need for delivery trucks and credit checks. Building supply stores now operate mainly this way, and more people venture to the public markets to take advantage of lower prices direct from the supplier.

There are functional intermediaries such as manufacturers' representatives, brokers, auctioneers, and sales agents who arrange buying and selling transactions but do not usually assume ownership. Their function is to find a buyer and a seller, and arrange an agreeable transaction. A manufacturers' representative usually handles lines of products from several suppliers that are related but not competitive. They usually have a specific territory and are paid commissions only for goods sold.

Figures 16.2 and 16.3 show the typical intermediaries in the channels of distribution.

ORDER AND INFORMATION SYSTEMS

The computer has revolutionized information processing in the modern distribution center. Companies with many warehouses often have

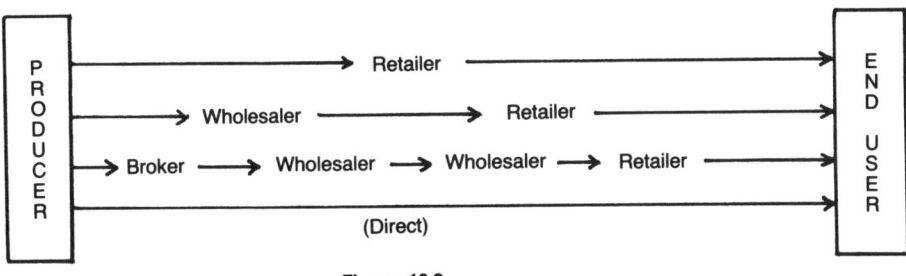

Figure 16.2
Channels of distribution for consumer goods

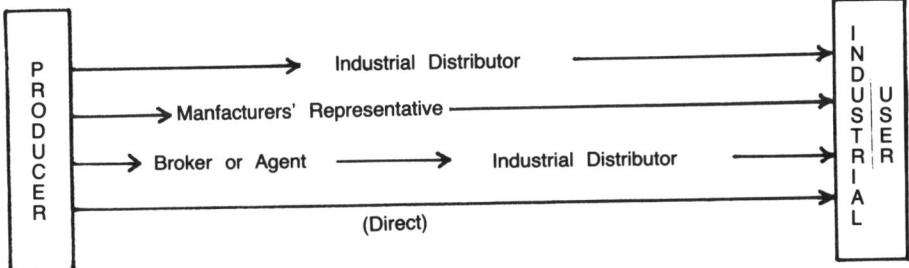

Figure 16.3
Channels of distribution for industrial goods

central data processing with terminals online to every inventory location, so orders can be quickly input, stock confirmed, shipping documents prepared, inventory debitted, and movement directed. Many systems have a loop for checking customer credit while on the phone to assure that financial affairs are in order, or else enable the customer order clerk to ask the customer for payment of past-due bills before the new order is shipped. The elements of the order-processing system are shown in Figure 16.4.

Emergency situations will inevitably arise in which the normal order and delivery system is not fast enough. Procedures should be established for such events to allow the special preparation of paperwork and picking of emergency parts for rapid shipment or pickup. A distribution system functions best on a planned basis with the work detailed at least a day in advance of the action, but there will always be a critical few who need an item fast. Strict accounting should be kept of those expensive actions, and controls established to keep the rate under 5 percent of the total. Since the costs of physical distribution are often 10–35 percent of sales, there will be considerable attention paid to cost control. After all, the leverage at a 20 percent level is such that reducing expenses $2 is at least equivalent to a sales increase of $10! The major planning inputs for PD are given in the following.

Inputs Required by Physical Distribution (PD) for Durable Goods

The development of practical and cost-effective distribution plans requires a continual dialogue between PD personnel and the technical and marketing organizations. Factors significantly affecting PD plans are as follows:

1. Physical characteristics of the product/accessories/spares/modifications/support equipment.
    a. a Physical size (dimensions, weight, etc.).
    b. Product modularity (subsystem physical breakdown).
    c. Transportation specifications (humidity, temperature, vibration, etc.).
    d. Storage specifications.
    e. Handling requirements.
    f. Packaging specifications.
    g. Dangerous article identification and special requirements.
2. *Physical characteristics of consumables.*
    a. Specifications for shelf life, temperature, humidity, etc.
    b. Special handling requirements or hazards.
3. *Demand levels forecast*
    a. Spares identification, documentation levels, manufacturing schedule, etc.
    b. Machine demand levels.
    c. Field start-up requirements.
    d. Training hardware requirements.
    e. Sales hardware requirements.
    f. Miscellaneous requirements (product consumable usage, service consumables, replacements for in-transit damage, etc.).

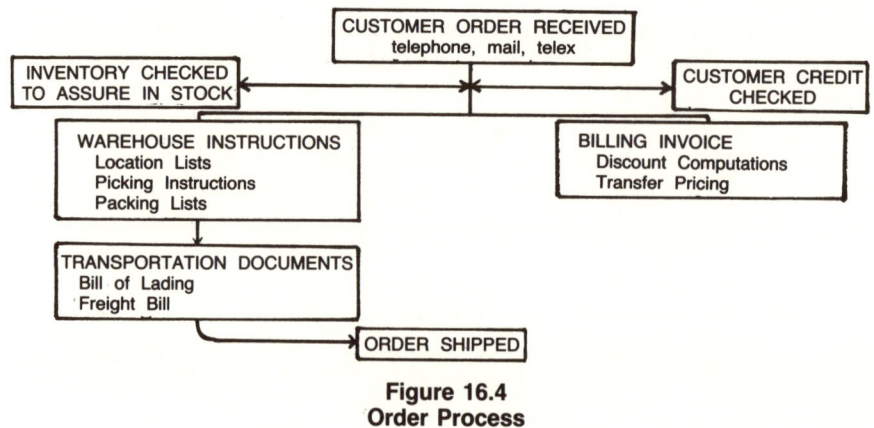

Figure 16.4
Order Process

4. *Installation/removal concept.*
    a. Approach (single person or team, Rigger, timing, etc.).
    b. Special handling techniques.
5. *Rehabilitation.*
    a. Defective product and parts repair/replace/scrap/return procedures.
    b. Minor refurbishing criteria and goals.
    c. Major rebuilding criteria and goals.
6. *Related business strategies.*
    a. Effect on other products.
    b. Price lists.
    c. Time schedules.

CHAPTER

17

Packaging, Handling, and Warehousing

Costs of packaging are currently above $25 billion annually for materials, equipment, and labor. Material-handling activities easily exceed $45 billion annually. These two areas, along with computer technology, represent the areas of logistics that have seen the greatest technological advances in recent years.

PACKAGING

Package design is a part of the product development process. Until recently packaging had been considered a minor element in the marketing mix for a product. The two traditional packaging concerns are protection and economy. The manufacturer wants packaging that will protect the product on its trip from the manufacturer to the customer, but at the same time, to keep packaging costs low, because packaging is often viewed as a straightforward cost without much marketing consequence. A third packaging objective which comes closer to considering the consumer is convenience. This means such things as offering size options and packages that are easy to open.

Over the years a fourth packaging objective has become increasingly recognized—its promotional function. It must attract attention, describe product features, give the consumer confidence, and make a favorable overall impression. Consumers are willing to spend a little more for convenience, appearance, dependability, and prestige. Packaging is an important vehicle for projecting these qualities, and is also an area where innovation can bring large sales gains. One need only think of pop-top beer cans, aerosol dispensers, boil-a-pack dinners, plastic animal bubble-bath containers, and L'eggs hosiery to appreciate this. Some companies base their whole advertising campaigns on the merits of their packaging rather than on the products it contains.

Developing a package for a new product should take into account inputs from packaging engineering, production, physical distribution, sales, traffic, purchasing, and installation service. The first step is to establish the packaging concept. This is a basic definition of what the package should be or do for the particular product. Should the package offer superior protection, introduce a novel selling message, provide a dispensing method, suggest certain qualities of the product or company, or something else? Once the concept is defined, many other decisions must be made on the component elements of the package design: size, shape, materials, color, text, and trademark.

The logistical system of packaging usually has individual unit packs that fit into master cartons, which in turn fit into containers. The master carton is the basic unit for material handling and provides major protection from damage. The weight, cube, and fragility of the master cartons determine the configuration of transportation and warehousing. The objective is to arrive at a configuration that is as standardized as possible, so as to facilitate materials handling, high-density packing, and efficient space utilization. The ideal carton is a perfect cube of equal width, length, and depth; but since this is not normally feasible, care should be taken to assure an assortment of cartons which are mutually compatible. This is shown in Figure 17.1.

PROTECTION

The master carton's major function is to protect the items inside from damage. The cost of achieving absolute protection is prohibitive, so a judgment must be made as to the value of the product, its fragility, and the cost of packing. Hazards are basically physical or elemental.

The most common causes of physical damage are vibration, impact, puncture, and compression, with combinations of all four experienced whenever packages are being handled or in transit. Shock damage can best be controlled by proper loading and securing. Typical methods of securing are strapping, tie-down, and use of various dunnage materials such as wood frames and air bags to prevent loads from shifting and to absorb shocks. The best way to prevent damage is to load the vehicle in a tight pattern to prevent shifting.

The packaging requirements also influence the logistics system. The shipping of electronic goods provides an example. The items are very fragile and of high value. Very expensive packaging would be required to protect the products. Instead electronic equipment is usually moved by specialized movers who use trucks with special shock-absorbing suspensions, special handling equipment, and training to avoid damage. Costs of transportation are higher, but costs of packaging are less and damage is reduced.

Temperature, humidity, and foreign materials such as solvents, gases, insects, and rodents can create environmental damage. Many items, such as photographic film, perishable food, and livestock, require refrigerated cars, secure containers, or conditions that must be specially designed to accommodate them.

There is considerable psychological implication in packaging. Packaging engineers sometimes feel that the more adequately protected packages become, the more careless freight handlers become. On the other hand, carriers feel that if they handle goods more carefully, packaging

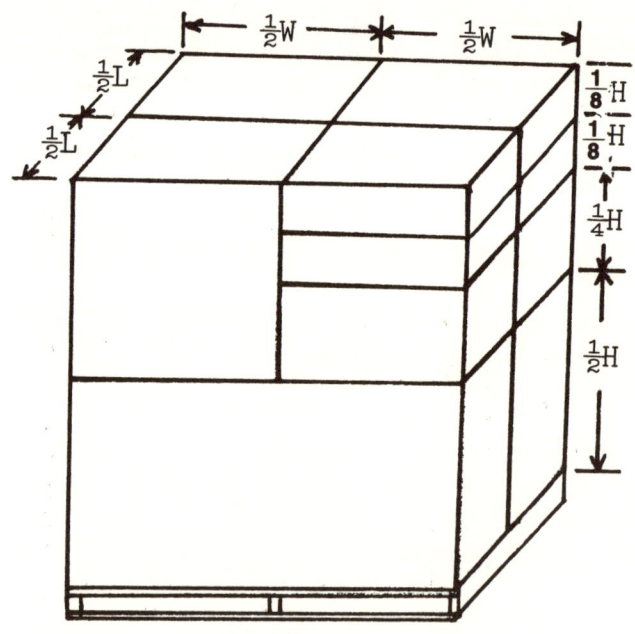

Figure 17.1
Compatible cartons

will be reduced and cheapened and there will be greater potential for damage. A novel response to this dilemma was seen in the case of overseas shipments of delicate office copiers being damaged even though they were in strong packaging. An innovative packaging engineer suggested substituting transparent polyethylene shrouds for all the wood and cardboard packaging, with the idea that handlers would be more careful if they could see what was in the package. The method has been very successful and is being used for most shipments. It has the added advantage of reducing theft since we can easily see if any component has been removed. There are also advantages for quality control.

One remaining problem is the disposal or reuse of spent packaging. The person who invents a self-destructing beer bottle will become rich. Expanded foams and plastics are a major problem since they are not biodegradable or combustible in normal waste-disposal facilities.

Containerization is becoming popular because of the savings possible with Contran. Long-distance shipments will often cost one third less shipped by Contran versus conventional methods. Modern airliners are designed to load quickly and easily with containers that fit the shape of the aircraft's freight compartment. These can be prepositioned while awaiting the plane's arrival, and later placed on the plane in one loading maneuver, utilizing mechanized handling equipment.

In summary then, good packaging design considers elements relevant to engineering, purchasing, production, storage, material handling and order picking, traffic and transportation, retailer/wholesaler, and the end user. Good packaging design should provide the best balance for optimal value.

MATERIAL HANDLING

Material handling differs in minor degrees depending upon whether it is supporting a distribution center of fast-moving goods, a production shop floor, or a slow-moving commodity. In all warehouses three main activities must be performed: receiving, processing, and shipping. There are variations in the degree to which automation is applied, so that warehouses may be grouped as either manual, mechanized, or automated. Labor is so expensive that manual material handling is uneconomical and any surviving operation must be looking at machines to replace humans to a large extent. Besides the economies of mechanization, humans could not achieve the production rates, high lifts, and accuracy required by modern distribution systems.

Combinations of the material-handling means are appropriate since each method has strengths and weaknesses. Guidelines for proper method selection should include:

1. Use standard equipment wherever possible.
2. Choose gravity in preference to power.
3. Work for continuous flow as opposed to batches.
4. Invest in equipment to speed movement.
5. Strive for high utilization rates.
6. Remember that efficiency depends on a high ratio of cargo weight to vehicle weight.
7. Keep it simple to operate and maintain.

AUTOMATION

Automation replaces human labor with automatic handling equipment, which is expensive, but uses less direct labor and works faster and more accurately. Besides the high capital investment, automatic equipment is complex and subject to the same problems of reliability and maintainability that befall any electromechanical system.

A typical automatic system consists of a series of racks containing coded slots where goods may temporarily reside. The racks may extend up to 200 feet vertically (although 50–75 foot racks are more common) and have long, narrow aisles in which the loading and picking equipment operates. The storage and retrieval equipment is a cross between a forklift truck and a stacker crane. It can operate at very high speeds to reach the programmed position and quickly withdraw the necessary amount of merchandise. The machine usually remains in one aisle and picks from both sides. Its directions come from a computer, either in the form of a punched card for each item wanted or direct electronic signals. There are discharge stations at the end of each row to transfer the picked items to the pack station. For maximum performance there will usually be separate transfer stations for goods in and goods out. The control logic may use any of several methods of allocating the incoming goods to a slot. It may always want the same sequence, or a special location considering bulk or weight. Control systems also accommodate FIFO or LIFO and configuration controls. An automated system must be utilized on high-turnover items. It is also effective where humans do not like to work, such as in a frozen-food warehouse.

PALLETS AND CONTAINERS

Pallets of wood, cardboard, metal, or plastic are the common method of organizing goods for handling. Pallet dimensions are standardized depending on their use, with the most common being 40 by 48, 32 by 40, and 32 by 36. Dimensions are in inches and the first number indicates the side where handling equipment such as a fork truck will enter the pallet. Four-way pallets are preferred but are not always practical. As a general rule, the larger pallets permit more economical material handling since more cubic feet or meters can be placed on each. However, many over-the-road trucks and trailers have interior widths of 90–92 inches, so it makes sense to use pallets that can fit two side by side. It is interesting that standard pallets do not fit particularly well without overhang of the load. A disposable pallet of cardboard can be made for about $1, but good hardwood costs $8–12, so is normally returned.

Master cartons can be stacked in many configurations on a pallet, with the arrangements classed as block, brick, row, or pinwheel in configuration. The stability of the load can be increased by interlocking the cartons, which is possible in all but the block arrangement. Usually the cartons are not secure enough themselves and so must have additional securing. If the load is many small boxes, an overpack of heavy cardboard or plastic shrink wrapping may be applied. Larger cartons may be strapped with steel or nylon bands, ropes, or corner posts.

Rigid containers are large wood or steel boxes into which many smaller items can be placed. The potential for increased productivity is obvious, since over half the cost of transportation is in dock handling, packaging, and claims for theft and damage. Several ships have been constructed and massive container terminals built with facilities for rapid transfer of containers. The projections in the late 1960s and early 1970s were for half the freight across the Atlantic to be in containers by 1975 and 90 percent by 1980. Those forecasts have not materialized and several large transportation firms have gone bankrupt.

The reasons that containers are used so little include:

1. Carriers resist change from current practices.
2. Domestic standards are lacking.
3. Coordination does not exist.
4. There is little leadership.

Carriers presently are not convinced that the investment in specialized containers and facilities is warranted. Rate reductions are not commensurate with those anticipated, and empty containers are hard to handle if volume is low. Development of containers themselves has not filled the need. There are few standards and no one wants to invest in a type or size that later might be unacceptable. The U.S. Postal Service evidences this problem in the different containers developed by each region independently; these are not mutually usable and must be returned by air empty from New York to Los Angeles, as one example. Container transportation has great potential but cannot be realized until leadership surfaces to show the way.

WAREHOUSE FUNCTIONS

Warehouse functions differ depending on the activity supported, but are common in the major functions of material handling and storage. The typical logistics warehouse mainly breaks down bulk shipments and regroups the items for shipment to production or outside customers. The five basic functions are receiving, transfer, storage, assembly, and shipping.

Receiving usually consists of manually unloading the trucks or rail cars that deliver the shipments, and inventorying the contents to assure control and accountability for any damage or missing items. The goods are then moved to a designated slot for storage until they are required. When they are needed to fill an order, they are moved in proper amount to the assembly area for packing and shipping. Control systems determine the movements and check to ensure the exact items are moving, and proper papers are prepared for receipts, invoices, bills of lading, and customer billing. The control system should also debit inventory when the order is initially approved and trigger reordering for inventory when necessary.

Storage in a warehouse will usually be temporary, but may be long term in some cases including:

1. Seasonal production of foods such as apples and shrimp.
2. Fluctuating demands that require safety stocks.
3. Speculation such as grain or fertilizer.
4. Conditioning if ripening or curing is required for foods.
5. Discount purchasing for economies of scale.

TYPES OF WAREHOUSES

Four arrangements for warehouses are possible: privately owned, privately leased, public, and combinations of these. The decision as to whether a private warehouse should be owned or leased is one of financial planning. Storage facilities are usually more easily found than are facilities suitable for fast-flowing distribution, so a special-purpose facility may need to be built just to serve the desired purpose. This is particularly true if special storage and movement conditions are required in response to temperature, humidity, flammability, large sizes, or other conditions not commonly found in mass distribution. The costs of a private warehouse will normally be lower than a public warehouse, because the operation of a private warehouse is designed to fit the specific needs of the owning firm and its products. This level of efficiency requires utilization rates of at least 75 percent.

Warehouses may also provide a combination facility to house marketing or purchasing staff in addition to distribution people. It is common, too, in firms handling small durable goods, such as office equipment, to locate a refurbishing center in the warehouse. Equipment demanding minor cleaning and repairs can be fixed on location and shipped out rapidly to the next paying customer.

Operated by individuals or companies, public warehouses provide the facilities and services of complete warehousing to anyone willing to pay for them. Public warehouses have been very progressive in developing facilities and services that can be made quickly available to users without the high capital costs or long planning cycles needed for a private facility. Naturally the variable costs of using public warehouses are higher than with private, since the prices are set to recoup capital investment costs and fluctuating utilization. Charges are usually derived on the basis of weight or number of cartons handled.

The decision as to whether to use private or public warehousing is similar to the make-or-buy decision in production. Since distribution is a vital link in the marketing channels, companies are reluctant to turn over all responsibility to outside organizations. The potential for customer relations problems, slow or erratic service, slow reaction times, and lack of firm control are often cited as reasons for not using public warehouses. On the other hand, they can be a valuable supplement to a private system and handle peak loadings, or low volumes in remote, but profitable markets. The tax situation may have an influence, since some localities do not tax goods in public warehouses, but do tax goods in private facilities. Tax considerations can have greater impact than the potential transportation or storage savings, which is one reason for "free port" popularity where goods can be stored free of customs or local taxes. The same type of inducement is being provided by many states and local governments to attract industry and distribution centers that will employ local people.

Public warehouses have advantages in the complete line assortments they can handle and their ability to break-bulk and provide in-transit mixing at efficient rates. They often provide local delivery service that can be shared by any firm using their facilities. Orders for several customers in the area can be shipped in truckload quantities to the warehouse, which will break the bulk down into individual orders and deliver them, perhaps with orders from other manufacturers going to the same customers. In-transit mixing, as shown in Figure 17.2, allows a company to ship products from several different production plants or procurement sources to a public warehouse for separation into customer orders and shipment. Special tariffs have been developed that reduce transportation costs since the shipments are treated as though they were going from producer to user, with minimal handling charges.

PLANNING A WAREHOUSE

The initial step in planning a warehouse is to decide on location, first taking into account the region of the country, then community, and finally specific sites. This necessitates establishment of objectives and detailed goals for the facility and basic determination of size and location requirements. Considerations should include access to rail, road, or air transportation; utilities for light, heat, cooling, and production movement; proximity to customers; room for expansion; taxes; insurance rates; acquisition costs, and material-handling systems. Too often a building is under construction before the interior is planned, and effective integration becomes impossible without major alterations. New floors torn out and redone to accommodate drag lines or guide wires, or walls demolished to permit entry of large equipment, are the result, expensive in both time and money, of poor planning. In good logistics planning, both the building and the functions to be carried out in and around it are considered together, and not as separate entities.

Policies of the company and its management must be carefully reviewed to ensure compatibility and complete coverage of the specifications. Recently a materials-handling group decided on conveyor systems

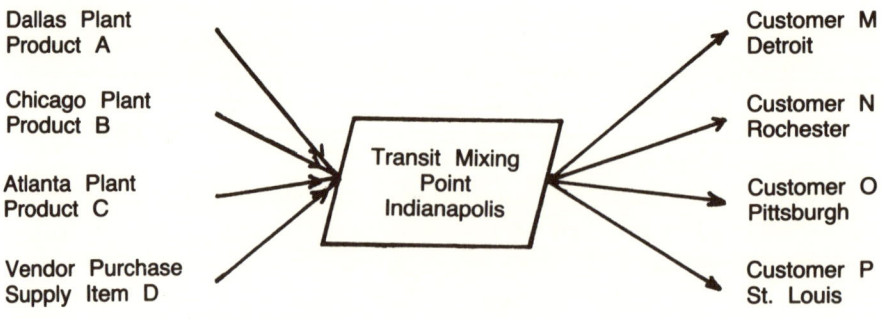

**Figure 17.2
In-transit mixing**

for an entire warehouse, unaware that transportation management had decided to convert to unitized pallets. The extensive conveyor system was installed to handle large, single items but could not handle the complete pallets that soon began to arrive. Special temporary arrangements had to be made for shipping nonpallet loads while the conveyor system was removed and pallet-handling equipment installed.

Layout depends on the material-handling system. If pallets are to be used, the first step is to determine the sizes to be stored, using standard sizes whenever possible. The second step involves positioning the pallets at either 90 degrees (square to the aisle) or at an angle of 10–40 degrees. The square method was used in early warehouses simply because it was easy to lay out and looked neat. The angle method, which most commonly uses 26½-degree placement, is more efficient and aisle width can be reduced since a fork truck can position a pallet without having to make a precise 90-degree turn with a long load. The space lost by angling is offset by the decreased aisle width. The positions are shown in Figure 17.3.

Once the equipment is selected, the material flow can be determined. If possible, the receiving areas should be separated from the shipping docks so materials flow smoothly from receiving into storage, and then are smoothly assembled for shipping without crossing paths. A typical warehouse layout is shown in Figure 17.4. There are many variations, and design firms specialize in the architectural design and engineering of warehouses with complete "turnkey" operations possible to assure total integration and practical efficiency.

Space requirements start with forecasts of sales volumes and utilization expected over the next five plus years. Given the tonnage, number of pallets, truckloads, product lines, and other applicable quantitative facts, the planners can make detailed projections of space required. Variations such as seasonal influences should be considered to assure high utilization, and additional space on the order of 10 percent allowed

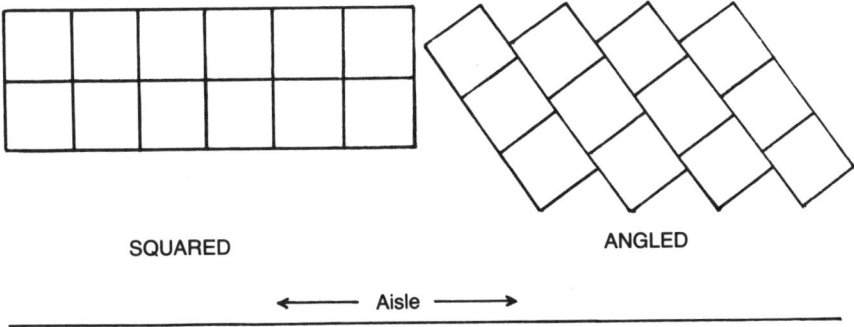

**Figure 17.3
Pallet placement**

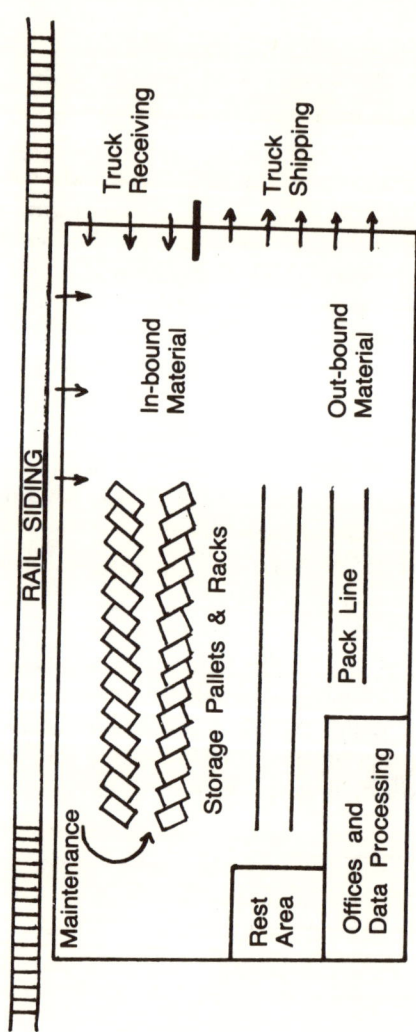

**Figure 17.4
Typical warehouse layout**

to accommodate increased volumes and contingency uses. The basic inventory can be numerically converted into pallet loads to determine floor and rack space requirements. Large, slow-turnover items will usually be kept in the main storage area until they are required for shipping, but fast-turnover items may be put in a special pick area closer to the pack line. Areas for vehicle maintenance and battery charging, offices, eating, smoking break areas, toilets, and data processing equipment are also necessary. Special considerations must be given to safety items and fire walls. Placement of equipment in relation to these items can have a great effect on capacity and efficiency. A modern warehouse does not, in fact, have much space to spare if it is being efficiently managed.

WAREHOUSE OPERATIONS

Operations entail personnel, work procedures, merchandise, control and information systems, and delivery means. Technical systems and machines are part of the modern warehouse. However, the most important element of the system is people.

Warehousing, even when automated, is a people business. People make the decisions and guide the machines that do the heavy work. It is not possible to have enough supervision to make up for incompetent or dishonest personnel. How can we prepare for effective operations? First a job description is required for each position. Each candidate must be investigated for honesty and reliability. References provided by the prospective employee will probably be positive, so other sources such as the most recent past employer should be checked. The telephone company is the best single credit check, since it usually comes last on the list of bills to be paid. While law now requires that employment tests relate directly to job performance and not be prejudiced against any group of people, it is still possible to use such tests to determine basic skills. A physical exam is vital since employees may be called on to do hard physical work that emphasizes lifting, accurate eyesight, and good hearing. Even though a person should only be hired after successfully passing through a series of checks, there should still be a period of 30–90 days' probation to evaluate progress and make a final decision to keep or terminate. Once an employee is hired, he or she must receive indoctrination as to:

1. Company history, objectives, and goals.
2. Products and services offered.
3. Customer requirements.
4. Work and safety rules.

5. Personnel policies on pay, sickness, vacation, etc.
6. Specific job training.

The immediate supervisor is the key to developing a new employee. Leadership is important, so first-line supervision must be emphasized in the selection and development of personnel because these supervisors influence the operating people who service the customer and produce profits or losses. Individual incentives are difficult to arrange in warehousing, but team plans are possible. While the wages must be fair and not become a point of contention, money is not as strong a motivator as are awards and public praise. Employee suggestions are valuable both to improve operations and to stimulate employee interest in the job. The best security systems can be outwitted by dishonest employees. However it is done, it is important to encourage honesty, as this is the only really effective way to prevent stealing. With dedicated people who have pride in their jobs, a warehouse system can work at its best.

Safety must be of paramount concern to all supervisors and employees. Insurance inspectors can assist in establishing safety stations, proper markings, and safe procedures; but day-to-day operations and enforcement of hard-hat, no-smoking, and look-before-moving practices keeps an operation safe.

The same attitudes work across the board—keeping products in as good a condition as they were when they arrived, assuring every outgoing item is billed, and matching packing materials with packing lists. Measurement standards can be established for those items as well as productivity in terms of weights or cartons per man-hour. No standard such as absolute work factors or cost per man-hour applies to every warehouse, since each is different regarding physical layout and items handled; but standards can be set within a warehouse on the basis of past experience and targets, and compared with similar warehouses. People in the business are usually pleased to compare figures and offer suggestions. Ideas are plentiful, but successful implementation determines loss or profit.

Fixed and variable costs should be determined separately so volume fluctuations can be planned and controlled. Fixed costs generally include depreciation on building or equipment, or their lease costs; utilities; taxes; maintenance of facilities and base equipment; and base management. Variable costs will include most labor, transportation charges, rental or depreciation of pallets, containers, and handling equipment, which vary with the need, and inventory tax. Overhead rates should be adjusted to assign proper loadings to expenses, but should also consider penalizing fast periods of high volume to subsidize slow, low-volume periods. Total costs must be evaluated, however, to assure that a warehouse is providing enough service and cost benefits to justify its existence.

CHAPTER

18

Facility Planning and Site Selection

Acquiring new facilities is a multibillion dollar function. In the United States alone, during the depressed mid-1970s expenditures for new facilities exceeded $50 billion per year. Acquisition of new facilities has a significant impact on a firm's current and future operations and expenditures. Suitable facilities that ensure economic operations and flexibility for potential improvements help assure future profitability. Replacement of destroyed facilities and the availability of new plants effect an organization's success and even survival. Efficiency of an organization is greatly affected by the location, quality, cost, and availability of facilities. Logistics and service have an increasing voice in the establishment of facilities, and in many organizations the logistics department is responsible for all facilities.

ACQUIRING A BUILDING

The most timely way of acquiring a building is to purchase or lease one already standing. Since the lead time for a new plant will exceed two years, the time savings can be great if the facility suits the needs and the cost is acceptable.

If no standing facility is available, then a building must be designed and constructed. This requires a team effort among the owner, designer, constructor, and user. Five major approaches are commonly employed to purchase building construction:

1. Conventional method.
2. Design and build to a firm agreed price.
3. Design and build with cost reimbursement.
4. Negotiation.
5. Do your own general contracting.

The conventional method is employed in about 50 percent of known situations. Usually a designer is selected and given a cost-plus-fixed-fee or percentage-of-cost-with-maximum-fee contract. The plan and specifications should be reviewed by a qualified engineer to ensure that requirements will be met. Then, in cooperation with the architects and engineers, potential contractors who have experience and resources and have done similar work of good quality and cost are determined. Proposals are solicited from qualified contractors and the contract awarded to the one whose bid is most attractive. Several bid procedures may be used, including bidding for both desired and the latest acceptable completion times, and incentive fees for savings below the target price and penalty charges for late completion. Contracts will often have a fixed-price-incentive-fee with a target price and guaranteed maximum total cost to the owner. The incentive fee should allocate about 25 percent of the savings below the target price to the general contractor.

Each of the other four methods is used 10–15 percent of the time. If time is of the essence, an experienced general contractor is selected who employs architects and engineers capable of designing and building a total structure. With this approach construction of a specific element of the building can proceed just as soon as design of that element has been completed, so design and construction can be done in parallel rather than serially as normally required. This cost reimbursement method tends to cost less than the conventional method, but this is not statistically significant.

The cost of a design-and-build firm-agreed-price facility is similar to the conventional method. The owner determines the basic facility requirements and price, and requests proposals from one or more contractors. The contract is given to the builder whose design and price proposal are most desirable.

In the negotiated method, the owner retains both a designer and a builder. In contrast to a conventional method, the builder is retained during the design phase to contribute information on cost procedures and time requirements not generally available to the architect. As the plans and specifications for a work element are completed, the work is either done with the contractor's own people or qualified subcontractors are hired. As with the other methods, the contractor oversees and integrates the efforts of the subcontractors.

The owner may act as general contractor to hire the various workers needed, and perform the integrating and controlling functions normally accomplished by a general contractor. This method is useful where an organization has its own qualified people, or on small projects where the cost must be kept low and risk is minimal.

Costs for a production or distribution facility will range from $30 to $90 per square foot, depending on construction, site preparation, utilities cost, supply and demand for construction, degree of automation, and design features. Determination of whether to lease or purchase a facility depends on the organization's need for capital. If the company has internally generated funds that can be best invested in its own facilities, then it should purchase. Most companies today lease buildings in order to make the equivalent capital available for other purposes. Savings of 5–10 percent should be possible during slack construction periods.

MANAGEMENT FUNCTIONS

Facility requirements should be part of corporate long- and short-range plans and goals. Facility plans should be included in both functional organizations and program-projects to assure that the needed facilities are covered. The more lead time available to those charged with acquiring new facilities, the better job they will be able to do.

It is preferable for an organization to assign or acquire specialists to provide a task group that can detail requirements for the facility, recommend several locations to top management, and advise on timing and purchase method. Top management should agree on the location for the new facilities.

PRODUCTION LOCATION

There are three factors that affect plant locations: least cost, profit maximizing, and intangibles. Location cost factors may be divided between transfer costs and production costs. Transfer costs are those that result in the movement of raw materials to the proposed plant site and those incurred by outgoing finished products shipped to market. Transfer costs are the dominant factor in plant locations and are readily quantifiable, and so provide a good starting point for solving location problems.

Production facilities should be near the source of raw materials if their costs are greatly influenced by a loss in weight of the raw materials during processing, their availability for extractive industries, or their perishability. On the other hand, processes that add weight during the production of finished products or produce a perishable finished product should be located near the marketplace. Beer and soft drinks, for example, would be produced near where they will be sold because the cost of shipping finished goods is much higher than the cost of shipping raw materials. Other industries, such as research and development firms, are quite independent of the transfer forces. In-transit privileges by transport companies also influence industrial dispersion. Particular industries locate plants at intermediate points depending on such economic forces as transportation availability, topography, rate boundaries, and labor availability.

Production costs include location costs, labor, and utilities. Location costs will vary depending on geography, accessibility to transportation, and demand for land in that area.

Labor is the greatest single influence on plant relocation; however, wage rates must be compared with productivity rates to assure good value. Firms that require highly skilled labor normally locate close to areas that offer such skilled laborers. It is possible to train and hire new skilled workers, but this is costly and time consuming. High labor turnover is expensive. Labor laws cause cost differences between areas, as can worker's compensation insurance rates, union activity, and the political climate.

The influence of taxes is at most secondary. Studies show that the incentives offered by lower taxes are not determining factors; in one study only 32 out of 272 respondents mentioned a favorable tax structure as an important location determinant. Taxes are primarily cost factors for firms with many assets that would be taxed under state or local ordinances. Capital must be available, but the location does not usually influence capital availability nearly as much as the financial status of the firm and its executives.

Utilities, particularly power and water, have a great influence on industries that require them in large quantities at low cost. Power-oriented industries such as steel production, which requires coal and coke, or aluminum refining, which requires electric power and water, will locate where these are readily available.

There are other internal and external factors that have minor influences. For example, geographical clustering of plants means ease of communication, transportation, labor pooling, and centralized control. There are also, of course, personal friendships, community contacts, large customers, human needs, educational facilities, and other influences that must be integrated into location decision.

INVENTORY LOCATIONS

Every industrial or commercial location is unique in relation to distance and time as well as units of cost. The decision by a potential customer to do business at a particular location is influenced by many factors including the accessibility of location, and the probability of its fulfillment capacity. William J. Reilly formulated a "law of retail gravitation" in which he stated that two cities will attract trade from an intermediate city in the vicinity of a breaking point which is approximately in direct proportion to the population of the two cities and in inverse proportion to the square of the distances from these two cities to the intermediate town. Thus:

$$\frac{B_a}{B_b} = \left(\frac{P_a}{P_b}\right)^1 \left(\frac{D_b}{D_a}\right)^2$$

where:

B_i = proportion of retail trade from the intermediate town attracted by city i
P_i = population of city i
D_i = distance from the intermediate town to city i
a, b = cities being compared

Business researchers have concentrated on definitions of primary, secondary, and tertiary (marginal) trading areas for competing retail operations. Estimates of the shape of such areas are based not only on the distance between the seller's location and that of the prospective buyer, but also on such factors as the type of goods being sold, the location of competing outlets, the buyer's economic capability to buy, the buyer's life-style, and any natural barriers to movement within the potential trading area.

Naturally costs of transportation for one firm in comparison with another will give competitive advantage to the less costly.

Regional self-sufficiency also has an influence, which is aided by the computer capabilities for regional advertising. Periodicals such as *U.S. News and World Report* now publish regional editions that are printed in many locations and distributed with ads for local businesses inserted as part of the magazine. Most population data can be obtained from standard metropolitan statistical areas (SMSAs), which are provided by the Census Bureau and also are available from most state commerce departments.

The problem in inventory location is where to place the inventory and how much to put there. One optimizing technique for the single inventory problem is the "center-of-gravity" approach. This method is based on the principle that however weights may be distributed on a surface, a point can be found at which the surface will be balanced. On a map this may be determined by simple coordinate geometry using X and Y matrix coordinates weighted by the units or pounds or dollars influencing that location. The center-of-gravity method is rather limited because it assumes a linear relationship between distance and transportation cost. It also does not reflect significant differences between crow flight distances and actual practical distances where a highway or waterway must be followed. Therefore, analysis is only the starting point and additional adjustments will be necessary to assure a realistic perspective in the final decision. For example, shifting a few miles in location could change the freight rate, giving an important advantage over competitors.

Usually increasing the number of inventory locations will improve the level of customer service through a reduction in delivery time. There is a corresponding increase in the cost of carrying inventory and operating the facilities as shown in Figure 18.1.

There are several ways to extend the center-of-gravity idea to evaluate simultaneous location of two or more inventories, but at best they are limited to cases where territories are not well defined and they can evaluate only the computed locations. Analysis of multiple inventory locations to determine plants to be served from alternate raw material sources, distribution centers to be served from alternate points, or customers to be served from a company location often require more powerful optimizing techniques than the center-of-gravity approach. The most useful of these are linear programming, the Baumol-Wolfe extension of linear programming, dynamic programming, and the Bowman-Stewart model. Linear programming has been basically covered under "Acquisition and Production/Construction Support." It is very useful for addressing problems with straight-line relationships among the critical variables. For example, transportation costs are nearly linear in relation to volume so that it costs twice as much to transport two items as it does to transport one. This assumption is important because freight rates, quantity discounts, and other factors may result in nonlinear parameters.

It is possible to introduce constraints such as "Never ship from Pittsburgh to Buffalo" or "Always give customer Big what he wants." These constraints are handled by setting the matrix values artificially high or low. To discourage allocation of merchandise from Pittsburgh to Buffalo, the intersecting square number should be set at least one higher than any other number in the matrix.

The major advantage of linear programming is that it gives a logical framework to the systematic appraisal of alternatives. If conditions are right, electronic calculators or computers can rapidly solve linear programming problems. On the other hand, linear programming solutions

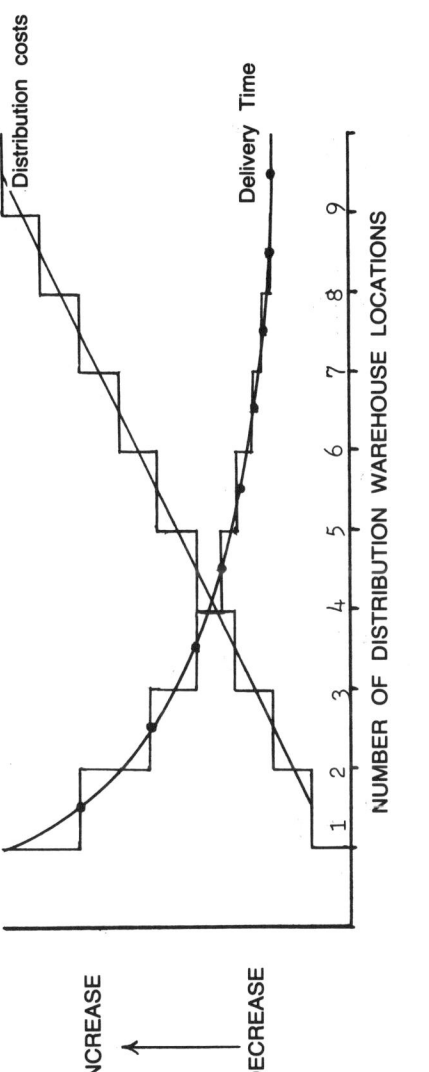

**Figure 18.1
Relationship of inventory locations and delivery time**

must be altered to consider practical realities. Three basic approaches are possible to cope with the linear limitation. First, curves may be reviewed to determine if they approximate linearity over short segments so that breaking a large curve into small portions may allow linear programming solutions of acceptable accuracy and validity. Also, nonlinear programming techniques have been developed that attempt to describe nonlinear cost functions by specially fitted equations. Finally, efforts such as those of Baumol and Wolfe have been made to combine linear programming with nonlinear program elements. Baumol and Wolfe represented transportation costs as three different matrices:

1. From factories to warehouses.
2. From warehouses to customers.
3. Those two matrices combined into a three-dimensional matrix for selecting the least-cost routes between any given set of factories, warehouses, and customers.

This solution method often indicates the need for more warehouses than are necessary; however, with appropriate weighting of conditions in the warehouse-to-customer matrix, the Baumol-Wolfe method is an adequate approach.

Bowman and Stewart assume that there is a low area in the total cost curve that is approximately the intersection of curves for delivery costs and warehouse costs. Some costs associated with materials handling and warehousing will vary inversely with volume. Other costs associated with transportation vary directly with the square route of the area served and other costs, such as utilities, space, and insurance, are assumed constant. Therefore, the expression of total costs is:

$$C = a + \frac{b}{V} + c\sqrt{A}$$

where
C = cost per dollar's worth of goods distributed (the measure of effectiveness)
V = volume of goods, in dollars, handled by the warehouse per unit of time
A = area in square miles served by the warehouse
a = cost per dollar's worth of goods distributed independent of either the warehouse's volume handled or area served
b = fixed costs for the warehouse per unit of time that will yield the appropriate cost per dollar's worth distributed when divided by the volume
c = cost of distribution, which varies with the square root of the area (e.g., gasoline, driver labor, maintenance, and so forth)
$K = \frac{V}{A}$ = density of sales per area

Facility Planning and Site Selection

Since we want to solve the equation for the area A to be served, we differentiate using K and get:

$$A = \frac{2b}{cK}^{2/3}$$

When we know A we can determine the radius of the circle that would be served using:

$$\sqrt{A/\pi} = \text{radius}$$

This model has disregarded any costs for shipping from plants to warehouses, because it is assumed that those costs would be incurred under any conditions. To determine the areas to be served directly from plants or warehouses, a simple additive cost formula was devised. This formula determines the break-even area at which the cost to serve customers directly from a plant warehouse equals the cost to serve them from a plant through a distribution warehouse.

$$\frac{2T^oP_d + T_f + T_dH_d}{P_h(H_d - 2P_dH_m - F_t)} = \frac{2T_oD_b + T_f + T_dH_d}{P_h(H_d - 2D_bH_m - F_t)}$$

$$+ \frac{S_1 + B_e + 2S^oD_p + S_f + 2S_dH_mD_p + I_w}{P_s}$$

where
T_o = truck operation cost per mile
P_d = plant delivery miles
T_f = truck fixed costs per day (amortization-type charges)
T_d = truck driver costs per hour
F_t = fixed driver time per day (check in, check out, coffee break, etc.)
D_b = miles from branch to delivery
S_1 = trailer loading and unloading costs
B_e = branch expense per semi
S_o = trailer operating costs per mile
D_p = miles from plant to the branch
S_f = trailer fixed costs per day (amortization-type charges)
S_d = trailer driver costs per hour
I_w = inventory costs per semi per week
H_d = hours per day
H_m = hours per mile
P_h = pieces per hour
P_s = pieces per trailer
2 = a multiplier reflecting cost per round trip

The information necessary to compute the Bowman-Stewart model can usually be obtained directly from the company's internal records or standard industry figures. The model can be solved for P_d, which is the distance from the plant to the farthest district within the plant warehouse area. Once the optimum to be served from the plant is determined, distribution centers can be spaced in accordance with relative efficiencies of scale and sales density to the outlying areas. It is interesting that most similar models produce a "teardrop" configuration rather than a circle as the optimum territory shape. This is illustrated in Figure 18.2 and is especially true when a distribution center lies within a few hundred miles of a plant warehouse.

Points outside the teardrop-shaped area A-B-C-D can be served more efficiently directly from the plant warehouse. The boundary line is the point at which transportation to the distribution center plus handling charges and small shipment charges to the customers equal the small shipment transportation charges directly from the plant to the customer.

SIMULATIONS

Simulation can be viewed as the adding up of costs or profits resulting from a specified action. It is a powerful technique for evaluating what will happen if particular decisions are made. Many simulations are extremely involved and require considerable time even using a computer. Heuristic programming has the advantages of:

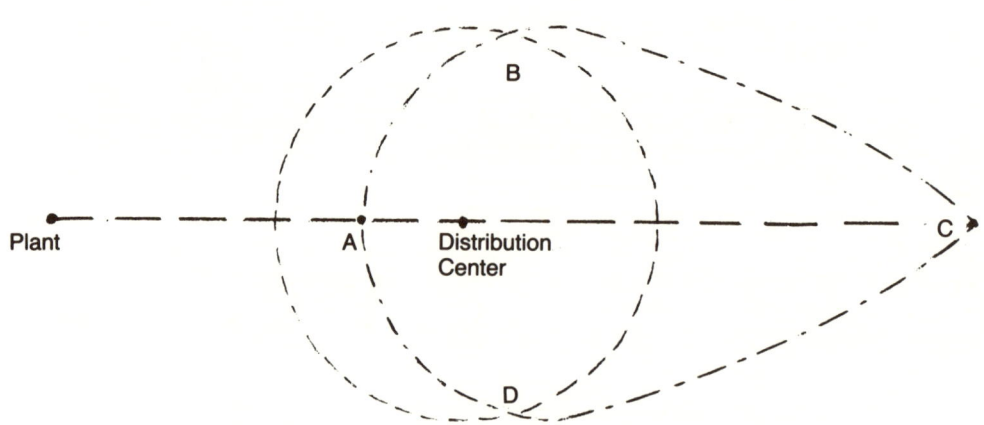

Figure 18.2
Optimal coverage from a distribution center: A-B-C-D

1. Paralleling the thought process used by a human.
2. Working toward optimum solution procedures rather than optimum solutions themselves, which are probably not achievable.
3. Allowing evaluation of many different possible warehouse combinations in a total logistics system.
4. Efficiently eliminating unnecessary and expensive search and analysis.

A flow diagram for a warehouse location heuristic program is shown in Figure 18.3.

It has been shown that near-optimum systems can be developed by locating warehouses one at a time and adding at each stage of the analysis that warehouse which produces the greatest cost savings for the entire system. All promising locations will be at or near areas of high demand.

The final decision as to whether inventory should be consolidated or decentralized will include many factors besides the time and cost of transportation. Reasons for consolidating inventories include:

1. To reduce factory-to-distribution-center cost of transportation.
2. Better warehouse management.
3. Consistent availability of stock items for filling orders.
4. Economies of scale.
5. To reduce total volume of safety stocks and dead and scrap items.
6. To eliminate cross-hauling of goods between inventory locations.
7. Improved inventory turnover.
8. Improved automation through large through-put.
9. Better negotiation for transportation and other services.

The reasons for decentralizing inventory locations include:

1. To fill customer orders more rapidly.
2. To reduce warehouse to customer transport costs.
3. Improved sales through greater availability.
4. Opportunity to use public warehousing and have costs variable with volume.

There may even be reasons for putting certain items such as high-value, slow-turnover Stock Keeping Units (SKUs) in central warehousing and put SKUs with high strategic value closer to the customer. This is an extension of the ABC stocking policies discussed in the inventory chapter. Distribution management must be continually alert to changes and willing aggressively to operate a dynamic system if the facilities are to provide the best value at reasonable cost.

1. Read in:
   a. The factory locations.
   b. The $\underline{M}$ potential warehouse sites.
   c. The number of warehouse sites($\underline{N}$) evaluated in detail on each cycle; that is, the size of the buffer.
   d. Shipping costs between factories, potential warehouses, and customers.
   e. Expected sales volume for each customer.
   f. Cost functions associated with the operation of each warehouse.
   g. Opportunity costs associated with shipping delays or, alternatively, the effect of such delays on demand.

2. Determine and place in the buffer the $\underline{N}$ potential warehouse sites which, considering only their local demand, would produce the greatest cost savings if supplied by local warehouse rather than by the warehouses currently servicing them.

3. Evaluate the cost savings that would result for the total system for each of the distribution patterns resulting from the addition of the next warehouse at each of the $\underline{N}$ locations in the buffer.

4. Eliminate from further consideration any of the $\underline{N}$ sites that do not offer cost savings in excess of fixed costs.

5. Do any of the $\underline{N}$ sites offer cost savings in excess of fixed costs?

   Yes → 6. Locate a warehouse at that site which offers the largest savings.
   No → 7. Have all $\underline{M}$ potential warehouse sites been either activated or eliminated?

   Yes

   No →

8. Bump–shift routine:
   a. Eliminate those warehouses that have become uneconomical as a result of the placement of subsequent warehouses. Each customer formerly serviced by such a warehouse will now be supplied by that remaining warehouse which can perform the service at the lowest cost.
   b. Evaluate the economics of shifting each warehouse located above to other potential sites whose local concentrations of demand are now serviced by that warehouse.

9. Stop

Figure 18.3
Flow diagram of a warehouse location heuristic program

CHAPTER

19

Traffic and Transportation

Traffic and transportation provide the utility that conveys goods from the producer to the user. Transportation costs are often the greatest logistics cost in any organization. In 1985 transportation expenditures were estimated at $103 billion per year. Naturally, traffic matters warrant a great deal of the total time and attention devoted to logistics management. However, they can be managed effectively only when they are considered as part of the total logistics system.

MODES

The five basic transportation modes are rail, highway, water, pipeline, and air. The relative importance of each mode is measurable in terms of distance, capacity, volume, revenue, and type of materials transported.

Railroads historically have carried the greatest number of ton-miles, although their share has been declining in recent years. There are presently about 200,000 miles of rails and the amount of well-maintained track is declining. The capacity of railroads to transport very large tonnages efficiently over long distances is the major reason they still command a significant share of tonnage and revenues. A railroad tank car, for example, can haul six to eight times as much liquid as can a large over-the-road tank truck and can do so much less expensively if it can reach both the producer and the user. Railway operations have high fixed costs and relatively small variable costs. Once goods are loaded on a train, they can be transported long distances at very low cost per ton-mile. Railroads are encountering severe problems from high labor costs and poor maintenance. The average speed between terminals is presently less than 20 miles per hour.

Vessels on water are the oldest form of transportation. In 1985 ships accounted for about 28 percent of total intercity tonnage, which is holding fairly stable. In terms of revenue, water accounts for about 3 percent of intercity revenues. There are about 26,000 miles of improved inland waterways in the United States, including rivers and the Great Lakes, in addition to the coasts. Water transport is oriented to hauling raw materials and basic bulk commodities, since extremely large shipments can be moved at low freight rates where speed is not important.

Highway transportation has expanded rapidly in recent years so that it now accounts for more revenues than all the other modes combined.

The trucking industry presently receives about 75 percent of all transportation revenues and carries about 16 percent of the ton-miles over more than three million miles of roads. Motor carriers have a relatively small investment in terminal facilities and the right-of-way is usually public. Although there are high license fees and tolls for operations, these expenses are regulated. Variable costs per mile are high since each rig must have a power unit and driver. The land trains often seen on thruways with two trailers per tractor are much more efficient, of course, for a long haul. Large tractor-trailers are not cheap (a good tractor will cost about $50,000 and a tanker trailer about $70,000), but relative to other means of transportation, trucks have low fixed cost coupled with high variable costs. They are more economically adapted to handling small shipments moving shorter distances. Increasing labor costs for drivers, maintenance, and platform wages are causing a great deal of pressure on the trucking industry. To counteract this trend, a great deal of attention is being paid to improved scheduling, administrative systems, terminal mechanization, and coordinated transport systems such as trailer on flat car (TOFC) (piggyback).

Aircraft is still the least utilized mode of freight transportation, accounting for less than 5 percent of intercity ton-miles and revenue. The speed of service possible between two distant points has the potential for reducing overall logistical costs through reduction of inventory and warehousing space. However, the erratic nature of freight has limited the assignment of pure freight aircraft so most intercity air freight is transported in the belly of scheduled passenger flights. Air transport does not have fixed costs as high as those as rail, water, or pipeline, however, the variable costs are extremely high for fuel, maintenance, and labor.

Pipelines have long accounted for large volumes of liquids such as petroleum. In 1980 they hauled about 22 percent of all intercity tonnage through the 220,000 miles of pipe. Since the pipeline operates around the clock, seven days a week, and is limited only by the need for minor maintenance, it is most dependable and offers most frequent service. The limitation is that it can transport only liquid commodities. Trials have been made to move solid products in liquid or gas suspension, but without success to date. Pipelines have the highest fixed cost and lowest variable cost of all the transportation modes.

The relative operating characteristics of these modes are displayed in table 19.1.

LEGAL FORMS

The four basic legal forms of carriers are common, contract, private, and exempt. Each type may exist within any mode of transportation and there may be more than one type of legal transport within the mode. The most frequent form is the "common carrier," a company that offers to transport property for revenue any time and any place within its operating authority without discrimination. Common carriers publish for public knowledge all rates charged for transport services, and the rates must be identical for similar movements of freight. Common carriers may be authorized to transport all commodities or they may be limited to specialties, and in geographic area and schedule.

Contract carriers perform selected transport services based on permits granted for specific shipment services. A contract carrier may negotiate an agreement with any shipper for a specified transportation service at mutually acceptable costs. This business contract becomes the basis for

Table 19.1
Relative Operating Characteristics

Operating Characteristic	Transportation Mode				
	Rail	Highway	Water	Pipeline	Air
Availability	2	1	4	5	3
Capability	2	3	1	5	4
Dependability	3	2	4	1	5
Frequency	4	2	5	1	3
Speed	3	2	4	5	1

receiving the permit. Contract carriers may work for more than one shipper and are not required to charge the same rate to all.

Exempt carriers must comply with licensing and safety laws, but do not confront direct regulation in terms of operating rights or pricing unless they operate in interstate commerce. Exempt carriers are most commonly involved with bulk agricultural products and raw materials. There may be association exemptions in which several shippers band together to consolidate small shipments in an efficient larger quantity.

Private carriage exists when a firm provides its own transportation service. The firm must own or lease the shipment and all goods being transported, must be transporting goods as an incidental rather than primary part of the business. Private cartage is efficient where specialized equipment or customized operations are required; however, it may be less efficient because of scheduling problems.

The main difference between legal types are the degree of restriction, operational flexibility, and financial commitment. The degree of restriction is determined by law. For example, a private carrier of one conglomerate subsidiary cannot legally backhaul goods of another subsidiary. This backhaul scheduling is an important part of operational flexibility. Deregulation is causing great changes in transportation as competition becomes more open.

MODAL COMBINATIONS

Several forms of transportation in general use involve more than one mode of transportation. Auxiliary users contract for legal forms of transportation and combine them to utilize the best characteristics of each, and justify lower rates. The auxiliary users include freight forwarders, shipper associations, and parcel post. REA Express, formerly known as the Railway Express Agency, was a major auxiliary user. One of the largest oldest auxiliary forms, it is now bankrupt.

Freight forwarders are a quasi-legal form of transportation, in the sense that they are treated as common carriers subject to federal regulation. They consolidate small shipments and then make a large bulk shipment with common carriers. The main advantage of the freight forwarder is a lower rate, and in many cases speedier transportation. Shipper associations are similar, but usually come from a single industry, such as department stores, garment manufacturers, or food processors. Parcel post is operated by the U.S. Postal Service to transport packages which are delivered to the post office. It is a major shipping means for mail merchandisers and utilizes the postal service delivery system.

Package services such as United Parcel Service (UPS) are furnishing intense competition to parcel post. UPS has done an excellent job of mechanizing its sorting system and has been able to keep labor costs under control. They operate both pickup and delivery service and, because of limits on package sizes, can do an effective scheduling job. UPS provides overnight service between cities within 150 miles, at rates less than or equal to parcel post. Greyhound and other bus companies offer package delivery service if the goods are delivered to the bus station and picked up at the other end.

Coordinated transportation arrangements refer to a combination of two common carriers that can provide point-to-point service on a regularly scheduled basis by using different modes of transportation. The TOFC mode, which is commonly known as piggyback, and the waterborne fishyback version are good examples of utilizing the best characteristics of each mode of transportation. There are seven available plans for TOFC service and a variant for containers on flat cars (COFC) is now being used.

RATES

Federal guidelines cover 100 percent of air and rail miles, 80 percent of pipeline, 43 percent of trucking, and 7 percent of domestic water, although deregulation will reduce the effect. All products normally transported are grouped together in uniform classifications. The purpose of the classification is to consider characteristics of a commodity or product that will influence the cost of handling and transportation. Similar products are grouped in a given class so that an infinite number of possible ratings can be reduced to a manageable number. The particular class assigned to the commodity or product is called its rating. A product's rating is not the price that must be paid; it is rather the classification placement. The actual price that must be paid is called the freight rate, which is found in a price list called tariffs. A product rating has a very real influence on the actual freight rate. The "National Motor Freight Classification" for basic motor carriers has 23 classes of freight. The "Uniform Freight Classification" for rail has 31. There may be additional classification listings in local or regional areas. Individual product classification is based on a relative percentage index of 100. Class 100 is the normal class with other classes running as high as 500 and as low as 35. Every product is assigned an item listing number and then a class rating. The higher a class rating, the higher will be the transportation cost for that item; thus a product classified as 300 would be three times more expensive to transport than a class 100 product. Classifications are also assigned based on the quantity shipped. A carload (CL) or truckload (TL) shipment is rated lower and therefore less expensive than a less-than-carload (LCL) or less-than-truckload (LTL) shipment of identical products. Many products have different ratings based on the packaging. Cost can be reduced by finding the correct classification for the product and recommending a change in the packaging or the quantity shipped that would reduce the product's rating. The rating is applied by a classification board to whom a written application for reclassification may be addressed. All changes other than corrections in classification require public hearings prior to publication, so that any interested persons have a chance to be heard prior to a decision on the proposal.

Rates are so complex that auditing of freight bills is a major activity. There are two kinds of freight audits: preaudit and postaudit. Auditing may be either internal or external. Often external specialized freight auditing companies are used since their personnel can be expert in specific commodity groupings and more efficient than internal personnel. Payment for external audit is usually based on a percentage of the amounts reclaimed through inadvertent overcharges in the original payment.

DOCUMENTATION

The major transportation documents are the bill of lading, the freight bill, and freight claims. The bill of lading provides:

1. The contract for the shipment.
2. A receipt for the goods shipped.
3. Terms and conditions for carrier liability.
4. A title and credit instrument.

There are several variations in bills of lading. In addition to the uniform straight bill of lading, there is a uniform order bill of lading whose purpose is to allow a supplier to obtain payment for goods when they are delivered and simultaneously transfer title. Since the order bill of lading is a negotiable document, it is used largely for financial purposes. There are other bills of lading for export, government goods, and livestock.

The freight bill represents the carrier's way of charging for transportation services. The freight bill is derived from information contained on the bill of lading. Since the large amount of paperwork involved is expensive, some shippers are trying combination forms. Freight bills may either be prepaid or collect. Bills for regulated motor carrier service must be presented within seven days of the effective date of a shipment and paid within another seven days. In the case of rail, 96 hours are allowed for carload shipments and 120 hours for LCL shipments. Some firms elect to pay at the time of creating the bill of lading, thereby combining the bill of lading and freight bill into one less expensive document.

Freight claims are documents that detail information about loss or damage to products in transit, unreasonable delay, or other problems. The shipper prepares the claim and negotiates settlement with the carrier. Shipments often go astray or get delayed en route, in which case tracing and expediting are required. If a shipper initiates a tracing action, the carrier must provide the desired information.

TRAFFIC MANAGEMENT

Traffic and transportation management is usually organized into a functional department with responsibilities including:

1. Freight classification.
2. Gaining lowest possible rates consistent with adequate service.
3. Equipment scheduling.
4. Documentation.
5. Tracing and expediting.
6. Auditing.
7. Claims.
8. Research.
9. Performance measurement.
10. Negotiations.
11. Influencing related items such as packaging and quantities.

Most of these items have been previously discussed, however, scheduling deserves specific attention. With the advent of computers to assist scheduling, significant reductions are possible in distance traveled, optimum load composition, and timing. In the area of school bus scheduling, which requires over $4 billion in taxes each year to support, computerized scheduling has been shown to save 15 percent in every case it was tried against manual scheduling and has achieved savings of 50 percent. These reductions in numbers of expensive school buses, mileage, variable costs, and time are very significant.

Finally, the traffic department has a research and engineering responsibility to assure that transportation is effectively interacting with the overall logistic system. There are many ways in which transportation can be effectively used to reduce total physical distribution costs. A slight packaging change might allow a lower classification rating for a product. Even though the packaging might cost slightly more, the expense could easily be offset by a substantial transportation (contran), which makes it possible to obtain an almost optimal weight and volume balance of office machines being shipped by truck. The first layer of machines was placed on the floor of the truck, four wide by 30 deep. An overfloor was installed and a second layer of 40 machines loaded, and then a third. This loading of 120 machines was a great savings over the 60 that could be loaded when machines were packaged in large wood and cardboard boxes.

Since transportation is the highest single-cost area in most logistical systems, the traffic department should at least be consulted in product design and development, and must be intimately involved in logistics planning.

CHAPTER

20

Personnel and Organizations

*H*uman beings are the most important part of any logistics system. The human brain is superior to any computer conceived to date and the human body is capable of many functions that can be duplicated by an electromechanical machine only at great cost. For some jobs investing in that high cost may be beneficial in the long term, because for such organizations as the U.S. Postal Service, where 85 percent of total costs are for labor, the costs are becoming prohibitively high.

Human asset accounting is proposed by many who recognize that humans are a valuable resource that should be included on a corporation's books along with facilities and machines. The technical problems of achieving this have prevented it from becoming a reality, but the direction is established. Failure to achieve human asset accounting is indicative of other human considerations such as reliability and productivity. Good techniques are established for measuring these characteristics on hardware, but only slow progress is being made with similar evaluations for humans, since they are complex, inconsistent, and emotional. It is apparent that while management is developing scientific characteristics, it will probably also retain many characteristics of an art.

WHAT MOTIVATES PEOPLE

Management has been concerned about employee motivation for many decades. Among systems that have been proposed and tried are:

1. More money for more work.
2. Attempts at better placement through psychological measurements.
3. Provision of better working conditions and greater security.
4. Human relations training for supervision.
5. More democracy through consultation and participation of employees.
6. Job enrichment.

Each of these systems has been valuable in some cases, but so far none has proved to be the universal panacea that management has been seeking. The problem is very complex. Some people will work harder for more money, somewhat more responsibility, and a chance to show what they can do. For some, no amount of money will motivate them unless they have some chance to plan and control their own work. The amount of responsibility different people want and can take is variable. There are probably also some people who really dislike work and will not produce unless they are driven to it. The real conclusion that can be drawn from the research is that managers can never hope to introduce a system that will relieve them of the directing part of their management jobs. They must consider each group and each person individually and treat them accordingly.

PERSONNEL REQUIREMENTS

Once organizational objectives and goals are established, the functions required to achieve them should be identified. Then the personnel requirements should be set before any specific individuals are named. This top-down approach is built around those who may not fit the need but are available and need work.

Persons are not all alike. Many different requirements exist within a discipline. A job description should be prepared for every generic position, and should include:

1. Purpose of the position (why does it exist?).
2. Principal activities and expected results (what is done, how it is done, and why).
3. Any complex problems and unusual aspects that differentiate this position from others.
4. Quantitative supporting data such as number of personnel reporting through the position, budget size, production rates, and machine services.
5. Special knowledge, experience, or skills required.

There is a tendency to overqualify positions, perhaps because present incumbents have those qualifications or because it seems desirable to upgrade the position. Certifications and licenses are one of the few bases for special qualifications and are a legal requirement only for medical doctors, lawyers, and similar professionals, although certification as a Certified Quality Engineer or Certified Reliability Engineer by ASQC or as a Certified Professional Logistician by SOLE is meaningful. Years of experience or formal education are not usually valid requirements and could result in Equal Employment Opportunity (EEO) discrimination claims.

Any skill level can be given a dollar value. If, for example, a machine of a particular design requires servicing by someone with an associate degree in electronics rather than a high school graduate only, the incremental cost difference can be determined on the basis of the salaries that would be paid to the two classes of individuals. Trade-offs can often be made to improve the built-in test (BIT) capabilities, self-diagnostics, and ease of service for equipment, but more often both equipment and the level of service personnel required can be improved just by the designer understanding the capabilities of the available work force.

HOW MANY PEOPLE

Many service organizations attempt to plan workloads for people according to quantitative factors similar to those used for machine loading. The first step is to determine demand, then establish what good production is in terms of time and effort. The time available is based on the available work-hours. For most organizations this is 40 hours per week for 52 weeks a year, or 2080 hours normal maximum. From this must be subtracted (typically) 10 holidays (80 hours), vacation days (averaging 10 days or 80 hours, and increasing), and sick time. Additional time is necessary for training, meetings, and other "overhead." An organization is doing well to get 1800 productive hours from an employee in a year, and active hours for a field representative are often less than 50 percent of the total possible.

The capabilities of a person can then be measured to determine how many machines can be repaired in a day, or the converse—how much time it takes to repair a machine. If mean active maintenance time ($\bar{M}$) is 1.5 hours and travel .5 hours, an efficient customer engineer could repair four machines in an eight-hour day: 8 (1.5 + .5) = 4. Several service organizations use "workload points," which are essentially minutes required to do an operation. Every activity, such as installation, customer training, retrofits, removals, refurbishing, preventive (scheduled), and corrective (unscheduled) maintenance, receive points proportional to the time normally required for their completion. The amount of activity in an organization is converted to points and this, divided by the point capacity of a person, determines the number of persons necessary. Naturally the system must be modified by the learning curve of the individuals—with a new, inexperienced person allowed more time than a skilled worker. Also, travel conditions and particular customer characteristics must be considered. Long travel time between service calls means fewer calls per time period. Particularly difficult customers will require a higher amount of attention than less particular ones, and should be given it if cost effective. The process of developing labor needs is outlined in Figure 20.1.

Workload planning factors allow evaluation of various alternatives prior to trial in the field. The work factors also provide good illustrations to the reliability and maintainability people, since the effect of their efforts on numbers of service people can be directly seen. However, it should be noted that the service organization and its operational policies

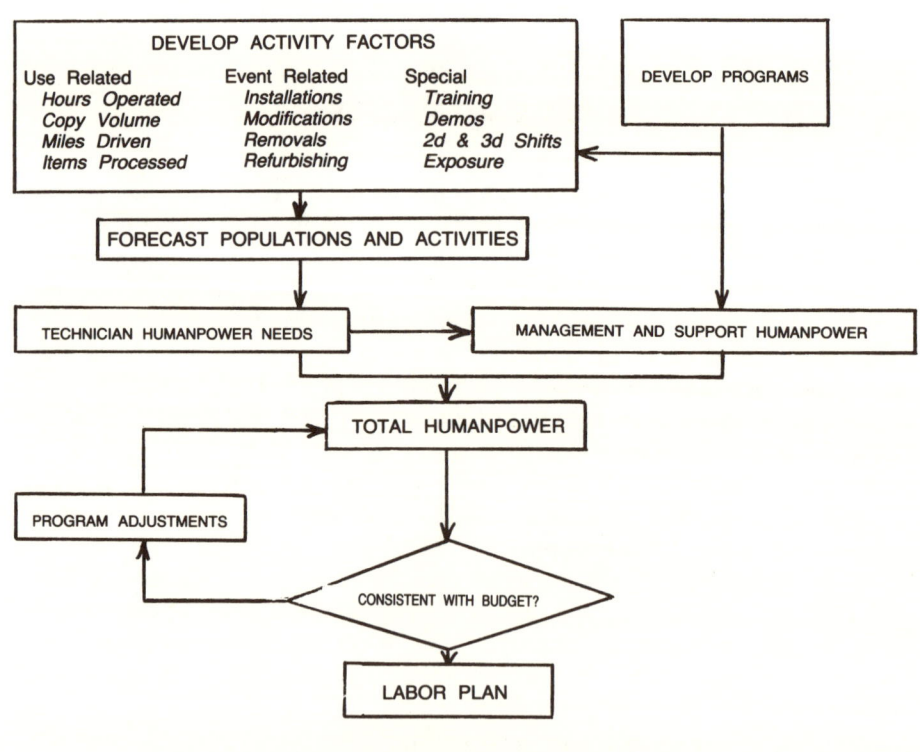

**Figure 20.1
Development of labor needs**

control the majority of time, often about 65 percent, with the minority variable by design changes.

Similar workloading can be done with other logistics functions. Field engineering can set factors for evaluation of engineering orders (for example, one hour average) and time spent on direct telephone advice to field customer engineers (15 minutes on the phone plus 35 minutes researching the solution). Each task in documentation preparation can be time-defined. These factors should be determined for every organization and job, so that work is distributed equitably and all are compensated fairly for their efforts.

There will be a split between exempt and nonexempt salaried and hourly personnel. The nonexempt personnel are under the protection of labor laws that require overtime pay for more than 40 hours per week, break periods, and other regulated treatment. The exempt people are normally management and professional specialists who are required by the nature of their work to put in whatever time is necessary to do the job, but are still guided by the same motivational factors as other workers.

HIRING

Selection of the right person to fill an open position is a difficult situation. The more successful a company is in recruiting applicants, the greater its chance of finding the kind of people it really wants and needs. But, of course, this is true only if it has effective means of selecting the right candidates for the jobs. For well over half a century, psychological tests have been available for use in the selection process but they still do not make selection automatic, nor is it likely they ever will.

The use of selection tests rests on assumptions that:

1. Any human ability follows a normal distribution. If we identify the ability we need for a particular job and the people who are in the high part of the distribution on that scale, we can select that segment of the population and improve our work force.

2. It is possible to construct tests to predict the ability in question. The test does not have to measure the ability directly but a high score should indicate the presence of a high level of the desired ability.

Tests are not perfect predictors and the cutoff scores are a function of the available work force. A test, to be shown reliable and valid, must be given to many people and the correlation proved with success or lack of success on the job. Certainly a screening test will eliminate applicants who have no understanding at all of the electrical or mechanical principles that may be required for a product support position. Three categories of jobs stand out as particularly likely areas for testing:

1. Jobs that are heavily loaded with easily identifiable skills and demand the relatively inflexible application of these skills in performance.
2. Jobs requiring very special or unusual characteristics.
3. Jobs requiring a long expensive training program before the applicant is useful.

In the case of some jobs, personality may be more important than intelligence or skill, provided the applicant has a reasonable quantity of each. Personality is much more difficult to judge than either intelligence or skill, and the personality characteristics that appear requisite for a job may actually be irrelevant to success in the work. Once the totally unacceptable candidates for a position are weeded out through testing, the high-scoring and marginal candidates should be personally interviewed. A customer engineer, for example, has two types of responsibility: technical repairs and human relations. The potential for good human relations can only be determined through face-to-face discussions. Trials may also be conducted during the interview so the potential supervisor can observe the applicant under realistic conditions. For example, a truck driver applicant should be called on to back a truck up to a loading dock while the potential employer watches. Or a potential computer programmer should be asked to describe how a sort routine would be written. These trials both bear a direct relationship to the job requirements and enable first-hand observation of the applicant's performance.

COUNSELING

Once a commitment to hire a new employee is made, the employee must be developed through counseling and training. It is often a good idea to put the new employee under an older employee's wing. The supervisor must take the time formally to indoctrinate the new employee in what is expected and what support will be available. Too often managers leave new employees alone to fend for themselves—and to pick up bad habits from others. A relatively small amount of time on the manager's part will be repaid many times over by the employee's improved activities.

A good rule for counseling is "public praise and private criticism." Performance reviews should be conducted frequently and not always formally. It is good policy to have formal reviews at three-, six-, and 12-month intervals after hiring a new person, and perhaps annually thereafter. Formal reviews, however, do not substitute for day-to-day contact between superior and subordinate. Although there are arguments against tieing promotional pay increases to performance reviews, most organizations do increase pay on the basis of performance.

SKILLS INVENTORY

Every organization should maintain an active file detailing the skills of its personnel and others it might utilize from time to time. The file might be as simple as the relevant resumés, or the information could be placed on edge-punched cards or entered into a computer.

Skills bank information is necessary for several purposes. First, human resources planning necessitates identification of possible replacements for every significant position in case of promotion, illness, or resignation. If replacements are not already prepared, training should be undertaken to develop them. Second, government contracts or others may require security clearances, certifications, or particular qualifications, and such data must be available. Third, the skills bank information helps an organization to evaluate itself in terms of having personnel with the required skills and experience and to plan ahead by developing those with potential.

LABOR RELATIONS

Most logistics and service organizations are not unionized. However, there are trends in that direction since the service segment of our economy is growing. The need for collective bargaining through union representation is normally felt only under poor management. The typical service person is independent and feels quite capable of dealing successfully without union assistance. The idea of large salary increases and other benefits publicized as union achievements is, however, a strong inducement. Since labor relations is a topic of great importance and legal significance, a person concerned with fair labor practices should consult experts in that field.

TRAINING

As was previously mentioned, training is critically important to developing and molding of the new employee into the desired form.

Most organizations conduct formal training for new employees shortly after they join the organization. This training may be accomplished in a classroom, through programmed instruction, by visual means, computer-assisted instruction, correspondence courses, or a combination of those methods. Informal instruction is normally conducted as on-the-job training (OJT) both before and after formal schooling. A flowchart for developing new product training programs is shown in Figure 20.2.

Humans learn best when all senses are involved—sight, sound, feeling, taste, and smell. We can give information fastest by speaking, but receive it best through our eyes. Depending on the importance of the information to the receiver, the retention may be virtually nil or may be 80–90 percent, but is rarely 100 percent. The second time the information is perceived, particularly if presented in a different fashion, a higher percentage will be retained through reinforcement. A third exposure at a later time provides additional reinforcement; however, beyond that the returns diminish in value. It is also important that both the organization's and the individual's needs are met by the training. Some alternatives are shown in Figure 20.3.

We learn best by doing. Motor skills, for example, which involve turning screws or measuring voltages cannot be learned from a book. They should be demonstrated and then the student should perform the activity. It can be a good idea to have one worker teach others, as this will inspire the teacher/worker to refine his or her own skills in order to teach properly.

Two-way interactions are desirable so that questions may be asked and clarified as they arise. Information should be presented and then reinforced. The material taught should be based on what management wants and has decided upon with respect to:

1. Difficulty.
2. Frequency of occurrence.
3. Time involved.
4. Dollar impact.

For example, maintenance tasks that must be carried out frequently, and thus consume many expensive hours of labor, should be carefully established according to good time and motion principles and the "one best way." Vacuum cleaning a machine, for instance, seems a simple, mundane task, but will consume many minutes during every preventive maintenance call. Technical representatives might vacuum the same spot on a machine six times because they failed to recognize the basic principles of removing dirty assemblies first, starting at the top and working down, and following a standard efficient pattern. It is observed that a minimum of five minutes (with a value of about $2.50) could be

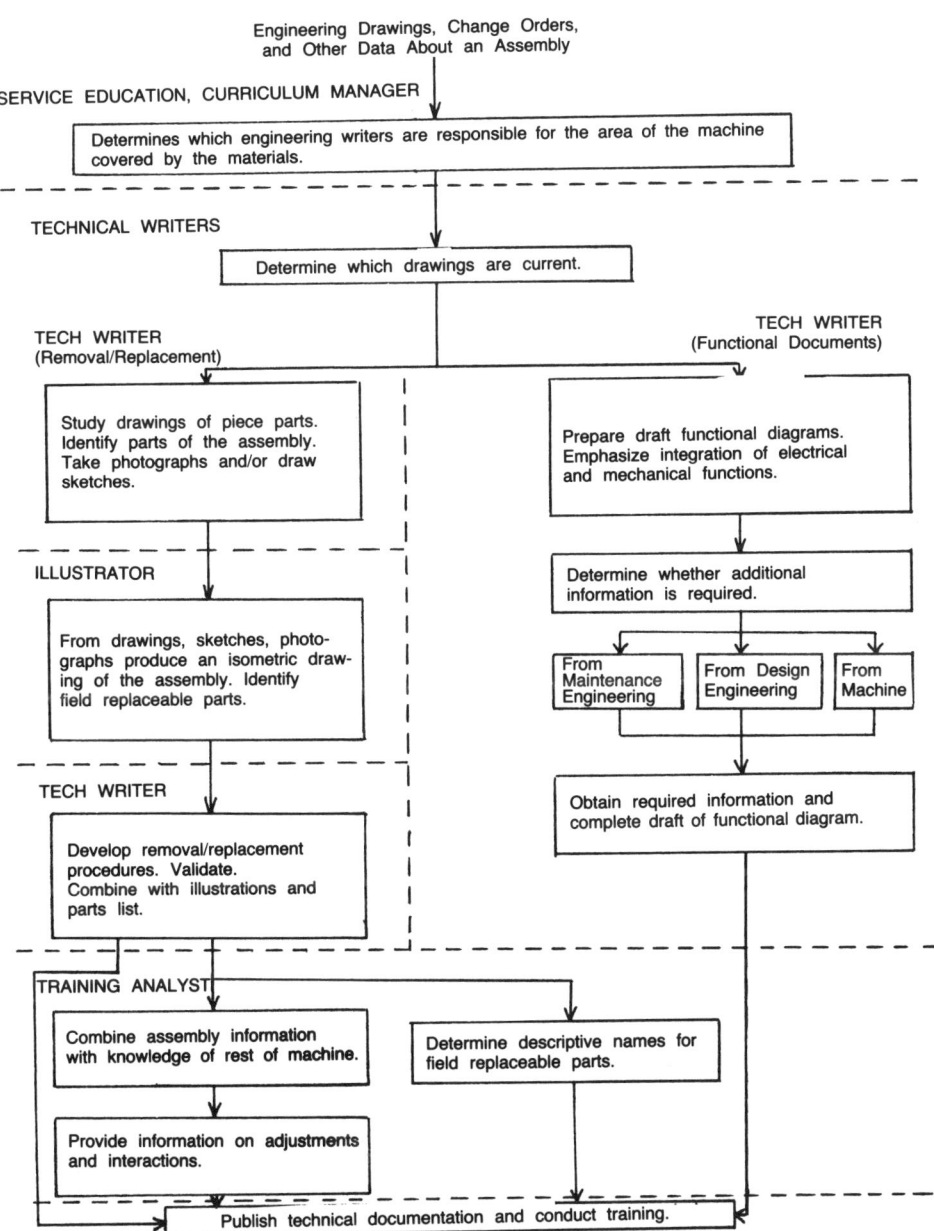

**Figure 20.2
Developing products training programs**

saved on every call for preventive maintenance for copiers or typewriters just by applying proper time and motion and training techniques.

If a task is very difficult and is characterized by interactions that require a "feel," these should be taught—assuming they will be encountered often enough for the learning to be retained. Since real learning comes by actually doing, the supervisor must be certain that the new employee is put to work immediately, utilizing the training. If not, the learning curve will never be developed. This is the curve showing the speed of accomplishment and reliability with which a person performs assigned tasks. A newly trained person, of course, will not be as efficient as someone with experience. The rate of development can be accurately established and is very useful in determining workload and reliability systems predictions.

Some kinds of training can be acquired only under realistic conditions. Installation of equipment, for example, can be learned best by installing products in a customer's location. Preventive maintenance cleaning can be learned best on a machine that has become dirty in a customer's operating environment. To learn well under realistic conditions, a newly trained employee should be placed under the supervision of a team leader or field instructor to assure that procedures will be practiced in the factory or field according to management precepts.

Human relations training can be conducted in formal settings through

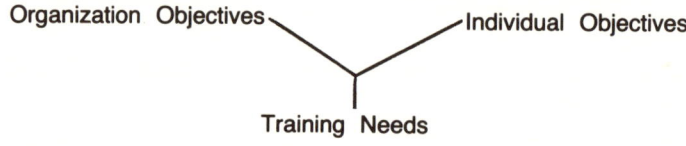

```
                Organization Objectives         Individual Objectives


                               Training Needs
SOURCES:
  WHO
    MANUFACTURER                        WHEN
    YOUR TRAINING DEPARTMENT              REGULAR SCHEDULE
    INDEPENDENT TRAINERS                  AS REQUIRED
    ON-THE-JOB


  WHERE                                 HOW
    THEIR FACILITY                        INDIVIDUAL PROGRAMMED
    YOUR FACILITY                         PROGRAMMED
    STUDENT'S LOCATION                    LECTURE/WORKSHOP
                                          HANDS-ON
                                          AUDIO-VISUAL
                                          WRITTEN
                                          CORRESPONDENCE
```

**Figure 20.3
Training**

the use of role playing. Audiovisual materials such as videotape are particularly valuable since they allow people to see how they react to situations, as well as giving them the rare opportunity to see themselves as others do. The penalties for failure in a classroom are far less serious than they are in a customer's location. Management development, too, can be learned through exposure, training, and reinforcement by experience. Seminars, workshops, night school courses, and continuing education programs are more effective in this area since they reinforce the learning experience of the work environment. Since change is inevitable, logisticians and service managers must continually educate themselves to provide improved leadership.

ORGANIZATIONS

Organization is indeed essential to sound management, particularly of a logistics service activity. On the other hand, there can be an overconcern with organizational structure, and a tendency to let the means create the end. This leads to the mistaken idea that changing the organization will solve all the problems. It can also inspire opposition for any new position that does not fit into an existing organization.

What is an organization? It is an entity made up of a logical combination of components to produce an ordered whole. It is a number of persons or groups having specific responsibilities and united for some purpose of work. Considered as a process, organization includes breaking down the work necessary to achieve the objectives into individual jobs, and providing a means of coordinating the efforts of job holders. The result of the process of organizing is "the organization"—the people employed and the network of relationships between them.

Legal Forms

The law requires anyone operating a business for profit to register as a sole proprietorship, partnership, or a corporation. The sole proprietor has title to all assets and all profits, but must assume all losses, risks, and debts of the business. It is well suited to a small enterprise such as a TV repair service or foreign car repair garage, and it can prove successful in much larger operations as well, as Howard Hughes clearly demonstrated.

A partnership is a voluntary "association of two or more persons to carry on as co-owners, a business for profit." A partnership is easily set up without the legal formalities which come with corporate organization. It pools the talents and money of the partners and sets forth in simple terms the sharing of profits or losses. Many large organizations such as architectural firms, doctors' clinics, and law offices are partnerships, though many are switching to the corporate form now that it is permitted for professionals.

A corporation was defined by Chief Justice John Marshall in the Dartmouth College Case of 1819 as "an artificial being, invisible, intangible, and existing only in contemplation of the law." A corporation is considered a legal person, a business entity that can sue, be sued, hold and sell property, and engage in business operations. A corporation is chartered under state laws. Its form is suited to large, complex organizations with extensive financial investments owned in shares by stockholders, and managed by professionals who may or may not also be owners. While sole proprietorships make up about 69 percent of all business establishments, they do about 25 percent of sales. Partnerships are 5 percent and do only 7 percent of sales. Corporations make up 23 percent of the organizations but their sales are 67 percent of the total. Other forms account for about 1 percent in each factor. Most logistics and service organizations use the corporate legal form because they are established by a parent organization which is itself a corporation. Also, the complexity, finances, legal liabilities, and ownership numbers are best met with the corporate entity.

Structural Forms

The most common form of organization is the bureaucracy. To many the word connotes a large, fumbling, structure. However, Max Weber in the translation of his *Bureaucracy* wrote, "The fully developed bureaucratic mechanism compares with other organizations exactly as does the machine with non-mechanical modes of production, precision, speed, unambiguity, knowledge of the files, continuity, discretion, unity, strict subordination, reduction of friction and of material, and personal costs—these are raised to the optimum point in the strictly bureaucratic administration." Weber's point was that bureaucracy substituted a rule of rational law for rule by the whims of those who happened to be in charge and also made it more probable that the various jobs would be distributed to those most competent to handle them. "The more complicated and specialized modern culture becomes, the more its external supporting apparatus demands the personally detached and strictly objective expert in lieu of the master of older social structures who was moved by personal sympathy and favor, by grace and gratitude."

Weber's ideal bureaucracy, in which the person(s) at the top can make decisions and be confident that the organization will move with speed and precision to carry them out, is still the goal of many practical administrators. Many of them accept his view that an organization will be built on specialization, a hierarchy of officials, each of whom possesses a bland amount of authority, impersonal rules, and managers trained for their jobs. People, however, are not like parts of a machine designed for a specific purpose. They are seldom so completely responsive that they will obey orders blindly. How people respond is affected by the extent to which they accept the goals of the organization, the way they interpret the instructions, and their relationship with others in the organization. Personal sympathy and favor are always present, no matter how rigid the structure. Most organizations have distinct cultures of their own. The "informal organization," in which the division of duties and the authority structure do not necessarily follow stated procedure, may grow up side by side with the formal structure. One of the aims in developing a formal structure is to produce a system which will function as planned and will insure that any informal organizations that develop within it will assist rather than interfere with the objectives of the formal organization.

While the bureaucratic form is most prevalent today, there are other forms including committee, overlapping/integrative, matrix/grid, and project/task/goal, that are very useful for specific purposes. They will be covered later in the section on logistics organizations.

Organization Charts

One of the simplest ways of presenting an organization is to picture it in an organization chart. This is simply a diagram of the formal authority structure in the organization which shows by job title who reports to whom, but it does not show the extent of that authority or the duties of each person in the organization beyond that implied by job titles. For this reason, companies often prepare organization manuals that include job descriptions in addition to the charts.

Together, the charts and job descriptions make up a plan of organizational behavior. They show who coordinates each segment of the organization, who is supposed to follow whose directions, what part of the necessary work each person is supposed to do, and what relationships should be maintained. They designate the official channels of communication and enable superiors to determine who to question if some part of the work is not completed on time or in the correct manner. Of course, it is not always necessary to reduce these things to writing. In a small organization, the division of duties and the authority structure may be so well understood that no written documents are necessary. However, as firms become large and more complex, they generally feel it is necessary to at least have charts so that everyone has a clear picture of the structure.

Classical Principles of Organization

The classical principles of organization include:

Objectives	Delegation
Specialization	Balance
Coordination	Unity of command
Authority	Span of control
Responsibility	Chain of command
Efficiency	

An organization should have defined objectives and each position should have goals that are logically related to the overall objectives.

Specialization is necessary so that the work of each person can be confined to one, or a few, functions, and related functions grouped together under one head. A means of coordinating all efforts must be established, with definite lines of authority from the top person or group down through the hierarchy.

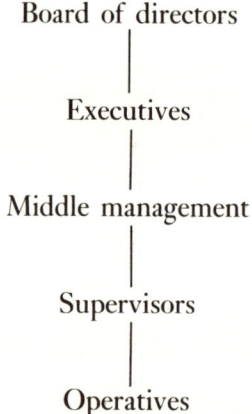

This principle is often referred to as the "scalar principle," and the resulting hierarchy is known as the "chain of command."

Authority should be commensurate with responsibility. The person responsible for achieving a given objective, should have the authority necessary to acquire resources, spend money, and engage in efforts necessary to meet the standard.

An organization should be planned so that objectives can be attained at the lowest possible cost in terms of money and resources. Decisions should be delegated to the lowest competent level. Each person should be accountable to only one superior, and a superior should direct instructions to subordinates to pass on to their workers rather than going around them in the chain of command.

A supervisor's span of control should be fairly small (from about four to 12 subordinates) and the chain of command should be as short as possible. While in a large organization it is not feasible to have both a short chain of command and a small span of control, it must be remembered that information received and passed on by many people becomes more garbled with each step in the chain.

Finally, an organization must be continually reviewed to ensure that there is a reasonable balance in the size of the various departments, between standardization of procedures and flexibility, and between centralized and decentralized decision making. Standard procedures are necessary in a larger organization but they should not be enforced so rigidly that swift and effective action cannot be taken should a particular situation require it. For example, it may be good policy for a company to require competitive bidding on large construction jobs, but to extend this to small alterations might mean holding up work to the point where new products could not come to market. Management must strike a balance between the need to have work done quickly and the need to have it done at the lowest possible cost.

It is usually possible to classify each person in the organization in one of four ways:

1. By the major purpose being served (e.g., firefighter, teacher, president).
2. By the process used, such as data processing, engineering, or accounting.
3. By the persons dealt with or served, such as production, field, or customer.
4. By the place where the work is done, such as loading dock or Boston branch.

There may, of course, be combinations of these classifications. A product support department is, for example, a purpose division because its objective is to support all the company's products. It is also a process division and may be subdivided according to products dealt with and places in which they are serviced.

People may be divided into units with common purpose simply by counting off—such as 100 men to a Roman Century, six centuries to a cohort, and ten cohorts to a legion. It may be divided by objects, such as products; by geographical areas; by alphabet or numerical sequence; by time, type, or incidents; or by the serial method of organizations for each part of a production process.

Line–Staff Organization

If each functional specialist were expert in some phase of work and gave orders directly to the workers, there would be no unity of command and no single line of authority running from the top to each person in the organization; hence the danger of conflicting order. Division of the jobs into line and staff activity gets around this difficulty. The line–staff organization is dictated by the scalar principle and the principle of unity of command. The distinction between line and staff in business is similar to the distinction between line and staff in armies.

A line organization is made up of those whose work contributes directly to the achievement of a fundamental goal.

The staff are those who assist the line in some way, either by providing services or developing plans, giving advice, or auditing performance.

The need for staff services in both armies and businesses has grown out of three developments:

1. Large-scale organizations.
2. Technical breakthroughs.
3. Laws and regulations that require detailed compliance.

In a small primitive army of a few hundred men, a general could shout his orders and be heard by anyone. There would be no need for a supply service, since such an army would not attempt to carry on a sustained campaign. Each man would carry his own provisions, or perhaps get them from the countryside by looting unfortunate inhabitants. Rudimentary staff services organized as groups apart from the line existed as early as 1600 B.C. However, development was not continuous even in the ancient world, and in the dark ages warfare reverted to small-scale operations again. It was not until the seventeenth and eighteenth centuries that staffs developed again in European armies. In 1645 Oliver Cromwell's army included a Chief of Staff and such specialized officers as a "Commissary General of Victuals," a "Commissary General of Horse Provisions," a "Scout Master General," treasurers, physicians, and a clerical staff. That is a simple organization compared with the present U.S. Defense Department Organization for Logistics. In addition, the Defense Supply Agency was organized to perform many of the functions that Cromwell's supply service once took care of for the clothing and feeding of soldiers.

The fact that the Joint Chiefs of Staff have line authority may seem confusing in view of the stress placed on purely advisory in-service capacity of the staff. This discrepancy is due to the fact that the

Constitution requires civilian control of the armed forces and the president, as commander-in-chief; coupled with the fact that highly specialized knowledge is now required for direction of the forces. On matters of policy, the Chiefs' function is advisory; but under the direct authority of the Secretary of Defense they administer the operations of certain joint or unified commands, and in addition they administer individually, under their respective secretaries, the operation of their specific armed forces.

Main Types of Staff

There are four main types of staff:

1. Personal.
2. Analytic.
3. Specialist.
4. Broad-based general services.

The personal staff consists of people such as secretaries, clerks, and administrative assistants whose main function is to handle the personal affairs of an executive so that time is available to concentrate on executive duties.

The specialized staff are those who handle functions requiring specific education and experience such as accounting, engineering, personnel, data processing, and research. It is impossible for one person to be familiar with all the various specialties needed in a large business or army. Hence experts in each field are required to perform supporting activities. In many businesses functions of this type are more properly called service departments or support facilities rather than staff, since they actually carry on a good deal of the work necessary in the business even though they do not produce or sell goods or services. The specialized staff people relieve the chief executive officer (CEO) of the need to become expert in many different specialized fields, but they also require that the CEO coordinate their work as well as that of the line people. The CEO must gauge the overall result of the proposed policies and projects because many of them will have far-reaching effects throughout the business and could impose burdens on the line departments that will offset the benefit seen by the promoters. Here is where the analytic staffs and general staffs come in. Figure 20.4 shows typical staff functions.

The analysis people have both the specialist's knowledge necessary to understand what is proposed, and the generalist's background to review all repercussions. The general staff person is most often "assistant to" the company president, although one may also be a vice-president, executive assistant, or have another title. An assistant-to is not second

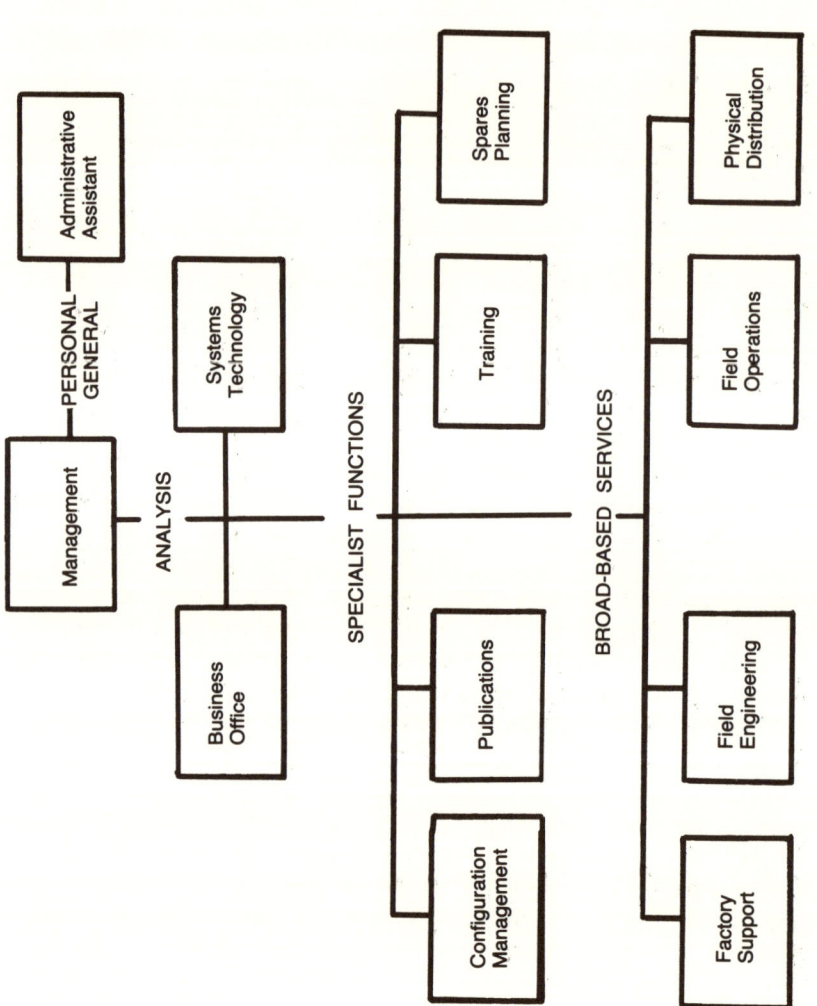

**Figure 20.4
Functional assistance in organizations**

in command and has no authority over the chief's immediate subordinates, even in the absence of the chief. What does this job mean then? Any decision that cuts across departmental lines must be made by the chief executive. However, the CEO does not have the time to devote to getting the views of many people and digging for information. The general staff will act as an extension of the eyes and ears of the chief executive.

Many people advocate what is called "completed staff work." This means that the chief executive officer (CEO) should not be concerned with long explanations and memos. Writing a memorandum to your chief does not constitute completed staff work, but writing one for your chief to send to someone else does. In most cases completed staff work results in a single document prepared for the signature of the chief, without accompanying comment. The final test of completed staff work is: If you were the chief, would you be willing to sign the paper you have prepared and stake your professional reputation on its being right?

There are inherent problems with line versus staff relationships. Specifically, the line has the following complaints against the staff: It usurps line authority; the staff tends to be more articulate and able to sell projects to management that are not necessarily realistic and cause extra trouble for the line; and the staff creates an excessive amount of paperwork.

The issues are not entirely one-sided. Many staff people think that the line does not take advantage of their services enough. Some feel that the line tends to push undesireable tasks onto them and when something goes wrong shirks the responsibility. Another complaint is that when the line asks for advice, it does not clarify the problem and does not allow an adequate amount of time for a proper answer. Finally, there are members of the staff who hesitate to report to operating people because they feel that by doing so, they limit the full scope of their own skills.

The obvious way to cope with line-staff difficulty is to encourage cooperation. Formal meetings are helpful but do not provide a complete answer. The issues are fundamental—caused by the formally prescribed roles. Some companies have attempted to put the relationship on a different basis so that the staff department services are not forced on the line, and, in fact, must be paid for out of the line budget. If the same services are available from an outside supplier at a lower cost, the line is free to buy from that supplier. While this arrangement is not suitable for all staff activities, it can be advantageous in the areas of training, maintenance, and construction.

Modern Approaches

Many critics argue that classical theory is too mechanistic and ignores major characteristics of human nature. Since formal organization structures are designed solely for the purpose of enabling people to work effectively together toward a common end, that is serious criticism. Several new approaches have been advanced including:

1. Behavioral.
2. Decision making.
3. Biological or mathematical.
4. Systems.

There is considerable overlap among these approaches.

The *behavioral* writers are conscious that an organization made up of human beings has a great many variables and an attempt to alter any one of them is likely to start a chain reaction. They point out that orders and policies, no matter how plainly stated, will always be subject to reinterpretation according to the psychological set of those who transmit them or carry them out, the environment in which those down the line find themselves, and the conflicting pressures to which they are subject. People who make up an organization are motivated by many forces besides those taken into account by the classicist, and may be seeking goals quite different from those assigned to them by the organization manuals. Chester Barnard, for example, writes that a person can and will accept the communication as authoritative only when the four conditions happen simultaneously.

1. The communication is understood.
2. At the time of decision, it does not seem inconsistent with the purposes of the organization.
3. At the time of decision, it appears to be compatible with personal interest.
4. One is able mentally and physically to comply with it.

Barnard realized that people are moved by a variety of incentives and that no organization could ever offer the full spectrum of positive motivating factors.

Herbert Simon identified the role concept "The captain goes down with his ship because he has accepted the role of captain and that is what captains do in our culture." People not only have notions of their own role identifications but also have set ideas regarding the roles of others. E. Wight Bakke viewed organization as a fusion process. The individual, he pointed out, hopes to use the organization to further personal goals while the organization attempts to use the individual to further its goal—the organization to some degree remakes the individual and the individual to some degree remakes the organization. Bakke listed the individual's goals as security, progress, and justice with respect to (1) possession of means, (2) optimum performance, (3) health or internal harmony, (4) understanding, (5) autonomy or freedom of movement and decision, (6) significant and effective integration, and (7) respect. Bakke termed the attempts to make the formal organization a means of reaching these goals the "personalizing process." His theory describes what actually happens within an organization rather than laying down rules for organizing. It notes, for example, the reciprocal character of each person's role. For example, if one person is to play the role of "benevolent supervisor" another has to play the role of "grateful subordinate." This may help to explain why industrial paternalism fails to produce desireable results in many cases. No person can play the role of "paternalistic employer" successfully unless others will play the reciprocal roles of "childlike employees."

Bakke's former associate, Chris Argris, believes that a basic conflict will exist between the personalizing and the socializing process as long as the socializing process requires people to work at jobs that:

1. Permit them little control over their work-a-day worlds.
2. Tend to place them in situations where they are expected to be passive rather than initiative.
3. Force them to occupy subordinate positions.
4. Permit them minimum degrees of flexibility and fluidity and emphasize the expression of one or a few relatively minor abilities.
5. Tend to make them feel dependent upon other agents, e.g., the boss.

Argris concludes that there is a basic incongruousness between the needs of a mature personality and the requirements of a formal organization developed in line with the classical principles. Moreover, this inevitable discrepancy increases as the formal structure becomes more clear-cut and logically tight, as one goes down the line of command, and as jobs take on more assembly line characteristics.

Several new organization specialists have pointed out that the demand for top management control can produce:

1. A reduction in personalized relations.
2. Internalization of the rules of the organization so that rules become ends in themselves.
3. Increased categorization in decision making.

These preclude the possibility of major contributions that require a breaking away from accepted practices. These trends to conformity have been pilloried in such books as W. H. Whyte's *The Organization Man* and Harrington's *Life in the Crystal Palace*. An interesting chain reaction might be

1. Management initiates a formal organization in which tasks are very detailed and closely supervised.
2. Because they have so little scope, employees become apathetic about their jobs.
3. Since the actual work is not satisfying, employees socialize during work hours and take longer coffee breaks.
4. Management views this as a failure on the part of the supervisors and therefore prescribes their roles more carefully.
5. Supervisors become apathetic themselves.
6. The failure of the supervisors to do more than blindly enforce rules leads management to insert another layer of supervision between the first line supervisors and the layer above them.

While many behaviorists take a motivational approach, a special motivational approach has been taken by Rensis Likert. He, like Elton Mayo, stresses the importance of the work group when he says, "Management will make full use of the potential capacities of its human resources only when each person in an organization is a member of one or more well knit, effectively functioning work groups that have high skills of interaction and high performance goals." Likert employs the idea of "linking pins" to help organizations and individuals perform their functions adequately. He feels it is usually desireable for superiors to hold group meetings not only with their immediate subordinates, but also incorporating two hierarchial levels. Strengthening the bonds of organization by the linking pin method is believed to insure three way communications, (up, down, and sideways between peers on the same level), and to permit each supervisor some opportunity to influence the boss.

The last major behavioral approach is called "*organic organization*," which was promoted by Warren G. Bennis. It holds that an organic organization is a temporary structure in which there is a minimum of formal duty division. *Everyone pitches in and contributes to the best of their ability to the solution of any problems that arise and there is more or less general agreement about who should do what since each person is known to possess certain skills and to lack others.* First of all, the key word is "temporary." Organizations become adaptive, rapidly changing temporary systems. Second, they will be organized around problems to be solved. Third, these problems will be solved by relative groups of strangers who represent a diverse set of professional skills. Fourth, given the requirements of coordinating the various projects, articulating points or "linking pin" personnel will be necessary to speak the diverse languages of research and relay and mediate between the different project groups. Fifth, the groups will be conducted on organic rather than on mechanical lines. They will emerge and adapt to the problems and leadership and influence will fall to those who seem most able to solve the problem rather than to programmed role expectations. People will be differentiated not according to rank or role, but according to skills and training. Crisis situations have been shown to develop this kind of organic organization, but so far nonstress situations seem to prefer other forms.

The decision-making approach emphasizes that the equilibrium or survival possibilities of an organization depend on its ability to induce cooperation. The CEO states the direction in which everyone should move and those instructions are passed down through each level to the last person in the chain of command, with each step becoming more and more specific. The idea of functional teamwork has been expanded as an approach to organization for ensuring that decisions regarding various areas are made by those most expert in those areas. All distinction between line and staff would be done away with and all functions given authority and decision making power in their own functional areas. There is teamwork, but only to the extent that decisions of one function impinge on the operating efficiency of another.

Biological-mathematical theories come from writers who conclude that an organization like an organism cannot grow and still function unless the balance between its various parts is maintained in fairly exact ratios. For example, Mason Haire has developed what he calls the "square-cube" theory. As the mass of an object is cubed, its surface is only squared, and Haire believes that something similar occurs in organizations. If, for example, the cube root of the number of inside employees doubled, the square root of the number of outside employees would also double. Thus, if an organization started with 27 inside employees (3^3) and nine outside employees (3^2) and it grew to the point where it had 216 inside employees (6^3), the square root of the number of outside employees would double and the organization would have 36 people in that category. Another line of exploration has been the possibility of predicting the results of various organization changes through the use of computers. However, the variables that affect the functioning of an organization are not only numerous, but difficult if not impossible to express in numbers, and the use of the computer requires quantification. Probability theory has been used to determine how large certain groups should be, but this is a different matter from using it to structure an entire organization.

The systems approach is characterized by elements of both the organic and the mathematical theories. It says that an organization should be studied, not merely as a formal arrangement of superiors and subordinates or as a social system in which people influence one another, but as a total system in which the environment, the formal arrangement, the social system, and the technical systems are constantly interacting. In this view, the organization is not a static arrangement of jobs that can be captured in an organization chart, but a pattern of inputs, outputs, feedback, delays, and flows. To say such an organization is in a "steady state" means merely that it is functioning in an orderly way. It does appear the net effect of a systems approach could be greater routinization of most work. Determining the effect of any particular decision or environmental change on the total organization would be very complicated, but there are many people who feel that such meaningful simulation can become a realistic organizational tool.

It is often possible to utilize the findings of the behaviorists within a largely classical structure. For example, it may be possible, as Volvo has done, to restructure the assembly process from individualized tasks to a team approach. This is known as job enlargement or job enrichment. Modern approaches alert organizers to many possibilities which might be overlooked if they were guided strictly by classical rules.

Coordination

Narrow specialization in middle-level professional jobs may not have the deadening effects it does at lower levels where a person may have to specialize in inserting four screws, but it does mean that activities are suboptimized when they should be aimed toward a common goal.

Coordination by committees is the most common method. A committee is usually a group of people that makes decisions or presents viewpoints and whose conduct is governed by a set of rules. Many hours are spent on committee meetings in the belief that when a group meeting takes place, the whole is somehow greater than the sum of its parts. On the other hand, many critics believe that committees tend to become mere sounding boards for a dominating personality, that they can not arrive at unified decisions, and that they waste time. Some generalizations may be made about committees.

1. High performance depends on the contributions of many people with extensive, rather than little, interaction.
2. Small groups tend to be superior to large ones when the material lends itself to immediate formation of opinions. Larger groups are better when it is desirable to reject faulty proposals quickly.
3. Potential for agreement diminishes with an increase in size.
4. The freer the discussion, the better the results.
5. Committees rarely end in consensus, but are useful for exploring options.
6. The effort to understand is the beginning of reconciliation.

Meetings

There are five basic types of meetings as shown in Table 20.1. Each requires a different approach to be effective.

Points to be considered regarding meetings include:
1. Members
   —Are the right people invited?
   —Could attendees be reduced?
   —Must everyone be there during the whole time?
2. Notification
   —Is the meeting really necessary?
   —Could it be special purpose rather than meeting routinely?
   —Should documents be sent with the notice?
3. Agenda
   —Are all items important?
   —Are all items mature enough for discussion?
   —Are we prepared to make decisions about these items?
   —Are the points arranged in order of importance?
   —Are experts available to handle each topic?
   —Would any topic be better handled by small outside meetings?
4. Minutes
   —Will minutes of this meeting serve any useful purpose?
   —Do all the names on distribution need copies?
   —Who else should receive copies?
   —Indicate action items and responsibilities.
   —Follow up to make sure everything is carried out.

Logistics Organizations

The most elaborate system of coordination ever devised is that used by the National Aeronautics and Space Administration (NASA) for the Apollo space program. *Fortune* hailed the techniques used to coordinate the work on the moon vehicle as "potentially the most powerful tool in man's history" since it made possible "the direction of thousands of minds in a close knit mutually enhancive combination of government, university, and private industry."

Production of the hardware was entirely the work of independent private corporations whose work had to mesh very closely, since the delay in one company's work would cause slippage in the schedule all along the line. To prevent slippages the director of launch operations met weekly with the top people in the contractor task forces to discuss mistakes and uncover problems that might result in delays. There were also daily meetings of NASA officials and contractor personnel to check on schedules, and if one contractor was causing delays, everyone knew about it. The system was characterized as "management by embarrass-

Table 20.1
Five Basic Types of Meetings

Type of Meeting	Leader's Style	Agenda Format	Postmeeting Action	Questions, Interruptions	Major Jeopardy
Communication Large or small group one-way	Highly directive, formal	Highly structured	Probably none or else already decided	No	Frustration at one-way style
Communication Small group, two-way	Controlled but open	Loosely structured	Dependent on situation	Yes, (invite many)	Turns into super bull session
Problem solving Clean-cut alternatives	Focused on problem solving	Structured	Critical, detailed, and specific	Some but within agenda	Wandering, reluctance really to solve problem
Problem solving No clear alternatives ("brainstorm")	Open, informal accepting	Almost no structure	Probably none, (except a list of ideas)	Yes, ("wide open")	Turns into super bull session
Scheduled "Staff meeting"	Directive but sensitive	Structured (but may have open time for new items)	Critical (detailed and specific)	Yes, addressing issue at hand	Boredom, repetition, poor preparation, nothing solved, and so forth

ment." There were also large amounts of paperwork. Every step was documented so that failures would be traced and responsibility assigned and everyone concerned would be notified of any changes so they could adjust their own activities accordingly.

The Apollo program is, however, a special case. Excitement and high motivation were involved in taking part in one of the greatest adventures humankind has ever engaged in and the knowledge that human lives depended on every detail. Large amounts of money were spent with no need to show a monetary return on the investment. All the meetings and documentation cost money and people were well paid for attending the meetings and reading and digesting the documents. The situation in most business organizations is entirely different. However, it may be that eventually, if companies continue to grow, they must afford the kind of coordination that existed on the Apollo program, and through the use of computers streamlined information systems will be developed to reduce the time spent on reading documents and attending meetings.

A typical aerospace organization is shown in Figure 20.5. This product support organization combines line and staff functions to coordinate a large group of people spread around the world. A program/project/task organization is shown in Figure 20.6 for a product that could be commercial or military. The idea behind program management is that functional activities cannot be efficiently directed toward development of new programs and that experts should form temporary teams to guide and develop new potential products. Each function normally assigns qualified people to do the program and they then have two bosses: the program director, and their functional management. A typical rule to ensure single-point authority is that decisions of the program manager will be followed in all cases of dissention, until—and only if—it is overridden by higher management. It is only in the last 20 years that logistics organizations have been combined into a single organization; and even today, few companies have a vice president of logistics or product support or service.

Service Organizations

The legal form depends mainly on the size and profits of the service organization and its parent organization, if any. Structurally, service organizations may be:

1. Independent profit centers.
2. Aligned with sales.
3. With manufacturing or engineering.

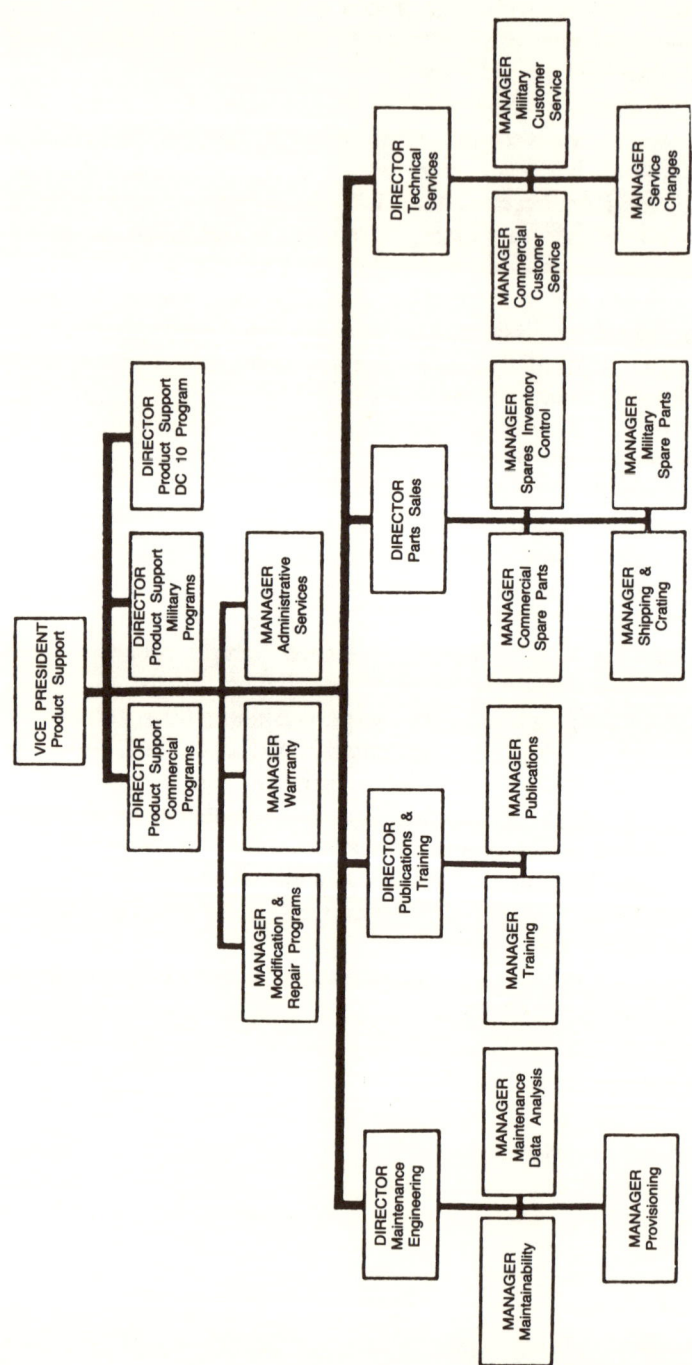

Figure 20.5
Typical aerospace product support organizations

The gas station operator, department store customer service, and most business equipment service organizations are with sales. Highly technical products will have service groups closely related to engineering. Custom-built equipment may be installed and supported by people in manufacturing.

The best reason for sales and service to be organized together is to present a united front to the customer. The disadvantages include conflict in the types of people involved, different goals, frequent lack of appreciation for each others' needs. Since service requires two main skills, technical and human, the organization should depend on which is greater. If human relations are major, then sales should be prime. If technical skills are major, then align with engineering or manufacturing. If there is a balance or the service organization is large and expensive, it should be independent.

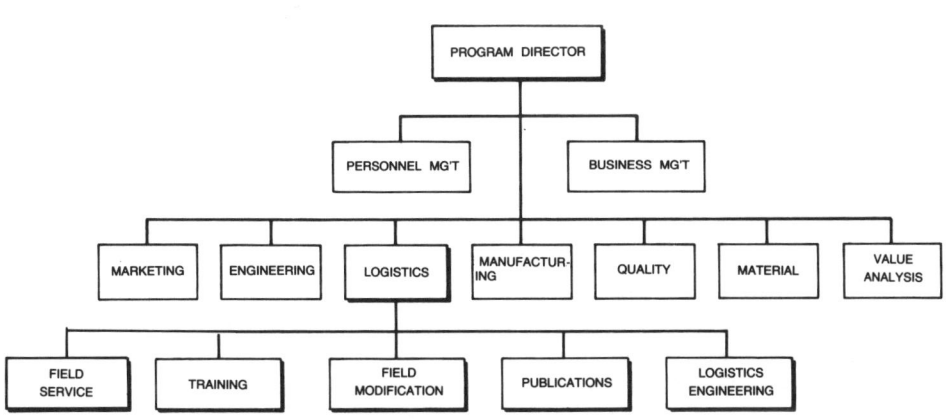

**Figure 20.6
A typical program/project/task organization**

CHAPTER 21

Customer Interfaces

The interface with the customer is the most important part of a company's external relations, but one of the least understood. Interactions with human beings tend to be subjective, inconsistent, colored strongly by our own experiences, not well controlled, and often accomplish (or undo) in a few words more than months of technical effort. There are two major parts to a customer engineer's job: technical maintenance and customer relations. The person who answers the telephone when you call to order parts for a dishwasher, the service representative at the car dealership who schedules you for service and then explains what was done and why, or the airline reservation clerk are all critical parts of the logistics system. They are the interface between the company and the customer.

Customer perceptions are more important than quantitative numbers. For example, customer-perceived reliability can be very different from the numbers indicated by a sophisticated data-reporting system. The technical representative may be performing scheduled preventive maintenance on the equipment, but if the passing manager thinks "that machine is broken again," the company's attitude toward the equipment will be negative. An answer to that specific problem is to have service personnel stay away from the customer and equipment unless maintenance is absolutely required. Customer relations calls should be done by sales personnel.

People who are going to interface with customers must be specially trained for the responsibility. Reading a book on "how to do it" will not suffice. There must be person-to-person development, preferably using role playing for initial training and then on-the-job guidance by supervisors. Successes and failures should be highlighted. If a customer writes commending one staff member, the letter should be prominently displayed so everyone can see it and be motivated to do likewise. Positive response should be publicly praised, while failure should be privately punished. There are lessons to be learned from mistakes, so customer interface problems can be used without names and details as training media.

The word *reliability* to a person not versed in the semantics of the logistics profession means dependability, durability, warranty, and value. Product service is a complete package in which the system components must be integrated to form an effective, efficient whole. Good product service means being able to deliver a CAD (capable, available, dependable) product.

Many users are dissatisfied, as illustrated by congressional inquiries, letters to newspapers, increasing workloads in the state attorney general offices, and a generally increasing level of customer complaints. On the other hand, organizations providing good customer service are seeing significant increases in business and profits.

How good are your customer relations? How good should they be? What is the reliability of your human systems? Have you asked your customers lately what they want, or are you sitting back afraid to stir up complaints? Goodwill is an expensive commodity and requires so much time to nurture that it must be continually cultivated. But do you have objectives and specifications that cover the customer service aspects of logistics? Most organizations do not, but should!

PRODUCT NEEDS

Every product requires prepurchase information, easy, ordering, prompt delivery, smooth installation, simple use, preventive maintenance, rapid repairs, and, finally, convenient termination and replacement. Successful service regards these elements as building blocks for the complete service system.

Prepurchase information is gained from advertising, salespeople, publications, owners' comments, and test use. The amount of prepurchase investigation depends on the value of the product to the prospective user, in terms both of cost and of utility.

Service is a very advertisable feature for products customers know will occasionally fail. Take, for example, the washer repairman in the TV commercial who is sad because he has no business.

A company's advertising and sales approach greatly influences the customer's expectations. Service personnel should work with sales to ensure that products are not oversold. If salespeople are not aware of the product's full capabilities and limitations, or are less than honest, they may place a product, but gain a dissatisfied customer who will probably cost the company money in the long run. If a car gets 20 miles per gallon instead of the 30 promised, the customer is going to harrass the service department. Long-term success with high-cost durable goods is not usually compatible with sales huckstering.

Easy ordering means that once the customer has decided on your product, that customer should be accorded courteous salespeople, expeditious credit approval, and prompt confirmation of the order.

Prompt delivery connotes that you either provide the product on the spot or arrange a suitable delivery schedule and deliver as promised. People appreciate being given accurate information even though it is not entirely satisfactory. The installer faces a problem when the customer opens the door if the sales representative promised that the item would be delivered weeks ago. Many companies now pay sales commissions at delivery, rather when the order is taken, so that the customer is kept happy and sales revenue coincides with the commission expense. Some companies furnish "loaner" equipment, such as typewriters or laboratory instruments, for the customer to use until the ordered product is delivered.

Smooth installation is another important factor. The best installation is the one the customer can accomplish simply by plugging in, or winding up, or turning on. The worst are those in which the product arrives in pieces at the user's location, to be assembled by a service engineer who is delayed for several days and finally appears to complain that the correct items are not all there. A situation such as this makes a lasting impression on the customer—a very poor one.

During the early design stage of the office copier which is now the Xerox 3100®, it was recognized that smooth installations are of critical importance. Performance of products then in the marketplace was evaluated and found to be very bad. In fact 35 percent of all installations were aborted. The general reasons were that in 10 percent of the cases, the location was not ready for the machine, and in 15 percent of the installations, the electrical wiring had to be modified. Finally, in 20 percent of the installations, the machine could not be operated because vital parts were missing. Various solutions were possible. The salespeople were made responsible for ensuring that the location was ready and the proper electrical connections were made. The service organization was alerted to problems of poor-quality manufacturing. When major problems began to occur, the service organization would have the products checked out prior to installation in the customer's office. This was quite expensive in terms of both time and labor; however, it ensured complete quality products ready for installation in the customer's office and reduced the defective rate at the customer's installation.

For the new 3100 Copier, design approaches were taken to make sure that it could be located anywhere there was space and that it would operate on any 15-ampere grounded electrical outlet. These pushes from the service and logistics organization proved to be positive sales features also. The problem of missing vital parts was often caused by components that were shipped separately. The solution to this was the concept of "Shipping Ready to Copy," which was presented at the 1973 International Logistics Convention in the paper "Quality Products, Ready-To-Use." The concept had the major advantages of checking out the copier in manufacturing final test with all new components and then shipping it with the components still in place. The idea has proved so practical that the product installation abort rate was usually under 3 percent.

Easy to use means that the new customer can operate the product with minimal information. Human factors design is the key, backed up by design reviews, trials, failure modes and effects analysis, and practical logistics assistance.

KISS ("Keep it simple, stupid") must be the watchword. Customers eager to use their new product will try to make it work first, then read instructions when they get into trouble. Self-guiding features are preferrable so that the combination of design, movement flow, numbers, letters, colors, and other features of the product direct the person's efforts in the proper sequence.

If specific training is required for primary operators, it should be conducted either at a central training location prior to the customer's product being installed, or at the customer's location coincident with the installation. A training location removed from the disturbances of the work location is preferred. If the product is to be used by casual operators, then self-guiding features are a must, and may be enhanced by gimmicks such as instructional "comic books."

Preventive maintenance should be avoided if possible. Very few products can be effectively maintained with parts or consumables replaced purely on the basis of time or usage. The conditions under which the products are used are so individualized that condition monitoring and on condition maintenance are significantly more effective than following a strict schedule.

Early-warning devices that measure decreasing resistance, weakening electron emissions, pressure drops, dirt-level buildup, and other changes in significant operating parameters are a better approach than replacing components on the basis of some statistical evaluation. Customers cannot be expected to check these parameters. They should either be checked by service personnel, or should have idiot lights to warn in ample time to prevent a major problem, and a fail-safe mechanism that takes over if necessary.

Rapid repairs make an angry customer happy again. All products are going to fail sometime—the best performing automobile occasionally runs over a nail and gets a flat tire. The customer is most unhappy between the initial detection of failure and when someone is taking care of the problem. The aggravation level over the maintenance downtime is very high before arrival of the service engineer, moderate during diagnostics and repair, and low during the final test and cleanup. Many business equipment service organizations have the technical representative call the customer within ten minutes of receiving dispatch notice of the product failure. This phone call confirms to the aggravated customer that a competent repair person is aware of the need for service. The customer's aggravation is reduced even when told that it will be several hours before the tech rep can arrive. The customer knows the problem is being attended to and has facts on which to make alternate arrangements.

The ability to do it yourself can save many service calls, but must be provided for in the product design. If product complexity precludes the customer from doing repairs, perhaps product mobility will allow the customer to bring the product to service, rather than bearing the cost and time of taking the service to the product. As technical labor becomes more expensive, the inefficiency of wasting a technical representative's time driving to a remote customer becomes more significant. It will always be required for some immovable products, but even large products can have built-in test equipment (BITE) with clear go/no go indications to the customer, and modular components that can be easily transported to service.

Little extras after the repairs are complete can help give the customer a satisfied feeling. How about the carwash after your automobile has just been overhauled? Two dollars worth of labor on top of a large repair bill is a minimal investment that makes the car seem to perform better. Even a correct, itemized bill accompanied by all replaced parts in a clear plastic bag helps reduce the stress caused by the customer's financial expenditure. It is an interesting commentary on the abuses of repair practices that the New York State Repair Shop Registration Act requires a detailed invoice listing parts and labor, including a list of terms and time limits for any guaranteed repairs.

Termination and replacement will inevitably become necessary. When a product wears out and becomes unreliable or obsolete, it will no longer be used. Most companies will try to obsolesce their own products on a planned cycle in order to have continuing business. The competition, of course, would like to have your products replaced with theirs. You should make it easy for the customer to discard or trade in your product. If it could present a safety or security hazard through chemical reaction or explosion, then you should ensure that it is rendered harmless. Preferable arrangements for durable products are to take the old product away when the new one is installed.

In many areas, too, it is found that customers will upgrade to advanced models of your equipment because they were happy with your service but need improved capability. If that is the case, service has done a good job.

LIFE-CYCLE PROFITS

Logisticians are preoccupied with life-cycle costs. It is time things are taken a step further to life-cycle *profits*. Cost is only one component; the other is income. The number of service organizations that are complete business centers is increasing. This is due in a small degree to government pressures, but mainly to the realization that service organizations are motivated more highly toward a total profit goal if they are responsible for both income and outgo.

Six guidelines for establishing smooth customer interfaces that will improve life-cycle profits are as follows:

1. Define the elements of service.
2. Determine the customer's viewpoint.
3. Design a competitive service package.
4. Develop a program to sell service.
5. Market test your program.
6. Establish performance controls.

It is obvious that stock-outs, excessive delivery time, and lack of repair service can all result in lost sales. It should be equally clear that providing a high level of service is costly, and the cost must be justified by achievement of a higher level of sales than would be the case if such service were not offered.

The sales and cost efforts related to customer service have in the past been often considered intangible, but they are rarely so nebulous as to be imponderable. Further, they can usually be quantitatively evaluated and are often measurable and predictable with considerable accuracy. These measurements *must* be made in order to have an efficient service organization.

It is especially important that the customer's view of service be carefully evaluated, taking into account the following:

1. Additional elements of service that could be important to the customer.
2. The economic significance to the customer of each element of service.
3. The customer's rating of your company's service level relative to competitors.

Field personnel often receive significant suggestions from customers. These should be consolidated into a list and put on a customer survey form with additional space for remarks and other suggestions. A customer will almost inevitably request better service or one of the elements not currently provided. However, if service is to be meaningful, it must have an economic significance to the customer in terms of either lowering cost or increasing selling effectiveness. That economic significance will also determine how much the customer is willing to pay for the additional service. A forced rating system is necessary to obtain this information accurately. Forced rating is also the reason that your company service level should be compared with those of competitors. You have an idea what your competitors are doing and what you think your company is doing. The best ratings and comparisons, and the only truly meaningful ones, are those made by your customers. Customers generally appreciate being asked for their comments and regard the opportunity as a sign of positive management.

As we consider the past 200 years, and particularly the technologies that provide comfort and convenience, we should keep in mind that customer perceptions may be more important than facts, and sooner or later the customer is always right!

CHAPTER

22

Product Introductions

More than 26,000 new products are introduced every year at a cost of more than $6 billion in research and development, according to *Time Magazine*. Additional insight into the purpose and nature of industrial R&D can be gained from a survey conducted by McGraw-Hill's department of economics. Slightly more than 40 percent of the firms that responded indicated that the principal purpose of their research and development programs was to "improve existing products" and slightly less than 50 percent indicated it was to produce "new products." Only 11 percent of the firms saw "new processes" as a principal output of these activities. In the same survey, respondents were asked how long they expected payoff from R&D expenditures to take. Here 39 percent stated "less than three years," 52 percent said "three to five years," and only 9 percent expected to wait six or more years to recover their investment. The close relationship of the percentages to the output types and payoff periods is not coincidental. The improving of an existing product typically consumes fewer resources than developing a new product. And when a new product represents a radical departure from the firm's current technological and marketing experience, the resources committed to development may be very large. Therefore, shorter acceptable payoff periods are associated with product improvement and longer payoff periods are indicated for major innovations.

How many product concepts make it to the marketplace? Booz Allen & Hamilton studied this question for 51 companies and discovered that out of approximately every 58 ideas, about 12 pass the initial screening test showing them to be compatible with company objectives and resources.

Of these about seven remain for a thorough evaluation of their profit potential. About three survive the product development stage, two survive the test marketing stage, and only one is commercially successful. Thus some 58 new ideas must be generated to find one good one. Another survey indicates that even among powerful and well-managed companies, seven out of eight hours devoted to technical product development by scientists and engineers are spent on products that fail at some stage in the process. The most vital ingredient for successful new product development and introduction is an effective organizational structure for processing new ideas and following through with them.

TIMING

Timing is important and the payoff for entering the market at an opportune moment can be substantial. It is not unusual to find products prematurely placed in the market. In this case, two sources of failure are common: the product or its introduction has not been fully developed, or the market is not ready to accept the product.

To investigate the effect of time and timing upon marketed products, the production, ongoing, and termination phases of a product's life cycle may be more finely divided as shown in Figure 22.1.

The major stages of a product's life cycle are as follows:

1. Announcement. This is the public notification that the company

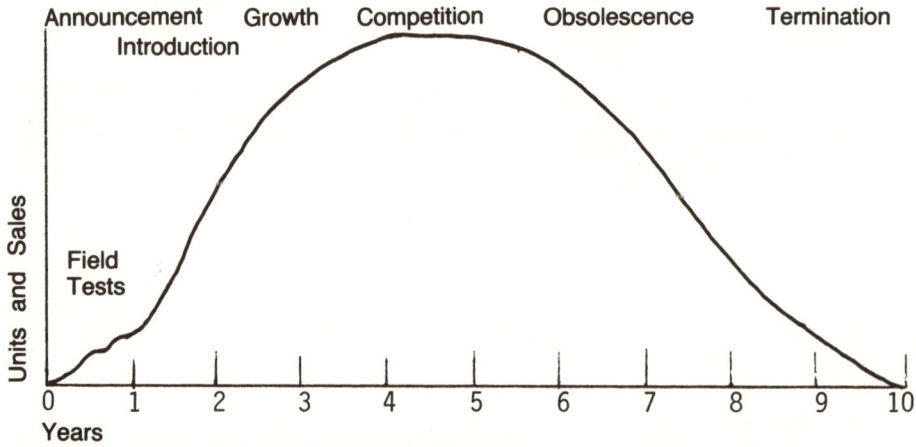

Figure 22.1
Distribution of units and sales during a product's life cycle

intends to market a new product. Legally the product must be available for the mass market within one year of this time, and could be so immediately following the announcement. When a new product is announced, prospective buyers will tend not to buy current products but wait for the new one, so announcement has a major effect on competitive sales. Publicly held corporations are required by the Securities and Exchange Commission to make announcements.

2. Introduction. This normally follows announcement as soon as product tests are successful, although tests may be continued after introduction.

3. Growth. This describes the period during which the product is gaining acceptance and finding its natural place in the market.

4. Competition. This occurs when other products appear and find their places in the market.

5. Obsolescence. The product's competitive disadvantages indicate that the product will soon need modification or replacement.

6. Termination. The product is phased out in favor of an improved product or is dropped from the line.

The coordination between termination of old products and introduction of new ones is important since it is to a company's advantage to have products become obsolete when economies make this reasonable. Financial implications must be emphasized since, as IBM found out in introducing the system 370 computers, new products can sometimes drive more profitable old ones from the marketplace, with a resulting reduction in total profits.

The process of successfully introducing a new product into a firm's product line is typically complex and should take into account many factors.

1. The timing is always later than desired.
2. Many activities are critical in the sense that a delay in any one of them will delay later stages.
3. Some activities are substantially more costly than other activities.
4. High degrees of uncertainty and risk are associated with the required time and cost.
5. Activities that are critical, high in cost, or uncertain must receive special attention.

The critical path method (CPM), program evaluation and review technique (PERT), Gantt charts, and other planning and control techniques are valuable for new product introduction.

INTRODUCTION SUPPORT PLANNING

An organization should have a general policy and procedure for new product introductions. A detailed support plan should be prepared for every significant new product to ensure that it gets reasonable care and attention. The top-level check list for a typical consumer or industrial durable product will include these sections:

1. Introduction and purpose.
2. Program overview
   a. Product
   b. Major events and timing
   c. Build schedule
   d. Revenues and return on investment
   e. International
   f. Timing
3. Personnel selection, training, and management
   a. Technical representatives
   b. Customer education
   c. Field technical and management support
   d. Sales
   e. Riggers
4. Publications and communications
   a. Service manual and updating information
   b. Customer publication
   c. Rigger publications
   d. Installation data sheet
   e. Product capability guide
   f. Administrative procedures
   g. Special publications
5. Tools
   a. Individual
   b. Repair centers
6. Spare parts
   a. Parts ordered document system
   b. Packaging and shipment
   c. Inventories
   d. Returns for repair
   e. Returns for special evaluation
7. Consumables
   a. Special packaging and shipment
   b. Forecasts and inventory
   c. Customer orders and billing

8. Product handling
   a. Packaging
   b. Allocations and shipment
   c. Installation
   d. Cancellation and removal
   e. Rejuvenation
   f. Retrofits
9. Budgets, plans, and controls
   a. Expense, personnel, and capital planning
   b. Facilities and resources
   c. Field data collection and analysis
   d. Configuration management
   e. Service cost analysis
   f. Life-cycle costs
10. Field studies, initial machine observation, and launch control
11. Field operation
    a. Technical service objectives
    b. Territory planning and management
    c. Staffing
    d. Organizations
    e. Reporting systems
12. International
13. Installation emphasis
    a. Sales
    b. Branch coordination
    c. Rigger
    d. Service support
14. Reliability emphasis

INSTALLATION EMPHASIS

Installation and the initial period of use have major impact on customer perception of whether a product is a good one from a competent supplier or a "lemon." Potential customers hear about products from many sources, including sales representatives, advertising, and others who use those products. The amount of investigation a prospective purchaser puts into a new purchase depends largely on the amount of money and effort that is required and what gains are anticipated.

For example, an automobile that is a relatively expensive purchase and will last several years receives considerable customer attention prior to purchase. A prospective customer will read every road test report or advertisement, query other owners, and visit several dealerships to determine the best price. Prominent in the purchaser's mind will be the amount of service that has been required on cars of that make and model in the past, particularly during the initial period of use. Availability of the automobile to provide dependable transportation is most important. The purchaser will also inquire into the number of defects that other owners discovered on their cars since automobile preparation is a responsibility that is shared by the production factory and the selling dealership. The first drive in a new car molds the customer's attitude of satisfaction or discontentment. When the salesperson turns over the keys to a new automobile, we expect it to be ready to run and to provide safe efficient transportation until the first *scheduled* maintenance.

How many parents have discovered late Christmas Eve that a child's new toy requires batteries to operate? How many of us have started to put together a new bicycle in time for a birthday surprise only to discover that critical special hardware has been left out? How many people read the instruction manual *before* trying to operate a new product? It appears that installation and the initial customer perception have often been neglected due to higher priority interests and lack of foresight. One of the most successful concepts for assuring smooth installations is shipping products ready-to-use. Basically this has the advantages of:

1. Increased customer satisfaction by ensuring a complete system.
2. Reduced costs.
3. Improved quality through production type controls.

Emphasis on quality installation will create initial fitness for use. Reliability is often singled out for additional emphasis so that it can be assured the product will continue to provide desired capabilities. If reliability is a major goal for the equipment, then early attention must be paid and special data systems created to evaluate achieved reliability, follow up with failure modes and effects analysis, evaluate retrofits, and provide the other activities a good reliability program will require.

TEST MARKETING

If management has confidence that a product will succeed in the marketplace without testing, then it should be immediately introduced to place as many items as possible in customers' hands before competition can do the same. This is obviously high risk, so most products are market tested prior to large-scale introductions. Figure 22.2 shows a decision tree with alternatives pending on the results of market tests.

Most product tests are integrated trials that evaluate all aspects of the product marketing, pricing, advertising, and packaging along with the distribution, service support, and other logistics elements. It may be seen from Figure 22.2 that the alternative decisions range from going with full introduction for the new product, through modification of the product to improve deficiencies, to dropping the product entirely.

Wise management must be alert to the possibility of terminating the product if market testing shows it is not financially viable. Too often management is reluctant to drop a product that has come so far, and continues to pour money into futile efforts.

Objectives and detailed goals must be developed for a market test so that the critical types of information are identified and methods of gathering this information carefully designed *prior to conducting the test*. The cost of testing includes the cost of setting up the test and analyzing the data and the valuable time that will be lost if the product could have been successfully introduced without the benefit of a test. This author maintains that any new or innovative product must be market tested, since the risk and high cost of failure are generally far more critical than the potential sales impact of earlier full introduction. If management is confident of potential success, then products can be manufactured and stockpiled while the tests are being conducted so that large quantities are available for initial introduction.

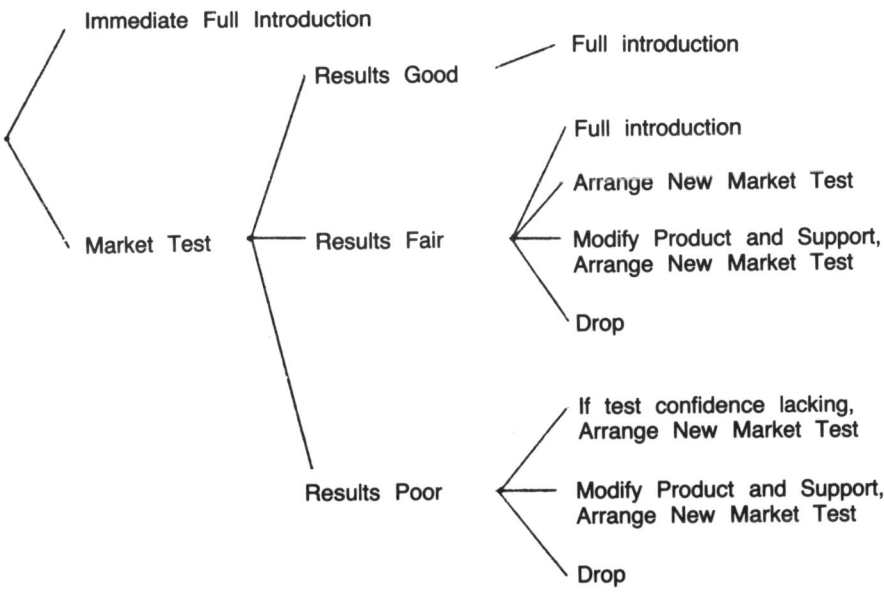

Figure 22.2
Alternative decisions following results of market tests

SUPPORT IMPACT ON INTRODUCTION

The logistics and service organization should have a major impact on location, quantity, timing, and other parameters of product introduction. Sales normally wants large numbers of products distributed to all corners of the globe during the first weeks of introduction. That may be possible, and simultaneous worldwide introductions of new goods are accomplished for publicity and other values, but it is of questionable desirability as common practice. Limited resources should be applied where the need is most critical and most profitable to meet. Particularly with consumer durable products that require service after sales, the service organization should plan a phased introduction so that personnel, spares, tools, information, and other necessary items can be fully established in one area before moving on to the next.

An important consideration in designing a test market concerns the way the population of potential and actual buyers may be classified. Some of the classifications include (see also Figure 22.3):

1. First purchases versus repeated purchases. In many instances it is relatively difficult to forecast customer satisfaction with a product until it has been used under typical conditions. Although it is helpful to know how many potential customers can be persuaded to buy a new product, it will be difficult to determine the product's "staying power" until satisfaction is demonstrated by long-term use or repeat purchases. If the consumption cycle is long, the time lags encountered lengthen and complicate the test process.

2. Test purchases versus full-scale purchases. A new transistor or integrated circuit may be purchased in very small quantities by buyers

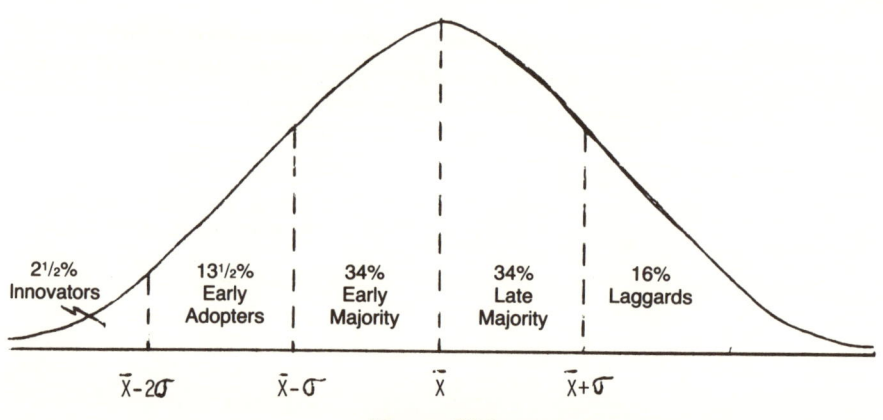

Figure 22.3
Classes of new products adopters

who want to determine how the product performs. Once proven successful in application, a large order may be forthcoming when the product is adopted as a component. In the consumer field, a wholesaler or retailer may buy a small lot of a new product to determine acceptance among customers. When an adequate level of sales to final buyers has been assured, larger normal orders will be forthcoming. In this form of repeat purchasing, order size and time lags justify careful investigation.

3. Purchases by innovator and by noninnovators. For some classes of goods, a distinct group of buyers are leaders or risk takers. This is illustrated in Figure 22.3. Initial sales will be heavily concentrated in this group, and if sales reach a particular level, the less adventuresome buyers can be expected to enter the market. The ability to forecast depends on a knowledge of the types of buyers and the timing of their purchases.

4. High-volume purchasers versus low-volume purchasers. Most types of goods are used in different quantities by different buyers. The extent to which a new product appeals to various segments of the market with different consumption rates can significantly influence the success of some new products.

5. Loyal purchasers and fickle purchasers. Other factors being equal, attracting buyers who can be expected to buy or use the product is more advantageous than gaining a temporary following. In some instances buyers can be identified as being of one type or another. For example, in both the consumer and industrial goods fields, price-conscious buyers may be identified who tend to switch from product to product on short-run price movements.

6. New purchasers and brand-switching purchasers. In most cases some buyers will be new entrants into the market and some will be former buyers of other brands. The number of new buyers and the market and sources of former buyers of another brand can be indicative of both the market size and share of market a new product may expect to attract.

7. Purchasers requiring exceptionally high quality or service levels. If there are significant differences within customer groups, they should be identified so it can be determined if the proposed service package is acceptable to all or what differences should be established. Some customers will require only basic functionality, where others will need consistently high performance. The latter will cost more, but can also be highly profitable.

Although other market segments could be enumerated, the point of looking at these classifications should be evident. Knowing who the users and buyers are will do much to enhance the value of sales information obtained from a test market. Of particular importance is the identification of decision makers as possibly different from the product initiators or operators. Most industries also have a "keystone" company that sets the pace for others. Assuming normal exchange of information within the industry, if probability of test success is high, the product should be placed in this keystone company so that word of the experience will be spread through the industry as a credible positive occurrence. Conversely, if the test is high risk, perhaps the product should be placed where it will get a good test but a possible failure would be kept quiet. If the latter is the case, the product is probably not ready for introduction anyway. A test often depends on the cooperation of the test company and its ability to do what is requested.

SECURITY

Competition will necessarily be very interested in market tests and introductions of new products. Since time is such an important factor in commercial products, secrecy is usually desirable until large quantities of the product are available for sale. For this reason questionnaires, surveys, market tests, and other product-related activities prior to announcement should be conducted using nondisclosure agreements so the information is not divulged. Given the complexity of the logistics system and the large numbers of people involved, it is extremely difficult to keep information secret. Physical distribution personnel are one of the best sources competition can have for information on how many units are being built and where they are being shipped. Service personnel are willing to discuss advantages and disadvantages of new products, too often on the basis of insufficient information. If a new product introduction is to be kept quiet, that fact should be carefully explained to all involved personnel, and their confidence solicited. If everyone knows the information is to be kept secure and why, the risk of exposure is reduced to those who intentionally release information. At least unintentional exposure will be reduced.

CONCLUSIONS

New product introductions can be most successfully accomplished if:

1. The new product is fully proved before its full-scale introduction.
2. Competition is not aware of the coming product until the official announcement.

3. Large quantities of the product are available for early mass distribution.

4. Careful plans are made for the many activities necessary to introduce a new product successfully.

5. Special emphasis is given to installations and the initial period of customer use.

CHAPTER

23

Repair, Rejuvenation, and Disposal

EQUIPMENT REPLACEMENT DECISIONS

The decision to replace a piece of equipment should be based on facts and figures. The judgment is the result of weighing the cost of keeping the old equipment in operation against the cost of its replacement. As time goes by, equipment deteriorates and becomes obsolete. Frequent breakdowns occur, defective output increases, unit labor costs rises, and schedules no longer can be met. At some point these occurrences become serious enough that positive action must be taken either to repair or replace the equipment.

The problem is that new equipment usually requires an initial outlay of capital. The question is whether it will have lower life-cycle costs than the older equipment it would be replacing. The decision is reached making financial calculations that include depreciation, interest, operating costs, and revenues.

Depreciation is one of the major costs connected with any type of capital equipment. For cost-comparison purposes, depreciation is simply the amount by which an asset decreases in value over some period of time. The Internal Revenue Service sets guidelines that say, for example, one should depreciate computers, typewriters, and calculators over a five-year period, office furniture over ten years, service tools over 13.5 years, and automobiles over three years. Other periods may be used if they can be justified. Depreciation rates may be figured either on straight line, so that an equal percentage is allowed each year; using sum-of-the-years digits; or using a high percentage declining balance, which will result in higher depreciation in early years that is reduced later in the equipment's life. If, for example, you bought a typewriter for $800 and sold it four years later for $250, the $550 difference is the depreciation that was one of the costs for owning the equipment those four years. When considering equipment replacement, you must calculate the future depreciation expense that you will experience with both the old and the new equipment. This requires knowing the acquisition cost, estimated service life, and expected salvage value.

The depreciation expense for old equipment is determined in the same general way, but with one important difference: no expenditure is required to acquire the equipment because you already own it. However, a decision to keep it does require an investment at the present time which is equal to the asset's market value—that is, the amount of money the asset would bring if it were sold. If this amount is not equal to the equipment's book value, the depreciation expense that was shown for accounting purposes should be corrected to show the actual depreciation.

In addition to depreciation, every piece of equipment generates an interest expense. This is so because owning an asset ties up capital that could be bringing some return if used for other investments. This "opportunity cost" is one of the costs of owning the equipment. For example, suppose that the current market value of service test equipment is $10,000. Also suppose that capital is costing 12 percent per year and that if the asset were converted into cash, that cash could be invested to realize a rate of return of 15 percent per year. The decision to own the asset, therefore, costs 15 percent times $10,000, or $1500 in interest per year.

A third type of cost—the cost of operation—is experienced with a piece of equipment. Typical operating costs include labor, materials, supervision, maintenance, and power. These costs must be considered because the choice of equipment affects them. Figures can be obtained for each unit of equipment by estimating next year's operating costs as well as the annual rate at which these costs are likely to increase as wage rates rise and the equipment deteriorates. For example, the operating costs of new equipment might be $15,000 during the first year of its life. After that first year, operating costs are projected to increase at a rate of $500 per year. The comparison problem may be simplified by estimating the costs either as an incremental difference between the operating costs of the compared units, or by ignoring those costs that are the same for the old and the proposed equipment. With this simplification the total costs calculated for each type of equipment will be understated by the same amount and the difference between the total costs will be the same, so the more economical alternative will be easily recognized.

If the revenues generated by the old and the new equipment will be the same, they may be ignored. But if revenues are affected by the choice of the equipment, they must be considered. For example, higher output from new equipment could increase annual sales by $2000. This difference in revenues can be handled either by showing the $2000 as an additional annual cost experienced with the old equipment, or by treating it as a negative annual cost associated with the new equipment.

To do a comparison, assume that an old piece of equipment has a market value of $7000. If retained, its service life is expected to be four years and its future salvage value will be $1000. Next year's operating costs are estimated to be $8000, but will probably increase at an annual rate of $200. The cost of money is 12 percent per year.

Depreciation is computed by

$$\text{Annual depreciation} = \frac{\$7000 - \$1000}{4} = \$1500$$

Annual interest expense is found by taking the average market value of the equipment times the annual interest. Since the equipment is worth $7000 today but will decline to $1000, the average investment is

$$\text{Average investment} = \frac{\$7000 + \$1000}{2} = \$4000$$

Annual interest = $4000 \times 0.12 = \$480$

The average annual operating costs are computed by taking the average of the costs expected for the next four years, which increase by $200 each year.

$$\text{Annual operating cost} = \frac{\$8000 + \$8200 + \$8400 + \$8600}{4} = \$8300$$

The total average annual cost is simply the sum of depreciation plus interest plus operating expenses. See Table 23.1.

Looking at the new piece of equipment that is the proposed replacement, the acquisition cost is seen to be $30,000. Its life is estimated to be ten years and it will probably have a salvage value of $6000. Operating costs are expected to average $5200 a year. Furthermore it is expected that there will be an annual revenue advantage of $300 over the old equipment. Annual depreciation and interest are calculated the same way as they were for the old equipment.

It can be seen that the expected annual cost for the old equipment is

$10,280 and for the new is $9460. It appears that the new equipment is more economical than the old. But is it? A person could argue that with the old equipment you are committed for only four years, whereas with the new your commitment is for ten years. This fact suggests a need to consider the kind of equipment that may be available for replacement purposes four years from now as compared with ten years from now. Since it is difficult to forecast that far into the future, this element should be ignored unless a new technology has already been announced that might mean improved products four years from now.

There may be other irreducible factors that should be considered. If total average annual costs are about the same, the equipment that requires the smaller investment and has the shorter life should be preferred. Also to be preferred is equipment that has advantages in safety, reliability, or output capacity even though the value of these parameters may be unknown. Finally, if interest rates for borrowing money are expected to increase in the future and the price of new equipment will increase significantly, the investment should be made in new equipment now, rather than later.

Table 23.1
Average Annual Cost

Item	Average Annual Cost
Depreciation	$1,500
Interest	480
Operating cost	8,300
Total	$10,280

Table 23.2
Average Annual Cost
Less Revenue Advantage

Item	Average Annual Cost
Depreciation	$2,400
Interest	2,160
Operating cost	5,200
Total	$9,760
Less revenue advantage	300
	$9,460

REPAIR/DISCARD ANALYSIS

Level-of-repair analysis (LORA), also known as level of repair (LOR), and optimum-repair-level analysis (ORLA) is now a well-established and accepted technique. The military services remain unable to agree on an acronym, but otherwise they and most commercial industries use the techniques, and often computerized models. The maximum benefit in performing level-of-repair analysis is obtained by doing so early in the life cycle and designing the equipment according to the analysis results. The results of an LOR analysis are used to prepare maintenance plans and determine logistics resource allocations. The analysis will delineate as outputs resources of workers, material, and money. The LOR analytic techniques can also be used to evaluate alternative design and support proposals. Examples include:

1. Repair versus discard.
2. Basic system design versus proposed alternatives.
3. Automatic test equipment versus peculiar support equipment.
4. Contractor support versus military support.
5. Modular versus piece-part replacement.

Repair/discard trade-off decisions may be classified into two types: repair level and design direction.

The repair-level decision is useful for developing logistic support concepts during the system planning phases for use during the operational phase after design has been completed. The decision to be made is concerned with optimizing the maintenance and support levels at which repairs are most economical to effect. For example, is it more economical to repair a repairable item at the using level or at a rear support level? The second type of repair/discard decision is design oriented for application during the late planning and the design phases of the system life cycle. Some models can be used for both design and repair-level decisions.

In a study titled "Criteria for Repair vs. Discard Decisions," the Logistics Management Institute noted the high interaction between repair/discard decisions and other system design and support economic (life-cycle cost) decisions. It identified five major decision points in the system life cycle where repair/discard decisions might logically be made (Figure 23.1). The first of these decision points, development of design specifications, occurs during the concept formulation and system definition phases. It depends upon operational, maintenance, and logistic support policies as well as cost effectiveness and other economic criteria established during concept and system studies. At this level repair/discard decisions are primarily broad policy decisions that become part of the

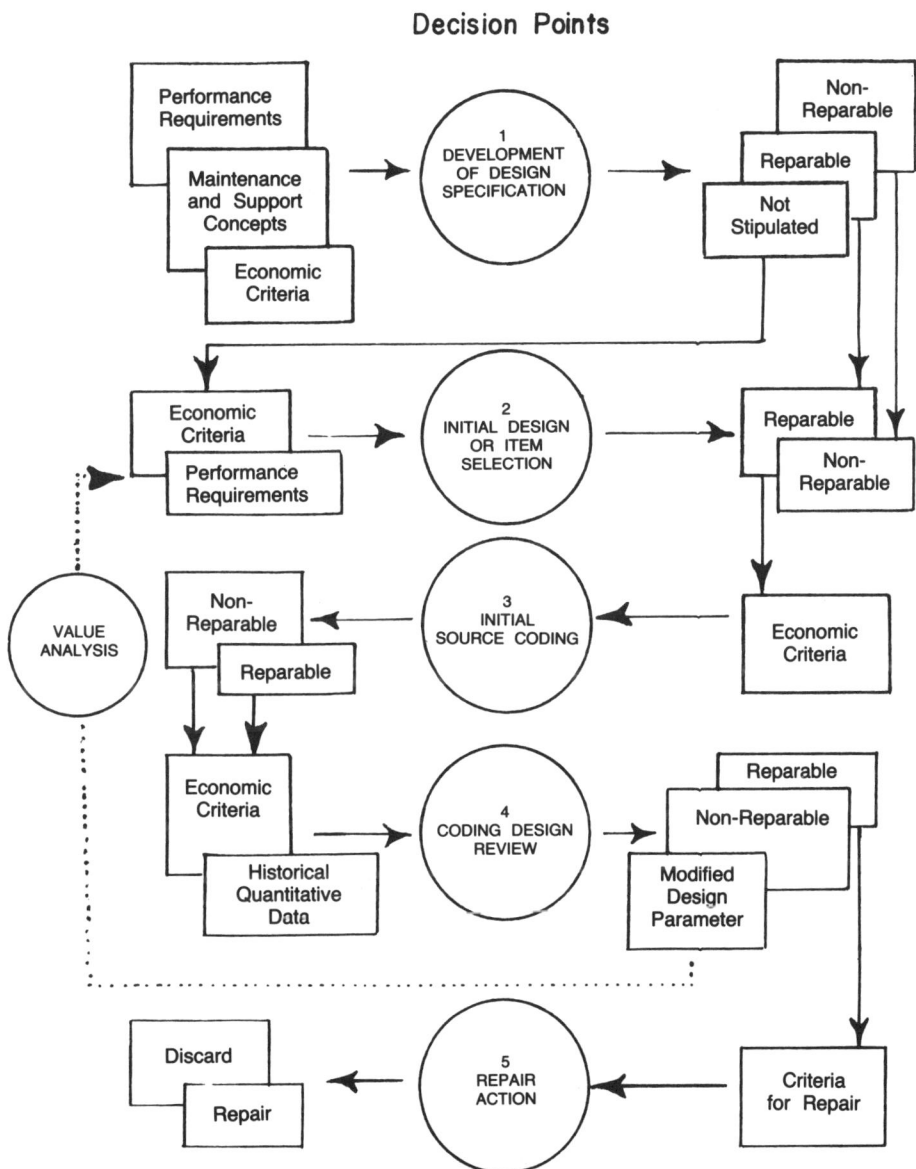

Figure 23.1
Decision points for repair discard analysis

overall maintenance and logistic support concept. They result in the establishment of both qualitative and quantitative criteria in system development specifications to guide system/equipment design engineers during the development and design phases.

The second point in the LMI model, initial design or item selection, occurs during engineering development. The policies and criteria previously established are now applied to assemblies, subassemblies, and modules based upon analyses using quantitative repair/discard cost models. The third decision point, initial source coding for provisioning, occurs during the late design and early production phases. At this point the major design decisions with regard to repair/discard have already been made. The decisions at this point, therefore, are primarily logistic support decisions, such as range and depth of spares, effect on operational readiness of maintenance and supply delays, transportation and pipeline effects, and numbers and locations of test and repair stations.

The fourth decision point in the LMI model, coding/design review, occurs during the operation and support phases of system deployment. At this point previously established repair/discard decisions and criteria may be reviewed for validity based upon historical operation and support data collected from the field use of the system/equipment. Such a review may result in a change in the repair/discard decision or in a modification to the design through the use of value engineering. The fifth decision point, repair action, is concerned with whether a repairable item is still economically worth fixing after a failure has occurred, or, upon a scheduled maintenance inspection, as a result of damage, the item's age, wear, or other condition.

Of these five decision points, the first two have significant impact upon system/equipment design for maintainability. The LMI report points out that the quantitative values of most decision criteria depend upon the results of a variety of design and support decisions other than the repair/discard decision.

REPAIR/DISCARD MODELS

Repair/discard models are economic decision models in which the cost of repairing an item is compared with the cost of discarding the item and replacing it with a new one, and the lower cost option chosen. The costs considered are usually total life-cycle costs. The comparison is often displayed in terms of a difference equation, such as

$$\Delta C = C_r - C_d$$

where
ΔC = cost difference
C_r = cost of repair
C_d = cost of discard and replacement

Thus, if C is positive, the discard option is selected; if it is negative, the repair option is selected. The cost equations are usually quite complex, but the models are readily computerized. The repair and discard cost equations may contain identical terms for some cost factors or terms that are relatively insensitive and thus can be treated as constants. These terms can then be eliminated from the difference equations. The difference equations are sometimes simplified into limited "delta cost models," and simpler screening rules are sometimes used to minimize the need to use the more complete cost models. In some cases, especially during early life-cycle phases, all the data required by the complete model may not be available. The screening rules are, therefore, useful for early decisions.

GRAPHIC SCREENING TECHNIQUES

It is both expensive and unnecessary to perform a detailed cost analysis on every spare. A screening technique has been developed that can, with minimum effort, indicate the economically correct repair–throwaway code for a large portion of spares. It is applied to all spares except the items that are always thrown away, such as common hardware, potted or welded materials, or materials with limited storage life.

There may also be noneconomic criteria that outweigh the economic screening, such as:

1. Weight. Very heavy parts might be made repairable to avoid having to transport the items for replacement.
2. Volume. Storage space may be at a premium and not available for replacements.
3. Mobility. Operating conditions may require local repair instead of resupply.
4. Downtime. Speed of restoration could be better with repair, or replacement may be faster.
5. Design differences. Materials, producibility, reliability, and maintainability can differ with intent.

Figure 23.2 illustrates a series of curves developed for graphic screening. The horizontal axis shows the total parts usage for all products over their life cycle. The vertical axis shows the average repair cost as a percent of the unit cost of the part. For example, if the average repair costs $3500 for an item of unit cost $5000, the vertical point is 70 percent (3500/5000). Part P of Figure 9.9 has usage of 100 over the life cycle. If it would cost $50,000 to have repair facilities for part P, then it should be coded "repairable" since the intersection point is below the $50,000 cost curve. If repair facilities would cost over $125,000, the part should be discarded. Note that there is a range of values since this type of graph is not precise and the sensitivities of specific parts can vary. If the point intersection is close to the decision curve, then more careful calculations should be made. Quantitative factors to be considered are shown in Table 23.3.

IMPACT ON MAINTAINABILITY

Equipment must be designed for discard instead of repair, with consideration given to the items shown in Table 23.4. Many benefits are possible if failed parts can be discarded, including reduced requirements for accessibility to lower equipment levels, reduced need for skilled personnel and test equipment, fewer test points, simpler displays, and possibly even elimination of an entire level of maintenance. Time

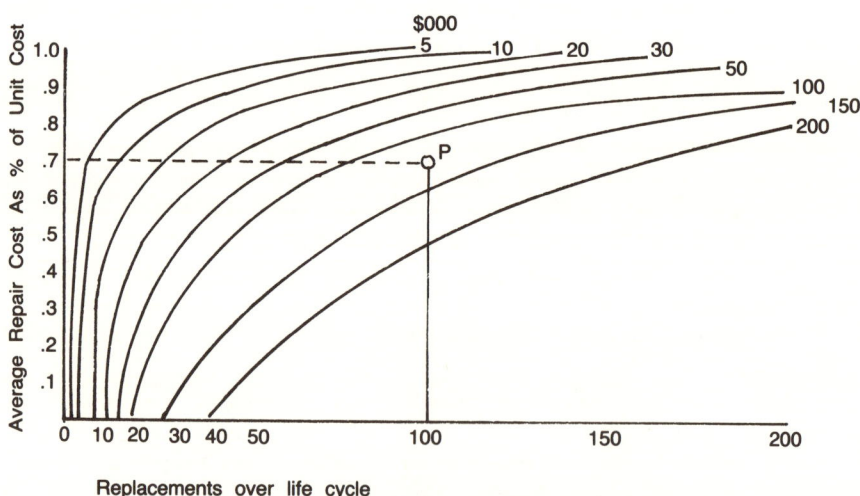

Figure 23.2
Graphic screening for repair/discard

to repair will usually be improved with resulting improvement on operational readiness. The number of individual line items in spares stocks will be reduced.

On the other hand, depending on module size, weight, and complexity, there may be a requirement for a greater number of larger, bulkier, heavier, more expensive modules in inventory.

The following guidelines are useful in making repair/discard decisions:

1. Repair unless a discard decision is justified.
2. Start analysis with the highest assembly and work downward until a discard decision is justified.
3. Screen all items before more exhaustive economic analysis is used.
4. Identify and evaluate significant related decisions and noneconomic factors prior to repair/discard analysis.
5. Finally conduct analysis, weighted by necessary constraints.

Factors that favor discard include:

1. Probable reliability improvement due to reduced exposure.
2. Probable design and manufacturing savings due to elimination of need for accessibility within throwaway modules.
3. Unit cost reduction since more modules would be produced.
4. Simplified retrofits by replacement of complete modules.
5. Reduction in skill requirements of repair persons.
6. Go/no go testers instead of variable devices.
7. Less need for repair space.
8. Freeing of expensive facilities freed for more important uses.

Factors against discard include:

1. Emotional feeling that discard is wasteful.
2. Loss of reliability information since parts are not often evaluated.
3. High inventory and storage requirements.
4. Capability for emergency repairs is reduced.
5. Probable increase in size and weight due to more connectors.

REJUVENATION

A piece of equipment often reaches the state of performing poorly, whether because of degraded capabilities, obsolescence, or wear-out; and it must either be replaced or rejuvenated. There are several "R words" that describe the rehabilitation, refurbishment, reconditioning, or rebuilding that may be done to rejuvenate a piece of equipment and restore

**Table 23.3
Quantitative Factors in Repair/Discard Models**

I. Dollar costs
   A. Calculated values
      1. Total life-cycle cost
      2. Discard cost
      3. Repair cost
      4. Cost of difference (Δ cost)
   B. Input costs
      1. Design cost
      2. Production cost
      3. Procurement cost
      4. Logistics cost
      5. Salvage value
      6. Constants

II. Resources
   A. Personnel
      1. Direct labor
      2. Indirect labor
      3. Training
   B. Equipment
      1. Prime equipment
      2. Support equipment
      3. Test equipment
      4. Tools and fixtures
   C. Materials
      1. Expendables
      2. Spares
      3. Repair parts
   D. Facilities
      1. Buildings
      2. Maintenance areas
      3. Supply areas
   E. Information
      1. Maintenance manuals
      2. Logistics data
      3. Provisioning data
      4. Maintenance engineering analysis data
      5. Drawings and specifications
      6. Test programs (software)

**Table 23.3
Quantitative Factors in Repair/Discard Methods (continued)**

III. Activities
  A. Maintenance
   1. Preventive maintenance
   2. Corrective maintenance
   3. Repair levels
  B. Supply
   1. Inventory and inventory control
   2. Entering and retaining a new line item
   3. Logistics processing
   4. Procurement
  C. Transportation and handling
   1. Packaging and preparation
   2. Storing and handling
   3. Transportation
  D. Miscellaneous
   1. Technical services
   2. Administration

IV. Other factors
  A. Quantity
   1. Item population
   2. Items per module
   3. Number of parts peculiar
  B. Reliability
   1. Failure rate
   2. Total number of failures
  C. Maintainability
   1. MTTR or repair rate
   2. Repair cycle time
  D. Time
   1. Item life
   2. Systems/equipment life
   3. Operating time
   4. Utilization rate
   5. Lead time
   6. Waiting times
  E. Effectiveness
   1. System availability
   2. Logistics availability
   3. Operational readiness

**Table 23.4
Effect of Repair/Discard Considerations on Maintainability Design Factors**

Factor	Repair	Discard
Accessibility	To lowest repair level	Reduced in equipment; none in modules
Test points	To lowest level	Fewer; perhaps as few as one per module
Controls	More with greater interaction among modules	Within module
Labeling and coding	To individual item	To module only
Displays	More complex; to lowest repair level	Simpler and fewer
Manuals, aids	More complex	Fewer and simpler
Test equipment	More specialized and manual; down to individual item for fault isolation	BITE and more automatic; simpler fault isolation
Tools	More	Fewer
Connectors	Probably fewer	Probably more for plug-ins
Mounting and fasteners	Hard wiring, fewer plug-ins and connectors	More plug-ins
Handles and handling	May require more handling	May require more handles on plug-ins; less handling
Safety	Greater hazard to workers and equipment	Less hazard
Skill level	Higher	Lower

it to prime operating condition. Refurbishment has the connotation of being the easiest to do, as it usually consists mainly of performing preventive maintenance and cleaning the equipment so it appears fresh again. This is usually done on rental equipment being removed from one customer after easy use, and can be reinstalled quickly with another customer. The "loaner" and "demo" equipment used by salespeople requires frequent refurbishment to keep it in top-notch condition. Modifications and retrofits are rarely done during a refurbishing process. It must be cost effective and therefore involves minimal labor and parts, and can be done only on equipment that is in relatively good condition to begin with. Equipment that is older, has had more use, suffered damage, or requires a modification must be routed to a more extensive rejuvenation process.

Rebuilding and reconditioning generally mean the same: to disassemble equipment completely and build it again using materials of the latest configuration so that a reconditioned product is considered equivalent to a new one. In fact a rebuilt product can be superior to a new one as early failure will have been eliminated from many components. As returned products are disassembled in the reconditioning plant, the parts should be carefully inspected to determine whether, on the basis of their configuration and remaining wear life, they should be scrapped, repaired, or cleaned and reused. The quality control on a reconditioning process must include the same stringent specifications as are used for new manufacture, with additional competence in the tear-down/receiving inspection because of the many variations in configuration and the wear that must be judged as acceptable or not. Great effort is required to establish the specifications for reconditioned equipment. Marketing will want equipment that looks and performs like new. Manufacturing wants to minimize costs. Both can be accomplished, but only through an integrated effort where all parties work together with the objective of improving life-cycle profit by both reducing life-cycle costs and balancing them with improved life-cycle revenues.

A cost-effective approach can be "as-required" conditioning. If only a few high-value items are to be rejuvenated, this can be very effective. Aircraft, for example, should always be rebuilt as required. This involves detailed evaluation of every component to determine whether it should be reused or replaced.

If large quantities of equipment are to be considered for rejuvenation, criteria should be established that will permit rapid screening to the best process. There will be some attributes that can be used as go/no-go criteria. These might include the presence of certain modifications or configuration features, possibly established by serial number. Variables measurements may be decided by a point system that assigns a value to usage, age, appearance, service history, and projected cost for rejuvenation.

The screening criteria should keep the equipment at the least-cost/least-effort rejuvenation level. However, it is recognized that the rejuvenation activity may be strongly driven by sales. If open orders exist for the product, then service and manufacturing people will be required to do whatever is necessary, with little regard to cost and time efficiencies, so that the equipment can be placed to produce revenue.

Another major reconditioning operation can be for major parts and assemblies. For example, printed wiring boards generally have high-density circuitry with sensitive components that require expensive computerized test equipment and specialized repair techniques. Motors, power supplies, transmissions, and similar high-value items can be replaced on location to get the customer's equipment running quickly and then returned to the reconditioning center for repair.

Credit is often used as a motivator to ensure that high-value parts are returned through the system. The amounts range from 50 to 100 percent of the part value. If the part is on warranty, the credit should be 100 percent since every item is to be returned to the manufacturer for repair. Other amounts may be set depending upon the need for the material, cost of the components, aggravation of returning it, and abilities of field customer engineers to repair the equipment. If field personnel have to pay high prices for replacement parts, they will avoid the replacement as long as possible and will then try to repair it themselves or have it done in the lowest cost fashion. This is not the best approach from a total dollar value or customer satisfaction point of view.

A credit system helps to motivate people to use the best method of repair. To have a credit system work well, every customer engineer must be aware of the credit amount for those parts that are to be returned. Those parts should also be packaged in a returnable shipping container so that the new replacement part will have the packing materials to return the defective part. The credit system must assure that the proper monetary credit is recorded, either in the same month as the cost of the replacement part, or no later than one month following. A credit tag is very useful for attachment to the returned goods. If it is in multiple copies, one can be retained by the customer engineer, and the other copies attached to the returned part box as a shipping record with a copy removed by each agency needing a record. The form should state what the part number is, why it is being returned, equipment serial number it came from, the customer engineer's name and number, and the date.

Attention must be continuously paid to the amounts of material accumulating and the time required to process that inventory. An amazing amount of material can gather during periods of inattention, since it is of less value than similar materials in usable condition. When one large business equipment company created an organization specifically to expedite repairs or disposition of excess and returned materials, it added over $2,000,000 to the company income the first year through repairing or selling excess materials.

DISPOSITION

Sooner or later every piece of equipment reaches the point where it is no longer serviceable and should be disposed of. Major products and systems should have a phase-out and termination stage planned as the last major program action. This is rarely done, however, as product planners like to think their creation is going to live forever. Still, withdrawal from the marketplace can be accomplished best in planned conditions, with a new product phased in while the obsolete one is being phased out. Planned obsolescence is, in fact, a necessary marketing strategy, which is translated into specific tactics at the end of the equipment's life.

Diminished system effectiveness—as a result of decreased capability relative to competitive equipment, declining reliability, or even changes in the style—may cause a product to be pushed from the market by dissatisfied customers or pulled back by the company, which realizes it is no longer profitable.

There is considerable tie-in in the marketplace between different products of one company. It is mandatory that the company continue to supply parts and service for equipment for at least seven years after it is officially withdrawn from active sales. Many products have markets well beyond the original one. For example, the DC-3 aircraft is still utilized effectively in underdeveloped areas. Basic equipment that has been surpassed by more sophisticated products in major American and European markets may be quite suitable elsewhere. Thus products may be withdrawn from a current market and rejuvenated for use in another geographic area. Similarly, items might be withdrawn from lease and sold outright for cash profits. For financial reasons depreciation should be taken on equipment as rapidly as possible so that it will have been fully depreciated by the time it is resold. Equipment or parts that have no further use to a company should be scrapped and their value written off the company's financial records as soon as possible. There is rarely any advantage in having obsolete or unnecessary equipment lying around—it is consuming space, labor, and financial resources that can be better utilized.

Several options exist for materials an organization no longer finds useful. They may be of value, for instance, to another division in the parent company, or to a company that deals in that specific item or commodity, or they may be sold for their scrap value. Research laboratories and model shops often need components that are being discarded, and they should be notified first so that they can screen such materials for possible use. The service or factory repair operations may also be able to save money by using components discarded by other operations. Any material that can be used within the same company saves the user the expense of buying new materials and thus retains more value for the company than it would if sold to outsiders.

Large quantities of scrap material such as motors, transformers, printed wiring boards, and other components in relatively common use can be sold to scrap marketing companies, which in turn sell them to short-run facilities and hobbyists.

Finally, if the materials cannot be sold for a functional use, they can at least be segregated by components and raw materials such as aluminum, steel, glass, and paper sold for recycling. The service and logistics departments should work closely with the procurement organization responsible for disposition in order to secure the best possible value for excess materials. It will occasionally even be economically prudent to sell materials that could be modified and use new ones instead, if someone else will pay a high price for the materials in their present state. While this situation is not common, it is another way in which participation by procurement experts can increase the life-cycle profit through improved repair, rejuvenation, and discard of materials.

CHAPTER

24

Logistics Models

*T*his chapter deals with a modern analytical tool called *modeling* and how it can be applied to solving complex logistical problems. The advantages and disadvantages of models will also be discussed and the application of two types of modeling techniques used throughout industry today explained.

DEFINITION OF A MODEL

A model is an abstract representation of real phenomena. Models can be grouped into five main types: verbal, iconic, analog, schematic, and mathematical.

Words are used to construct verbal models. Written and spoken verbal models construct images in the receiver's mind that depict the real occurrence. This type of verbal modeling is a sign of intelligence and a level of abstraction that sets humans apart from other animals in capability.

Iconic models are three-dimensional creations, usually in scale proportion to the real thing. A child's model airplane and a full-scale mockup of the Trident submarine are both iconic models.

Analog models are built on the premise that the behavior of full-scale systems may be studied and analyzed by studying the behavior of other systems with similar characteristics. Prototype aircraft (iconic models) may be tested in a wind tunnel to predict operation under flight conditions. The flow of water through pipes has been shown to be analogous to the flow of electricity through wires. The most immediate application of analog models is in research and development, product design, and plant operations.

Schematic models are based on the adage, "A picture is worth a thousand words." Using pictorial form avoids many of the communication difficulties inherent in the use of verbal models, and reduces ambiguity. The most frequent use of schematic models is to describe complex systems in summary form. Drawings and charts such as PERT diagrams, maps, organization charts, and decision-tree diagrams are very useful.

Mathematical or symbolic models represent the highest level of abstraction in model construction. The fields of operations research and management science are devoted almost exclusively to developing and using mathematical models to provide management with more and better information for decision making. Mathematical models offer a degree of precision that is limited only by our ability to count or measure and the perceptions of the model builder.

Mathematical models may be classified as either stochastic (probabilistic) or deterministic models. Stochastic models deal with uncertainty through the use of probability and statistics. Deterministic models, on the other hand, do not recognize the element of chance in a system and compute the dependent variable exactly. Common business examples of deterministic models are break-even analysis, linear programming, and economic order quantity determination. Math models may also be characterized as either descriptive or optimizing in purpose. Descriptive models describe a single relationship or a set of relationships, usually at a single point in time. For example, the equation A (assets) = L (liabilities) + NW (net worth) is a financial descriptive model. The basic goal of optimizing models is to find the best possible allocation of scarce resources among competing opportunities as in determining least-cost solutions for level-of-repair determination.

SOME BASIC ADVANTAGES OF USING MODELS

When one sets out to study the interactions among the interrelated elements of a system, such as reliability, maintainability, performance, effectiveness, and logistical support, one quickly discovers the difficulty of creating total system visibility. A model can be developed to represent the total system in a realistic integrated manner, and will allow a productive analysis effort. One might ask, "How will an increase in reliability affect spare parts provisioning?" "Is shorter maintenance downtime worth the cost of achieving it through parts redesign?" These and thousands of other questions may be answered through the judicious use of properly constructed models.

Models broaden the base of investigation. They can be used to assess alternatives rapidly and permit the decision maker to investigate many more alternatives than would be possible otherwise. Models often permit the solution to problems that are too cumbersome to solve by other means.

CHECKING FOR MODEL LIMITATIONS

Models are well accepted as a means of performing analyses of various alternatives. However, since many significant decisions are based in large part on the results of such analyses, it is important to be aware of some of the limitations of the modeling approach. There are four important questions every analyst should consider before selecting and using a model:

1. Is the model applicable and usable?
2. Are the available data adequate?
3. Are the results applicable to the real world?
4. Are the results optimal?

Every model has its limitations. Analysts must recognize them and adjust their thinking accordingly.

APPLYING MODELS THROUGHOUT THE PRODUCT LIFE CYCLE

Modeling can be an effective analytical tool at almost every stage of a product's development cycle. Models are also useful in assessing the effectiveness of logistical support programs even after the product is in operation in the field.

During the conceptual design and advanced system development phase, models can be used to compare alternative operational concepts, utilization rates, performance parameters, logistic support policies, and related factors. During the early phase of system development (at program inception), the system designer should establish an overall maintenance philosophy to determine whether an equipment will be repaired or discarded at failure, whether intermediate and/or depot maintenance will be required, whether preventive maintenance will be feasible, and so on. A firm policy cannot be established at this point, but it should at least be thought about. Feasible approaches may be identified and included as part of the maintenance concept through the use of models that evaluate the many possible alternatives identified for consideration. The most fruitful method of reducing ownership costs is to influence design from its inception, thereby ensuring that the downstream logistic costs to operate, maintain, and sustain the hardware are considered. It is here where the greatest payoff opportunity lies.

The logistics community, and the logistics engineer, must become involved at the start of the equipment life cycle during the conceptual phase. The reason is clear when one understands that by the conclusion of the conceptual phase, at least 70 percent of the total life-cycle costs have already been dictated. The logistician must be involved from the inception of a system's or equipment's life and must play an active role in any analysis leading to program decisions. In arriving at a design approach, or a method of satisfying the operational need, acquisition costs, performance, and schedule are the three prime considerations utilized in making trade-offs. They form the three sides of the acquisition decision triangle. The triangle must become a square, however, and a fourth factor must be considered: the support costs associated with the design approach arrived at during the conceptual phase.

Trade-offs must weigh performance against support costs, and hard decisions must be made at this point no matter how agonizing they may be. Modeling gives the decision maker a tool that helps promote such decisions.

Modeling can also be useful for comparing alternative design configurations during the detailed equipment design phase. Equipment packaging schemes, testing approaches, accessibility, size and weight, standardization, and other related reliability, maintainability, and human factors design characteristics significantly impact the various elements of logistic support. Models may be employed to aid the designer in defining the ultimate equipment design configuration.

As the equipment design approaches maturity, it is necessary to evaluate the various alternative methods for supporting the equipment in the field. This includes the many approaches that become evident through life-cycle cost analyses and maintenance analyses. The use of logistic support models facilitates this evaluation.

The final phase in a total program cycle is the assessment of the logistic support effectiveness; the evaluation of equipment supportability and the effectiveness of logistic support throughout system/equipment operation in the field. After initial deployment of the prime equipment and its associated elements of logistics support, it is necessary to measure overall cost/system effectiveness. Several questions should be asked. "Are the acquired elements of logistics support adequate in terms of type, quantity, and location?" "How should logistic support provisioning factors used in reprocurements be changed to meet the needs better?"

"What is the impact of a prime equipment change on the various elements of logistics support?" These and other factors need to be evaluated on a continuing basis to assure that system operational effectiveness is maintained, and the logistics models may be employed accordingly.

USING MODELS FOR DETERMINING SENSITIVITIES

Modeling in general has tremendous educational benefits as well as being an effective tool in decision making. The analyst can readily identify relationships among system parameters, and is better prepared to respond to the "what if . . ." questions. For instance, what is the impact on spare/repair parts if equipment reliability is degraded? What is the impact on support equipment if the prime equipment packaging design changes? What is the impact on overall system maintenance if the equipment is utilized to a greater extent than initially planned? There are many questions of this type to which an analyst with experience can readily respond, and these responses should be preplanned to avoid possible future problems.

Caution in Use of Models

There are things a model cannot do. It will not solve a problem without correct logic and input. And it is not a substitute for good judgment.

A single, complex, all-inclusive model cannot offer some of the advantages available through the use of multiple models designed to function as an integrated set. Computer storage may be quickly exceeded, it may be difficult to acquire the required time on the computer, the model may not incorporate the desired flexibility and/or growth potential, it becomes difficult and costly to incorporate changes in the model, and the model may not provide timely results. On the other hand, developing a set of models (each model in the set having the capability to evaluate a specific class of problems) does provide the necessary flexibility required to solve the large variety of problems listed. Individual models can be tailored and are more responsive to evaluating the impact of a design change on spare/repair parts, and of a waiting line or repairable item demands on support equipment loading and utilization, and similar lower level problems. If changes to the model are required, they can be incorporated without affecting other models in the set. Thus, when developing models, the modular approach is preferable. Both individual evaluations and the total system evaluation effort must be considered so that different models in the set may be employed singly or on a combined basis.

The usual dangers inherent in abstraction are present. A mathematically feasible model or series of expressions may require gross oversimplifications. There is no guarantee that the time and effort invested in model development will provide the results desired. The analyst must be careful to ascertain that the model does indeed reflect a realistic situation.

There is danger that the analyst, after playing with the model for a long time, will become too attached to it—some analysts so much so that they will insist the model is the real world and is directly applicable to all problems at hand. Again, care must be exercised to ensure that the model selected is compatible with the problem(s) being solved.

Models are only a decision-making tool and cannot be considered a substitute for experience and judgment. As such, their use in a variety of situations has produced successful results.

Two popular models are level-of-repair analysis (LOR) and long-range environmental planning simulators (LREPS).

Level-of-Repair Analysis Model

Most LOR models calculate the fixed costs involved with acquiring initial spares, repair facilities, training, and publications; and the variable costs associated with such tasks as performing maintenance, replacing consumable items, updating publications, training replacements, and keeping an item in the inventory. They do this for a preset number of maintenance concepts under an operating scenario that generates maintenance requirements, repair, and replacement of the items being analyzed. These costs are then summed over some specified number of years. That maintenance concept with the lowest cost is considered to be the optimum repair level.

The model used must take into account the various levels of maintenance, which may vary from customer to customer, and it must represent the possible flows of items through those repair and supply channels. It must then consider all the factors that cause costs to be incurred and treat those in an appropriate manner while avoiding the necessity where possible for input data that are difficult and/or expensive to obtain. A balance must be struck between including all factors that significantly impact the life-cycle cost while excluding those that make a minimal contribution.

Another consideration is when during the life cycle the model is to be used. The LOR analysis task itself will normally be performed during full-scale development of the system. However, the same basic model can (and should) be used during early development to perform trade-off studies to ascertain the most optimum combination of system design features and support characteristics. It should also be used after deployment to evaluate the cost effectiveness of proposed changes to the system.

Decisions on provisioning, reprovisioning, product improvement, and modification all should receive the benefit of economic analysis. Support policies must receive continued scrutiny and evaluation throughout a system's useful life.

Data requirements vary greatly from model to model. Whatever its requirements, a model's effectiveness is dependent upon the quantity and quality of the data available to drive it. In general the longer a system has been in development, the more data there are to describe it. (And the less effect analyses and trade-offs can have.)

Instances could occur where the customer might override the LOR recommendations produced by the model. For example, some particular support posture (e.g., establishment of a new centralized repair facility) that might be unattractive in the context of only one system could be highly desirable when its costs are spread across a number of systems. Thus there must be sufficient interaction between the support system designer and the customer so that support alternatives, which are optimal when aggregated across all systems, are not rejected because they are unattractive in the context of a single system. This is an area where producer–user relationships are particularly significant.

Because these models deal with marginal costs, occasions can arise where the recommendations conflict with established maintenance policies. When this occurs the analyst should take a more detailed look at the real world and try to ascertain the reason for the policy. The model can be adjusted to reflect that additional aspect of the real world, or it can be recommended that the policy be changed, or neither. The last course would be followed when there are subjective noneconomic criteria influencing the repair-level decision.

The prevalence of certain conditions would help to alleviate the problem of subjective influences on decisions. In particular, the data, models, and personnel must be available in order to make the analyses. The data must represent the engineers' best estimates of the system and equipment descriptive parameters. The models must be credible, and must represent the support process. They must be readily usable and economical to operate. Their products must be easily interpreted and capable of iteration and adaptation. The personnel in both industry and the services must be trained and motivated concerning the use of analysis and models and must understand the context of their roles.

The consequences of support decisions should be explored as early in the life cycle as possible. It is less costly to make mistakes then, it is easier to adjust design objectives, and it makes studies and trade-offs more meaningful since they influence the broader set of specifications at the operation and support levels.

Management and policy levels must be aware of the analysis objectives and the support procedures and trade-offs that reflect this philosophy so that early trade-offs can have their impacts on design, and hence on operating capability and life-cycle cost. The ultimate purpose is not merely cost minimization, but cost avoidance wherever that is possible without jeopardizing mission success.

The results of the analyses and trade-offs must be operationally feasible or they will not be acceptable. LOR analysis therefore must take into account system availability and the cost of achieving that availability. Most often the optimization will be minimize cost to achieve a specified level of availability. Ways to achieve availability include:

1. Buy many spares.
2. Make the item very reliable.
3. Fix the item quickly.

What must be done in LOR analysis is to quantify the impacts of maintenance on cost, other scarce resources, and system availability in order to choose the most efficient way of obtaining such system availability. The analysis is not done in a vacuum, but in conjunction with other factors. Such questions as "Repair forward or rear?" "Throw away?" or "Replace assembly or module?" must be asked in the context of an n-dimensional trade-off space composed of the various design, operational, and support factors.

The (low-cost) LOR for a particular combination of factors is optimized to see what the total life-cycle cost is. Then some of the factors are changed, LOR for that combination optimized, and life-cycle cost examined again. This process continues until the system designer is satisfied that some particular combination of design parameters is optimum for that system in its operational context. Throughout, level-of-repair analysis is a subroutine of the total system design process.

LONG-RANGE ENVIRONMENTAL PLANNING SIMULATOR

This model is specifically suited for evaluation of a physical distribution system. The LREPS system model consists of three echelons that can be arranged in a variety of product flow channels from point of manufacturing to geographical point of demand satisfaction.

The initial level of the model is manufacturing. The manufacturing control center (MCC) produces either a complete or partial product line that is automatically placed in an adjoining replenishment warehouse (RC). All product flow reorders to the second echelon are supplied from the RC.

The second level consists of distribution centers (DC) and consolidated shipping points (CSP). The primary function of the second echelon is to provide inventory replenishment and product delivery to satisfy customer service requirements. Three different types of distribution center alternatives exist at this point. A primary distribution center (PDC) functions within the model as a full-line regional distribution center. A second type of distribution center is classified as a remote facility (RDC) in the sense that it services a limited market area within a region on a full-time basis. If the remote distribution center inventories less than a full product line, it becomes the third type of distribution center (RCD-P). The alternative of consolidated shipping points (CSP) is also an option. The CSP does not stock inventory, but serves as a geographical point where customer orders can be consolidated for purposes of transportation economies with subsequent break-bulk and local delivery.

The third echelon consists of customer locations. Specific customers can be identified on an individual basis, or, when desirable, agglomerated demand units (DU) can be employed. In mass marketing applications, the 560 geographic Zip sectional center areas are grouped into 400 geographic DUs. Hub cities of these 400 DUs serve as points of simulated customer demand.

The flexible structure of echelon arrangement allows the stimulation of a variety of different physical distribution systems with respect to both echelons and alternative product flow paths. The range and scope of the simulated situation allow a wide variety of combinations regarding product, market, and competitive profiles, in addition to components of the physical distribution system.

The model can be defined more specifically as one involving:

1. Unlimited conditions of product, market, and competitive profiles.
2. Multiple facility locations in an echeloned arrangement.
3. Multiproduct, multilocation inventory.
4. Multiecheloned communication network.
5. Multiecheloned transportation capability.
6. Varied material-handling capability.

Appendix

Classes of Models

SYSTEM OPERATIONAL ANALYSIS, AND LOGISTIC SUPPORT MODELS

1. *Support Availability Multisystem Operations Model (SAMSON).*

This model simulates operational events (alert requirements, aircraft flight capabilities, and readiness postures) and associated logistic support requirements (personnel, equipment facilities, and spares) for one or more aircraft at one or more operational sites. The model takes into account weather, resource shortages, flying schedules, alert commitments, flight configuration requirements, abort rates, attrition estimates, and operating policies governing flight cancellation and makeup practices. The model can be used to evaluate the impact of changes in concepts, policies, and resource mixes upon operational capability. It is used in conceptual design for performance/support trade-off analysis, and in support planning.

2. *Logistics Composite Model (LCOM)*

This model simulates overall operations and support functions at a single air base. It includes the flying of aircraft, servicing tasks such as refueling, occurrence of malfunctions, accomplishment of flight-line aircraft maintenance, item repair in intermediate shops, utilization and interaction of maintenance resources, and changes in resource availability based on different work shifts. The model has the capability to optimize resource levels, and can be used to evaluate interaction between maintenance policy, resource availability, and operational effectiveness. The model is used in conceptual design and support planning.

3. *Computer Analysis of Maintenance Policies (COAMP)*

This model estimates the support costs of an end item consisting of *n* similar assemblies for 20 basic maintenance postures. Including all the stockage options, there are 80 distinct four-echelon, three-indenture postures that can be analyzed. Support equipment requirements are estimated by computing the number of service channels required to handle the material flows at the various repair points. COAMP can analyze complex decisions, including various types of built-in test equipment; however, to handle such postures, COAMP must approximate optimal stock levels and optimal support equipment requirements. The model supplies default values for all variables. Thus one can start runs initially with very little information, and then become more precise as valid data become available. Sensitivity tests can be run automatically for a number of specified variables. This model can be used in concept evaluation, detailed design, and support planning.

LEVEL-OF-REPAIR ANALYSIS MODELS

1. *O*ptimum *R*epair *L*evel *A*nalysis (ORLA) Model

ORLA evaluates alternative support postures (i.e., discard-at-failure, intermediate-level repair, or depot-level repair) in terms of total life-cycle cost. Also, it allows for the trade-off evaluation of any two or more elements of logistics support. The model is used in the conceptual and early design process to make repair-level decisions.

Input data include equipment deployment, system utilization, maintenance rates and times, and operation and maintenance cost factors. ORLA approaches the data uncertainty problem by considering several levels of variable factors (i.e., parametric analysis approach) such as system utilization and item costs.

2. *S*ystem *C*ost and *O*perational *R*esource *E*valuation (SCORE) Model

This model provides estimates of life-cycle cost (research and development, investment, operations, and maintenance) for up to 15 years for various component estimates, and aggregates these into a total cost for a system. Cost estimates are based on historical accounting records and on cost-estimating relationships. Costs are arranged in a two-dimensional matrix (program element and time).

3. *L*evel of *R*epair for *A*eronautical *M*aterial (LORAM)

LORAM is used for making level-of-repair decisions (i.e., discard-at-failure, intermediate-level repair, or depot repair) for assemblies, modules, and other elements of a system. The model also includes screening methods and noneconomic criteria, and is used for design decisions and support planning. The model ties in closely with the maintenance analysis.

LIFE-CYCLE-COST MODELS FOR PROCUREMENT AND PROGRAM EVALUATION

1. *A*cquisition *B*ased on Consideration of *L*ogistics *E*ffects (ABLE)

ABLE computes life-cycle cost by item by cost type (storage, repair, etc.), and sums cost for all items in the system. The model could be used in support of detailed design, but is intended primarily for developing and specifying contract incentives regarding logistics.

2. *L*ife-*C*ycle *C*ost *M*odel (LCCM)

LCCM calculates life-cycle costs by item by period. Costs can be entered directly into the model or calculated by cost-estimating relationships, standard formulas, or summation of other costs. Learning curves are considered and costs are discounted to the present value. This model is used in program management.

SPARES AND INVENTORY POLICY MODELS

1. *Base Depot Stockage Model* (BDSM)

This model determines intermediate base and depot stock levels that will minimize back orders within a fixed spares budget. The model assumes a compound Poisson demand at *n* identical bases. It considers basing posture, failure rates, repair-cycle times, condemnation rates, procurement costs, procurement lead times, reorder quantities, and cost constraints.

2. *Spares Kit Evaluator Model* (SKEM)

This model determines optimum types and quantities of spare parts for the support of a deployed unit, subject to multiple constraints. Also, the model computes supply effectiveness in terms of probability of no stock-out or expected time to stockout. The model is used in support planning.

3. *Spares Provisioning Model* (SPM)

SPM computes spare part levels and fill rates and investment for each station in an airlift network. The model is oriented to commercial airline operations, and is used in support planning.

References

Asimov, Morris, *Introduction to Design*. Prentice-Hall, Englewood Cliffs, N.J., 1962.
Buffa, Elwood S., *Modern Production Management*. Wiley, New York, 1969.
Duncan, R. J., *Quality Control and Industrial Statistics*. Irwin, Homewood, Ill., 1965.
Grant, E. I., and R. S. Leavenworth, *Statistical Quality Control*. 4th ed. McGraw-Hill, New York, 1972.
Hall, Arthur D., *A Methodology for Systems Engineering*. Van Nostrand, Princeton, N.J., 1962.
Hall, Arthur D., "Three-Dimensional Morphology of Systems Engineering," *IEEE Transactions on Systems Science and Cybernetics*, vol. SSC-5, no. 2, April 1969.
Heskett, J. L., Nicholas A. Glaskowsky, Jr., and Robert M. Ivie, *Business Logistics*. Ronald Press, New York, 1973.
Integrated Logistic Support. Implementation Guide for DOD Systems and Equipment. U.S. Government Printing Office, Washington, D.C., March 1972.
Juran, L. M., and F. M. Gryna, *Quality Planning and Analysis*. McGraw-Hill, New York, 1970.
Magee, John F., *Physical-Distribution Systems*. McGraw-Hill, New York, 1967.
Starr, Martin, K., "Evaluating Concepts in Production Management," *Proceedings of the 24th Annual Meeting*, Academy of Management, Chicago, 1964, pp. 123–133.
Systems Engineering Management Procedures. U.S. Air Force Systems Command Manual AFSCM 375-5, March 1966.
Timms, Howard L., and Michael F. Pohlen, *The Production Function in Business*, 3rd ed. Irwin, Homewood, Ill., 1970.
Webster's New International Dictionary, 2nd ed., unabridged. Merriam, Springfield, Mass., 1958.

BIBLIOGRAPHY

BOOKS

ARINC Research Corporation, *Reliability Engineering*, Prentice-Hall, Englewood Cliffs, New Jersey, 1964.
Berry, Dick, *Managing Service for Results*, Instrument Society of America, Research Triangle Part, North Carolina, 1983.
Blanchard, Benjamin S., *Engineering Organization and Management*, Prentice-Hall, Englewood Cliffs, New Jersey, 1976.
Blanchard, Benjamin S., *Logistics Engineering and Management—3rd Edition*, Prentice-Hall, Englewood Cliffs, New Jersey, 1986.
Bleuel, William H. and Patton, Joseph D., Jr., *Service Management: Principles and Practices—2nd Edition*, Instrument Society of America, Research Triangle Park, North Carolina, 1986.
Brown, Robert G., *Advanced Service Parts Management*, Materials Management Systems, Thetford Center, Vermont, 1982.
Buffa, Elwood S., *Elements of Production/Operations Management*, John Wiley & Sons, New York, New York, 1981.
Buffa, Elwood S., *Modern Production/Operations Management—7th Edition*, John Wiley & Sons, New York, New York, 1983.
Capacino, W. F., *Modern Logistics Management: Integrating Marketing, Manufacturing and Physical Distribution*, John Wiley & Sons, New York, 1985.
Chase, Richard B. and Aquilano, Nicolas, J., *Production and Operations Management: A Life Cycle Approach—4th Edition*, Irwin Publishing, Ontario, Canada, 1985.
Evans, J. Thomas, *The Field Service Manager's Handbook*, Association of Field Service Managers, Fort Myers, Florida, 1977.
Fogarty, Donald W. and Hoffman, Thomas R., *Production and Inventory Management*, Southwestern Publishing Company, 1981.
Greene, James R., *Production and Inventory Control Systems and Decisions—3rd Edition*, Richard D. Irwin, Homewood, Illinois, 1979.
Jardine, A. K. S., *Maintenance, Replacement and Reliability*, Pitman Publishing Company, Toronto, Canada, 1973.
Joseph William, *Professional Service Management*, McGraw-Hill, New York, New York, 1983.
Lee, W. B. and Steinberg, E., *Service Parts Management: Principles and Practices*, American Production and Inventory Control Society, Falls Church, Virginia, 1984.

Locks, M. O., *Reliability, Maintainability, and Availability Assessment*, Hayden Book Company, Lexington, Massachusetts, 1976.
Mann, Lawrence, *Maintenance Management*, Lexington Books, Lexington, Massachusetts, 1976.
Mather, Hal, *How to Really Manage Inventories*, McGraw-Hill, New York, New York, 1985.
McCafferty, Donald N., *Successful Field Service Management*, AMACOM, New York, New York, 1980.
Military Handbook 217 series *Reliability of Electronic Components*, Available from Defense Documentation Center, DSA, Cameron Station, Arlington, Virginia 22314, or from Naval Publications and Forms Center, 5801 Tabor Avenue, Philadelphia, Pennsylvania 19120.
Military Standard 470 *Maintainability Program Requirements for Systems and Equipments*, Available as above.
Military Standard 471 *Maintainability Verifications/Demonstrations/Evaluation*, Available as above.
Military Handbook 472 *Maintainability Prediction*, Available as above.
Patton, Joseph D. Jr., *Maintainability and Maintenance Management*, Instrument Society of America, Research Triangle Park, North Carolina, 1980.
Patton, Joseph D. Jr., *Preventive Maintenance*, Instrument Society of America, Research Triangle Park, North Carolina, 1982.
Patton, Joseph D. Jr., *Service Parts Management*, Instrument Society of America, Research Triangle Park, North Carolina, 1984.
Rosander, A. C., *Applications of Quality Control in the Service Industries*, ASQC Quality Press, Milwaukee, Wisconsin, 1985.
Sasser, W. Earl, and Wyckoff, D. Daryl, *Management of Service Operations: Text, Cases and Readings*, Allyn and Bacon, Newton, Massachusetts, 1979.
Tersine, Richard J., *Principles of Inventory and Materials Management—2d Edition*, Elsevier North-Holland, Inc. 1982.
Wellemin, John H., *The Handbook of Professional Service Management—Caring for the Customer Before, During, and After the Sale*, Studentlitteratur, Lund, Sweden, 1984.
Witt, Phillip R., *Cost Competitive Products—Managing Product Concept to Marketplace Reality*, Reston Publishing Company, Reston, Virginia, 1986.

ARTICLES

Angier, R. C., "Organizing Space Shuttle Parametric Data for Maintainability," (IBM, Houston, Texas, USA) *Journal of Guidance, Control, and Dynamics*, Volume 6, Number 5, September-October 1983, p. 407-413.
Anonymous, "Integrating Reliability, Maintainability, and Quality," *Automotive Engineering* (Warrendale, Pennsylvania) Volum 91. Number 6. June 1983, p. 67-70.
Anonymous, "Fatigue Reliability: Quality Assurance and Maintainability," *American Society of Civil Engineers, Journal of the Structural Division*, Volume 108, Number ST1; January 1982, p. 25-46.

Arendt, J. S.; Fussell, J. B., "System Reliability Engineering Methodology for Industrial Application," (JBF Assoc. Inc, Knoxville, Tennessee, USA) *Loss Prevention: A CEP Technical Manual*, Volume 14, AIChE Loss Prev Symp, 14th, at 88th Natl Meet, Philadelphia, Pennsylvania, USA, June 8-12, 1980, (Publ by AIChE (CEP Tech Man), New York, New York, USA, 1981, p. 18-28.

Arthur, Jeffrey L.; Lawrence, Kenneth D., "Multiple Goal Production and Logistics Planning in a Chemical and Pharmaceutical Company," (Oregon State University, Corvallis, USA) *Computers and Operations Research* Volume 9, Number 2, 1982, p. 127-137.

Bagione, Frank, "Parts and the IRS," *Computer/Electronic Service News*, March 1986.

Bajaria, H. J., "Integration of Reliability, Maintainability and Quality Parameters in Design," (Multiface Inc, MI, USA) SAE Specification Publication SP-533, February 1983, 24 p.

Berns, Gerald M., "Assessing Software Maintainability," (Science Applications Inc, Arlington, Virginia, USA) *Communications of the ACM*, Volume 27, Number 1, January 1984, p. 14-23.

Billinton, Roy; Allan, R. N., "Reliability Engineering—A Basic Component in an Undergraduate Curriculum," (Univ. of Saskatchewan, Department of Electrical Engineering, Saskatoon, Sask, Canada) *International Journal of Electrical Engineering Education*, Volume 21, Number 2, Apr 1984, p. 159-168.

Bojanowski, R., "Improving Factory Performance with Service Requirements Planning (SRP)," *Production and Inventory Management, Second Quarter*, 1984. P. 31-44.

Bolton, R., "The Importance of MRO Purchasing," *Purchasing World*, June 1984, p. 92-93.

Burgess, Robert M.; Koens, Kathleen B.; Pignetti, Emil M. Jr., "Semiconductor Final Test Logistics and Product Dispositioning Systems," (IBM, Hopewell Junction, New York, USA) *IBM Journal of Research and Development*, Volume 26, Number 5, Sep 1982, p. 605-612.

Cleveland, J. W., Regenie, T. R., Wilson, R. J., "Nuclear Power Generating Station Operability Assurance, Reliability, Availability, and Maintainability Application for Maintenance Management," (GDS Associates Inc, San Jose, CA, USA) *IEEE Transactions on Power Apparatus and Systems*, Volume PAS-104, Number 4, April 1985, p. 786-789.

Collier, Courtland A., Jacques, David, E., "Optimum Equipment Life by Minimum Life-Cycle Costs," (Univ. of Florida, Dep of Civil Engineering, Gainesville, Fla. USA)
Journal of Construction Engineering and Management, Volum 110, Number 2, June 1984, p. 248-265.

Coppola, Anthony, "Reliability Engineering of Electronic Equipment: A Historical Perspective," (US Air Force, Rome Air Development Department, Griffiss AFB, New York, USA) *IEEE Transactions on Reliability*, Volume R-33, Number 1, April 1984, p. 29-35.

Davies, A., Skinner, K. J., "Application of a Life Cycle Cost Model to Modular Electronic Systems," (Univ of Wales Inst of Science and Technology, Department of Mechanical Engineering and Engineering Production, Cardiff, Wales) *Radio and Electronic Engineer*, Volume 53, Number 5, May 1983, p. 209-215.

Davis, Peter, "Transfer of Systems Technology: Logistics Systems for Underdeveloped Countries," (Univ of Pennsylvania, Philadelphia, Pennsylvania USA) *European Journal of Operational Research*, Volum 7, Number 3, July 1981, p. 232-241.

Der Kiureghian, Armen; Moghtaderi-Zadeh, Masoud, "Integrated Approach to the Reliability of Engineering Systems," (Univ of California, Department of Civil Engineering, Berkeley, California, USA) *Nuclear Engineering and Design*, Volum 71, Number 3, August 1982, Procedure of the International Semin on the Reliab of Nucl Power Plants, 3rd, Paris, France, 1981, p. 349-354.

DeVries, Larry, G., "Managing an Centralized Service Parts Inventory," *American Production and Inventory Control Society Service Parts Seminar Proceedings*, 1983, p. 58-65.

Dhillon, Balbir S., "Life Cycle Cost: A Survey," (Univ of Ottawa, Ontario, Canada) *Microelectronics and Reliability*, Volume 21, Number 4, 1981, p. 495-511.

Dun's Review "The High Cost of Bad Maintenance," August 1979, p. 51-52.

Ellis, T. M. R. (Ed.); Semenkey, Oleg Ignatevich (Ed.), "Advances in CAD/CAM Proceedings of the International IFIP/IFA Conference on Programming Research and Operations, Logistics in Advanced Manufacturing Technology, 5th, Prolamat 82 (Computer Aided Design/Computer Aided Manufacturing), 1982," (Univ. of Sheffield, Sheffield, England) Adv in CAD/CAM, Proceedings of the International IFIP/IFAC Conf on Program Res and Oper Logist in Advanced Manufacturing Technology, 5th, PROLAMAT 82, Leningrad, USSR, May 16-18 1982 Published by North Holland Publishing Co, Amsterdam, Neth and New York, New York, USA, 1983 720 p.

Engi, Dennis, "Maintainability Analysis Using Q-Gert Network Simulation," (Sandia National Laboratory, Geo-Systems Division, Albuquerque, New Mexico, USA) Simulation Volume 44, Number 2, Feb 1985, p. 67-74.

Feldmann, Herbert C., Patton, Joseph D., Jr., "Managing Repairable Parts." *Computer/Electronic Service News*, January 1986.

Green, A. E., "Maintainability versus Disposability," (UKAEA, National Center of Systems Reliability, Warrington, Lancashire, England) *Nuclear Engineering and Design*, Volume 71, Number 3, Aug 1982, Proc of the International Seminar on the Reliability of Nuclear Power Plants, 3rd, Paris, France, 1981, p. 435-438.

Gronland, Stein Erik, "Logistics and the Shipping Industry-Concepts-Importance-Methods," (Ship Research Institute of Norway) *Norwegian Maritime Research*, Volume 10, Number 2, 1982, p. 13-23.

Govil, K. K., "New Analytical Models for Logistics Support Cost and Life Cycle Cost vs Reliability Function," *Microelectronics and Reliability*, Volume 24, Number 1, 1984, p. 61-63.

Govil, K. K., "Optimum Design of Reliable Systems for Specified Life Cycle Cost," *Microelectronics and Reliability*, Volume 25, Number 2, 1985, p. 239-241.

Govil, K. K., "Slection Factor Algorithm for Reliability and Maintainability Tradeoff to Optimize Availability Allocation Subject to Cost Constraint," *Microelectronics and Reliability*, Volume 24, Number 3, 1984, p. 411-413.

Gruver, William A.; Canady, Robert M., "Modern Technology for Computer

Control and Logistics Support of Large Scale Robotics Systems," Logist Technol. Int. SME Tech Rep Ser MSR 80-13, 1980, 37p.

Hall, D. D., "Active Reliability Engineering—Technical Concept and Program Plan. A Solid-State Systems Approach to Increased Reliability and Availability in Military Systems," (Final report May-October 1982) (Naval Ocean Systems Center, San Diego, California) Report No.: NOSC/TD-654, 5 October 83, 105p.

Hanslovan, James J., Mayercheck, William D., "Logistics in Underground Mining: A Close Examination," (Skelly & Loy, Clearfield, Pennsylvania, USA) *Coal Mining & Processing*, Volume 20, Number 2, February 1983, p. 36-39.

Harvard Business Review Reprints, Soldiers Field, (Boston, Massachusetts) *Book 18051 Service Management; Book 18041 Inventory Policy*.

Hellyer, F. G., "Application of Reliability Engineering to High Integrity Plant Control Systems," (Protech Instruments & Systems Ltd, Luton, England) *Measurement and Control*, Volume 18, Number 5, June 1985, p. 172-176.

Holderby, William S., "Maintainability Considerations in a Fault Tolerant/Faultproof Systems Design," (Autech Data Systems, Pompano Beach, Florida, USA) *IEEE Transactions on Industrial Electronics*, Volumes 19-31, Number 2 May, 1984, p. 120-129.

Hyman, William A.; Hughes, Dennis J., "Computer Model for Life-Cycle Cost Analysis of Statewide Bridge Repair and Replacement Needs," (DOT, Division of Planning & Budget, Madison, Wisconsin, USA) Transp Res Rec 899 1983 p 52-61.

Iwane, Masahiko; Sato, Fumitaka, "Maintainability Design of Large Scale Computer," Toshiba Corp, Ome, Jpn *Systems—Computers—Controls*, Volume 11, Number 2, March-April 1980, p. 18-26.

Longworth, J. D., McFarland, R. H., Phipps, W., d'Estaintot, T., Jamil, M., "Engineering and Technical Services to Improve Reliability and Maintanability of Instrument Landing System Components," (Ohio University, Athens. Avionics Engineering Center.) (Sponsor: Federal Aviation Administration, Washington, DC. Program Engineering and Maintenance Service.) Report No.: OU/AEC/EER-62-1; DOT/FAA/PM-84/7. January 83, 293p.

Jenkins, B. M., Arthur, J. F., Miller, G. E., Parsons, P. S., "Logistics and Economics of Biomass Utilization." (University of California, Davis, Agricultural Engineering Department, Davis, California, USA) *Transactions of the American Society of Agricultural Engineers (General Edition)*, Volume 27, Number 6 November-December 1984 p 1898–1904, 1910.

Keller, A. Z., Kamath, A. R. R., Peacock, S. T., Selman, A. C., "Proposed Methodology for Assessment of Reliability, Maintainability and Availability of Medical Equipment," (Univ. of Bradford, Postgraduate Sch of Studies in Industrial Technology, Bradford, England) *Reliability Engineering*, Volume 9, Number 3, 1984, p. 153-174.

Klitz, J. Kenneth, "Simulation of an Automated Logistics and Manufacturing System," (IBM, Boulder Colorado, USA) *European Journal of Operational Research*, Volume 14, Number 1, Sep 1983, p. 36-39.

Kodama, Masanori; Sawa, Isao, "Reliability and Maintainability of Multicomponent Series-Parallel System Under Several Repair Disciplines," (Kyoshu University, Faculty of Economics, Fukuoka, Japan) *Microelectronics and*

Reliability, Volume 22, Number 6, 1982 p. 1135-1153.

Kodama, Masanori; Sawa, Isao, "Reliability and Maintainability of a Multicomponent Series-Parallel System with Simultaneous Failure and Repair Priorities," (Kyushu Univ, Department of Economic Engineering, Fukuoka, Japan) *Microelectronics and Reliability*, Volume 24, Number 1, 1984, p. 147-164.

Lau, H. T., "Reliability, Maintainability and Cost-Effectiveness: A Bibliographical Note," (Vanderbit Univ, Computer Science Department, Nashville, Tennessee, USA) *Microelectronics and Reliability*, Volume 23, Number 1, 1983, p. 21-40.

Montag, Geraldine M., "Life-Cycle Cost Analysis Versus Payback for Evaluating Project Alternatives," (Iowa State University, Ames, Iowa, USA) *Heating, Piping and Air Conditioning*, Volume 56, Number 9, September 1984, p. 75-78.

Multhaup, H. A., "Design for Reliability and Maintainability Life Cycle Cost Minimization," (GE, Schenectady, New York, USA) *Proceedings for the Annual English Conference on Reliability for the Electric Power Industry, 7th*, Madison, Wisconsin, USA, April 29-30, 1980, Published by American Society for Dual Control, Milwaukee, Wisconsin, USA, 1980, p. 88-92.

Munson, John B., "Software Maintainability—A Practical Concern for Life-Cycle Costs." (System Development Corp., Santa Monica, California, USA) *Computer*, Volume 14, Number 11, Nov 1981, p. 103-109.

Murphree, E. Lile Jr., "Economic Analysis Models for Evaluating Costs of a Life Cycle Cost Data Base," US Army Construction Engineering Research Laboratory, Champaign, Illinois, USA, *Technical Report US Army Corps of Engineering Construction Engineering Res Laboratory*, P-164 September 1984 57p.

Musick, Victor S., "General Electric Design and Manufacture of Large Steam Turbine-Generator Sets for Reliability, Availability and Maintainability," (GE, Schenectady, New York, USA) *Proceedings for the Annual Engineering Conference on Reliability for the Electric Power Industry, 7th*, Madison, Wisconsin, USA, April 29-30 1980 Published by American Society for Quality Control, Milwaukee, Wisconsin, USA, 1980, p. 15-19.

Ntuen, Celestine A., "Availability-Based Life Cycle Cost Model: A Simulation Approach," (North Carolina Agricultural & Technical State University, Department of Industrial Engineering, Greensboro, North Carolina, USA) *Microelectronics and Reliability*, Volume 25, Number 2, 1985, p. 331-342.

O'Connor, P. D. T., "Computer Programs for Design Safety, Reliability and Maintainability Analysis," (British Aerospace Dynamics Group, Reliability Technology Department, Stevenage, England) *Quality Assurance*, Volume 10, Number 2, June 1984 p. 36-40.

Patki, V. B.; Patki, A. B.; Chatterji, B. N., "Reliability and Maintainability Considerations in Computer Performance Evaluation," (Tata Engineering & Locomotive Company, Poona, India) *IEEE Transactions on Reliability*, Volume R-32, Number 5, December 1983, p. 433-436.

Patton, Joseph D., Jr., "The Logistics of Service," *Field Service Manager*, February 1986.

Petroski, Michael R., "Some Computer Applications for Reliability and Maintainability," (US Army, Tactical Vehicle Systems, Warren, Michigan, USA) *Computers & Industrial Engineering*, Volume 9, Number 4, 1984, p. 339-345.

Pollard, Brian W., "RAM for Robots (Reliability, Availability, Maintainability)," (Unimation Inc) *SME Technical Pap Service*, MS 80-692, 1980, 15 p.

Pollard Brian W., "Reliability, Availability, Maintainability," (Unimation Inc.) *Proceedings—AUTOFACT West*, Volume 2, Assemblex 7, Predict Maint 2, PEMCON, Qualinspex 2, Mater Flow 2, Robotics, Anaheim, California, USA, November 17-20, 1980, (Published by SME, Dearborn, Michigan, USA) 1980, p. 577-590.

Remer, Donald S., Abdul-Ganiy, Saleem; Khan, Khalid, "Model for Life Cycle Cost Analysis with a Learning Curve." (Harvey Mudd Coll, Claremont, California, USA) *Engineering Economist*, Volume 27, Number 1, Fall 1981, p. 29-58.

Retterer, Bernard L., Kowalski, Richard, "Maintainability: A Historical Perspective." (ARINC Research Corp., Annapolis, Maryland, USA) *IEEE Transactions on Reliability*, Volume R-33, Number 1, April 1984, p. 56-61.

Richter, Horst P., "Verifying the Reliability of Engineering Software." (Bechtel Power Corp., San Francisco, California, USA) *Computers in Mechanical Engineering*, Volume 2, Number 4, January 1984, p. 53-56.

Russon, Larry; Streifer, Stephen, "Systems Engineering Approach to Support Design of the Navy's SL-7/T-AKR Fast Logistics Support Ship Conversions," (National Steel & Shipbuilding Co, San Diego, California, USA) *Marine Technology*, Volume 22, Number 3, July 1985, p. 267-285.

Seger, James K. "Reliability Investment and Life-Cycle Cost." (Lockheed-California Co., Burbank, California, USA) *IEEE Transactions on Reliability*, Volume R-32, Number 3, August 1983, p. 259-263.

Seminara, Joseph L.; Parsons, Stuart O., "Nuclear Power Plant Maintainability," Lockheed Misseles and Space Co, Sunnyvale, California, USA Applied Ergonomics Volume 13 Number 3 September 1982 p 177-189.

Shun-ichi, Abe, "Asymptotic Method of Evaluating Reliability and Maintainability of Highly Reliable Networks and Its Application," (Railway Technical Research Institute, Transportation Systems Analysis Laboratory, Tokyo, Japan) *Q Rep Railw Tech. Res. Inst.*, (Japan) Volume 24, Number 2, June 1983, p. 77-80.

Singpurwalla, Nozer D.; Talbott, Carlos M., "Time Series Analysis of Some Interrelated Logistics Performance Variables," (George Washington University, Washington, DC, USA) *Naval Research Logistics Quarterly*, Volume 29, Number 4, December 1982, p. 571-583.

Srivastava, Sanjaya; Soi, Inder M., "Hardware vs Software Maintainability: A Comparative Study," (Regional Engineering College, Department of Electronics and Communication Engineering, Kurukshetra, India) *Microelectronics and Reliability*, Volume 22, Number 6, 1982 p. 1077-1079.

Soi, Inder M.; Aggarwal, K. K., "Life-Cycle Cost Viewpoint of Softward Maintainability," (Regional Engineering College, Kurukshetra, India) *Computers & Electrical Engineering*, Volume 8, Number 4, December 1981, p. 277-282.

Soi, Inder M., "Software Complexity: An Aid to Software Maintainability." (Haryana State Electricity Board, Faridabad, India) *Microelectronics and Reliability*, Volume 25, Number 2, 1985, p. 223-228.

Tombari, H., "Designing a Maintenance Management System," *Production and Inventory Management*, Volume 23, Number 4, Fourth Quarter, 1982, p. 139-147.

Tripp, Robert S., Pearson, John M., Rainey, Larry B., "Application of the Cybernetics to the Air Force Logistics Command. Command, Control, Communication and Intelligence System," (USAF, DCS/Plans and Programs, Wright-Patterson AFB, Ohio, USA) *Cybernetics*, Volume 28, Number 2, 1985, p. 145-157.

Tripp, Robert S., Rainey, Larry B., "Cybernetic Approach for the Design and Development of Management Information and Control Systems (MICS): An Illustration Within the Air Force Logistics Command," (US Air Force Logistics Command, Directorate of Special Projects, Plans and Programs, Wright-Patterson, AFB, Ohio, USA) *Cybernetica*, Volume 26, Number 4, 1983, p. 281-305.

Turiel, Isaac; Estrada, Henry; Levine, Mark, "Life-Cycle Cost Analysis of Major Appliances." (University of California, Berkeley, USA) *Energy* (Oxford) Volume 6 Number 9 September 1981 p 945-970.

Vessely, Jack E.; Cowdery, James W., 'Reliability, Availability, Maintainability—A Management Challenge," (Fla Power & Light Company, Miami, USA) *Proceedings for the Annual Engineering Conference on Reliability for the Electr Power Industry*, Seventh, Madison, Wisconsin, USA, April 29-30 1980 Published by American Society for Quality Control, Milwaukee, Wisconsin, USA, 1980, p 70-72.

Walters, R. J., "Derivation and Application of Reliability and Maintainability Values," (Ontario Hydro, Canada) *Engineering Journal* (Montreal) Volume 64 Number 2 April 1981 p 6-10.

Wang, P. Y.; Mavec, J.; Wolosewicz, R. M.; Calm, J. M.; Chopra, P. S., "Reliability, Maintainability, and Availability Engineering for Integrated Community Energy Systems." (Argonne National Laboratory, Illinois, USA) *Argonne National Laboratory Energy Environ System Division Rep. (ANL) CNSV.* 6 December 1979 84 p.

Wohl, Joseph G., "Maintainability Prediction Revisited: Diagnostic Behavior, System Complexity, and Repair Time," (Alphatech Inc, Burlington, Massachusetts, USA) *IEEE Transactions on Systems, Man and Cybernetics* Volume SMC-12 Number 3 May-June 1982 p 241-250.

RELATED PROFESSIONAL SOCIETIES AND PUBLICATIONS

Annual Reliability and Maintainability Symposium (ARMS)
Proceedings available
from IEEE Service Center.
Piscataway, NJ

Association of Field Service Managers (AFSM)
3475 Presidential Court, Suite B
Fort Myers, FL 33907
(800) 237-5044
Publication:
Field Service Manager

American Society for Quality Control (ASQC)
230 West Wells Street
Milwaukee, Wisconsin 53203
Publication:
Quality Progress, and others
(414) 272-8575

American Production
and Inventory Control Society (APICS)
500 West Annondale Road
Falls Church, Virginia 22046-4274
Publications:
Production and Inventory Management Review
Service Parts Management Seminar Proceedings
Bar Coding Seminar Proceedings, and others

Computer/Electronic Service News
P O Box 428
Peterborough, New Hampshire 03458

Council of Logistics Management
2803 Butterfield Road
Oakbrook, Illinois 60521
(312) 655-0985

Equipment Maintenance Council
60 Revere Drive, Suite 500
Northbrook, Illinois 60062
(312) 480-9080
Publication:
Equipment Maintenance

Institute of Industrial Engineers (IIE)
25 Technology Park / Atlanta
Norcross, Georgia 30092
(404) 449-0460
Publications:
Industrial Engineering,
and others

Institute of Electrical
and Electronic Engineers (IEEE)
345 East 47th Street
New York, New York 10017
Publications:
IEEE Spectrum,
and others
(212) 644-1900

International Maintenance Institute (IMI)
P O Box 266695
Houston, Texas 77207
(713) 481-0869

Microservice Management
P O Box 12901
Overland Park, KAnsas 66212-9981

National Association
of Service Managers (NASM)
60 Revere Drive, Suite 500
Northbrook, Illinois 60062
(312)480-9575
Publication:
Service Management

Quality—for Better Product
Assurance and Reliability
Hitchcock Publishing Company
Hitchcock Building
Wheaton, Illinois 60188

Plant Engineering
Technical Publishing Company
1301 South Grove Avenue
P O Box 1030
Barrington, Illinois 60010

Society of Logistics Engineers (SOLE)
303 Williams Avenue, Suite 922
Huntsville, Alabama 35801-6061
(205) 539-3833
Publications:
Logistics Spectrum
Annual International Logistics Symposium Proceedings
and others

Society of Reliability Engineers (SRE)
P O Box 392
Wilsonville, Oregon 97070

Index

ABC inventory policy   183,235
Acceptable quality level (AQL)   162
Access   1
Achieved availability   77
Ackoff, Russell   46
Acquisition   1,31,106,118
Acquisition Based on Consideration of Logistics Effects (ABLE) model   319
Activity   26
AFSCR-80-9   90
Air transport   238
Algain, George   120
Allocation   80,97,196
Alpha error   160
American Production and Inventory Control Society (APICS)   47
American Society for Quality Control (ASQC)   166
Analog model   309
Analysis of Variation (ANOVA)   165
Apollo program   269
Appraisal costs   153
AR-705-50   90
Argris, Chris   265
Asimow   63,66
As required conditioning   305
Assembly line   119
Atomic clock   156
Attribute   156
Audit   104,165
Autocorrelation   137
Automation   97,216
Availability   24,74
Average outgoing quality limit (AOQL)   163
Average measurements (X) chart   164

Bakke, E. Wight   264
Barnard, Chester   264
Barometric forecasting   137
Base Depot Stockage Model (BDSM)   320
Baseline   108
Baumol-Wolfe linear extension   230
Behavioral management   264
Bennis, Warren G.   266
Beta error   160
Binomial distribution   162
Biological-mathematical organization   267

Blanket buying   121
Block control   112
Block diagrams   84
Booz, Allen, & Hamilton   26,281
Bowman-Stewart model   230
Branch and bound   126
Built-in test   97
Built-in test equipment (BITE)   46,97,178,247,278
Bureaucracy   256
Burn-in   80,174
Business Conditions Digest   138

Camp's formula   185
Capacities   133
Car purchase   37
Carload (CL) shipment   241
Cash flow   201
Cash-in-fist (CIF)   125
Causal factors   136,145
Center-of-gravity inventory approach   230
Certified Quality Engineer (CQE)   166
Certified Professional Logistician (CPL)   247
Chain of command   258
Change order (CO)   116
Change impact analysis   40
Change control   108,116
Changeover points   142
Channels of distribution   206
Check digit   49
Chief executive officer (CEO)   261
Collection agency   114
Combinations   112
Common carrier   239
Competitive evaluations   143
Completed staff work   263
Component reliability   84
Computer Analysis of Maintenance Policies (COAMP) model
Concept phase   33
Conceptual design review   103
Concessions   110
Condition monitoring   171
Conditional demand analysis   141
Configuration management (CM)   108,112
Consolidated shipping point (CSP)   316

333

Consumable 21,112
Consumer intention survey 139
Consumer risk 160
Consumption 72
Containerization 215
Container on flat cars (COFC) 241
Contingency procedures 195
Continuous process 119
Contract carrier 239
Contran 215
Control charts 147,164
Coon, Charles 19
Corporation legal form 256
Corrective Maintenance 16,60,91
Cost analysis 37
Cost breakdown structure (CBS) 38
Cost effetiveness 35
Cost plus fixed fee (CPFF) 123,226
Cost 46,61,88,98,108,152,201
CPM 24,26,50,54,283
Counseling 250
Criteria 108
Critical few 32,125
Critical Path 25,27
Critical design review 103
Criticality 88
Cromwell, Oliver 260
Cumulative distribution 193
Cumulative frequency 191
Customer satisfaction 97
Customer perceptions 77,274
Customer interfaces 274

Davidson, Ralph 45
Davis, Ralph 47
DC-3 aircraft 307
Debug 80
Defect number (C) chart 164
Defense Supply Agency 260
Definition phase 104
Delphi approach 141
Demand 141, 177
Demographic analysis 141
Demonstration 92, 100
Dependent variable 150
Depreciation 39, 292
Deregulation 240
Design reviews 103
Design to life cycle cost 35
Design to cost (DTC) 35
Design to unit cost (DTUC) 35
Design of experiments 165
Design disclosure 110
Design phase 39
Designer-planner 118
Design-planning process 66
Deterministic models 310
Development phase 33
Development 22
Deviations 97, 108
Discard 97
Discount 39

Disposal 31, 207
Distribution 71
Distributor 207
Do it yourself maintenance 174
Documentation for transportation 242
Documentation 36, 108, 110, 112
Dodge-Romig plans 162
Dollar value 42
Double-sampling plan 163
Downtime 79, 103
Drop shipper 206
Dual-Parallel combination 83
Dummy variables 128
DuPont 142

Econometrics 137
Economic level of repair screening model 202
Economic order quantity (EOQ) 185
Economies of scale 132
Effectiveness 92
Emergency Maintenance 16
Engineering model 112
Engineering change order (ECO) 116
Engineering order (EO) 116
Equal employment opportunity (EEO) 247
Error of forecast 146
Essentiality 88, 181
Estimating 126
Excess 46, 196
Exempt carriers 240
Expectation 78
Expedite 195
Explanatory variable 150
Exponential distribution 158
Exponential 80, 157
Exponential smoothing 145, 190
External failures 153

Facility planning 225
Factor-listing forecasting 137
Fagan, William 26
Failure rate 80
Failure 22, 1002
Fayol, Henri 47
Feasibility study 67
Field change order (FCO) 116
Final design review 104
Finite replenishment rate 189
First in, first out (FIFO) 183
First in, still here (FISH) 183
Fitness for use 12, 151
Fixed cost 224
Flow diagrams 115
Flow sequencing 126
Flow-through production 119
FMEA 87, 179, 203
Forced rating 280
Ford, Henry 108
Forecasting 133
Free port 219
Functionality 104

INDEX 335

Galbraith, Frank and Lilian 47
Gantt, Henry 24, 47
George Washington University 88, 181
Gluck, Fred 1
Goals 21, 57
Graphic screening 299

Haire, Mason 267
Hall 63
Hands-off-until-failure 80
Harrington 266
Heskett, Ivie, and Glaskowsky 2
Heuristic programming 234
Hiring 249
Home appliances 31
Human factors 36, 87
Human engineering 103
Human asset accounting 245
Hypergeometric distribution 162

IBM 283
Iconic model 309
Incentive 226
Indifference 43
Indifference quality level (IQL) 163
Industrial logistics 118
Industrial engineering 125
Infant mortality 169
Inflation 29
Information systems 21
Information theory 45
Inherent reliability 80
Inherent availability 76
Inherent design 78
Initial demand 202
Initial production model 112
Input 86, 135
Input/output analysis 137
Inspection 171
Installation emphasis 285
Installations 61
Insurance 195
Integrated logistics support 74, 108
Interdependence 147
Interest 294
Interface compatibility 104
Intermediate design review 104
Intermittent process 119
Internal Revenue Service 292
In-transit mixing 219
Inventory management 176
Iteration of design 69

Job shop 119
Jobbers 206
Joint Chiefs of Staff 260
Juran, Joseph 152
Just-in-Time (JIT) 48, 120

K factors 78, 149

Kaiser Aluminum Corporation 125
Kevlar 142
Keystone company 290
KISS (Keep it simple, stupid) 277

Labor 228
Labor relations 251
Ladder charts 115
Lambda 80
Last in, first out (LIFO) 183
Launch 112
Lead time 191
Leading indicators 138
Learning 252
Learning curve 128
Lease 227
Least commitment principle 69
Least squares 146
Least squared linear regression (LSLR) 149
Legal forms of ownership 255
Leontief input/output analysis 147
Less-than-carload (LCL) shipment 241
Less-than-truckload (LTL) shipment 241
Level of Repair for Aeronautical Material
   (LORAM) model 319
Level of repair analysis (LORA) 296
Levitt, Theodore 172
Liability 30
Life-cycle cost 29, 88, 107, 126
Life cycle profits 30, 40, 279
Life-cycle models 143
Likert, Rensis 266
Line of Balance (LOB) 25
Linear programming 127, 230
Linear regression 137
Line-staff organization 260
Linking pins 266
Lockheed 88
Logistics Composite Model (LCOM) 318
Logistics supply time 93
Logistics Management Institute 296
Long range environmental planning simulator
   (LREPS)
Lorenz 152
Lot tolerance percent defective (LTPD) 162

Maintainability 32, 36, 76, 103, 152, 300
Maintainability demonstrations (MDs) 55
Maintenance concept 92, 167, 178
Maintenance task analysis (MTA) 55
Maintenance 90, 167
Maintenance, repair, and operating (MRO)
   parts 125
Make or buy 123, 219
Manufacturability 110
Manufacturing control center (MCC) 316
Manufacturing engineering 126
Marginal 22
Marketing concept 205
Marketing mix 206
Master cartons 213
Material handling 212, 215

Material flow 221
Material Requirements Planning (MRP) 48, 120
Mathematical models 310
Matrix organization 53
Mayo, Elton 266
McDonnell Douglas Aircraft Company 115
McGraw-Hill 281
Mct 93, 98
MDT 77, 98
Mean logistics delay time (MLDT) 176
Mean time between failure (MTBF) 59
Mean (average) 158
Measurement 24
Meetings 269
Merchant middlemen 206
Method time and motion (MTM) studies 126
Methods engineering 126
Military Handbook 217 87
MIL-STD-105 162
Mission 23
Mmax 93
Modal transport combinations 240
Model limitations 311
Model T 108
Models 37, 82, 309
Modes of transportation 237
Modification 33, 117
Modification labor 129
Modularization 97
Money constraints 201
Monte Carlo analysis 192
Morphology 63
Motivation 245
Moving average 144, 190
Mpt 93
MTBF 76, 79, 93, 96
MTBM 76, 93
MTTR 77, 93
Multiple-sampling plan 163

NASA 78, 269
National motor freight classification 241
NAVORD-OR-39223 90
Nomograph 82
Normal distribution 157
Not operationally ready-supplies (NORS) 181

Objectives 20
Obsolescence 72, 195, 283
On-condition maintenance 171
On-the-job training (OJT) 252
Operating days 186
Operating cost 294
Operating characteristic (OC) curve 160
Operating cost 31
Operation and Support (O&S) 39
Operational readiness 23
Operational requirements 92
Operational availability 77, 176
Operations plan 68
Opportunity identification techniques 141

Opportunity cost 182, 293
Optical Character Reader (OCR) 49
Optimistic 26
Optimization 21
Optimum level of repair analysis (ORLA) 296
Optimum 22
Optional replenishment model 196
Organization charts 257
Organization 52, 245, 255
Organization plan 68
Output 20, 87, 135
Overhead 224

P fixed order point model 196
PACE 50
Packaging 212
Pallet placement 221
Pallets 216
Parallel combination 83
Parameter analysis 142
Pareto 32, 152
Partnership 255
Parts for new products 178
Patton's principle 57
Percent defective (P) chart 164
Percent-of-cost-with-maximum-fee 226
Permutations 112
Personnel 245
PERT 24, 26, 50, 54, 283
PERT/Cost 26
PERT/Time 26
Pessimistic 26
Phased program planning and management (PPP&M) 55
Phase-in 72
Physical distribution (PD) 205
Piggyback 238
Pipelines 239
Planning 24
Plant engineering 126
Plant location 227
Pohlen 71
Poisson 80
Poisson 157
Poisson 162
Poisson 193
Polaris 88
Population 158
Prediction 87
Predictive maintenance 171
Preliminary design review 103
Pre-production model 112
Prepurchase information 275
Present value (PV) 37, 39, 43
Pressure indices 138
Prevention costs 153
Preventive maintenance 91, 171, 277
Pricing 121
Primary trading area 229
Printed circuit board (PCB) 173
Private carriage 240
Probability distribution 156

INDEX

Problem identification   55
Procurement   120
Produceability   104
Producer risk   160
Product planning   52, 53
Product assurance   153
Product introductions   281
Production planning and control   126
Production plan   68
Prodution phase   33, 57
Production and Inventory Control   121
Production concepts   119
Production units   112
Production/Construction support   118
Production-consumption cycle   68
Productive hours   247
Profit   43
Program phases   112
Progress/learning curve   128
Project organization   53
Proposals   122
Protection   213
Prototype model   112
Public warehouse   219
Purchase order draft (POD)   125
Purchase orders (PO)   121, 122
Purchasing Handbook   120
Purchasing   120
Purchasing reviews   107

Q fixed order quantity model   196
Quality Assurance (QA)   151
Quality control (QC)   151
Quality costs   153
Quality   48, 72, 88, 120, 151
Quality control   126
Quality cost budgeting   153
Quality standards   155
Quotations   122

Railroads   237
Random failure   168
Range (R) chart   164
Ready-to-use   277
Reciprocal agreements   124
Redundancy   46
Regression analysis   137, 165
Rejectable quality level (RQL)   162
Rejuvination   301
Relative value   202
Relevancy   46
Reliability   24, 32, 36, 46, 76, 103, 152, 275, 286
Reliability bathtub curve   169
Reliability growth   179
Remedial maintenance   16
Reorder point(ROP)   185
Repair   97
Repair level   97
Repair, rejuvination & disposal   292
Repair/discard analysis   296
Repairable credit   306

Replaccement decisions   292
Replace   97
Request for proposal (RFP)   122
Request for Quote (RFQ)   122
Research and Development (R&D)   39
Resource   26
Response time   79
Responsibility   97
Resume   123
Resupply   192
Retailers   206
Retirement Phase   33, 73
Retrofit   117
Return on investment (ROI)   43, 61
Risk   22, 42, 53, 104, 108
Roll-in changes   114
Rosenstein, Louis C.   1

S curve   143
Safety   22, 36, 90, 103, 168
Safety stock   183, 195
Sales forecasting   139
Sample   158
Scalar principle   258
Schedule   152
Scheduled maintenance (SM)   171, 175
Schematic diagram   115
Schematic model   310
Seasonal influences   146, 189
Securities and Exchange Commission (SEC)   283
Security   290
Sensitivity   38, 43, 313
Series reliability   82
Series-parallel combinations   83
Service cost   31, 79
Service life   72
Service system matrix   170
Service level   192
Serviceability   90, 110
Shewhart, W. A.   152
Ships   238
Shock   213
Short takeoff and landing (STOL) aircraft   52
Significant few   3
Simon, Herbert   264
Simon, William   45
Simplification   87
Simulations   234
Single-sampling plan   163
Skills inventory   251
Slack   27
Sole proprietorship   255
SOLE   1, 247
Span of control   259
Spares Provisioning Model (SPM)   320
Spares inventory   36
Spares Kit Evaluator Model (SKEM)   320
Specialization   258
Specifications   21, 57, 93, 108, 114, 121, 210
Speculative stocks   183
Square-cube theory   267

Standard Metropolitan Statistical Area (SMSA) 229
Standard deviation 158
Standardization 87, 97, 104
Statistical quality control 152
Step function 141
Stochastic 149, 310
Stock records 197
Stock-keeping unit (SKU) 182
Stock-keeping unit location (SKUL) 182
Stock-out 177, 191
Strategic evaluation 143
Stress 87
Structured process 64
Suboptimization 21, 22
Substitution growth curves 142
Support Availability Multisystem Operations model (SAMSON) 318
Supportability 104
Survey forecasting 139
Synergism 104
System effectiveness 32, 36
System definition phase 33
System 19
System Cost and Operational Resource Evaluation (SCORE) model 319
System design 63
System design review 103
System integration 92
Systems engineering 19, 93, 103
Systems approach 24, 40
Systems analysis 143

T fixed order time model 196
Tariffs 241
Tax 228
Taylor, Frederick 47
Technological mapping 143
Technological forecasting 140
Termination 34, 36, 39, 276, 283
Test marketing 286
Testing 112
Theoretical limits test 141
Throwaway maintenance 172
Time magazine 281
Time and motion 100
Time 79
Time horizons 133
Time-series analysis 137, 146
Timms 71
Tolerance 156

Total quality control 152
Trade-off curves 95
Trade-off 38, 92, 103
Traffic and transportation 237
Traffic management 243
Trailer on flat car (TOFC) 238
Training 21, 44, 251
Transformation 70
Tranship 195
Trends 137
Truckload (TL) shipment 241
Trucks 238
Turnover 180

U.S. News and World Report 229
U.S. Postal Service 217, 240, 245
Uncertainty 134
Uniform freight classification 241
Uniform Product Codes (UPC) 49, 199
Unit packs 213
United Parcel Service (UPS) 240
Unscheduled maintenance 77
Usage 177
Use to failure 175
Utilities 228
Utilization 22, 92, 124

Validity 46, 101
Value 120
Value of information 194
Variability 157
Variable cost 224
Vendor stocking 125
Verification 108
Video Display Tube (VDT) 50
Volvo 268

Warehouse 218
Warranty 48
Wearout 80, 168, 179
Weber, Max 256
Webster 64
Weibull distribution 157, 160
Wholesalers 206
Whyte, W. H. 266
Wilson lot size formula 185
Work factor analysis 126, 224
Work Breakdown Structure (WBS) 25
Workload points 247
Workload planning factors 248

Zero defects 153